PCs
ALL-IN-ONE

FOR

DUMMIES®
5TH EDITION

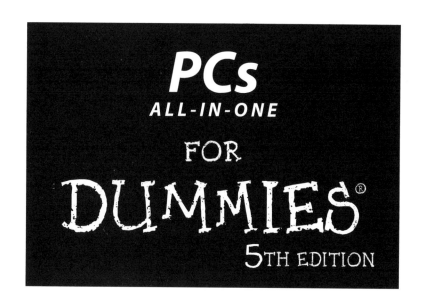

PCs
ALL-IN-ONE
FOR
DUMMIES®
5TH EDITION

by Mark L. Chambers

WILEY

Wiley Publishing, Inc.

PCs All-in-One For Dummies®, 5th Edition

Published by
Wiley Publishing, Inc.
111 River Street
Hoboken, NJ 07030-5774
www.wiley.com

Copyright © 2010 by Wiley Publishing, Inc., Indianapolis, Indiana

Published by Wiley Publishing, Inc., Indianapolis, Indiana

Published simultaneously in Canada

For general information on our other products and services, please contact our Customer Care Department within the U.S. at 877-762-2974, outside the U.S. at 317-572-3993, or fax 317-572-4002.

For technical support, please visit www.wiley.com/techsupport.

Wiley also publishes its books in a variety of electronic formats. Some content that appears in print may not be available in electronic books.

Library of Congress Control Number: 2010929414

ISBN: 978-0-470-61454-9

Manufactured in the United States of America

10 9 8 7 6 5 4 3 2 1

WILEY

About the Author

Mark L. Chambers has been an author, a computer consultant, a BBS sysop, a programmer, and a hardware technician for more than 25 years — pushing computers and their uses far beyond "normal" performance limits for decades now. His first love affair with a computer peripheral blossomed in 1984 when he bought his lightning-fast 30bps modem for his Atari 400. Now he spends entirely too much time on the Internet and drinks far too much caffeine-laden soda.

With a degree in journalism and creative writing from Louisiana State University, Mark took the logical career choice: programming computers. However, after five years as a COBOL programmer for a hospital system, he decided there must be a better way to earn a living, and he became the Documentation Manager for Datastorm Technologies, a well-known communications software developer. Somewhere between writing software manuals, Mark began writing computer how-to books. His first book, *Running a Perfect BBS*, was published in 1994 — and after a short 1.5 decades or so of fun (disguised as hard work), Mark is one of the most productive and best-selling technology authors on the planet.

Along with writing several books a year and editing whatever his publishers throw at him, Mark has also branched out into Web-based education, designing and teaching a number of online classes — WebClinics — for Hewlett-Packard.

His favorite pastimes include collecting gargoyles, watching St. Louis Cardinals baseball, playing his three pinball machines and the latest computer games, supercharging computers, and rendering 3D flights of fancy with TrueSpace. And during all that, he listens to just about every type of music imaginable. Mark's popular worldwide Internet radio station, MLC Radio (at www.mlcbooks.com), plays only CD-quality classics from 1970 to 1979, including everything from Rush to Billy Joel to the *Rocky Horror Picture Show*.

Mark's rapidly expanding list of books includes *MacBook For Dummies*, 2nd Edition; *MacBook All-in-One For Dummies*; *Apple TV For Dummies*; *iMac For Dummies*, 6th Edition; *Mac OS X Snow Leopard All-in-One For Dummies*; *Build Your Own PC Do-It-Yourself For Dummies*; *Scanners For Dummies*, 2nd Edition; *CD & DVD Recording For Dummies*, 2nd Edition; *Mac OS X Tiger: Top 100 Simplified Tips & Tricks*; *Microsoft Office v. X Power User's Guide*; *BURN IT! Creating Your Own Great DVDs and CDs*; *The Hewlett-Packard Official Printer Handbook*; *The Hewlett-Packard Official Recordable CD Handbook*; *The Hewlett-Packard Official Digital Photography Handbook*; *Computer Gamer's Bible*; *Recordable CD Bible*; *Teach Yourself the iMac Visually*; *Running a Perfect BBS*; *Official Netscape Guide to Web Animation*; and the *Windows 98 Troubleshooting and Optimizing Little Black Book*.

His books have been translated into 14 different languages so far, and his favorites are German, Polish, Dutch, and French. Although he can't read them, he enjoys the pictures a great deal.

Mark welcomes all comments about his books. You can reach him at mark@mlcbooks.com, or visit MLC Books Online, his Web site, at www.mlcbooks.com.

Dedication

This book is dedicated to my daughter in-between, Chelsea Chambers — movie fanatic, Johnny Depp expert, Color Guard star, and audiophile — with all my love.

Author's Acknowledgments

Books don't produce themselves — and no book that I've written is complete without a round of sincere thanks (and applause) that's due to everyone involved!

First, my appreciation to my technical editor, Lee Musick, who spent weeks checking every fact and verifying every menu item (and Ribbon button, and pop-up selection . . .) in this book. I do a lot of technical editing myself, and I can tell you that it's no simple task to wade through this many chapters — it takes a combination of long nights and lots of soda.

Again, the Wiley Composition Services team has outdone itself in designing and preparing the material. All the beautiful formatting in this book (including every single figure and screen shot, all the step-by-step procedures, and the regular appearances of Mark's Maxims) is a testament to this team's hard work.

As with all my books, I'd like to thank my wife, Anne, and my children, Erin, Chelsea, and Rose, for their support and love — and for letting me follow my dream!

And I won't forget the support, the patience, and the guidance of Kyle Looper, my acquisitions editor; Jean Nelson, my project editor; and Teresa Artman, my copy editor. Kyle, I hope I kept any headaches to a minimum, even with a tome this size — and Jean and Teresa, your direction has improved every chapter in this edition, and I appreciate all your hard work! My heartfelt thanks to all three.

Publisher's Acknowledgments

We're proud of this book; please send us your comments at http://dummies.custhelp.com. For other comments, please contact our Customer Care Department within the U.S. at 877-762-2974, outside the U.S. at 317-572-3993, or fax 317-572-4002.

Some of the people who helped bring this book to market include the following:

Acquisitions, Editorial, and Media Development

Project Editor: Jean Nelson

Acquisitions Editor: Kyle Looper

Senior Copy Editor: Teresa Artman

Technical Editor: Lee Musick

Editorial Manager: Kevin Kirschner

Media Development Project Manager: Laura Moss-Hollister

Media Development Assistant Project Manager: Jenny Swisher

Media Development Associate Producers: Josh Frank, Marilyn Hummel, Douglas Kuhn, and Shawn Patrick

Editorial Assistant: Amanda Graham

Senior. Editorial Assistant: Cherie Case

Cartoons: Rich Tennant (www.the5thwave.com)

Composition Services

Project Coordinator: Katherine Crocker

Layout and Graphics: Joyce Haughey, Stephanie D. Jumper

Proofreaders: Melissa Cossell, Cynthia Fields

Indexer: Steve Rath

Publishing and Editorial for Technology Dummies

    Richard Swadley, Vice President and Executive Group Publisher

    Andy Cummings, Vice President and Publisher

    Mary Bednarek, Executive Acquisitions Director

    Mary C. Corder, Editorial Director

Publishing for Consumer Dummies

    Diane Graves Steele, Vice President and Publisher

Composition Services

    Debbie Stailey, Director of Composition Services

Contents at a Glance

Introduction *1*

Book I: PC Hardware *7*

Chapter 1: Starting with the Basics 9
Chapter 2: Additional Toys Your PC Will Enjoy.. 21
Chapter 3: Connectors, Ports, and Sundry Openings 35

Book II: Windows 7 .... *43*

Chapter 1: Shake Hands with Windows 7 45
Chapter 2: The Many Windows of Windows 63
Chapter 3: Windows 7 Basics 79
Chapter 4: Advanced Windows 7 103
Chapter 5: Taking Control of the Control Panel... 127

Book III: The Internet *153*

Chapter 1: Making Sense of the Internet... 155
Chapter 2: Adding an Internet Connection to Windows 7 169
Chapter 3: Protecting Your Internet Privacy.. 177
Chapter 4: Cruising the Web with Internet Explorer...................................... 187
Chapter 5: Harnessing Your E-Mail... 205
Chapter 6: Instant Messaging Done Right.. 227

Book IV: PC Troubleshooting and Maintenance *239*

Chapter 1: Easy PC Troubleshooting 241
Chapter 2: Maintaining Windows 7.. 253
Chapter 3: Maintaining Your Hardware 273

Book V: Office 2010 .... *283*

Chapter 1: Introducing Office 2010.. 285
Chapter 2: Using Word 297
Chapter 3: Putting Excel to Work.. 325
Chapter 4: Performing with PowerPoint 351
Chapter 5: Doing Database Magic with Access 377
Chapter 6: Staying in Touch with Outlook... 387
Chapter 7: Working with SkyDrive 407

Book VI: Fun with Movies, Music, and Photos 415

Chapter 1: Scanning with Gusto 417
Chapter 2: Dude, MP3 Rocks! 433
Chapter 3: Making Movies with Your PC 445
Chapter 4: I Can Make My Own DVDs? 457
Chapter 5: I'm Okay, You're a Digital Camera 465

Book VII: Upgrading and Supercharging 483

Chapter 1: Determining What to Upgrade 485
Chapter 2: Adding RAM to Your Hot Rod 493
Chapter 3: Adding Hard Drive Territory to Your System 499
Chapter 4: Partying with USB, FireWire, and eSATA 509
Chapter 5: Pumping Up Your Sound and Video 517

Book VIII: Home Networking 527

Chapter 1: Do I Really Need a Network? 529
Chapter 2: Ethernet to the Rescue 537
Chapter 3: Going Wireless 555
Chapter 4: Sharing Your Internet Connection 565
Chapter 5: Securing Your Home Network 573

Index 585

Table of Contents

Introduction *1*

What's Really Required 1
What's Not Required 2
About This Book 2
Conventions Used in This Book 2
    Stuff that you type 2
    Menu commands 3
    Display messages 3
How This Book Is Organized 3
    Book I: PC Hardware 3
    Book II: Windows 7 3
    Book III: The Internet 4
    Book IV: PC Troubleshooting and Maintenance 4
    Book V: Office 2010 4
    Book VI: Fun with Movies, Music, and Photos 4
    Book VII: Upgrading and Supercharging 4
    Book VIII: Home Networking 4
Icons Used in This Book 5

Book 1: PC Hardware *7*

Chapter 1: Starting with the Basics 9

Basic Terms 9
    Hardware 10
    Software 11
    Peripherals 12
The Common Components of a Desktop PC 13
    The computer 13
    The monitor 15
    The keyboard and mouse 16
    Speakers 17
Desktop PCs versus Laptop PCs 18
RAM and Processors: The Keys to Performance 18
Your Friend, Your Operating System 20

Chapter 2: Additional Toys Your PC Will Enjoy 21

Printers 22
    Inkjet versus laser printers 22
    Photo printers 24
    Label printers 24

Scanners 25
Keyboards, Tablets, and Pointing Things 26
    Tickling keys wirelessly 26
    Putting a tablet to work.. 27
    Repeat after me: Buy a trackball!... 28
Big-Time Game Controllers 29
Video and Digital Cameras 30
External Drives.. 31
    Portable hard drives and DVD/Blu-Ray recorders 31
    Backup drives... 32
    USB flash drives 33
Surge Protectors and UPS Units 33

Chapter 3: Connectors, Ports, and Sundry Openings **35**

Using USB Stuff... 35
Riding in the Fast Lane with FireWire 37
Your Fossilized Serial Port 38
The Once-Renowned Parallel Port 39
Meet Your Video Port 40
Audio Connectors You Likely Need 41
Keyboard and Mouse Ports on Parade 42

Book II: Windows 7 .... **43**

Chapter 1: Shake Hands with Windows 7 . . . .**45**

A Windows 7 Primer.. 45
    Why Windows 7, anyway?... 45
    Flavors à la Windows... 47
    Upgrade or clean install 47
    System requirements for the Big 7 48
Starting and Shutting Down Windows 7 49
    Shutting down completely.. 49
    Restarting your PC... 50
    Using sleep mode... 50
    Yes, your PC can hibernate 51
    Multiuser options.. 51
Your Windows 7 Controls... 52
    Icons 52
    That constantly changing cursor... 53
    The Start menu... 54
    The taskbar... 55
    Menus and toolbars... 56
Using Bill's Funky Keys 57
    The Windows keys.. 58
    The Shortcut key.. 59
    Other important keys... 59

Using the Windows 7 Help System 60
    Displaying Help 60
    Searching for specific help 61
    Yelling for assistance 62

Chapter 2: The Many Windows of Windows. 63

Managing Windows Means Productivity 63
    Opening and closing windows 64
    Scrolling windows 65
    Minimizing and restoring windows 66
    Maximizing and restoring windows 68
    Moving windows 68
    Resizing windows 69
    Switching windows 69
A Field Guide to Icons 70
    Hardware icons 71
    Program icons 72
    File icons 72
    Folder icons 74
    Shortcut icons 74
    System icons 75
Selecting Icons 76
    Selecting a single icon 76
    Selecting multiple contiguous icons by dragging 76
    Selecting multiple contiguous icons by clicking 77
    Selecting multiple separated icons by clicking 77
Using the Toolbar 77

Chapter 3: Windows 7 Basics 79

Running Applications from the Start Menu 80
Running Applications from Your Hard Drive 81
Running Applications from a CD-ROM or DVD-ROM 82
Running Applications from a Network Drive 82
Exiting a Program 83
Putting Your Files in Order 84
    Copying and moving stuff 85
    Creating a new folder 86
    Deleting stuff with mouse and keyboard 87
    Displaying properties 87
    Renaming items 88
Emptying the Recycle Bin 88
Recovering Items from the Recycle Bin 89
Putting the Start Menu through Its Paces 90
    Tossing the Recent Applications list 90
    Using the Run item 91
    Accessing printers 92
    Working with your network 94
    Configuring the Start menu 95

Handling the Taskbar 96
Switching programs 96
Controlling the notification area 97
Adding icons to the taskbar 98
Configuring the taskbar 99
Terminating a Program with Prejudice 100
How to Avoid Formatting a Floppy Disk 101

Chapter 4: Advanced Windows 7 103

Personalizing Your Desktop 104
Changing the background 104
Using themes 105
Changing system sounds 106
Adding the Sidebar and gadgets 107
Switching Views and Sorting Items 108
Don't Forget the Preview Pane! 109
What's This Stuff in the My Users Folder? 110
A Word about Libraries 112
Share the Documents . . . and Other Stuff 113
Using Your HomeGroup 114
Creating a Shortcut 116
Multiuser Operation For Dummies 116
Logging in 117
Be my guest 118
Fax Me, Please 119
Setting up faxing under Windows 7 119
Sending faxes 120
Doing the Multimedia Thing 121
Playing your MP3 files 122
Viewing and downloading digital photographs 123
Recording your own CDs 124
Watching a DVD movie 125

Chapter 5: Taking Control of the Control Panel 127

First, Put the Control Panel on the Start Menu! 128
Configuring the Date and Time 129
Date and Time tab 130
Additional Clocks tab 130
The Internet Time tab 131
Changing Personalization Settings 131
Theme 131
Desktop background 132
Sounds 133
Screen saver 133
Adjusting Display Settings 134
Choosing AutoPlay Options 135
Adjusting the Power Options 136

Tweaking the Keyboard 138
    The Speed tab.. 138
    The Hardware tab 139
Adjusting Thy Mouse 139
Configuring Internet Options 140
    The General tab 140
    The Security tab 142
    The Privacy tab 143
    The Content tab 144
    The Connections tab 145
    The Programs tab 146
    The Advanced tab.. 147
Uninstalling and Repairing Programs and Features.................... 147
Fine-Tuning User Accounts 149
Configuring Phone and Modem Options 150
    The Dialing Rules tab... 150
    The Modems tab 151
    The Advanced tab.. 151

Book III: The Internet *153*

Chapter 1: Making Sense of the Internet **155**

Exactly What Is the Internet, Anyway? 156
Exploring the Potential of the Web 158
    Surf the Web 158
    Build a Web site 159
    Blogging... 159
    E-mail and instant messaging... 160
    FTP file transfer 161
    Newsgroups 162
    Webcams and Web videoconferencing............................ 163
    Enjoy digital media over the Internet............................. 163
Understanding Internet Connections... 164
    Dialup connections 164
    DSL connections 164
    Cable modem connections 165
    Satellite connections 166
"What Exactly Do I Need?".. 167

Chapter 2: Adding an Internet Connection to Windows 7.........**169**

Gathering the Account Incantations 169
Making the Physical Connection 171
Creating a New Dialup Connection in Windows 7 171
Creating a New DSL, Satellite, or Cable Connection in Windows 7 173
"Is My Connection Alive?" 175
"My Connection Appears to Be Dead" 175

Chapter 3: Protecting Your Internet Privacy **177**

What Can Really Happen?...177
Common Sense Goes a Long Way...179
    Passwords...179
    Risky behavior...180
    E-mail..182
Using the Built-in Windows 7 Firewall 183
Using Antivirus Software 186

Chapter 4: Cruising the Web with Internet Explorer **187**

Running Internet Explorer 187
The Explorer Window and Basic Controls 188
    More buttons for your buck...190
    Finding a home page...193
Navigating the Web 193
    Simplifying surfing with Favorites 194
    Searching for the hay in the needlestack............................196
    Doing the Tab thing 198
Downloading Files 199
Keeping Track of Where You've Been...201
Printing and Saving Web Pages..202
    Putting the Web in print...202
    Saving the best (for last)..203

Chapter 5: Harnessing Your E-Mail **205**

Introducing the Mail Window...206
Setting Up Your Mailbox..208
The Three R's: Receiving, Reading, and Replying 211
    Receiving e-mail 211
    Reading e-mail 211
    Replying to and forwarding e-mail.......................................213
    To Bcc, or not to Bcc...214
    E-mail housekeeping: Deleting and filing 216
Creating and Sending E-Mail...216
    Formatting a message 217
    Creating and sending a draft 218
    Windows Live Mail 102...218
Sending and Receiving File Attachments.....................................220
Spam: I Hate It — Truly I Do! 222
Working with Your Contacts..223

Chapter 6: Instant Messaging Done Right **227**

Selecting a Chat Client 227
    AIM..228
    ICQ 228
Running Windows Live Messenger..229
Configuring Windows Live Messenger 230

Keeping Track of Friends and Family..................................232
Chatting with Your Brethren...233
Selecting a Status..235
Squelching the Unwelcome Few 236

Book IV: PC Troubleshooting and Maintenance 239

Chapter 1: Easy PC Troubleshooting............................241
Relax and Breathe Easy 241
The Troubleshooting Process, Step by Step.........................243
Drastic Things That You Won't Do Often.............................249
    Using System Recovery Options.................................249
    Reinstalling Windows 7..250
HELP! Additional Troubleshooting Resources 251
    The Windows 7 Help system 251
    Microsoft tech support 252
    The Microsoft Web site 252
    Those unsupported newsgroups 252

Chapter 2: Maintaining Windows 7 253
Device Manager: The Hardware Tool.................................253
Checking Your Hard Drives in Windows 7 256
Defragmenting Just Plain Rocks 258
Be Smart: Back Up Your Stuff...261
Safeguarding Your System with System Restore....................265
Have at Thee, Foul Virus!..267
Using Windows Defender...268
Windows 7 Boot and Recovery Options 269
    Using Safe mode 270
    Using the last known good configuration 270
Using Windows Update...271
    The fully automatic way..271
    The (somewhat) manual way...................................272

Chapter 3: Maintaining Your Hardware......................273
When Should You Move Your PC? 273
Avoiding Dust Bunnies...274
Watching Your Cables..275
Cleaning Monitors and Scanners.....................................276
Cleaning Your Mouse and Keyboard 277
Cleaning and Maintaining Your Printer 278
    Cleaning laser printers 278
    Changing inkjet cartridges.....................................279
    Calibrating your printer 280
    Cleaning inkjet cartridges 281
    Refilling inkjet cartridges......................................282

Book V: Office 2010 283

Chapter 1: Introducing Office 2010 285

The Components of Office 2010 286
    Word 2010 286
    Excel 2010 288
    PowerPoint 2010 289
    Access 2010 290
    Outlook 2010 291
Putting the Office Clipboard to Work 292
Using the Office Help System 293
    Displaying the Help system 294
    The three controls of justice 294

Chapter 2: Using Word. 297

Running Word 298
The Elements of Word 298
A Word about Views 301
    Draft view 301
    Outline view 301
    Print Layout view 302
    Web Layout view 302
    Full Screen Reading view 302
Typing, Selecting, and Editing Text 303
    Typing like the wind 304
    Selecting what you will 304
    Editing text in Word 305
Finding and Replacing Stuff 306
Building Tables 308
Adding Bulleted and Numbered Lists 310
Adjusting Tabs and Margins 312
    Setting margins with the ruler 312
    Setting margins from the Ribbon 313
    Setting tabs with the ruler 314
    Setting tabs from the Ribbon 314
Applying Formatting 315
    Font formatting 315
    Paragraph formatting 316
    AutoFormatting 318
Adding Graphics 319
Doing the Collaboration Thing 320
    Using revision marks 320
    Using comments 321
    Using highlighting 322
Printing Your Document 323
Creating Web Pages with Word 323

Chapter 3: Putting Excel to Work 325

Running Excel..326
Waltzing Around the Excel Window.................................326
Selecting, Entering, and Editing Cell Data 328
    Filling a cell to the top..328
    Moving around the worksheet 328
    Selecting cells the easy way 330
    Editing cell contents..331
Working with Numbers and Dates....................................332
Working with Rows and Columns......................................334
    Resizing rows and columns 334
    Inserting blank cells...335
    Inserting cells from the Clipboard.........................336
    Inserting rows and columns 336
Formatting in Excel...337
    Font formatting 337
    Cell alignment...338
    Changing borders and shading 338
The Basics of Excel Formulas 340
Working with Graphics in Excel.......................................343
Adding a Chart 344
Linking Cells 346
Adding Headers and Footers...347
Printing Your Worksheets 348

Chapter 4: Performing with PowerPoint 351

Getting Your Bearings in PowerPoint 352
Changing Views..354
    Normal view..354
    Slide Sorter view 354
    Notes Page view 355
    Reading view...355
    Slide Show view...356
Creating Slides 356
    Inserting slides 357
    Inserting a document..358
Typing, Selecting, and Editing Text..................................359
    Adding text 359
    Moving within text fields.......................................360
    Selecting text and objects.....................................361
    Editing text...361
    Moving slide elements..362
Installing Graphics in Your Slides 363
Applying a Theme...364
Entering Notes 366
Using Movies and Sound..367
Building and Running a Slide Show...................................369

Making a Transition 'twixt Slides...371
Using Package for CD...372
Printing Your Document...374

Chapter 5: Doing Database Magic with Access. 377

Running Access...378
A Quick Tour of the Access Window...378
Creating Access Tables...380
Creating a Form with the Wizard...381
Entering and Editing Fields Manually 385
Using Access Templates..386
Printing Your Data..386

Chapter 6: Staying in Touch with Outlook. .387

Running Outlook...388
Elements of the Outlook Window...388
Configuring Your Mail Account 390
Reading and Replying to E-Mail..392
Composing and Sending Messages 396
Using File Attachments...397
Keeping Track of Your Contacts..399
        Entering a contact...400
        Editing a contact...401
Using the Outlook Calendar 401
        Creating an appointment 403
        Displaying appointments in Outlook Today........................405
Printing within Outlook...405

Chapter 7: Working with SkyDrive. 407

Answers to Your Online Storage Queries....................................407
Signing In to SkyDrive...408
Marking Your Own Territory and Adding Files 409
Saving Files within Office Applications......................................412

Book VI: Fun with Movies, Music, and Photos.............. 415

Chapter 1: Scanning with Gusto 417

What Happens inside a Scanner? 417
Your Friend, the Flatbed...419
Popular Scanner Features 421
Basic Scanning with Windows Live Photo Gallery 422
        Acquiring the image..422
        Rotating and cropping images 424
        Converting and saving the image.......................................427
Scanning Do's and Don'ts 429
Those Irritating (Or Invaluable) Copyrights 430

Chapter 2: Dude, MP3 Rocks! **433**

   An MP3 Primer 434

   Ripping Your Own MP3 Files 435

   Listening to Your Stuff 438

   Downloading to an MP3 Player 440

   Using Other Sound Formats 441

      WAV format 441

      WMA format 442

      AAC format 442

      AU format 442

      AIFF format 442

      MIDI format 442

   Burning Audio CDs from MP3 Files 443

Chapter 3: Making Movies with Your PC **445**

   Getting the Lowdown on Windows Live Movie Maker 445

   Rounding Up Clips and Images 447

   Building Your First Movie 448

   Adding Transitions without Breaking a Sweat 450

   Adding Special Effects without Paying George Lucas 451

   Adding Sound 452

   You've Just Gotta Have Titles! 453

   Previewing Your Oscar-Winning Work 454

   Saving and Sharing Before Traveling to Cannes 455

      Creating a digital video file 455

      Sharing your masterpiece on YouTube 456

Chapter 4: I Can Make My Own DVDs? **457**

   Welcome to Windows DVD Maker 457

   Clips 'R Easy! 459

   Time to Preview 463

   Burning Your DVD and Celebrating Afterward 464

Chapter 5: I'm Okay, You're a Digital Camera **465**

   How Does a Digital Camera Work? 466

   The Pros and Cons of Digital Photography 468

   Digital Camera Extras to Covet 471

      External card readers 471

      Rechargeable batteries 471

      Lenses 472

      Tripods 473

   The Lazy Man's Guide to Composing Photographs 473

      The rule of thirds 474

      The rule of asymmetry 475

      Using lighting creatively 477

   Organizing Your Pictures 478

   Downloading Your Images 478

Book VII: Upgrading and Supercharging 483

Chapter 1: Determining What to Upgrade 485

Making Performance Upgrades: CPU, Motherboard, and Memory....... 486
    Upgrading your CPU and motherboard 486
    Adding memory... 487
Expansion Upgrades: eSATA, USB 2.0, and FireWire 488
Making Storage Upgrades: Internal and External Drives..................... 489
    Adding a hard drive 489
    Adding a recorder or a tape drive 489
Making Sound and Video Upgrades: Sound and Video Cards 490
    Sound cards on parade 490
    Deciding which video card is right for you 491

Chapter 2: Adding RAM to Your Hot Rod 493

Defining the Different Types of RAM.. 493
    DDR.. 494
    DDR2... 494
    DDR3... 494
    RDRAM.. 494
    SDRAM.. 494
Figuring Out Which Type of RAM to Buy.................................... 495
Deciding How Much RAM Is Enough... 496
Installing Extra RAM... 497

Chapter 3: Adding Hard Drive Territory to Your System 499

The Tale of Virtual Memory 499
Recognizing a Well-Dressed Hard Drive 501
    Size definitely matters.. 502
    How fast is your access? 502
    What does rpm have to do with hard drives?................. 502
Internal versus External Storage 503
Adding a Second Internal Hard Drive.. 504

Chapter 4: Partying with USB, FireWire, and eSATA 509

A Tale of Three Fine Ports.. 509
    Comparing USB ports 510
    I vote for FireWire.. 511
    The latest power user port: eSATA 512
Or Do You Just Need a Hub? 512
Installing a Port Card... 513

Chapter 5: Pumping Up Your Sound and Video..................517

Sound Card Features to Covet... 517
    3D spatial imaging.. 518
    Surround sound support 518

MP3 encoding support 519
Game and FireWire ports 519
MIDI ports 519
Shopping for a Monster Graphics Card 520
Just say, "PCI Express" 520
Exploring the differences between chipsets 520
Other video card features that you'll want 521
Installing Sound and Video Cards 523

Book VIII: Home Networking 527

Chapter 1: Do I Really Need a Network? 529

Discovering the Advantages of a Network 529
File transfer 530
Sharing that-there Internet 531
One word: Games! 531
Shared documents and applications 531
What Can I Connect To? 533
What Hardware Do I Need? 534
What Software Do I Need? 535

Chapter 2: Ethernet to the Rescue 537

A Quickie Ethernet Primer 537
The Hardware You Need 539
Cables 539
Switches 541
NICs 541
Doing the Cable Dance 542
Configuring Windows 7 for Your Network 543
Ah, sweet DHCP 543
Browsing the neighborhood 546
Sharing folders and documents 548
Printing across the Network 550
Using a Standard Switch with a Cable or DSL Modem 550
Troubleshooting Your Network 551
Windows 7 doesn't recognize my NIC 551
No lights show up on my network card(s) or switch 552
Nothing shows up when I browse 552
I can't connect (or print) to a shared printer 553

Chapter 3: Going Wireless 555

Understanding Wireless Networking 555
Comparing wireless with wired 555
Keeping track of the standards involved 556
AC and phoneline networking 562

Using Wireless Hardware in Windows 7 563
    Preparing to install 563
    Installation tricks 563
    Making the connection 564

Chapter 4: Sharing Your Internet Connection 565

Why Share Your Internet Connection? 565
Sharing through Hardware...566
    Wired sharing devices...566
    Wireless sharing devices 570
Sharing through Software in Windows 7 571

Chapter 5: Securing Your Home Network 573

Common Sense Tips for Wired Networks..573
Ensuring Security on Your Wireless Network..576
Using Shared Folders (The Right Way)...578
Knowing Why You Need NAT...579
Marveling at the Magic of Virtual Private Networking...........................580

Index *585*

Introduction

*W*hat's the definition of a reference book? Well, I like to think of this book as a snapshot. Sure, it's an extremely heavy photograph, weighing in at more than 600 pages. But nevertheless, it captures the current state of PCs, including hardware, the most popular applications, and of course, the latest and greatest incarnation of the Windows operating system that we all cherish (in this case, Windows 7).

That covers a lot of ground, especially when you consider how the PC has branched out into all sorts of new directions in the past 15 years. What used to be primarily a simple word processing platform in the early days of DOS has now become a hub for digital video and audio, an optical recording center, an Internet communications system, a digital darkroom, a 3D gaming console, an office productivity center — the list goes on and on. Therefore, fitting the features and functionality of today's PCs into a single volume was a challenge for me — *and* it proved singularly rewarding because PCs are both my career and my favorite hobby!

With that comprehensive approach in mind, this book still holds true to the *For Dummies* format: step-by-step instructions on each major feature within Windows 7, Microsoft Office 2010, and other popular PC applications, with a little personal opinion, my recommendations, and my attempts at humor mixed in to add spice. I take the time to explain each topic for those who have just entered the PC universe, but you'll uncover plenty of advanced information as well. With this book in hand, you can set up a wireless network, navigate an Excel spreadsheet, diagnose hardware problems, and even work magic with your digital camera.

I sincerely hope that you enjoy this book and that it will help open up the countless possibilities offered by your PC. Thanks to the efforts of all those software developers, engineers, and hardware manufacturers, you and I get to play!

What's Really Required

Here's a short section for you — for this book, I assume that you have a PC or laptop/netbook, preferably running Windows 7.

(I told you it was short.)

What's Not Required

If you've read any of my earlier books, you already know the score. But just in case you haven't (hint, hint), here's the list of what you don't need:

✦ **A degree in computer science:** Computers are supposed to be *easy*. I like 'em that way, and I get *very* testy when faced with anyone who tries to make a PC artificially complex. 'Nuff said.

✦ **All sorts of expensive software:** Because Microsoft Office 2010 is so doggone popular, I cover it here, but virtually everything else is either included in Windows 7 or is inexpensive.

✦ **An Internet connection:** Some folks should be reminded that PCs are quite productive by themselves. Naturally, you need an Internet connection to use Internet Explorer and Windows Live Mail or Outlook, but you **don't have to be online** to enjoy your computer.

About This Book

Each of the eight minibooks in this desk reference squarely addresses a specific topic, and there's no need to read this whole book in a front-to-back fashion. You certainly can, if you like, but it's not necessary. Instead, each minibook (and on a lower level, each individual chapter) is self contained. That is, you can jump from chapter to chapter to pursue information about what you're working on right now — happy in the knowledge that when you decide to invest in an external hard drive (or a scanner or a memory upgrade), it's covered!

Conventions Used in This Book

Like other *For Dummies* books, this volume uses a helpful set of conventions to indicate what needs to be done or what you'll see onscreen.

Stuff that you type

When I ask you to type something, like a command or an entry in a text box, the text appears like this, in bold:

Type me

Press the Enter key to process the entry.

Menu commands

When I give you a specific set of menu commands to use, they appear in this format:

Edit⇨Copy

In this example, you should click the Edit menu and then choose the Copy menu item. (This format applies to programs with old-fashioned menus.)

I describe selecting items from the Ribbon in Office programs similarly. For example, when I ask you to "choose Insert⇨Picture," this is shorthand for "click the Insert tab of the Ribbon and then click the Picture command button."

Display messages

If I mention a specific message that you see on your screen, it looks like this on the page:

```
This is a message displayed by an application.
```

How This Book Is Organized

Here's a quick summary of what's included in those eight minibooks (with cross-references where appropriate, included at great expense).

Book I: PC Hardware

It's not a PC without the hardware. In this minibook, I discuss the standard equipment (like your monitor, keyboard, and mouse) as well as optional items that you can attach (like a scanner or a game controller). I also cover the different ports on your PC and the proper methods of maintaining your PC hardware.

Book II: Windows 7

A minibook for the Big 7 generation — with everything you need to know about today's most popular PC operating system, including the basics, advanced customizing topics, maintenance, the included applications — and (insert ominous chord here) troubleshooting.

Book III: The Internet

The obligatory Internet information fills this minibook. Discover how to navigate the Web, read all that incoming e-mail, fritter away countless hours with instant messaging, and — most important — keep your computer secure while you're online.

Book IV: PC Troubleshooting and Maintenance

Every PC owner should be familiar with basic hardware and software troubleshooting, and this minibook walks you through the process. I also cover the maintenance steps you should follow to keep your PC running smoothly. (Someday, PCs will be smart enough to clean themselves.)

Book V: Office 2010

Okay, so I decided to cover the behemoth. The major components of Microsoft Office 2010 are Word, Excel, PowerPoint, Access, and Outlook — and the gang's all here, with each application covered in a separate chapter, along with Microsoft's new online SkyDrive storage system. If you use Office 2010, you'll treasure this minibook. And if you don't use Office, you'll still enjoy it as a spellbinding work of nonfiction. (Sure, Mark.)

Book VI: Fun with Movies, Music, and Photos

Your PC is now a digital, multimedia production center — and an excellent combination for watching video and listening to music, to boot. In this minibook, I show you the latest cutting-edge fun you can have with your DV camcorder, your MP3 player, and your digital camera. Wait until you show your home movies on DVD!

Book VII: Upgrading and Supercharging

The gloves come off in this minibook: If you're hankering to turn the corner and become a PC power user, use these chapters to help you upgrade your PC's hardware, including your system RAM, your graphics card, and even external connections like eSATA. "To the BatCave!"

Book VIII: Home Networking

The final minibook is devoted to one of the fastest-growing segments of the PC population: those folks who are adding a home (or small-office) network. In these chapters, I demonstrate how to install your own wired network as well as how to expand with the latest wireless technology. Then I turn your attention to security so that you can use your network without fear of intrusion.

Icons Used in This Book

In a book stuffed to the gills with icons, my editors have decided to use — you guessed it — more icons. Luckily, however, the book's set of icons acts as visual signposts for specific information that you don't want to miss.

Mark's Maxims represent way-important stuff, so I call your attention to these nuggets, like this:

> **These are My Favorite Recommendations — in fact, I'll bet just about any PC power user would tell you the same. Follow my maxims, and you'll avoid the quicksand and pitfalls that I've encountered with all sorts of PCs!™**

A Tip icon points to a sentence or two that might save you time, trouble, or, quite possibly, cash.

Consider these tidbits completely optional, but if you're captivated by all things technical — as I am — you'll find trivia of interest here. (The information in these paragraphs is intended for those who enjoy cutaway drawings of the *Titanic* and those who know what JPEG means.)

Speaking of the *Titanic, always* read the information next to this icon first! Your PC is usually quite a safe harbor, but icebergs can appear from time to time, if you're not careful.

As you might expect from its name, this icon highlights information that you might want to, well, remember.

Book I

PC Hardware

The 5th Wave   By Rich Tennant

"Good news! I found a place where the router works with the PC upstairs and the one in the basement."

Contents at a Glance

Chapter 1: Starting with the Basics 9

Basic Terms...9
The Common Components of a Desktop PC 13
Desktop PCs versus Laptop PCs...18
RAM and Processors: The Keys to Performance........................18
Your Friend, Your Operating System...20

Chapter 2: Additional Toys Your PC Will Enjoy 21

Printers 22
Scanners 25
Keyboards, Tablets, and Pointing Things 26
Big-Time Game Controllers 29
Video and Digital Cameras 30
External Drives...31
Surge Protectors and UPS Units 33

Chapter 3: Connectors, Ports, and Sundry Openings. 35

Using USB Stuff..35
Riding in the Fast Lane with FireWire 37
Your Fossilized Serial Port 38
The Once-Renowned Parallel Port 39
Meet Your Video Port 40
Audio Connectors You Likely Need 41
Keyboard and Mouse Ports on Parade 42

Chapter 1: Starting with the Basics

In This Chapter

- ✔ Defining hardware, software, and peripherals
- ✔ Identifying the common components of all PCs
- ✔ Comparing desktop and laptop PCs
- ✔ Understanding RAM and your PC's CPU
- ✔ Defining the operating system

*I*f your name is Hemingway or Faulkner or King, the first chapter is always the toughest to write. For me, however, this chapter was fun to write because it tackles the basic questions, such as which components make up your PC and why you need an operating system. You'll discover more about the specific parts of your PC that determine how fast it is, and I also discuss the pros and cons of choosing a laptop (or netbook or notebook) over a desktop PC.

If you're a hardware technician or a PC power user, you might decide to eschew these basic concepts and move on — and that's okay. But if you're new to the world of personal computers running Windows 7 or you're going to buy your first PC running Microsoft's latest and greatest version of Windows, this chapter is a great place to start. In fact, you would be amazed by how many folks I talk to who have owned their PCs for a year or two and still don't know some of the terms that you'll read here!

Here's the first Mark's Maxim for this book:

It takes a solid foundation to build a power user.™

So read on!

Basic Terms

My high school English teacher, a wonderful lady whom I have always admired (even then), always told us, "Never jump into anything before defining your terms." (I owe her a lot.) No small coincidence that my favorite editors at Wiley say the same thing!

Before you venture further, commit these terms to memory to take a giant first step toward becoming a PC power user.

There's no reason to walk around with these definitions tattooed on your arm; you certainly don't need to know these technicalities just to check your e-mail or use Microsoft Word. However, when you grow more knowledgeable about Windows and your PC, you find that these terms will crop up in your computer conversations more and more often.

Hardware

In the PC world, *hardware* is any piece of circuitry or any component of your computer that has a physical structure. For example, your computer monitor is a piece of hardware, as is your keyboard. Even those components that you normally can't see or touch — the ones buried inside your case — are considered hardware, too, like your PC's motherboard and power supply. (And yes, your computer's case is technically a piece of hardware even though it's not electrical.)

Figure 1-1 illustrates a common piece of hardware — in this case, a video card with a PCI connector.

Figure 1-1:
Hardware,
like this PCI
video card,
is, well,
hard.

Software

The other side of the PC coin is the software you use. *Software* refers to any program you run, whether it resides on your hard drive, a floppy disk, a CD or DVD, or somewhere on a network.

When you hear folks discussing a software *upgrade, patch,* or *update,* they're talking about (you guessed it) *another* piece of software! However, the upgrade/patch/update program isn't designed to be run more than once; rather, its job is to apply the latest features, bug fixes, and data files to a piece of software that's already installed and running on your PC, to update it to a new *version.* (Virtually all software developers refer to successive versions of their software, such as Version 1.5 or Version 3; the later the version, the more features the software includes.)

Typically, think of software as an application that you buy or download, such as Microsoft Office 2010 or Nullsoft's Winamp (see Figure 1-2). However, the term *software* applies to any program, including Windows itself and the driver programs that accompany the hardware you buy. Unfortunately, computer viruses are software as well.

Figure 1-2:
Use
software
to perform
tasks, such
as listen to
your digital
music
collection.

From time to time, you might see the word *firmware* in a magazine or on a hardware manufacturer's Web site. This sounds like a strange beast, but I can explain: *Firmware* consists of the software instructions you find stored in the internal memory or the internal brain of a piece of hardware, so it's not quite software, and it's not quite hardware. For example, your DVD recorder has a firmware chip inside that controls the mundane tasks required to burn a disc; likewise, your video card's firmware contains instructions for all sorts of 3D magic that can be turned on and off by those games you play. Generally, you don't have to fool with firmware, but a manufacturer might release a firmware upgrade to add support for a new version of Windows, or fix bugs that have cropped up with a piece of hardware (or even add new features). To upgrade firmware, you run a software utility program supplied by the manufacturer.

And software might be cheap!

You'll probably encounter two other types of "ware": freeware and shareware. A *freeware* program has been released into the public domain — in which case the author generally releases the programming code needed to modify it or maintains the rights to it — but you can still use it for free. *Shareware,* on the other hand, is not free. You get to try it before you buy it; if you like it, you send your payment directly to the author. Because there's no middleperson (you won't catch me using a sexist term) and you're not paying for an expensive box or advertising, shareware is usually far cheaper than a similar commercial program.

Before using freeware or shareware, check to make sure that the author offers regular updates. When you work for peanuts, you usually can't afford a Quality Assurance department or comprehensive beta testing!

Peripherals

Peripherals are items that reside outside your PC's case, which can include all sorts of optional hardware. Examples include

+ Printers
+ External DVD recorders (such as the model shown in Figure 1-3) and hard drives
+ Webcams
+ Graphics tablets
+ Portable music players
+ Joysticks and other game controllers
+ Network hardware, such as Internet-sharing devices
+ Scanners and digital cameras

Figure 1-3:
This external DVD recorder peripheral enjoys sunshine and clean air.

Three pieces of external hardware that are found on every PC — your monitor, keyboard, and mouse (or trackball or touchpad) — are generally *not* considered peripherals because they're required in order to operate your PC. Call 'em "hardware" instead.

Peripherals connect to your computer via the ports built into the back (and often the front) of your PC. I go into more detail on ports in Chapter 3 of this minibook; any PC power user worthy of the name can identify, on sight, any common port on a computer. (If you're a hardware technician, you can identify the ports in the dark, the way a soldier knows his weapon. Just don't ask me why — I'm not at liberty to discuss it.)

The Common Components of a Desktop PC

Although a PC is hardly a living thing, your system can grow like one — and it can become quite unwieldy and tough to move. Turn your attention to the components that you find equipped on just about any PC you buy (or assemble) these days.

The computer

The computer itself is housed in a case, which protects all the internal parts from damage. (Unfortunately, dust still finds its way inside, which is why I recommend that you remove the case at least once a year and blow out all that dust by using a can of compressed air.)

Lingo alert: You'll hear techs refer to your PC as *box, CPU, chassis,* or possibly even *$*Q(#*$*!%* (reserved for special occasions). You meet your PC's *CPU* — central processing unit; a single integrated chip — later in this chapter.

Consider thy form factor

Not all PCs are created equal; several different *form factors* are available. (Jeez, another two-dollar term for a 50-cent concept.) A *form factor* determines the height and "footprint" of your computer, depending on the size of its case. (In the original days of the IBM PC, all computer cases were designed to straddle your desk, parallel to the floor; however, folks soon realized that a PC takes up far less room when standing vertically.)

Your desktop PC's case can look like any of the following:

+ **The standard tower machine:** Because a tower case (see Figure 1-4) gives you the largest number of expansion bays and room for multiple fans, it's the case favored by PC power users and network administrators. A tower case is often placed on the floor because it's sometimes too tall for your computer desk.

+ **The minitower machine:** The standard case offered with most PCs, the minitower is simply a shorter version of a tower case. The minitower is suitable for home and standard office workstation use — however, don't expect it to have as many expansion (or *card*) slots or as many empty drive bays waiting for you to fill with additional hard drives and another DVD recorder.

+ **The lunchbox and pizza box machines:** These are the smallest PC cases, built for those areas where space is at a premium (or you know ahead of time that expansion won't be required later). These machines are often used in larger corporate offices, hospitals, banks, and the like. Figure 1-4 shows a pizza box case, which sits flat on your desktop rather than stand upright.

Pizza box

Pizza box

Figure 1-4: No tower in Middle Earth can compete with the tower PC case!

Minitower

Tower

You might be interested in buying a PC with a special color scheme. Typically, these machines are black or brushed aluminum, but I've seen them in every color of the rainbow as well. (I particularly fancy the neon green and Florida orange.) Many high-performance gaming machines use wild color schemes that will knock you back a few feet. Use caution, though: Finding a neon green CD-ROM drive in any store — online or otherwise — is more difficult than getting a teenager to stop texting.

The monitor

Monitors come in two varieties:

✦ **The traditional CRT monitor:** A cathode ray tube (CRT) monitor is big and brassy and offers better color quality than a liquid crystal display (LCD) monitor in all lighting conditions, but CRTs use more electricity, get hot while you use them, and emit all sorts of radiation (nothing harmful, mind you, but it's there all the same). Because CRT monitors use older technology that's similar to a TV set, they're bulky, especially at larger screen sizes, such as 19" and 21". Most CRT monitors are flat-screen models; older designs with curved screens tended to distort the image you see.

✦ **The LCD monitor:** LCD monitors — also called *flat-panel* monitors — share the same technology as laptop computer screens, so they're very thin and use much, much less electricity than CRT monitors. (Many are even designed to hang on the wall.) LCD screens don't emit heat or radiation. LCD monitors have generally replaced dinosaur CRT monitors globally, and most LCD monitors are available in widescreen displays (good for watching DVD movies or working in a graphics program). See Figure 1-5.

Figure 1-5: LCD monitors: lithe, lean, and lissome.

Either type of monitor is fine for a home or office environment, but I recommend (naturally) using an LCD monitor. The larger the monitor size, the easier it's likely to be on your eyes, and the more windows and documents you can stuff on your desktop at one time.

The keyboard and mouse

Keyboards are rather mundane. All models now have the Windows-specific keys, which will help any PC power user — but I still have a suggestion or two:

✦ **Consider using an ergonomic keyboard.** The cool, curved appearance that makes ergonomic keyboards, such as the Microsoft Natural Ergonomic Keyboard 4000, stand out in a crowd isn't just for looks. You can type longer and faster and with less strain on your wrists if you use an ergonomic keyboard like the one shown in Figure 1-6.

✦ **Keyboard tasks are easier with one-touch buttons.** Many keyboards now on the market — and most that ship with new systems — feature one-touch keys that you press to automatically display your e-mail program or Web browser, print a document, or mute your computer's audio. Even if you don't use the standard functions for these keys, they can generally be reprogrammed to work with other applications. For example, I reprogrammed the Print key on my server's keyboard (which isn't connected to a printer) to run my network management application instead.

Figure 1-6:
Ergonomic keyboards are friendly to your wrists; trackballs are friendly to your fingers.

On the other side of the coin, most PC power users eventually look for a different mouse or pointing device; the standard-equipment mouse rarely gets the job done unless you're buying a more expensive system that comes with a premium mouse. Mouse-y features to consider include

✦ **Cordless:** This mouse type is sans tail: Instead, it uses a built-in infrared (IR) emitter or Bluetooth wireless connection to communicate with a separate base station, which in turn connects to your PC. The base station often acts as a battery charger for the mouse when you're not using your PC. Many folks find this type of mouse liberating because it has no tail to drag around and you can place the mouse farther away from the computer.

✦ **Optical operation:** Optical mice advantages include no mouse ball to clean, far fewer moving parts, and better control — it's no wonder that optical pointing devices are so popular! If you're still using an old mouse with a ball, jettison it and pick up an optical mouse.

✦ **Multiple buttons:** Most new offerings have a programmable third button and a scroll wheel, which you use to scroll the contents of a page just by turning the wheel with your fingertip. (For example, I have the middle button programmed as a double-click.) Some mice meant for gamers have additional buttons that can be programmed to "type" several keys automatically when clicked.

✦ **Trackballs and touchpads:** Many tech types swear by these alternatives to the traditional mouse. To use a *trackball,* which is kind of like a giant stationary mouse turned on its back, you move the ball with your thumb or the tips of your fingers. (Refer to Figure 1-6.) With a touchpad (like what's found on many laptops), you move the tip of your finger across a pressure-sensitive pad.

Speakers

Today's multimedia PCs are just as attractive to an audiophile as traditional stereo systems. If you think that you're limited to two desktop speakers and a chintzy volume knob, I invite you to contemplate the latest in PC speaker technology:

✦ **Flat-panel speakers:** As LCD screens are to CRT monitors, flat-panel speakers are to older PC speakers. Most flat-panel speakers are less than a half-inch thick yet provide the same power and punch as their older brethren.

✦ **Dolby Surround sound:** I get into more detail about high-fidelity PC audio in Book VII, Chapter 5. For now, suffice it to say that with the right sound card and multiple speakers, your PC can equal the clarity and realism of a home theater system. Your ears become just as important as your eyes when you play the latest 3D games!

✦ **Universal Serial Bus (USB) digital connections:** For the ultimate in sound quality, the best digital speakers now connect to your system through the USB port — you can say goodbye to old-fashioned analog forever.

Desktop PCs versus Laptop PCs

Should you buy a desktop or a laptop PC? Naturally, if the portability of a laptop PC is a requirement for you — say, your job or your lifestyle demands plenty of travel every year — you really have no other choice than a laptop computer. (There are those who take portability even more seriously — many PC owners choose a *netbook,* which is typically significantly smaller than a laptop, for its light weight and long battery life.) Laptops are as powerful as desktop PCs, with features such as high-resolution graphics, larger hard drives, and CD/DVD recording, which used to be very expensive options in the laptop world. Oh, and don't forget the all-important wireless networking that all laptops include these days — no longer just for students, either, since these days everyone craves wireless networking!

However, if you're sitting on the fence and portability is a lesser require-ment, I generally recommend a desktop system, for the following three reasons:

✦ **Laptops aren't as expandable as desktops.** Although you can hang plenty of peripherals off a modern laptop (using USB, eSATA, and FireWire ports), desktops are just plain easier to expand and upgrade (especially the processor and your graphics card, which are practically impossible to swap on a laptop).

✦ **Laptops are more expensive than desktops.** My friend, you pay dearly for that portability. (The cost exception is today's netbooks, which are very inexpensive, but they have fewer features and less power than a typical laptop, and lag far behind any desktop.) So if you don't need it, jump to the desktop side of the fence. It's as simple as that.

✦ **Laptops cost much more to repair.** If the sound card fails in your desktop, you can replace it yourself with a new, relatively inexpensive adapter card. However, if the sound hardware fails in your laptop, it's time to pull out your wallet because you can't fix it yourself and the entire motherboard inside the unit probably needs to be replaced. (Remember: Part of that portability stems from the fact that laptop man-ufacturers put all the graphics and video hardware on the motherboard to save space.)

Luckily, most of this book is still valuable to laptop owners. Just ignore the parts about upgrading the components you can't reach.

RAM and Processors: The Keys to Performance

When you hear PC owners talk about the speed and performance of their computers, they're typically talking about one of three different components (or all these components as a group):

✦ **System memory, or random access memory (RAM):** The more memory your PC has and the faster that memory is, the better your PC performs — especially Windows, which enjoys memory like the proverbial hog. I tell you more about slops — sorry, I mean *memory* — in Book VII, Chapter 2.

✦ **Central processing unit (CPU):** Most PCs now use either an Intel Core 2 Duo or Core 2 Quad, or Intel's less-expensive and slower cousin, the Celeron. The other popular processor is the AMD Athlon II X4 or the Phenom II along with AMD's less-expensive and slower cousin, the Sempron. The speed of your processor is measured in gigahertz (GHz), with 1 GHz equaling 1000 MHz. The faster the speed of your processor, the faster your PC performs. (I go into this topic big-time in Book VII, Chapter 1.)

✦ **Graphics processing unit (GPU):** This item is the chipset used on your video card. The better the chipset, the faster and the more realistic 3D graphics that your PC can produce. For the skinny on graphics cards, visit Book VII, Chapter 5.

To display which type of processor your PC uses, its speed, and how much RAM your PC has, click Start and then right-click My Computer in Windows XP (or Computer if you're running Vista or Windows 7). Choose Properties from the pop-up menu that appears, and you should see a dialog box, like the one in Figure 1-7, with these interesting facts.

Figure 1-7:
Display your System Properties in Windows 7.

Processor type

Your Friend, Your Operating System

Windows, which is your PC's *operating system,* is the program that you run to

+ Navigate through the files on your hard drive.
+ Run other programs.
+ Listen to music, view pictures, or watch movies.
+ Copy, move, and delete things, and much more.

Windows is composed of hundreds of smaller programs, but you rarely notice anything else running. Instead, Windows presents a cohesive and relatively easy-to-use interface to the world. (The tech word *interface* simply refers to the design of the screen and the controls you see when you're using software.)

In this book, when I refer to Windows, I'm talking about Windows 7. In my opinion, Windows 7 is the easiest-to-use and most stable version of Windows that I've ever encountered, and I heartily recommend that you upgrade to it if your PC meets the minimum requirements. (Book II is completely dedicated to Windows 7 — there's another reason to upgrade!)

I should mention, however, that Windows 7 isn't the only operating system that runs on a PC. For example, you can run Unix, Linux, Windows Vista, Windows XP, or even good old-fashioned DOS. To be honest, your PC's hardware couldn't care less — but it's a good bet that the programs you want to run are designed for Windows, and much of your PC's hardware either won't work or will be harder to configure if you use another operating system. Therefore, I heartily suggest that you stick with either Windows XP (for a machine more than three or four years old) or Windows 7 (for a PC designed or rated as compatible with the Big 7). Although the initial problems with Windows Vista have been largely solved, Windows 7 is a far superior operating system, and it has my recommendation.

Chapter 2: Additional Toys Your PC Will Enjoy

In This Chapter

- ✔ Comparing printers
- ✔ Adding a scanner to your system
- ✔ Upgrading your input devices
- ✔ Adding a game controller
- ✔ Introducing digital cameras and digital video (DV) camcorders
- ✔ Adding new storage to your system
- ✔ Protecting your PC with a surge protector or an uninterruptible power supply (UPS)

You bought a PC — congratulations! — or you decided to finally turn on that totem pole of a desktop computer that you've been looking at for the past six months. Here's a friendly warning for you in the form of a Mark's Maxim:

Serious computing requires serious peripherals.™

In other words, PC owners who are hoping to get the maximum return and explore the maximum power of their computers need additional stuff (*peripherals*, as you can read in Chapter 1 of this minibook) that connects to your PC to take care of specific jobs. Printers are a good example; a PC certainly doesn't produce hard copy without one.

In Chapter 1 of this minibook, I discuss hardware and software. This chapter is designed as both a showcase and an introduction to PC peripherals that will familiarize you with the most popular additional toys for your computer. Some of these devices are covered in great detail later on (for example, scanners have Book VI, Chapter 1 to themselves), and others are covered primarily right here.

This chapter can be hazardous to your wallet or purse.

Printers

The first stop in the world of peripherals is the most common (and most folks would say the most useful) device: the system *printer,* which allows your PC to produce hard copies of documents, artwork, and photographs.

Inkjet versus laser printers

In the digital days of yore (in other words, more than 20 years ago), making a choice between an inkjet and a laser printer was ridiculously easy. After all, laser printers were prohibitively expensive, and they couldn't print in color. Therefore, every home PC owner picked up an inkjet printer (or got an inkjet printer as a bundled peripheral with a new PC) and got on with his or her life. These days, however, the line between inkjet and laser printers has blurred; this section lists the advantages of each one so that you can shop with the right type of printer in mind.

Laser printer advantages

Monochrome laser printers now start at around $100 (all dollar amounts in this chapter are in U.S. greenbacks), which is still mind-bendingly weird for an old hardware hacker like me who still remembers the days when the *absolute* cheapest (and likely refurbished) laser printer you could find set you back $1,500 to $2,000. Advantages of the laser printer include

✦ **Speed:** Most laser printers can turn out pages more quickly than the average inkjet printer can.

✦ **Low cost:** Over time, toner costs for a laser printer total far less per page than refilling and replacing inkjet printer cartridges.

✦ **Quiet operation:** A laser printer is generally quieter than a low-cost inkjet printer — which is a big deal in a quiet office, where the printer usually occupies a central location.

✦ **Best-quality text:** No inkjet printer — no matter how much you pay for it — will ever turn out black text and line graphics as crisply as a laser printer does.

Also, if you can afford to pony up $300 or so for a color laser printer, you'll find that it offers better-quality color output than most low-cost inkjet printers. With these advantages in mind, pick a monochrome laser printer if most of the pages you print are text and if color isn't a requirement. You'll be glad that you chose the laser model after you go three months without changing a single toner cartridge!

The monochrome laser printer shown in Figure 2-1 can produce 12 pages per minute without blinking an eye (if it had one).

Figure 2-1:
Invest in a low-cost mono-chrome laser printer for document printing.

Inkjet printer advantages

Inkjet printers are still somewhat cheaper than laser printers. You can find an acceptable color inkjet printer for well less than $100 anywhere on the planet, and it's still the color printing solution for the home PC owner. Other advantages include

✦ **Versatility:** A color inkjet can print on many types of media, including craft paper, T-shirt transfers, and even printable CDs/DVDs.

✦ **Smaller size:** Save some space on your desktop.

✦ **Larger paper sizes:** If you spend more, you can add to your system a large-format inkjet printer that can print 11-x-17-inch or larger items.

The inkjet printer shown in Figure 2-2 costs less than $100 yet includes both Ethernet and Universal Serial Bus (USB) connections. It can print near–laser-quality black text and photo-quality color images. You can even set this model to print on both sides of the paper.

Figure 2-2:
This inkjet printer produces stunning photo-quality color.

Photo printers

Photo printers are specifically designed to create photographs that rival any 35mm film print. They either use the best-quality inkjet technology or rely on dye-sublimation (dye-sub) technology (also called *thermal wax* printing). A *dye-sub* printer transfers heated solid dye from a ribbon to specially coated paper, producing the same continuous tones that you see in a photograph produced from a negative. Photo printers can often accept memory cards from digital cameras directly (or by using a USB cable connection to the camera), so you don't need a PC to print your digital photographs.

Most photo printers on the market are smaller than typical inkjet printers. (They can't use standard 8.5" x 11" paper, and they're lousy at printing black text, which makes an inkjet printer far more versatile.) Both photo and inkjet printers can produce borderless images (just like a film print), but a true dye-sublimation photo printer is far slower than an inkjet, and the special paper and dye ribbon it requires make it much more expensive over the long haul.

If you're a serious amateur or professional digital photographer, a photo printer is worth the expense. For a typical home PC owner, however, a standard color inkjet printer is the better path to take.

Label printers

Before I move on, I want to discuss the popular personal *label printer,* like the DYMO LabelWriter I use. The LabelWriter 450 Turbo uses a USB connection and sells online (www.dymo.com) for about $140.

This printer might look a little like a toy — it's not much bigger than the label tape it uses — but I've found that a label printer is worth twice its weight in gold (see Figure 2-3). For example, the LabelWriter 450 Turbo can produce all these materials with aplomb:

+ **Address and shipping labels**, complete with your logo
+ **Bar codes and U.S. mail codes**
+ **CD and DVD labels**
+ **File folder labels**
+ **Floppy disk labels** (for those who still use floppy disks, anyway)
+ **ID badges**
+ **VHS tape and cassette labels**

Figure 2-3:
A personal label printer is a convenient tool for printing all types of labels.

When you design your labels, the software that ships with the LabelWriter gives you control over fonts, time and date stamping, line drawings, and even thumbnail photographs. You can rotate and mirror text or set up bar coding with ease. Plus, you get the capability to print labels directly from applications such as Outlook, Word, and QuickBooks.

Just as valuable as the output, however, is the sheer convenience you get from one of these printers! A label printer frees you from the hassle of designing and preparing labels on your inkjet or laser printer, and you don't have to hunt for your label sheets every time you need to print a new batch. (Anyone who has fought tooth and nail to align and print a bar code or address labels on a standard laser printer knows just what I mean.)

Scanners

Scanners are interesting beasts — and man, you get a lot of bang for your buck! In fact, a perfectly serviceable USB scanner (as shown in Figure 2-4) is waiting for you at your local Maze O' Wires store for less than $100, and it can do all this:

✦ **Produce digital images from magazine and book pages, photographs, and just about any other printed material.** These images can later be edited to your heart's content, sent as an e-mail attachment, or recorded to CD or DVD.

✦ **Read text from a printed document into your word processor.** This trick — optical character recognition (OCR) — can save you hours of typing and prevent introduction of typos and finger fumbles.

✦ **Produce images that you can fax with your PC's fax/modem.**

✦ **Produce images from transparencies or slides (with the right attachment).**

✦ **Create copies of a document (in concert with your printer).**

Figure 2-4:
Use a scanner to bring all sorts of printed material to your PC.

The scanner shown in Figure 2-4 features seven one-touch buttons on its front. You can e-mail, copy, or even create PDFs from the original — or even run your OCR software with a single punch of a button. *Sassy!*

Specialized scanners are designed especially for things such as bar codes — perfect for those who collect audio and video — and business cards. I go into more detail on scanners in Book VI, Chapter 1. For now, just remember that they're the very definition of the cat's pajamas. (In fact, many printer manufacturers include scanning and faxing features with specific printer models, calling them *multifunction printers* or *all-in-one units*. Talk about a Swiss Army Knife!)

Keyboards, Tablets, and Pointing Things

Gotta have 'em. Using a PC without an input device is . . . well, I guess it's like playing Ping-Pong without paddles. In this section, I discuss the upgrades you can make to your PC's existing keyboard and mouse. (Although they're technically not peripherals, as I mention in Chapter 1 of this minibook, some of these hardware devices are too cool not to cover.)

Tickling keys wirelessly

As I discuss in the previous chapter of this minibook (and as you can read in Book II, Chapter 1, when I start talking Windows 7), Mr. Bill has remodeled the hoary PC keyboard in his own fashion, by adding extra keys that make it easier to control Windows. If you're using a PC built in the past five years, you already have these keys handy. I mention a few keyboard features to look for in Chapter 1 of this minibook, such as ergonomic keyboards that can help reduce the strain of typing on your wrists. But what if you want to relax in a better chair several feet away from that big-screen monitor?

Enter the wireless keyboard, which is the perfect complement to a wireless mouse or trackball. The wireless keyboard shown in Figure 2-5 also comes with a wireless mouse and uses the Bluetooth short-range wireless network technology (covered in Book VIII, Chapter 3). This keyboard is festooned with no less than 11 one-button hotkeys and even includes a set of audio CD player controls for listening to your music.

Figure 2-5:
This wireless keyboard/ mouse combo is the nomad's dream.

Putting a tablet to work

If you're a graphic artist, a professional photographer, or someone who wants to paint or draw freehand, consider getting a *graphics tablet* (shown in Figure 2-6), on which you draw or make notes with a stylus in the familiar old-fashioned method. Like an ergonomic keyboard, a tablet can also help ease the strain on your wrist.

Figure 2-6:
A graphics tablet makes drawing a breeze.

"But what about the fine control I get with paper or canvas?" No problem! Today's tablets can recognize thousands of different levels of pressure. Some can even detect the angle of the stylus, allowing you to tilt your virtual brush in graphics applications like Photoshop and Corel's Painter 11 (www. corel.com) for special effects with watercolor, chalk, and pencil filters.

A typical tablet, like the Intuos4 from Wacom (www.wacom.com), has no batteries or cords on its stylus, and it even comes with its own mouse. The tablet uses a USB connection to your PC, and it sells online for about $350 — that's the 5.5" x 8.8" model. (The 8" x 12.8" model is about $120 more.)

Repeat after me: Buy a trackball!

I can't work with a traditional mouse any longer — I'm now firmly set in the trackball camp. A trackball offers a number of benefits:

+ **Compact:** Trackballs require far less space on your desktop because just the trackball moves (rather than the entire device).

+ **Control:** Many folks find that using a trackball provides a finer level of cursor control.

+ **Clean:** A trackball stays cleaner than a mouse. (Even optical mice get dirtier than trackballs.)

Figure 2-7 illustrates a trackball mouse that you control with your thumb; on other trackballs, you use your index finger to control the ball. This particular model uses either a USB or PS/2 connection to your PC and sells for about $35 US online. (For more detail on PS/2 and USB connectors, visit Chapter 3 of this minibook.)

Figure 2-7: A trackball is much more efficient than the traditional mouse.

Big-Time Game Controllers

Ah, do you remember the old Atari joysticks that ushered in the age of the video game (and the Atari personal computer after that)? A plastic tube, a base with a single red button, and a cord — what more could you possibly want, right?

Because modern game players want a lot more than one button, witness the arrival of the game controller (which I think has a much grander sound than just *a joystick*). For example, check out the controller shown in Figure 2-8 — does that look like an old-fashioned joystick to you? In fact, this model is more like a combination of a mini-keyboard and a gamepad (reflecting the current complexity of PC games, which rely as much on the keyboard as on the pointing device you're using). Your entire hand fits on top of the controller, much like with a trackball, and your fingers press the keys while your thumb operates the gamepad directional control. (You can also use this controller along with your regular mouse or trackball.) This model, which sells for about $30 U.S. online, can even be programmed to fit your preferences for each individual game you play. *Sweet!*

Figure 2-8:
It's a
bird, it's a
plane —
no, it's a
modern
PC game
controller!

Another popular feature of today's game controllers is *force feedback*, where the controller rumbles or provides resistance to your hand that matches the action onscreen, such as a steering wheel that gets tougher to turn in curves or a joystick that shakes each time your WWII fighter is hit by enemy fire.

Consider the Logitech MOMO steering wheel, which has the same optical tracking mechanism as today's optical mice and trackballs. It even has its own onboard processor, which keeps track of what's happening within the game and activates the wheel's internal motors to provide the matching feedback. (Naturally, it also has programmable buttons. What a surprise.) Anyway, you get the steering wheel and a set of pedals to boot for about $100, making you the hit of your NASCAR crowd!

Video and Digital Cameras

Images and full-motion video have traditionally been based on film (which retains an image when exposed to light) or magnetic tape. That whole approach, however, is now strictly '90s — and very early '90s to boot. Digital cameras and digital video camcorders now have heavy-duty advantages over film cameras and tape camcorders:

+ **No processing at your local MegaMart is required.** Your digital images can be downloaded directly to your PC (or printer).

+ **Editing is easy,** using programs like Adobe Photoshop (static images) or Adobe Premiere (for video).

+ **No film to buy.** Instead, you simply delete images from your digital camera's memory card after they're downloaded.

+ **Images and videos can be saved to a CD or DVD for permanent storage.**

+ **Images can be sent by e-mail or displayed on your Web page.**

+ **You can create your own DVD movies from your video clips.**

A specialized model of DV camcorder (about the size of a golf ball) is designed especially to sit atop your desktop PC: a webcam. Folks use them to send digital video over the Internet, to add a video signal to their Web pages, or to record simple movies from their chairs. Webcams have been in use as Internet videoconferencing tools for years; most cost less than $100; and they use either a FireWire or USB cable connection to your PC. Many laptops are equipped with built-in webcams as well.

Figure 2-9 illustrates a typical digital camera, which looks and operates much like its film counterpart; it also shows a camcorder, ready to record straight to digital video, which you can transfer over a USB or FireWire connection to your PC.

Figure 2-9: The image and video makers of the new millennium: the digital camera and the camcorder.

For the skinny on digital cameras, see Book VI, Chapter 5. And, for a look at how the video clips you take with your DV camcorder can be turned into movies, see Book VI, Chapter 3.

External Drives

Now consider how simple it is to add fast storage — or the ability to record your own CDs and DVDs — to today's PCs. If you're the least bit nervous about digging inside your PC's innards to add more hard drive space, you'll be pleased to know that you can easily connect a fast external hard drive to your system — as long as you have the FireWire, USB 2.0, or external SATA ports available on your desktop or laptop PC. (If you're not familiar with these types of high-speed connections, fear not: I launch into a complete discussion of all three in Book VII, Chapter 4.)

In fact, not every form of external storage even needs a cable. Read on to see what I mean.

Portable hard drives and DVD/Blu-Ray recorders

Forget the huge external hard drives of just five years ago. Those doorstops have been replaced by slim, trim models (see Figure 2-10) that run faster and are more reliable, yet are no bigger than a pack of playing cards. At their current prices, you can pick up an external 500GB hard drive for less than $100 that's a mere one inch thick and shock resistant yet can connect effortlessly to PCs with either FireWire or USB 2.0 ports. These drives are usually bundled with backup software that can automatically safeguard your PC's data — more on this in the next section.

Figure 2-10:
This external drive means mobile storage.

On the DVD and Blu-Ray recording scene, you find six major types of drives:

✦ **CD-R/CD-RW drives:** Can store around 700MB on a CD

✦ **DVD-R/DVD-RW drives:** Can store 4.7GB on a DVD

✦ **DVD-RAM drives:** Can store 9.4GB on a double-sided DVD

✦ **DVD+R/DVD+RW drives:** Can store 4.7GB on a DVD

✦ **Dual Layer (DL) DVD+R drives:** Can store 8.5GB on a DVD

✦ **Blu-Ray BD-R/RE drives:** Can store 25GB on a Blu-Ray disc

The *RW/RE* in the drive moniker stands for *rewriteable,* which means that you can reuse a CD-RW, DVD-RW, DVD+RW, or Blu-Ray BD-RE over and over. All these recorders can produce audio CDs and standard data CDs and DVDs, but only the drives that can record the DVD-R and DVD+R formats are likely to create DVD movies that can be played in your standalone DVD player. Unfortunately, the rewriteable DVD-RW and DVD+RW standards aren't compatible with each other, and they're not compatible with older, standalone DVD players, either; you have to watch your discs on your PC. (Insert sound of palm slapping forehead here.)

Backup drives

Backup drives used to mean inexpensive, slow-running tape drives — however, typical 1 terabyte (TB) and 2TB drives are now simply too humongous for such tapes to be worth much anymore. Heck, I remember when everyone backed up to floppy disks, and now even the highest-priced digital audiotape (DAT) drives are losing ground fast in the backup storage world.

Instead, you now have three choices to pick from when backing up your system:

✦ **Blu-Ray recorder:** As I mentioned earlier, 25GB per disc makes optical backup reasonable.

✦ **Online backup:** Use a commercial Internet backup service. ***Note:*** This solution is viable only if you're using a broadband connection to the Internet; backing up a big hard drive takes too long over a pokey 56KB modem.

✦ **External FireWire and USB 2.0 backup hard drive:** An example is the 1TB Western Digital My Book (www.westerndigital.com), which provides full, automated backups of your system on a regular schedule.

The My Book drive isn't cheap at $120, but how much are your documents and files worth? No matter which backup method you use, I strongly urge you to do your duty as your PC's guardian and *back up your system!*

USB flash drives

One storage toy is something different: a *USB flash drive,* which is a keychain-size unit that needs no batteries and has no moving parts! Instead, it uses the same method that digital cameras use to store images. Your files are stored on memory cards (either removable cards or built-in memory inside the unit). Most USB drives now range anywhere from 2GB to 256GB of storage. Just plug one into your PC's USB port and copy data there. Then, just unplug and go: the ultimate in portable data storage. These drives don't need any extra software — Windows recognizes them instantly — so they make a great "digital wallet." These drives are now so common and downright handy that you can find novelty drives in different shapes and colors (for the style-conscious individual)!

Figure 2-11 illustrates a 16GB flash drive that sells for about $40 online. It even has a write-protect switch so that you can safeguard your data from being accidentally erased.

Figure 2-11: Carry 16GB in your pocket with a USB flash drive.

Surge Protectors and UPS Units

You know, one clear sign of a PC power user is at the end of the PC's power cord. True power users use either surge protectors or UPSs to safeguard their systems. However, I always make sure that I stress the following fact when I'm talking about surge protectors and UPS units: Neither can protect your PC from a direct lightning hit on your home or office wiring! (That's just too much current for any commercial surge device to handle.)

Otherwise, using either a surge protector or a UPS helps guard against less serious power surges, and both provide additional AC sockets for your rapidly growing system. If you can afford to spend $200 to $300, a UPS is the better choice because of the following reasons:

+ **Safety nets:** A UPS provides a number of extra minutes of AC power if your home or office experiences a power failure — generally enough so that you can close any documents you're working on (like that Great American Novel you've been slaving over for 20 years) and then shut down your PC normally.

+ **Auto shutdowns:** More expensive UPS models can automatically shut down your PC in case of a power failure.

+ **Current cleaners:** Most UPS units filter the AC current to smooth out brownouts and noise interference from other electronic devices.

+ **Audible alerts:** Some UPS units sound an alarm whenever a power failure or significant brownout occurs.

How long (in minutes) your UPS will last during a power failure depends on the power rating of the battery and the power drawn by your PC.

If you're using a dialup or any broadband modem connection, make sure that you get a surge protector or UPS that also protects your modem from electrical surges. That juice can travel just as easily across a phone line as across your power line. (For this reason, some electric utility companies are now offering insurance safety plans that cover your home against surge damage.)

Chapter 3: Connectors, Ports, and Sundry Openings

In This Chapter

✔ Connecting USB devices

✔ Connecting FireWire devices

✔ Putting the antique serial and parallel ports to rest

✔ Connecting your monitors

✔ Locating the jacks and ports on your sound card

✔ Connecting your mouse and keyboard

*I*n the beginning (okay, last century), there were the serial port and the parallel port — who would have needed anything else? If you could afford a printer back then, it was connected to the parallel port, and your modem (or perhaps your mouse) was hooked to your serial port. End of story.

The typical PC of today might not have either of those original two ports, though. The serial port is all but extinct, and although some current motherboards still provide a parallel port, it's on the way out as well. Modern PCs rely on a number of relatively new connectors that greatly expand the range of peripherals you can add to your system. In this chapter, I help you make sense of the various ports and sundry openings that you find on the back and front of your PC.

Using USB Stuff

The first port on the tour is the most important standard PC connector on the planet these days. A *Universal Serial Bus* (USB) port (see the following figure) allows you to connect all sorts of peripherals, and it's just as popular for connecting keyboards and mice. Intel is responsible for this most versatile of ports.

USB

A USB connection is the cat's pajamas because

✦ **It's plug and play.** You don't even need to reboot your PC after you connect a USB device because Windows automatically recognizes the connection, and you can start using your USB peripheral immediately.

✦ **One port supports dozens of devices.** A single USB port can support as many as 127 different devices, either connected in a daisy-chain configuration or by using a USB hub. I doubt that you have that many connections to handle. (If you do, please take a photo of your system with your digital camera and send the picture to mark@mlcbooks.com because I can hardly wait to see it.)

✦ **It's relatively fast.** USB devices come in two flavors. The older USB 1.1 standard (which still delivers data transfer speeds that are many times that of a traditional serial port) has all but disappeared. However, the USB 2.0 standard (one of the fastest external connections available for the PC) is backward compatible, so you can still use that USB 1.1 2X external CD-ROM that Aunt Harriet gave you. (Or not. I certainly wouldn't.)

Note that many USB cables have a different type of connector on each end, as shown in Figure 3-1. One end will connect only to your PC, while the other connects only to the device (like a cellphone, scanner, or digital camera). As long as you use the cable supplied with the external device, all is good!

I discuss USB connections in greater detail in Book VII, Chapter 4; for now, just remember that any device with a USB port connection is a better choice over the same device with a serial port or parallel port connection.

Figure 3-1:
USB
connectors.

Riding in the Fast Lane with FireWire

Until two or three years ago, the FireWire port (sometimes referred to by its more official name, *IEEE 1394*) was the fastest port on any personal computer. For a time, it was the standard for digital video (DV) camcorders and high-resolution scanners — both of which produce honking big files that need to be transferred to your computer as quickly as possible. Apple Computer is the proud parent of FireWire.

IEEE 1394
FireWire

The original FireWire standard has now been overtaken in raw speed by USB 2.0, but because FireWire has been around much longer, it's in no danger of disappearing any time soon. In fact, I would pick FireWire over USB 2.0 every time for my digital video equipment because many older pieces of my digital movie gear will never recognize USB 2.0.

Unlike USB ports — which are now included with every new PC — FireWire ports are generally available as optional equipment, so make certain that you have a FireWire port before spending the big bucks on that new DV camcorder. (Of course, you can always buy an adapter card to add FireWire ports to your computer.) Like USB, FireWire is a plug-and-play connection; a FireWire port can support 63 devices (using a daisy-chaining technique).

Find more information about FireWire in Book VII, Chapter 4, where I introduce the FireWire 800 standard, which ups the ante in the port speed race by churning an incredible 800 Mbps (megabits per second) — or twice as fast as original FireWire!

Your Fossilized Serial Port

Okay, perhaps the serial port isn't *fossilized,* but it is one-half of the original dynamic duo that first appeared with the premiere of the IBM PC.

Serial
port

Most new peripherals nowadays are USB. However, you can still find the following serial devices from time to time (usually used, and probably on eBay):

✦ Modems

✦ Game controllers (especially the more complex joysticks)

✦ Scanners and older ZIP drives

✦ Digital cameras

✦ Personal digital assistant (PDA) docks for Palm and Pocket PC units

Serial devices aren't plug and play, so you have to reboot your PC before Windows recognizes them, and most serial peripherals need drivers for Windows that have to be installed for things to work. Also, serial devices — especially modems — might require additional manual configuration inside Windows, such as editing files with Notepad and turning off certain port features. Oh, and did I mention that serial ports are slow as molasses compared to USB?

All in all, go USB. Everyone else is, and it's A Good Thing.

The Once-Renowned Parallel Port

Ah, I remember those days: the early 1980s, when the parallel port was truly the Queen of the PC Connections. Printers were hideously expensive peripherals that only a doctor, lawyer, or Supreme Court justice could afford. And, if you did have a printer, it was connected to your PC's parallel port (see Figure 3-2) with all the pomp, grace, and grandeur of the *RMS Queen Elizabeth II.* (Perhaps I need more Diet Coke.)

Figure 3-2:
The antique 25-pin parallel port.

Parallel
port

Again, I'm sorry to report that the parallel port's days are numbered. The popularity of the USB port as a printer connection has doomed the parallel port to obsolescence, and we can wave goodbye to her with a wistful smile. As with the serial port, this Mark's Maxim prevails:

Buy USB. You'll be happier.™

Laptop Connectivity 101

Like their desktop brethren, today's laptops lean heavily on USB 2.0 ports to provide all the connections to printers and other external devices. However, there are two types of ports that are generally considered specific to laptops that you may encounter from time to time:

✔ **Infrared:** Many laptops feature an infrared port (commonly called an IrDA port, short for Infrared Data Association) that can be used to communicate with devices such as PDAs and other laptops. Windows provides full support for an infrared connection. However, these ports don't do diddly-squat if the external peripheral you're trying to communicate with doesn't

have its own IrDA port — and not many do, so you can't use this whiz-bang technology with many devices.

✔ **PC Cards:** Speaking of laptops, PC Cards are used with laptop computers to provide all sorts of external connections: wireless network adapters, FireWire and eSATA ports, external hard drives, and even cellular phone service. Most laptop models can accommodate either two or three of these credit-card-sized adapter cards. When you pack up your laptop, your PC Cards can be ejected to streamline your computer for the road — when you get to your destination, it takes only a second to pop them back in.

Meet Your Video Port

At last, a port that has been around for many years and still (occasionally) rocks! Yes, friends and neighbors, most video cards still offer the same 15-pin, D-SUB video port that originally appeared with the IBM Video Graphics Array (VGA) specification. However, the 29-pin DVI-I port has gained ground fast. A *DVI-I port* is used to connect digital flat-panel (also called *liquid crystal display,* or LCD) monitors to your PC, as well as many flat-panel televisions. Figure 3-3 shows the business end of a typical video card that offers both ports onboard.

Figure 3-3:
A VGA and
a DVI-I
connector.

Standard VGA
monitor connector

DVI-I
connector

If you're wondering, virtually every card that has both these video ports can use two monitors at a time (either showing an *expanded* desktop, where your mouse moves seamlessly from one monitor to the other, or two separate and discrete desktops). Figure 3-4 illustrates this kind of rig.

Figure 3-4:
Two side-
by-side
monitors
offer a huge
desktop.

In a pinch, a DVI-VGA adapter allows you to use the DVI-I port to connect a legacy cathode ray tube (CRT) monitor, so you can use two analog monitors instead.

Audio Connectors You Likely Need

Today's speakers connect to your PC's sound card in one of four ways:

✦ **Standard analog Line Out/Speaker jacks on the card:** You find these familiar audio jacks on the card itself, just like the headphone jacks on an MP3 player or a boombox. Most PC speakers use these jacks, shown in Figure 3-5.

Figure 3-5:
A typical PC sound card shows off its speaker jack and game port.

✦ **Standard analog RCA jacks on the card:** Some cards also have the RCA jacks that most folks associate with a stereo system or VCR. These jacks are more convenient than the Line Out/Speaker jacks because you don't need a miniplug-to-RCA adapter to use your stereo system with your PC's audio output.

Analog audio   S/PDIF   USB

✦ **Standard optical (TOSLINK) and coaxial digital (SPIDF) connectors:** Audiophiles who truly want the best sound reproduction are willing to spend the extra dollars on an all-digital connection betwixt card and speakers (or card and high-end stereo system). These connectors are also standard equipment on most Dolby Surround sound systems.

✦ **The USB port:** Surprise! Our new-old-friend makes another appearance. This time, your speakers can use any USB port on your system for a digital audio connection — analog gets tossed out the door, and audiophiles can wax enthusiastic about their pristine digital sound.

You might also find a PC game port on older audio cards, allowing you to connect a joystick or another game controller. The game port is going the way of the dodo (thanks once again, as you might guess, to USB game controllers), but it's still quite common on today's sound cards.

Keyboard and Mouse Ports on Parade

The final stop on the port tour is the ubiquitous PS/2 keyboard-and-mouse port. Figure 3-6 illustrates the plug that fits in these ports. Each port is typically color coded and marked with an icon to indicate which piece of hardware gets connected where.

Figure 3-6: A PS/2 keyboard-and-mouse connector. Awesome sight, isn't it?

Make sure arrow is on top

I hate to bring it up, but at the risk of sounding like a broken record, virtually all PC hardware manufacturers are turning to USB keyboards and USB mice. (See why I stress just how important USB is to the modern PC?) In this case, however, I see no real advantage to using a USB keyboard or mouse over a PS/2 keyboard or mouse because the latter really doesn't require any configuration, and it's not continually being unplugged and reconnected. Plus, today's PCs still include PS/2 ports for keyboards and mice, so we're not quite to the point of an "orphan" PS/2 connection yet.

Book II

Windows 7

"Well, the first level of Windows 7 security seems good – I can't get the shrink-wrapping off."

Contents at a Glance

Chapter 1: Shake Hands with Windows 7 ....**45**

A Windows 7 Primer...45
Starting and Shutting Down Windows 7 49
Your Windows 7 Controls...52
Using the Windows 7 Help System 60

Chapter 2: The Many Windows of Windows. **63**

Managing Windows Means Productivity 63
A Field Guide to Icons 70
Selecting Icons 76
Using the Toolbar 77

Chapter 3: Windows 7 Basics **79**

Running Applications from the Start Menu...............................80
Running Applications from Your Hard Drive.............................81
Exiting a Program 83
Putting Your Files in Order 84
Emptying the Recycle Bin...88
Putting the Start Menu through Its Paces 90
Handling the Taskbar...96
Terminating a Program with Prejudice....................................100

Chapter 4: Advanced Windows 7 ....**103**

Personalizing Your Desktop..104
Switching Views and Sorting Items 108
What's This Stuff in the My Users Folder? 110
A Word about Libraries 112
Share the Documents . . . and Other Stuff 113
Using Your HomeGroup..114
Creating a Shortcut 116
Multiuser Operation For Dummies...116
Doing the Multimedia Thing..121

Chapter 5: Taking Control of the Control Panel **127**

First, Put the Control Panel on the Start Menu!........................128
Configuring the Date and Time 129
Adjusting Display Settings..134
Choosing AutoPlay Options 135
Adjusting the Power Options 136
Tweaking the Keyboard 138
Adjusting Thy Mouse 139
Configuring Internet Options 140
Uninstalling and Repairing Programs and Features....................147
Fine-Tuning User Accounts 149
Configuring Phone and Modem Options 150

Chapter 1: Shake Hands with Windows 7

In This Chapter

✔ Celebrating the advantages of Windows 7

✔ Starting and shutting down Windows 7

✔ Introducing Windows controls

✔ Using the keyboard

✔ Searching for help

✔ Contacting Microsoft for support

The Windows 7 operating system offers the most current appearance, performance, and functionality available for your PC — that is, as long as you're using an Intel or Advanced Micro Devices (AMD) processor with sufficient muscle. If you're using an older Pentium or Athlon single-processor machine, consider sticking with Windows XP because your PC doesn't have the necessary horsepower to provide real performance in Windows 7.

In this chapter, I present you with the beginning of your Windows 7 manual — the invaluable, indispensable paper volume that you *didn't* get when you bought Windows 7 or your PC. (Can you tell that I used to write software user manuals?) This book assumes no experience with Windows, so I start with shutting down your PC and the most important controls and keys that you use in the following chapters.

A Windows 7 Primer

Start off by seeing what's new in Windows 7. And for those readers on the fence trying to decide whether to upgrade — and whether your current machine has the juice to support Windows 7 — I've got you covered.

Why Windows 7, anyway?

If you're wondering why Windows 7 is the pick of the Microsoft litter — and why it's time to upgrade from an older Windows version, such as 2000, XP, or Vista — allow me to point out the advantages of Windows 7:

✦ **Attractive:** Microsoft has done a lot of work to make Windows 7 a graphics jewel — menus fade in and out, 3D effects are prevalent, high-resolution graphics abound on your desktop, and even your mouse can have a fashionable shadow under it. Of course, this graphics banquet has its cost, which I talk about more in the upcoming "System requirements" section.

✦ **Fast:** Run on a PC built within the past year or so, Windows 7 performs better than older versions of Windows — and that includes Windows Vista, which was used as the foundation for Windows 7.

✦ **Customizable:** You can tweak, remove, and reengineer such elements as toolbars, menus, and your desktop within Windows 7. (In this chapter, however, I stick with the default settings, to avoid confusing you with my crazy preferences!)

✦ **Easier to use:** No downside here! Older versions of Windows made it harder to take care of common tasks, such as creating an Internet connection and adding a printer to your system. The folks in Redmond have been working overtime to help automate these processes.

✦ **Supports the latest standards:** Again, this is nothing but the very definition of Good. Windows 7 can handle all the acronyms you want (but might not yet know): MP3, MPEG, JPEG, USB, Wi-Fi, DSL, and many more.

(All those cryptic escapees from a bowl of alphabet soup are explained in this book.) Unlike some earlier versions of Windows — which either don't even support the latest technology or require additional software to use — Windows 7 has built-in support for today's neatest toys.

✦ **Harder to attack:** Windows 7 includes better protection against all sorts of malware (without being as intrusive as Vista when it comes to protecting your system). With better defenses, you can get up from your PC for lunch without worrying whether it will still be running when you return.

Flavors à la Windows

Windows 7 comes in three editions: Home Premium is by far the best seller, Windows 7 Professional fills a more specialized need, and Windows 7 Ultimate is the Cadillac, including all the features Microsoft can pack into Windows. You can tell which version you have when you start your PC because Windows 7 displays an identifying welcome screen while it's loading.

The Home Premium edition is probably the best low-cost choice. (At the time of this writing, the full Home Premium edition is selling for under $200 on www.amazon.com, with an upgrade from Vista Home Premium going for about $110.) For a typical home PC owner or small office PC user, the Home Premium and Professional editions are just about identical in look, taste, and smell. (Professional Edition includes better backup capabilities and better compatibility with older software.) Everything you find in this chapter applies to both the Home Premium and Professional versions of Windows 7. (When disparities occur later in this minibook, I send up a flare.)

Upgrade or clean install

To upgrade, or to perform a clean install? A question worthy of the Bard himself (if he were using Windows Vista, that is). If you've never heard the term, a *clean install* involves backing up your existing personal data from your Vista system — the files and information that you created — and then formatting your hard drive and installing Windows 7, fresh as a daisy. You have to reinstall all of your data and programs, of course, but your system should perform at its best with a clean install.

Upgrading from Windows Vista to Windows 7 is possible, but it also involves backing up your data, and takes a considerable amount of time. You're also more likely to encounter minor problems and bugs, and you'll likely have to reinstall at least some of your applications. Also, your PC may not perform as well as it would if you had done a clean install.

Personally, I recommend a clean install, which results in the best possible performance for Windows 7, and also allows me to "clean house" by determining what programs I really need to reinstall.

**Book II
Chapter 1**

**Shake Hands with
Windows 7**

System requirements for the Big 7

If you're upgrading to Windows 7, it's time for that moment that you've feared all along: coming to grips with the demands that the Big 7 will make on your PC. Is it ready for the upgrade? Do you need to add RAM, or will you run out of hard drive space?

I cover the basics in this section, but don't forget that Microsoft offers the Windows 7 Upgrade Advisor, which scans your PC's current configuration and provides you with a listing of possible issues that you might have while upgrading. You can download the Advisor at

```
www.microsoft.com/windows/windows-7/get/upgrade-advisor.aspx
```

Processor and RAM

For a typical 32-bit installation of Windows 7, you need at least a 1GHz processor (preferably with multiple cores) and at least 1GB of random access memory (RAM).

These are the minimum requirements as recommended by Microsoft. I wouldn't run Windows 7 on any PC with less than a dual-core processor and at least 2GB of RAM.

Hard drive space

Installing Windows 7 Home Premium costs you at least 16GB in hard drive space, and that's the very definition of A Bare Minimum.

Those figures don't include the extra hard drive territory that Windows 7 demands for features such as temporary files and virtual memory, so you should add another 5GB (or even 10GB) to those totals. With today's hard drives, a spare gigabyte of space is easy to come by, so there's no reason to feel claustrophobic. My call? I'd opt for a minimum of 30GB for Windows 7.

Mr. Potato Head on parade

Over the years, Windows has inflated like a Macy's parade balloon on Thanksgiving Day. On my desk is an original copy of Microsoft Windows/286 — version 2.1 of Windows, which dates back to the late 1980s and was designed for 80286-powered PCs. I keep it as a conversation piece. The entire installation took a whopping seven low-density floppy disks, and only one holds the operating system! (The other six disks store applications, fonts, printer drivers, and such. And you can forget the floppies — Windows is available only on DVD-ROM now.)

Graphics card

You need a graphics card of recent manufacture — one that supports at least DirectX 9 — to enjoy these visual perks without slowing down your PC.

And now for the rest of the story

To enjoy some features of Windows 7 to the fullest, I would also recommend the following "luxuries" (luckily, most of them are either included with a PC of recent vintage, or they're easily obtained at your local Maze O' Wires electronics store):

✦ To use the full power of Windows 7 and the programs I describe in this tome, you'll need an Internet connection

✦ For those interested in watching or recording TV directly, a TV tuner is a must

✦ Sharing files and printers using HomeGroup requires a network and PCs running Windows 7

✦ DVD/CD authoring requires a compatible optical drive

Starting and Shutting Down Windows 7

Starting (or, as technotypes continue to call it, *booting*) your Windows 7 PC is as easy as pressing the power switch. Some diagnostic and trouble-shooting options are available during the startup process, but I cover those in detail in Chapter 5 of this minibook. For now, just remember the power switch.

There's more to consider, however, when you're ready to shut down Windows 7. In this section, I discuss the five methods you can use to shut down completely or partially.

Shutting down completely

The first option is the full deal: turning off your PC completely. Click Start and then click the Shut Down button in the lower-right corner of the Start menu. Your PC (eventually) turns itself off.

Windows tries to be a friend by automatically closing any applications you're running before it shuts down. However, if a program has an open document or file that hasn't been saved, the application is *supposed to* prompt you to save your changes first. Note that I said *supposed to*: Some misbehaving or badly written programs *don't* prompt you before they zap themselves out of existence, so don't use the Shut Down or Restart options (see the next section) unless you manually saved all open documents (or you trust any application that's open, such as Microsoft Word).

Restarting your PC

Restarting your PC consists of shutting down Windows and then immediately turning it back on. (Restarting is also called *rebooting*.) To restart your computer, close all open programs and documents, choose Start and click the right arrow button (next to the Shut Down button) on the Start menu; then choose Restart from the pop-up menu. You don't need to press the power button to turn your PC back on again. Dame Windows, she can do it all.

You might need to restart when you install new software or upgrade existing software. (You typically see a dialog box that displays a Restart button.) I also recommend rebooting if your PC starts acting flaky — like when error messages keep appearing, programs refuse to close, or strange graphics appear on your desktop.

Using sleep mode

Sleep mode immediately puts your PC in a low-power mode: The monitor goes black, and Windows appears to shut down. However, you can return to your work just as you left it by pressing one of the arrow keys on the keyboard or moving the mouse. It's rather like your monitor waking up from a screen saver snooze: It saves time and electricity, and makes it easier to return to your work "already in progress." To go into sleep mode, choose Start, click the right arrow button (next to the Shut Down button) on the Start menu, and then choose Sleep from the pop-up menu.

Not all PCs support sleep mode. Check your PC or motherboard manual to see whether you can use this feature. If you can use Windows's sleep mode, you may also be able to set your PC's power switch to activate sleep mode rather than turn off the computer. Or, your PC can go into sleep mode automatically after a certain amount of inactivity.

Manually save your documents before putting your PC in sleep mode because putting your machine into sleep mode does *not* save to your hard drive the files you're working with — instead, they're saved to your PC's memory. You lose everything if your PC is hit with a power failure and you haven't saved your documents.

Yes, your PC can hibernate

Hibernation is a variation of sleep mode that's popular with laptop owners. It takes longer for your PC to switch to hibernation mode or to return from hibernation, but that's because a snapshot of your PC's current state (including all open applications and files) is saved to your hard drive. Unlike in sleep mode, a power failure while your PC is hibernating doesn't result in lost files!

As with sleep mode, your PC's motherboard must support Windows 7 hibernation mode. When you want to put your machine in hibernation mode, choose Start, click the right-arrow button (next to the Shut Down button) on the Start menu, and then choose Hibernate from the pop-up menu. (You can also set your PC to automatically hibernate when a certain period of inactivity has passed, and most laptops can be set to hibernate automatically when you close them.)

Multiuser options

The last three system choices available from the right-arrow button (next to the Shut Down button) on the Start menu are useful in a *multiuser* environment: in other words, when multiple people are sharing the same PC at different times and using a different user account for each person.

+ **Switch User:** If another user simply needs the PC for a short time, you can choose the Switch User menu item, which allows another person to log on and take care of business. Unlike logging off, however, your applications continue running (in a *hidden* state). When that other person has finished with her account, she can log off, allowing you to return to your far more important tasks! In other words, Windows 7 is allowing *two* accounts to run at the same time but allowing only one person to use the PC.

+ **Log Off:** Leave your PC running but allow others to log on to the PC if they enter a valid username and password. Like a true shutdown, logging off in Windows 7 automatically closes most applications and any open documents. To pass the computing torch to someone else, choose

Start, click the right-arrow button on the Start menu, and then choose Log Off from the pop-up menu.

✦ **Lock:** Choose Lock, and Windows 7 immediately displays a password-protected screen that prevents anyone from logging in or using the machine until the proper password is provided. (If you're thinking security while you visit the restroom, you're a winner.) In effect, a Locked system operates just like it would with a password-protected screen saver.

Windows 7 keeps track of each different user's account data and documents, so you can be assured that everything you don't want seen by others remains private. I go over multiuser operation in Chapter 4 of this minibook, so don't worry — all will become clear there.

Your Windows 7 Controls

After you become an expert in starting and shutting down your PC, survey the landscape of Windows 7. I show you the various graphical WUDs (short for *Wondrous User Devices*) represented on your desktop and how you can use them to exercise your will within.

Icons

The first stop on your journey is the lowly icon — often jeered and often the target of a string of impassioned and unprintable words. Yet, icons are still the building blocks of today's graphical user interfaces (GUIs; that's a 10-cent synonym for operating systems such as Windows, Mac OS X, and Linux, which all use a mouse). Believe me, icons will be around long after you and I are no longer worried about PCs.

Icons look like a picture, and that's no accident because they're simple representations of different locations and items on your computer. For example, Windows 7 displays different types of icons to represent items such as these:

✦ **Files and folders**

✦ **Programs you can run**

✦ **Hardware, such as hard drives, DVD drives, and printers**

✦ **Internet connections**

✦ **Other computers on your home or office network**

Figure 1-1 shows a gaggle of different types of icons in their natural environment. I go into much more detail about what you can do with icons in the next two chapters of this minibook. For now, just remember their versatility and that they represent something else on your system besides a thumbnail-size picture.

Figure 1-1:
I have always depended upon the kindness of icons.

That constantly changing cursor

Within Windows 7, your mouse cursor is more than just a focus for your clicking finger — although that is its main use. When your cursor isn't pointing the way (depending on the desktop action you're performing or the application you're running), it can also show

✦ **Status:** PC activity, such as loading a file or applying a command

✦ **Selection:** Select text or graphics (to do something nefarious, I'm sure)

✦ **Location:** Your position in a document

✦ **File movement:** Progress while you're copying or moving files

By the way, you can also click your right mouse button *(right-click)* when the mouse cursor is resting atop something to display a pop-up menu that includes commands that are specific to the item you're hovering over. (To technonerds, the term for this pop-up is a *contextual menu.* Geez.) For example, if you right-click a digital photograph that you saved to your hard drive, you can choose to preview it, edit it, or print it. Personally, I'm a big fan of contextual menus because they usually contain everything that applies to a particular file. Some programs, such as Photoshop, even add their own commands to the contextual menu.

The Start menu

Another familiar face that you see often in Windows 7 is the Start menu, shown in Figure 1-2. (Someone at Microsoft should get a free steak dinner for this one.) The name actually fits its purpose because you can start from this single menu virtually every activity and task that your PC can perform.

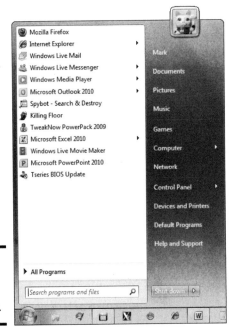

Mozilla Firefox
Internet Explorer
Windows Live Mail
Windows Live Messenger
Windows Media Player
Microsoft Outlook 2010
Spybot - Search & Destroy
Killing Floor
TweakNow PowerPack 2009
Microsoft Excel 2010
Windows Live Movie Maker
Microsoft PowerPoint 2010
Tseries BIOS Update

Mark
Documents
Pictures
Music
Games
Computer
Network
Control Panel
Devices and Printers
Default Programs
Help and Support

All Programs

Search programs and files

Shut down

Figure 1-2:
The
invaluable
Start menu.

Your Start menu might look different from mine. You can customize your Start menu to fit how you work, like how I did.

To use the Start menu, move your mouse cursor to the bottom of your desktop until the Start button appears in the lower-left corner. Click the Start button, move your cursor to an icon or a command, and then click.

Highlights of the Start menu include

+ **All Programs list:** Run any program installed on your PC.

+ **Recent Applications list:** It's on the left, which makes it easy to run a program that you used, well, recently.

+ **Documents link:** Quickly access any document that you created or saved to your hard drive (such as photos, videos, and music).

✦ **Control Panel:** Configure Windows 7 to your preferences. (Chapter 5 of this minibook centers on Control Panel.)

✦ **Pictures and Music links:** Go directly to your digital photographs and digital music files.

✦ **Games link:** Does this one need an explanation? (I thought not.)

✦ **Start Search text box:** Track down specific files, folders, or locations within your system.

✦ **Access to your network locations:** Examples are your Internet connection and any home or office network that your PC can use.

I discuss all these controls in later chapters of this minibook — but you've got to admit that it's *sassy* to have them all them in one place!

Book II Chapter 1

Shake Hands with Windows 7

The taskbar

The next stop on the Windows 7 Express is the *taskbar,* which is that little strip of buttons and miniature icons that runs along the bottom of the screen. Like the Start menu, the taskbar is another useful control that you can use to accomplish all sorts of tasks, and it remains out of sight until you need it. (Depending on the settings you choose for your taskbar, it might remain hidden until you move your mouse cursor to the bottom of the screen.) I talk more about configuring the taskbar in Chapter 3 of this minibook.

Don't worry if your taskbar doesn't look like mine in the figure here. The appearance of the taskbar varies according to the programs you're running and the custom controls you added to it. You can use the taskbar to

✦ Switch quickly between open applications (and even multiple documents or windows open in the same program, as shown in Figure 1-3).

✦ Run the programs that you specify with a single mouse click.

✦ Control background programs that normally run hidden, such as your antivirus software.

✦ Control hardware, such as your printer and modem.

✦ Connect and disconnect Universal Serial Bus (USB) and FireWire peripherals, such as digital cameras and external DVD recorders.

✦ View the time and date.

✦ Access the Start menu.

You can find the full scoop on the taskbar in Chapter 3 of this minibook.

Figure 1-3:
Use the
taskbar
to switch
between
multiple
documents
in one
program.

Figure 1-3:
Use the
taskbar
to switch
between
multiple
documents
in one
program.

Menus and toolbars

Here's one more set of Windows 7 common controls, which are found in just about any program you run because they're part of Microsoft's grand user interface design standard. (It makes all Windows programs easier to understand and use, often without the need to refer to that ridiculous Web-based user manual you got with your latest application.) Both these common controls — menus and toolbars — are shown in the multipurpose Figure 1-4.

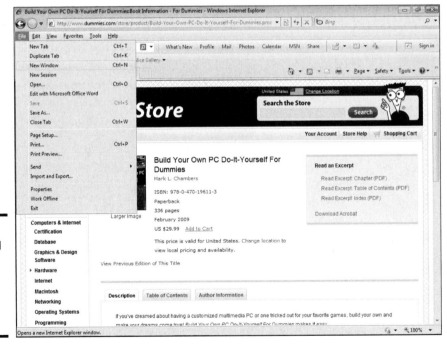

Figure 1-4:
Menus and
toolbars
abound
in the
Windows
world.

The miracle of menus

Menus are the drop-down secret to life itself. Each menu contains either a group of similar commands or a group of commands that fall under the same category. To use a menu, you can either

✦ **Go mousing.** Click the menu name and then click the command from the list that appears.

✦ **Go digital.** Hold down the Alt key, press the underlined letter (the *hot key*) in the menu name, use your cursor keys to choose a command, and then press Enter to use the command.

For example, to open a file in virtually any Windows application, click the File menu at the top of the window and then choose Open from the drop-down list that appears. Alternatively, while holding down the Alt key, press F (the hot key for the File menu) and then press O (the hot key for the Open menu).

Book II
Chapter 1

**Shake Hands with
Windows 7**

Those tremendous toolbars

A *toolbar* is a collection of buttons that allows you to use the most common menu commands in a program with a single click. Typically, toolbars appear at the top of a program window, but many applications (Adobe Photoshop, for example) have either floating toolbars that exist as separate windows or toolbars that can be resized and relocated anywhere in the application window. Some applications let you go even further, allowing you to customize your toolbars with buttons for the menu commands you use the most. (In the world of Microsoft Office 2010, the toolbar is a huge oversized monster called the Ribbon . . . but it's still a toolbar down deep inside.)

To illustrate how easy it is to use a toolbar, consider opening a file. If the application you're using has a File Open button on the toolbar, click it — end of story. (The moral is, toolbars rule!)

To display the name of a toolbar (which is usually all you need to identify it or to jog your memory), leave your mouse pointer motionless on top of the toolbar button for a moment or two. Such motionless conduct is called *hovering* among technotypes, and the snippets of text that appear are called *tooltips*.

Using Bill's Funky Keys

Not all Windows-specific controls are meant for your mouse. Thanks to the Power of Bill, PC keyboards now come complete with additional keys that are tied directly to Windows, so you can use your keyboard, rather than your mouse, for navigation. As any PC power user will tell you, the mouse that can move faster and more efficiently than your fingertips hasn't been (and likely never will be) invented. Just wait until Bill gets those new letters that he wants in the alphabet!

Most of the keys on your computer keyboard work like they do on standard typewriters. For instance, pressing Shift in combination with another alphabetic key still creates a capital letter. PC keyboards, however, also sport nifty special keys for navigation, functions, and (sometimes) Windows-specific commands. For your reference, Figure 1-5 illustrates a typical modern 104-key PC keyboard.

Figure 1-5:
The PC keyboard — still the fastest Windows controller around.

The Windows keys

Ah, the Windows keys — they rest snugly between the Alt and Ctrl keys on both sides of the spacebar on your keyboard. You can press either of these keys at any time to display the Start menu. Additionally, a number of other keys can be used in combination with a Windows key. Just hold down a Windows (Win) key and try one of the keys listed in Table 1-1.

Table 1-1	Windows Key Combinations
Key Combination	**What It Does**
Win+D	Displays the Windows desktop (even with other programs running)
Win+E	Opens the Computer window, where you can manage your files
Win+F	Opens the Find dialog box, from which you can locate a file or folder
Win+L	Locks your computer (or allows you to switch users, if multiple accounts are active)
Win+R	Opens the Run dialog box, from which you can run a program by typing its name

In fact, just press the Windows key by itself, and Windows opens (or closes) the Start menu. What will they think of next?

The Shortcut key

Remember how enamored I am of contextual menus? A quick poke at the Shortcut key — located on the right side of the keyboard, between the Windows and Ctrl keys — acts as a right-click (displays a contextual menu) when you select an icon anywhere in Windows. After the pop-up menu appears, you can use your cursor keys and the Enter key to choose a command.

Other important keys

These old friends have been around since the days of Genghis Khan — or at least the beginnings of the IBM PC, whichever came first. (Scary thing is, I remember the latter vividly.) Anyway, these keys still come in quite handy in the Windows world:

+ **Enter:** PC keyboards have two of these beauties: one above the Shift key on the right side of the alphabetic keys and the other in the lower-right corner of the numeric keypad. Within your word processor, of course, pressing Enter creates a new paragraph. But elsewhere within Windows, pressing Enter almost always starts a command or selects an item. (A friend of mine still calls it the *Submit key*. He's great fun at parties.)

+ **Arrow (navigation) keys:** This tightly-knit group of four keys performs a number of different functions, depending on what you're doing at the moment, but it's always something to do with movement. For example, you can scroll through a document in a word processor or spreadsheet, or move through the items in a list. Heck, many games you play will even use the arrow keys to select a direction or move your character forward or backward.

+ **Escape (Esc):** Press Esc (in the far upper-left area of your keyboard), and you're jetted off to your favorite vacation spot with a ton of cash to spend and your favorite movie star. (No, not really — although Bill is rumored to be working on the new enhanced Escape key for the next version of Windows.) Actually, you use Esc to back out of things. Pressing Esc can cancel many commands, close some windows, and close dialog boxes.

+ **Num Lock:** Press this key (in the upper-left corner of the numeric keypad) to toggle those keys between the numbers — useful for spreadsheets and data entry — and navigational keys. (Note the cursor arrow symbols on the 2, 4, 6, and 8 keys.)

+ **Ctrl (Control):** These two keys (on either side of the spacebar) are used in conjunction with other keys for editing and keyboard commands within many applications. For example, pressing the combination Ctrl+B within Microsoft Word makes selected text bold.

✦ **Alt (Alternate):** Like the Ctrl keys, your Alt keys are used in league with other keys, typically for invoking menus and special features within your applications.

✦ **F (Function) keys:** These 12 sentinels across the top of your keyboard are used for different purposes throughout Windows — and in many cases, even within specific applications (hence the generic name). They're usually abbreviated as *F1* through *F12*.

 Other keys on your keyboard — for example, Home, End, Page Up, and Page Down — also have specific uses within every application. To become a power user of a certain application, consult that program's Help system for the special keystrokes it uses. You'll zip through documents while others plod along!

Using the Windows 7 Help System

Speaking of help, I'm happy to say that Windows 7 comes with the best Help system that has ever shipped with any version of Windows. It even has online components that you can refer to for the latest information on features (and the *occasional* bug). With the Help system, you can

✦ **Locate specific help.** Find help for nearly any topic.

✦ **Follow task tutorials.** They guide you step by step through all sorts of procedures (such as printing, troubleshooting, and updating Windows with the latest patches).

✦ **Search the Microsoft Windows 7 communities.** All you need is an Internet connection.

✦ **Scan tips and tricks.** Get help from Windows experts (if you have an Internet connection).

✦ **View the latest headlines.** Read all about new Windows 7 features (if you have an Internet connection).

Displaying Help

The two methods of displaying Help within Windows itself are

✦ **Press F1 while on your desktop.** Click anywhere on your desktop and then press the F1 key to load the top-level Windows Help system window, which you see in Figure 1-6. (Check out that spiffy toolbar at the top of the window!) *Note:* When you're using a program, pressing F1 displays the Help system for that program.

✦ **Click Help and Support from the Start menu.** It's another neat function of the Start menu.

Figure 1-6:
The oracle
of all things
Windows
7 — the
Help system.

Searching for specific help

After the Windows 7 Help and Support window displays, feel free to click any
of the *links* (the bolded words) to display the corresponding topic. However,
you usually visit the Help system to search for specific help on a Windows
feature or command. To search for a word or phrase within Help, follow
these steps:

1. **Click within the Search Help box, at the top of the Help and Support
    window.**

2. **Type the word or phrase you want to search for and then press Enter.**

    The fewer words you enter, the better the chance of getting a match that
    addresses your topic.

    The Help system hums happily to itself for a few seconds and then dis-
    plays a results page like you see in Figure 1-7. (I searched for the phrase
    burning a cd in this example.)

3. **To display the information in a topic, click the topic name (in the
    Search Results area).**

Some steps have *links* (look for underlined text), which you can click to open
the dialog box or window in question or run the program mentioned in the
Help text. (This really makes it easy to fix something, especially when you
don't quite know where a particular setting is within the Windows 7 behemoth.)

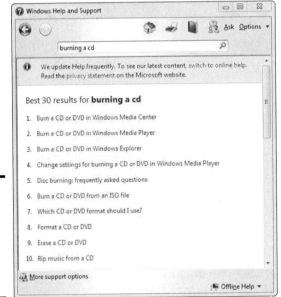

Figure 1-7:
The results
of a typical
search
through
the Help
system.

To move backward through Help topics to where you started, click the Back button on the toolbar in the upper-left corner of the Help window.

Some search results return *technical articles* — consider them *Tips for Technonerds* — that relate to the topic you found. Technical articles can include bug fixes, workarounds, or just explanations of what precisely is happening when you use a Windows feature.

Yelling for assistance

If you can't find what you're looking for within the Help system, you can turn to Microsoft for direct support. In the bottom-left corner of the top-level Help menu (refer to Figure 1-6), click the More Support Options button.

Unless you have a very knowledgeable friend who has already mastered the Windows Remote Assistance feature of Windows 7, I *strongly* urge you to avoid using this option. This process involves your friend connecting to your PC over the Internet and gaining control of Windows 7 — with all the possible nastiness that entails. Personally, I recommend that you turn to Microsoft support instead.

If you lost your Internet connection or you don't have an e-mail address, naturally you can also contact Microsoft for support by telephone — at least for now. (Insert ominous chord here.) The number is always included in your Windows 7 installation documentation.

Chapter 2: The Many Windows of Windows

In This Chapter

- ✔ Managing windows
- ✔ Recognizing icons
- ✔ Selecting one icon (or many icons)
- ✔ Using toolbars in Windows 7

Doing things graphically is what Windows 7 is all about. The idea of visual control is at the heart of today's graphical user interfaces (GUIs), like Windows and Mac OS X (and Linux, when it's wearing the right makeup).

In this chapter, I introduce you to the graphical building blocks of Windows 7. Plus, I show you the "antique" keyboard combinations that are even faster than a speeding mouse. (Hey, any power user will tell you that pressing a sequence of two or three keys is often faster than clicking!)

Managing Windows Means Productivity

What's that on the horizon? Oh, boy — it looks like another of those weighty Mark's Maxims:

Learn the Zen of the window and become a power user.™

In this section, you do just that — and your efficiency and speed in Windows 7 will amaze your friends and family. (And that's what it's all really about, right?)

Windows 7 has a helpful feature that displays a short pop-up description of the controls in a window. If this book isn't handy, you can find out the function of a button or widget by leaving your mouse pointer sitting motionless on top of the control in question. (Interesting trivia fact: This mouse action is *hovering,* and the descriptive text that appears is a *tooltip.*)

Opening and closing windows

You rarely need to manually open a new window in Windows 7, which is a trademark of good design from the Redmond troop. Windows 7 automatically opens a window when you

✦ **Run Explorer** (as shown in Figure 2-1). Just double-click the Computer icon on your desktop. Explorer is the tool that you use for navigating through the files on your hard drive, copying and moving things from place to place, running programs, and opening documents — for example, using Explorer, you could open your USB flash drive and load the family reunion photos given to you by your kids.

Windows Explorer is your navigation and file management tool. On the other hand, Internet Explorer is a Web browser that you'll use to visit sites on the World Wide Web, like www.dummies.com.

✦ **Run most Windows applications.** Some programs, however, run in the background or don't automatically create new document windows.

✦ **Create a new document in a Windows application, such as Word.**

Toolbar

Close button

Figure 2-1:
The most common window you'll encounter is the Explorer window.

Expand/Collapse

By default, the left portion of the Explorer window contains common locations within Windows 7. You can expand any heading with a right-facing triangle icon next to it; just click the triangle to expand the item (such as a folder or hard drive) and click it again to collapse the item.

You do need to close windows, however, to keep your desktop tidy and to free system resources for other tasks. To close a window, move your mouse pointer over the *Close button* — the red button with an X in the upper-right corner of the window, as shown in Figure 2-1 — and then click the left mouse button. Alternatively, you can usually choose File⇨Close from the window's menu. (You can see the File menu button in upcoming Figure 2-2. If the menu is hidden within the Explorer window, press and hold the Alt key to display the menu.)

And no worries that you might close a window by accident and lose all your work because a safety net is in place within any well-behaved Windows application (such as Word 2010 or Photoshop, for example): The program first asks you for confirmation before it closes a window containing an unsaved document.

Scrolling windows

Suppose that you're reading page 1 of a six-page document and you decide to jump ahead to page 5 — unfortunately, page 5 is nowhere in view. (In the same vein, you could be using an Explorer window to navigate a hard drive with dozens of folders, and the folder you want is farther down within that gaggle of folders.) How do you get to the item or the information you want to see?

That's the job of those unsung heroes, your scroll bars (as shown in Figure 2-2). To move through the contents of the window, just click in the area above or below the scroll button or click the up and down buttons at the top and bottom of the scroll bar. (*Note:* If your document is wider than the application window, you see a horizontal scroll bar as well. It works the same way, by just moving the contents of the window to the left or right.)

To really move like the wind within a window (bad pun that I won't repeat), you can even click the scroll button and drag it. When you drag something, you first click it — in this case, the scroll button — and then hold down the mouse button while you move the mouse in the desired direction. You can find more uses for dragging later in this chapter.

Many applications allow you to scroll through the contents of a window with your keyboard arrow (navigation) keys or with a scroll wheel on your mouse. And, pressing the Page Up and Page Down keys should move an entire page at a time through the contents of a window.

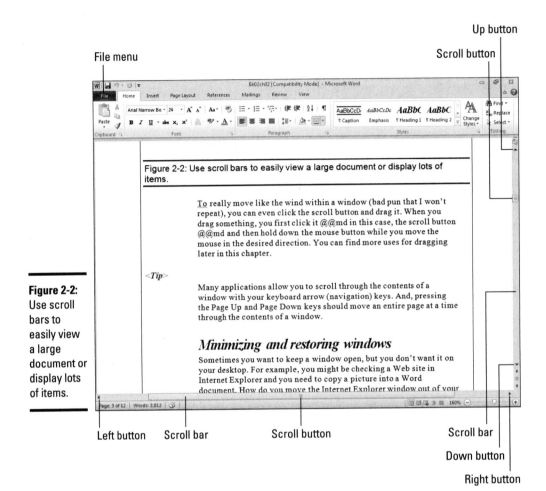

Figure 2-2:
Use scroll
bars to
easily view
a large
document or
display lots
of items.

Minimizing and restoring windows

Sometimes you want to keep a window open, but you don't want it full-screen on your desktop. For example, you might be checking a Web site in Internet Explorer and you need to copy a picture into a Word document. How do you move the Internet Explorer window out of your way temporarily without closing it? This is a job for the Minimize button, as shown in Figure 2-3.

Maximize/Restore button

Minimize button

Figure 2-3:
The window
control
buttons are
old friends
of any
power user.

Minimizing a window hides it. Well, more accurately, the window is stored as
a button on your taskbar, at the bottom of the screen. To return the window
to its original glory, simply click the button on the taskbar. If you have a lot
of windows open, the taskbar might sprout its own set of scroll buttons so
that you can scroll through the minimized windows within the taskbar. (To
minimize all open windows at one time, move your mouse pointer to the
taskbar and click the Show Desktop button. I tell you more about the taskbar
in Chapter 3 of this minibook.)

The taskbar also uses another trick if you have a large number of windows
open. Separate windows within a single application are grouped together as
a single taskbar button — and, when you hover your mouse over the button,
Windows 7 displays each window as a thumbnail. Click the desired thumbnail to select it.

"So does a program continue to run when it's minimized?" Good question. Most do, but some applications pause when minimized (such as games or video players) and then restart when the window returns to the desktop.

Maximizing and restoring windows

If you already guessed that maximizing a window is the opposite of minimizing it, pour yourself another soda as a reward! *Maximizing* a window expands it to fill the entire screen, giving you plenty of elbowroom to work with. In fact, applications such as Microsoft Word take advantage of a maximized window by displaying as much of your document as possible, using automatic word wrap (or even displaying multiple pages in one window).

If the window isn't maximized, click the Maximize button once — it's the middle button in the group in the upper-right corner (refer to Figure 2-3). After the window expands, the multitalented Maximize button toggles to the Restore button. When you click the Restore button, the window returns to the original dimensions it had before you clicked the Maximize button, and that doggone button morphs back into the Maximize button again. ("Ethel, make it stop!")

Moving windows

When you need to move a window from one area of your desktop to another, Windows 7 is there for you. On a typical day, I end up juggling multiple windows like the world's worst circus clown. (Alternatively, you can buy a larger monitor. Yeah, right.)

To move a window to another piece of desktop real estate, click and drag the window's *title bar* — the colored strip at the top of the window that displays the application or document name — and the entire window follows. When the window is in the correct place, release the mouse button to drop it. (Of course, you can't do this when the window is maximized. Go figure.)

To arrange multiple document windows within an application, choose Window➪Arrange All, and the document windows line up in an orderly fashion so that you can choose one.

Resizing windows

A window can be resized to different dimensions as necessary — sorry, no triangles or parallelograms, though. Simply move your mouse pointer over the lower-right corner of the window or to one of the sides of the window until the mouse cursor changes to an arrow icon. Then click and drag to move that window in the indicated direction. (As you might expect, you can't resize a window if it's fully maximized. Go figure.)

Switching windows

Although you can easily open 10 or 15 windows within your Windows 7 desktop, keep in mind that only 1 window at a time is *active*. And, the active window takes precedence, appearing on top of other windows, because it's the window you're viewing, editing, or using. Windows that are open on your desktop — and not minimized — are *inactive* windows. They're dimmed (or shaded) to indicate that they're offline. (Note, however, that you can still copy or move files to an inactive window, which I demonstrate in Chapter 3 of this minibook.) You can see both the active and inactive window in Figure 2-4; in this case, Internet Explorer owns the lucky active window.

Active window   Title bar   Inactive window

Figure 2-4:
The active window is the belle of the Windows 7 ball.

To switch to a different window, you can

✦ Click anywhere within the desired inactive window.

✦ Move your mouse cursor to the taskbar and click an application button or a window button.

✦ Cycle through the open applications by holding down the Alt key and repeatedly pressing Tab until the window you want becomes active.

Note that you can still use a window's Minimize, Maximize/Restore, and Close buttons even when the window is inactive. Also, an application might continue to run while its window is inactive.

A Field Guide to Icons

Now I begin my discussion of icons with a classic Greek comedy. (Readers familiar with my books will already know about my propensity for vignettes.)

7 and *The Iliad*
(with apologies to Homer)

As the play opens, Hector is tussling with his new installation of Windows 7. He's knee-deep in an Explorer window that's filled to the brim with icons.

Hector: "I want to run Microsoft Word! Which of these furshlugginer little pictures stands for the program, and which of these are my documents? What do I double-click? *Help!*"

[Enter proud Odysseus, hero of the Trojan War and experienced Windows 7 power user.]

Odysseus: "Do not panic, good Hector. You see, Microsoft Word has its own *program icon,* and each Word document that you create uses the Word *document icon.* The same is true for everything from Excel to Adobe Acrobat."

Hector: "So how do I learn which is which?"

Odysseus: "Read the manual that you got with the application or open an Explorer window and look in the folder where you saved a document from the application. Each software developer creates a unique program and document icon combination, but most of them are pretty self-explanatory."

Hector: "Or I could eschew icons completely by running Word from the Start menu, and then I can load the document that I want from Word's File menu, right?"

Odysseus: "That's right, or you can even double-click the document icon itself within that Explorer window, and it will automatically load Word with that document."

Hector: "Hey, bud, that's in the next chapter. And where's that Trojan horse you promised me?"

Odysseus: "Whoops — busted again. I'm out of here!"

Fin

In this section, I help Hector (and you) by identifying each type of icon and showing some common examples.

Don't be afraid to right-click an icon to see its properties. Just put your mouse pointer over the icon in question and press the right mouse button once, which displays a pop-up contextual menu. Click Properties, and you can see which application created a document — or, as Windows 7 calls it, *opens with* — as well as other nifty stuff that I discuss at several points in later parts of this book.

Hardware icons

Only a select few hardware devices have their own icons in Windows 7, but you'll be surprised at which ones do, including rather nebulous things such as network and Internet connections. These hardware icons tend to hang out on your desktop or in a top-level Explorer window.

Here's a representative list of hardware that's represented by Windows 7 as icons, many of which are shown in Figure 2-5:

✦ **Hard drives**

✦ **DVD and Blu-Ray drives**

✦ **Printers**

✦ **Removable storage,** such as floppy drives and portable Universal Serial Bus (USB) flash drives

✦ **External devices,** such as MP3 players and digital cameras

In general, you can open, activate, or control a hardware device by double-clicking its icon (depending on which type of hardware device it is). Find more on this topic in the appropriate spots later in this minibook.

Figure 2-5:
A well-ordered passel of hardware icons.

Program icons

Because you already know about program icons (thanks to Hector and Odysseus), I don't go into much detail here. Double-clicking a program icon runs the application from an Explorer window or your desktop, and a single click will suffice from the Start menu or a pinned item on the taskbar.

If you've used earlier versions of Windows, wave a fond farewell to the Quick Launch toolbar — now the taskbar offers the same functionality with the *pin* command. You can drag an item to the taskbar and click the Pin to Taskbar pop-up that appears, and that item remains on the taskbar. To open or run the item, just click on the pinned icon in the taskbar.

Figure 2-6 illustrates a number of well-known program icons. (I've made the icons larger so you can see them more clearly — you discover how to do this in Chapter 4 of this minibook.)

File icons

Technically, document icons are a subspecies of *file icons,* which can represent any type of data file on the planet. Windows 7 uses a couple of generic icons to represent files it doesn't recognize, so every file on your system — and I mean *every* file — can be represented by some kind of an icon.

Figure 2-6:
A number
of program
icons
caught on
camera.

Like it does with a document icon, Windows 7 attempts to open any data file you double-click. If Windows 7 knows the application that created the file, the program runs automatically to display the file. On the other hand, if Windows 7 doesn't recognize the file type, you see a dialog box that looks like Figure 2-7, where you can choose to

✦ Browse for the program that should open the file.

✦ Select the program from a list that you want to use to load the file.

Figure 2-7:
Specify
which
program
Windows
7 should
use for this
document.

Folder icons

A *folder* is nothing more than a container to hold and organize other items, which can include both icons and subfolders. All folders use the ubiquitous manila file folder icon. If the folder is empty, the icon looks, well, empty. The icon for a folder that contains files displays miniature thumbnail images of the items it contains, as shown on the right side of Figure 2-8. Chalk up this cool effect to the eye candy in Windows 7.

Figure 2-8: The unsung hero — the common folder icon, empty and full.

Shortcut icons

A *shortcut* is represented by a unique icon. Although a shortcut looks much like a regular icon, a thorough examination reveals a curved arrow at the bottom of the image. (The phrase *Shortcut to* might also appear at the end of the icon label.)

Think of a shortcut as a signpost or a link to another item within your Windows 7 system. For instance, you can set up a shortcut to *World of Warcraft* that runs the program just as though you had clicked the program icon directly on the Start menu or had double-clicked the program icon in the Explorer window.

However, because shortcuts take up only a few bytes of hard drive real estate, they come in handy when you're customizing your desktop or organizing a folder. You can set up a program to be run from any folder (without requiring that you dig down with Explorer). Too, a shortcut can be easily tossed into the Recycle Bin after you're finished with it because it's not a part of the original application.

In fact, many games and applications now offer to add a shortcut to your desktop during installation, and I usually take them up on the offer. A desktop shortcut is quite convenient, and the software developer knows that you can delete it quickly and easily, if necessary. If a program doesn't offer to install a shortcut on your desktop and you'll be using that program often, I would recommend manually creating a shortcut on the desktop (which I'll cover in Chapter 4 of this minibook).

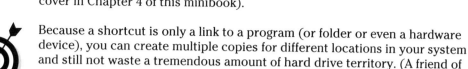

Because a shortcut is only a link to a program (or folder or even a hardware device), you can create multiple copies for different locations in your system and still not waste a tremendous amount of hard drive territory. (A friend of mine always creates a folder on his desktop with shortcuts to all the documents and files relating to his latest project. That way, he can immediately work on anything relating to that project and just delete the folder with the shortcuts after the job is done.)

"But Mark, can't I take matters into my own hands and just move the application?" Let me put out this potential fire with a well-placed Mark's Maxim:

Never try to simply copy or move an application that you've installed in Windows 7 from one folder to another.™

Not only is the application unlikely to work (because it can't find any of its support files), but you also can't use the Programs and Features screen within Control Panel to uninstall the application later! (I tell you more about uninstalling software the *right* way in Chapter 5 of this minibook.) Instead, create a shortcut (which I demonstrate in Chapter 4 of this minibook) and move that shortcut to the desired location.

Figure 2-9 shows off a number of shortcut icons, along with their original source icons.

System icons

The final type of icon represents a system function or a system location in Windows 7, such as Computer, the Recycle Bin, or the Network. Like other icons, you can use them or right-click them to display a context-sensitive pop-up menu. For example, right-clicking the Recycle Bin displays a menu with a number of choices that directly apply to deleted files.

I discuss these icons and what they represent in various spots throughout this book (especially in Chapter 4 of this minibook).

Book II
Chapter 2

The Many Windows
of Windows

Figure 2-9:
Shortcut
icons are
an excellent
way to
organize
your stuff.

Selecting Icons

After you become familiar with icons, you might be wondering how you can manipulate them. I go into more detail in the next two chapters of this minibook, but for now, you need to know how to select one or more icons: that is, how to highlight the icon (or icons) that you want to use when performing the next action, such as copying, moving, or deleting the selected icons.

I should note at this point that Windows 7 offers different ways to view the contents of a folder, which I discuss later in Chapter 4 of this very minibook. For example, you can display icons in a list format as well. The methods of selecting icons, however, do not change.

Selecting a single icon

To select a single icon, click it once — and notice that Windows 7 has highlighted it to indicate that it has been selected.

Selecting multiple contiguous icons by dragging

To select a group of icons that are next to each other, click your mouse in a part of the window above and to the left of the first icon, and then drag the mouse down to a spot below and to the right of the last icon you want to select. Any icons within the box are selected and highlighted.

Selecting multiple contiguous icons by clicking

Another method of selecting a group of contiguous icons is to select the first icon in the group by clicking it, holding down the Shift key, and then clicking the last icon you want to select. This method is especially handy when viewing files in List view.

Selecting multiple separated icons by clicking

What if you want to select a number of icons that aren't contiguous? How do you select them? In this case, click the first icon you want to select, hold down the Ctrl key — don't stop holding it down — and then click each additional icon you want to select. After you select everything you need, release the Ctrl key.

To deselect an icon you pick by mistake, click it again. ***Remember:*** You must continue holding down the Ctrl key until you finish selecting (and deselecting) what you want.

Using the Toolbar

The final stop in the graphical Windows world — at least in this chapter — is the toolbar. Most Windows applications now use toolbars; you can see in Figure 2-1, earlier in this chapter, the Explorer window has its own toolbar. Each button typically replicates one of the application's popular menu commands and performs the same function as though you had selected the menu command.

If you already know how to click a button in Windows, you know how to use a toolbar: Just move your mouse pointer on top of the desired button and click the left button once. Whoosh!

However, not all toolbars are stuck at the top of a window. Some applications have toolbars across the top and both sides of the screen, along with — gasp! — floating toolbars that you can click and drag to wherever you like!

Where am I going with this? Well, I'm suggesting that you read the manual for an application thoroughly because often you find that you can customize that application's toolbars with just the commands you want. Why take up valuable space on that toolbar with a Print button if you don't have a printer? I show you how to customize toolbars in several spots throughout the book, but for now, just enjoy using toolbars because they can save you all kinds of time.

Chapter 3: Windows 7 Basics

In This Chapter

✔ **Starting and exiting an application**

✔ **Moving, copying, and deleting items**

✔ **Creating new folders and renaming items**

✔ **Recovering valuable stuff from the Recycle Bin**

✔ **Using and configuring the Start menu**

✔ **Working with printers**

✔ **Using and configuring the taskbar**

✔ **Terminating a misbehaving program**

*B*oot camp is over — now it's time to discover some of the more advanced tasks within Windows 7.

For example, no PC owner can ever hope to become a power user without becoming good friends with both the Windows 7 Start menu and taskbar. You need to know how to run programs, whether they're installed and appear on the Start menu or whether you have to track 'em down and run them from your hard drive or CD-ROM drive.

Files and folders need to be copied, moved, or removed; deleted files need to be permanently erased (or recovered, in the case of an accident); and new folders need to be created while you're using your PC. You might need to change printer settings, shut down a program that's no longer responding, or locate another computer on your local network with the shared file that you have to copy to your hard drive. All these tasks are basic, yet a surprising number of PC owners are in the dark about them — they still know only one way to close a program, or they aren't aware that you can change the characteristics of a printer by just right-clicking it and choosing Printer Preferences!

That's what this chapter is all about — delving into the different methods of taking care of basic tasks within Windows 7.

Running Applications from the Start Menu

First things first: Windows 7 becomes a lonely place indeed if you can't run any applications. To run a program from the Start menu, follow these steps:

1. **Move your mouse pointer to the lower-left corner of the screen and click the Start button on the taskbar.**

Or, if you have a keyboard with Windows keys, press one of them to display the Start menu. (Your keyboard probably has two of these critters. Just look on either side of the Alt keys, which are on either side of the spacebar. The Windows keys look like the fluttering Windows flag.)

Figure 3-1 illustrates the Start menu and the taskbar. Any applications you recently used probably appear in the Recent Applications list, on the left side of the Start menu.

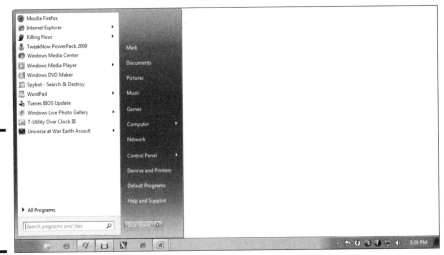

Figure 3-1:
The Start menu and taskbar — truly a dynamic duo!

2. **To run a recently used application again, click the application name in the list on the left, and dance around the room because you were able to do things The Convenient Way.**

3. **If the program doesn't appear on the Recent Applications list, click All Programs — or just hover your mouse pointer over the All Programs button.**

Whomp! Windows 7 displays in a list all applications installed on your PC. Program groups (think of them as subfolders) are displayed as folders, whereas individual applications appear at the top. (The All Programs link morphs into the Back link, allowing you to back up if you like.)

4. **Click the program group that contains the application you want to run.**

Sooner or later, you have to track down the doggone program you want, so be patient. (I've seen program groups that have two or three sub-folders!) If the program appears by itself at the end of the All Programs menu, you can rejoice.

5. **Click the application name to run it.**

Many software developers include supplementary programs with the actual application, such as utilities, game editors, and the like. That's nice of them — but unfortunately, those additional application icons can get kind of confusing, so make sure that you're clicking the Real Deal to avoid embarrassment (and the hassle of closing a program that you didn't want to run in the first place).

Running Applications from Your Hard Drive

Often you want to run a program from the forested undergrowth that is your hard drive. Perhaps you downloaded a program from the Web or you're running a shareware application that doesn't install itself on the All Programs menu. Follow these steps:

1. **Click the Start button and click the Computer item to open the Explorer window (behold it in Figure 3-2).**

Back button

Forward button

Figure 3-2:
You can
always run
programs
from the
Explorer
window.

2. **Double-click the hard drive that contains the program you want to run.**

   If necessary, continue clicking folders and subfolders until you see the application you want. This, good reader, is *navigating,* and I do a lot of navigating in this book!

3. **Double-click the application icon to run it.**

Running Applications from a CD-ROM or DVD-ROM

By default, Windows 7 loves to be helpful. So, usually when you load an application's CD-ROM into your drive to install the program, Windows 7 automatically runs the installation program for you. However, from time to time, you might need to venture onto Planet Optical and run a program directly from a CD-ROM or DVD-ROM. Follow these steps:

1. **Press the button on your CD-ROM/DVD-ROM drive to eject the tray; load the disc (shiny side down) and press the button again to retract the tray.**

   If the application's installation menu appears, just click the Close button or click Exit or Quit to shoo it away.

2. **Click the Start button and click the Computer item to open the Explorer window.**

3. **Right-click the CD-ROM or DVD-ROM drive that contains the desired application and choose Explore.**

   If necessary, navigate to the location of the program by double-clicking any folders and subfolders. (See? I told you that you'll be navigating Windows 7 all the time!)

4. **Double-click the application icon to run it.**

Running Applications from a Network Drive

If your PC is connected to a LAN (engineer-speak for a wired or wireless network), you might have access to programs located on other network computers. As my grandfather used to exclaim, "Zounds!" (It's really not magic, though.) Follow these steps:

1. **Click the Start menu.**

2. **Choose the Network item from the Start menu.**

   Windows 7 obligingly displays a Network window, displaying all shared folders and hard drives on your network.

Don't have a Network item on your Start menu? It's easy to place one there. Right-click the Start button, choose Properties from the menu that appears, and then click the Customize button on the Start Menu tab. Locate the Network check box in the list, click it to enable it, and then click OK to save your change. From now on, you're in Network heaven!

3. **Double-click the network folder or hard drive that contains the program you want to run.**

4. **Double-click the application icon to run it.**

Before you imagine a wonderland where anyone on your network can run any program on your PC, keep in mind these two caveats to running an application over a network:

✦ **You need the proper user access.** The person using the "host" PC must give you proper access to run the program.

✦ **The program must support networking.** Not only does the application need to support network operation, but you may also need a separate user serial number to run it from another PC on the network.

For more information on the ins and outs of networking, visit Chapters 1 and 2 in Book VIII, which covers home networking (and tell them I sent you).

Exiting a Program

After you perform whatever magic you need within an application, I recommend exiting the program. Of course, you can leave it running, like a Web browser, but most of the time, you avoid slowing down your PC's performance by closing applications you're not using. (Even when you're not directly using a program, Windows 7 spends processor time and memory keeping it ready for you, as well as maintaining all the eye candy of translucent window frames and shiny 3D buttons.)

To shut down a program, use one of these methods:

✦ **Click the Close button (the big X) in the upper-right corner of the window.**

✦ **Choose File⇨Exit from the program's menu.**

✦ **Press Alt+F4.** This one doesn't work on all programs, but many still honor the old Exit keyboard shortcut.

Where the @#&! is the @#&! Alt+F4 key?

If you're scanning your PC's keyboard in vain for the Alt+F4 key, you should stop now: There's no single key named that way on any keyboard. Instead, Alt+F4 stands for a key *sequence* — it's two keys pressed together. When you see two keys conjoined by a plus sign, press the first key and hold it while pressing the second key. For example, if I tell you to press the sequence Ctrl+C (which copies a selection), I'm asking you to hold down the Ctrl key while you press the C key. After you press the C key, you can release the Ctrl key.

Most Windows 7 shortcut key sequences use one of three keys as the first key: Alt, Shift, or Ctrl. You can press the specified key on either side of the keyboard, so lefties might press

the Shift key that's under the Enter key. It's all gravy to the Big 7. In fact, most PC owners are familiar with the Ctrl+C (copy), Ctrl+X (cut), and Ctrl+V (paste) sequences. (No need to hold down the Shift key or use Caps Lock, a lower-case c, x, or v works just as well.)

Some rare key sequences involve three keys: The first two keys are held down while you press the third one. The most famous three-key sequence, of course, is the infamous Three Finger Salute — the legendary Alt+Ctrl+Delete sequence that would reboot a PC running DOS. In Windows 7, applying the Three Finger Salute displays the Windows Task Manager, which I discuss a bit more later in this chapter.

If you haven't saved any open documents and you try to exit an application, most Windows programs prompt you for confirmation so that you don't lose your stuff accidentally — as shown in Figure 3-3, where I'm trying to close Word without saving this chapter. No, Mark, don't do it!

Figure 3-3:
Don't exit
without
saving.

Putting Your Files in Order

Have you considered how to manage files in Windows 7? Don't worry, the folks in Redmond are one step ahead of you — you can use the Explorer window to take care of your chores, as you see in this section.

You can find file management alternatives to Windows Explorer. One of my favorites is Total Commander (shown in Figure 3-4), which has been a popular shareware favorite for many years, and for $38 (US), it's a bargain. Total Commander is list based, so you see and select from more than the traditional icon view in Explorer. (I show you how to switch views in Chapter 4 of this minibook.) You can download a copy to try out from www.ghisler.com.

Before you buy software — either shareware or a commercial program — don't forget to check and make sure your new toy is fully compatible with Windows 7, and keep in mind that there's a *big* difference between the 32-bit and 64-bit versions of our favorite operating system. Programs that are written for one version of Windows 7 often refuse to even *install* on the other version!

Figure 3-4: Total Commander is an excellent alternative to Explorer.

Book II
Chapter 3

Windows 7 Basics

Copying and moving stuff

To copy selected files and folders from one Explorer window to another — or to the desktop or to a drive — you can use one of these methods:

✦ **Click the selected items and drag them from one Explorer window to the destination Explorer window.** Of course, this method requires you to open two Explorer windows, but that's life in the Big 7. Also, note that in order to copy from one location on a drive to another location *on the same drive,* you must hold down Ctrl while you drag. Otherwise, Windows 7 assumes that you want to *move* the items instead. (If you're copying something from Drive C to a location on Drive D, you don't have to hold down the Ctrl key.) You can always tell when you're copying something with the mouse because Windows 7 adds a small plus sign (+) to the items while you drag.

✦ **Right-click the selected items and drag them to their destination.**
IMHO (short for In My Humble Opinion), this choice is always better
than copying with the left mouse button. Why? Well, you don't have
to hold down Ctrl — Windows 7 pops up a menu when you release the
mouse button and asks whether you want to copy or move the file. It's
much more civilized, don't you think?

✦ **Copy and paste the items.** Right-click the items and choose Copy from
the pop-up menu, click in the destination Explorer window, and then
right-click and choose Paste. From the keyboard, you can press Ctrl+C
to copy or Ctrl+V to paste.

To move selected items, use one of these methods:

✦ **Right-click the selected items and drag them to their destination.**
Again, it's my favorite — release the mouse button and choose Move
from the pop-up menu that appears.

✦ **Cut and paste the items.** Right-click the items and choose Cut from the
pop-up menu, click in the destination Explorer window, and then right-
click and choose Paste. From the keyboard, you can press Ctrl+X to cut
or Ctrl+V to paste.

If you attempt to copy or move a file that has the same name as another file
in the target location, Windows 7 prompts you for confirmation before over-
writing anything. (Feel free to rename the file and try the operation again.)

If you need to reverse direction when navigating — for example, if you
click one subfolder too many and now you need to return to the previous
folder — don't forget about the Back button in the upper-left area on the
Explorer toolbar, which functions just like the Back button in Internet Explorer.
You can move forward as well, returning to your original position — just click
the Forward button.

Creating a new folder

Creating new folders is the cornerstone to good organization in Windows 7.
Dumping everything in your Documents Library folder is a bad idea because
it will rapidly resemble a sold-out rock concert (complete with additional
files struggling to get in).

To create a new folder within the current location in Windows Explorer, use
one of the following methods:

✦ **Click the New Folder button on the Explorer toolbar.** Explorer adds
the new folder icon and also opens a text box underneath it, in which
you can type a name for the new folder.

✦ **Right-click any open spot in the Explorer window and then choose New⇨Folder from the pop-up menu that appears.** Note that I said "open spot" — if you happen to right-click an icon or a control, you see a completely different pop-up menu, so pick an unoccupied parcel of territory.

Deleting stuff with mouse and keyboard

That heading kinda sounds like "Deleting stuff with moose and squirrel," don't you think? (Boy howdy, sometimes I turn into a real laugh riot — usually when I've had very little sleep.) Anyway, if you need to delete unnecessary files or folders from your system, Windows Explorer can handle that task as well.

Use your mouse to select the items you want to trash, click the Organize button on the Explorer toolbar, and then choose Delete from the menu. Alternatively, you can right-click the selected items and then choose Delete from the pop-up menu that appears. If you're into dragging things, you can drag an item from the desktop or an Explorer window and drop it on top of the Recycle Bin on your desktop.

From the keyboard, just select the unwanted items and press Delete. It doesn't get any easier than this, folks.

Deleted stuff is whisked away to the Recycle Bin — but that stuff may not be permanently deleted yet. (Read more on your Recycle Bin later in this chapter.)

Displaying properties

You might want to display an item's Properties dialog box, for a number of reasons:

✦ **If it's a shortcut:** You can find the location of the original file.

✦ **If it's a folder:** You can see how much total space the folder uses and how many files it contains.

✦ **If it's a file:** You'll see the file type, who created it, and when the file was last modified.

✦ **If you're displaying a drive's properties:** You can see how much free space the drive has left, or you can scan it for errors and then defragment it. (Read more on scanning and defragmenting in Book IV, Chapter 2.)

Here's the point: Every item on your Windows 7 desktop and in an Explorer window has a Properties panel, and the contents change depending on what the item is. Throughout the rest of this book, I show you how to use the Properties settings for all sorts of items.

To display the properties for an item, right-click it and then choose Properties from the pop-up menu that appears. For example, Figure 3-5 illustrates the properties for my drive C.

Figure 3-5:
Displaying the Properties dialog box for a hard drive.

Renaming items

You have three ways to rename an item in an Explorer window. Here's the first half of the process (telling Windows which item you want to rename):

+ **Click the item once, pause a second or two, and then click again.** Unfortunately, this method takes a bit of experience to do reliably.

+ **Click the item to select it and then press F2.**

+ **Right-click the item and then choose Rename from the pop-up menu that appears.**

Regardless of which method you use, Windows 7 opens a text entry box with the current name. To delete the current name completely, just type the new name. To use a portion of the original name, click in the text box and use your cursor keys and the Delete key to remove the unwanted characters.

Emptying the Recycle Bin

"Mom, where do we empty the recycled files?" Technonerds still chuckle about "recycled" ones and zeroes, but the Windows 7 Recycle Bin is a popular spot on your desktop, and you eventually have to empty it. (You can tell whether it's holding deleted items because the icon shows a discarded document in the bin.)

To delete the contents of the Recycle Bin, right-click it and then choose Empty Recycle Bin from the pop-up menu that appears.

Windows eventually deletes older items from the Recycle Bin automatically — or when you use Disk Cleanup. (If you've never used the Disk Cleanup utility, click Start and type **Disk Cleanup** in the Search box; then click the Disk Cleanup utility in the search results.) However, you free up space every time you empty the Recycle Bin, and sometimes that extra space can come in quite handy on a drive that's filled to the brim.

By default, Windows prompts you for confirmation before deleting your trash. If you feel that such clucking is overdoing things and you want to banish this file deletion confirmation, right-click the Recycle Bin and choose Properties to display the settings you see in Figure 3-6. Deselect the Display Delete Confirmation Dialog check box, and then click OK.

Figure 3-6: Turning off that darned file-deletion dialog box.

Recovering Items from the Recycle Bin

Here's a feeling we've all shared from time to time: You suddenly realize that you just dropped your Great American Novel into the Windows 7 Recycle Bin by mistake. (**Hint:** If you back up your files regularly, you won't panic nearly as much as the poor PC owner who has never backed up.)

However, there's still a chance that you can recover from your mistake and recover that orphaned Word document from the Recycle Bin! (The quicker you try a rescue after you realize the error, the better; read on to discover why.) Follow these steps:

1. **Double-click the Recycle Bin to display its contents.**

2. **Select the item you want to restore.**

3. **Right-click the item you want to restore and then choose Restore from the pop-up menu that appears.**

The Recycle Bin is useful, but it's not a perfect solution because Windows 7 might use the space occupied on your hard drive by a deleted item to store new data, which makes restoration impossible. That's why I recommend that you restore a deleted item *as soon as possible* — I try to do it immediately after I catch my mistake.

Putting the Start Menu through Its Paces

Ready to disassemble the Start menu? That's what this section is all about: helping you gain control of the somewhat ungainly (yet extremely useful) Start menu and customizing it for your specific needs. (I don't discuss the Documents folder here because I cover that topic in Chapter 4 of this minibook.)

Tossing the Recent Applications list

You can read how to use the Recent Applications list at the beginning of this chapter, but if security is an issue, you might want to disable it. After all, does your boss *really* need to know that you recently played *Tetris* and *Bioshock 2*? I think not.

To disable the list, follow these steps:

1. **Right-click the Start button and then choose Properties from the pop-up menu that appears.**

This step displays the Taskbar and Start Menu Properties dialog box, which you see in Figure 3-7.

2. **From the Start Menu tab, deselect the Store and Display Recently Opened Programs in the Start Menu check box.**

The Recent Items list works the same way as the Recent Applications list, except that it displays recently opened *documents* rather than recently used programs. Again, if you're worried about your security (or your reputation) and you don't want others to know what you're doing, you can disable the list entirely with the Store and Display Recently Opened Items check box.

3. **Click OK.**

Figure 3-7:
Yep, the
Start button
has its own
Properties
dialog box.

Using the Run item

You can launch any application from the Run item. Choose Start⇨All
Programs⇨Accessories⇨Run, and you see the dialog box shown in
Figure 3-8.

Figure 3-8:
Run
programs
with aplomb
from this
dialog box.

Click in the Open text box and type the filename of the application you want
to run; or, you can click the Browse button to navigate to the application. If
you recently used the Run dialog box to start the same application, click the
arrow at the right side of the Open drop-down list and choose that application from the list.

When the filename appears in the Open box, click OK to run it.

When you're using the Run dialog box, remember that the name of the
program you want to run might *not* be the same as the actual application
filename — and you must enter that actual application filename! For example, you can run Microsoft Word 2010 from the Run dialog box, but entering
word or **word.exe** results in an error. In fact, the filename you need to enter

is **winword.exe**. (The Start Search box on the Start menu can be used in the same way — enter **winword.exe** and press Enter.)

Accessing printers

To add a printer, choose Control Panel⇨Devices and Printers from the Start menu. Your Printers window likely contains different printers than mine does, shown in Figure 3-9, but the items on the window's toolbar are the same. (You may also see a Fax icon in your Printer window — read more about Windows 7 fax support in Chapter 4 of this minibook.)

Figure 3-9:
My
Windows
7 Devices
and Printers
window.

Check mark indicates default printer.

This window is also the place for changing the settings provided by your printer manufacturer's Windows 7 driver. For example, you can likely change the print quality, and perhaps you can clean your inkjet's print nozzles or check your ink levels. Right-click a printer icon and then choose Printing Preferences to see what you can change. What you see depends on your printer manufacturer. In Figure 3-10, which illustrates the Printing Preferences dialog box for my Epson inkjet printer, is an example of what you might see.

To choose your default printer throughout Windows 7, right-click the desired printer and then choose Set as Default Printer. Windows 7 adds a spiffy check mark symbol to the printer's icon to indicate that it's the default printer.

Figure 3-10:
Display the
Preference
settings for
your printer.

Note that Windows 7 also displays several advanced printer settings in a printer's Properties dialog box, including printer sharing (which I cover in Book VIII) and color management for color printers.

Windows applications are likely to use one of three different methods to print:

+ **Choose File➪Print from the application's menu.**
+ **Click the Print icon on the program's toolbar.**
+ **Press Ctrl+P.**

To display (and control) pending printing jobs, click a printer to select it and then click the See What's Printing button on the Devices and Printers window toolbar. This action displays a Print Jobs window with details about the pending printer jobs. You can pause all your print jobs on the selected printer by choosing Printer➪Pause Printing from the Print Jobs window menu; to restart the printer, click the Pause Printing menu item again. (If your printer is on a network, you need Administrator rights to pause all print jobs.)

To pause a single print job, click the job in the Print Jobs window list and then choose Document➪Pause. To resume printing, click the job in the list and then choose Document➪Restart.

Working with your network

Click the Start button and choose Network to open shared folders on other networks (including File Transfer Protocol [FTP] servers on the Internet). From here, you can

+ **Open a shared location for moving, copying, or opening documents.** Just double-click the network icon to open it.

If other PCs on your network are using Windows 7, you can use the Homegroup feature to conveniently share files and printers — to display your network kin and what they have to offer. (More on Homegroup in Chapter 4 of this minibook.)

+ **Open a shared location for running an application.** Again, double-click the network icon to open it.

+ **Add a new network connection.** Click the Network and Sharing Center button on the Network window toolbar, and then click the Set Up a New Connection or Network option in the window's Task pane to run the wizard, which walks you through the short process of creating a new icon in the Network window.

The properties of your network connection are always available from the Network and Sharing Center window, allowing you to control things like file sharing.

+ **View network connections.** Display the Network and Sharing Center window to view all available network connections recognized by Windows 7; note that not all these connections might be active at this moment.

+ **Set up a network.** Click the Network and Sharing Center button on the Network window toolbar, and then click the Set Up a New Connection or Network link. (I explain more about network setup in in Book VIII, Chapter 2.)

+ **Add a printer.** Click this button on the Network window toolbar to add a local or network printer to your collection. (First, though, make sure that the printer you want to add is powered up and connected.)

+ **Add a wireless device.** Click this button on the Network window, and Windows 7 will lead you through the process of installing all sorts of wireless gear to your network. Again, it's important to turn the device on (and set it as discoverable) so that Windows 7 can pick it up and display it for your selection.

I refer to many of these network windows and toolbar buttons throughout later chapters of this book, so remember how you got here.

Configuring the Start menu

I'm not quite ready to leave the Start menu yet — at least, not until I discuss the Advanced panel of the Customize Start Menu dialog box. Right-click the Start button, choose Properties, click the Start Menu tab, and then — finally! — click the Customize button to display the settings you see in Figure 3-11.

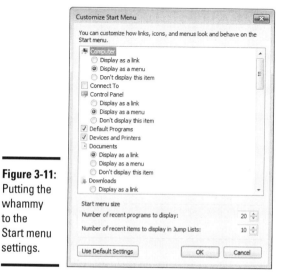

Figure 3-11: Putting the whammy to the Start menu settings.

From this dialog box, you can modify a number of features on the Start menu:

✦ **Sort All Programs Menu by Name:** Although you have to scroll down to find this feature, it's worth the trouble: Enable this check box, and Windows 7 automatically displays the programs and program groups in your All Programs list, with the individual applications on top of the list. If you have a huge number of installed programs, use this feature to locate that new application much more easily. (Folders are placed before filenames in the menu.)

✦ **Number of Recent Programs to Display:** You can ratchet this number up to 30 (resulting in a Recent Programs scrolling list) or reduce the number to clean up your Start menu.

✦ **Start Menu Items:** This scrolling list allows you to specify what you want shown on the Start menu and whether certain items should be shown as a link (which opens a separate window) or as a menu. The party guests include the Computer, Control Panel, Documents, Games, Homegroup, Music, Pictures, and Personal folders. (You can also turn off each item to tidy up your Start menu.)

TIP

Windows 7 introduces *Jump Lists*, which are submenus of recently opened documents, folders, Web sites, and other items arranged under the program that opens them. You can tell a Jump List when it appears in the Start menu by the right arrow that appears by the program name. Just hover your mouse cursor over the program to see the list pane and then click an item to run the program using that item.

Handling the Taskbar

Yep, it's yet another Windows 7 control. This time, I'm talking about the *taskbar,* which is that loyal strip of screen real estate that appears at the bottom of the screen — or at the side or the top. (Read more on this in a second.) In this section, I tell you more about the often-neglected taskbar.

Switching programs

The primary use of the taskbar — and one that has been around since Windows 95 — is to allow you to easily switch between the windows of the programs you're running. You can switch between programs by clicking your mouse pointer on the taskbar button for the program you want to use.

Will you flip over Flip 3D?

That all depends on your graphics card and your color scheme — but allow me to explain! Windows Flip 3D is the window-switching feature available to users of Windows 7 Home Premium, Professional, and Ultimate — it's part of the Windows Aero color scheme, which is well known for the high demands it requires from your PC's CPU and graphics card. (In other words, if you're not using one of these versions of Windows 7, or you're not using the Aero scheme because your PC isn't powerful enough, you can stop reading here.)

Still with me? Then you're in for a visual treat with Flip 3D because it makes switching windows into a special effects show! Click Ctrl+Windows key+Tab to display the Flip 3D stack, an overlapping side-on view of the application windows that are open in Windows 7, and then press Tab to cycle through the windows. (You can also move your mouse wheel to switch between windows in a hurry.) To choose the selected window, press Enter or click the window you want to switch to.

Personally, I like speed and efficiency rather than too much eye candy, so I continue using the old-fashioned familiar Alt+Tab shortcut to switch between windows.

Shhh . . . there's also another method of switching programs that doesn't use the taskbar — and because we're on the topic, I tell you about it here. You can press Alt+Tab to move between the programs you're running. To step through the programs, hold down Alt while you press Tab repeatedly, and you advance through your programs like Tiny Tim tiptoeing through the tulips.

Controlling the notification area

Another item on the taskbar Hit Parade is the *notification area* — that's the far right end of the taskbar, shown in Figure 3-12. Most of these icons represent a program that's running, such as your antivirus program. The Volume icon lives here (which you can click to set your PC's volume or mute sound altogether) as well as network connection icons.

Figure 3-12:
Your
taskbar,
your friend.

Icons pinned to the taskbar   Notification icons

So what did you glean here? ("Bueller? Bueller? Anyone?") Not everything in the notification area is a program; rather, the icons that appear there indicate (or notify you about) programs that are available and events that are happening on your PC. You can, however, right-click most notification icons to display pop-up menus. Typically, the menu allows you to control whichever program or feature the notification icon represents (including the ability to close or exit, if the icon represents a program that's running).

If you see a tiny yellow or red medieval-looking shield appear, right-click it immediately to display the Windows Defender, Windows Update, or Windows Security windows, which displays the reasons why you're seeing a warning icon. Typically, Windows 7 is shooting a flare to warn you that your firewall or virus protection has been limited or disabled; in addition, if you disable automatic updates, you also see the warning icon. When you have set things up right, the shield icon disappears from the notification area.

If you see an arrow pointing up at the end of your notification icons, Windows 7 is hiding the icons you haven't used recently, to make more room for program buttons. To see these hidden icons, click the arrow.

If you're dissatisfied with the contents of your notification area, right-click in any open space on the taskbar, choose Properties, and click the Taskbar tab. Click the Customize button in the Notification Area section — now you can configure which items you want to appear in the notification area, as shown in Figure 3-13.

Figure 3-13: Customizing the notification area settings.

Adding icons to the taskbar

Within Windows 7, you can right-click and drag any program icon, file icon, or folder icon down to the taskbar, where Windows 7 displays the Pin to Task Bar bubble — click the bubble to pin the item to the taskbar. From that point on, clicking the icon on the taskbar runs the application, opens the document, or opens the folder.

Naturally, space on the taskbar is limited, so I recommend that you add only the programs, folders, and items you use the most.

"Hey, I can't pin anything on the taskbar!" That's probably because the taskbar is *locked,* which prevents anyone (including you) from inadvertently dragging a pinned icon off to the desktop or from making any changes to the dimensions or location of the taskbar. Right-click anywhere on the taskbar itself (and not on an icon or control), choose Lock the Taskbar to unlock it, and then try again. After you're done arranging the taskbar as you like it, it's a good idea to lock it again.

Configuring the taskbar

Would you rather have your taskbar on the left or right side of the Windows 7 desktop? How about at the top of the desktop? No problem. First, make sure that the taskbar is unlocked (see the preceding section); then click in the center of the bar and drag it to any other side of the screen. (Check out Figure 3-14.)

Figure 3-14:
Zounds! For those who gravitate to the right. . . .

While the taskbar is unlocked, you can also expand it by clicking the edge closest to the desktop (where the thin strip appears) and dragging it up. (Some folks prefer a larger, easier-to-read taskbar.)

Now that you see how easy it is to alter the taskbar, you understand the necessity of locking it! Don't forget to batten down the hatches after you have things just as you want them.

Even many Windows 7 power users don't know that you can also add toolbars to the taskbar! Right-click any open part of the taskbar, choose Properties, and then click the Toolbars tab. Now you can add extras like an *Address toolbar* (where you can type or copy a Web or FTP site and go to that location, right from the taskbar) and a *Desktop toolbar* (which displays the items directly on your desktop). To remove a toolbar, just click to deselect the check box and then click Apply.

Terminating a Program with Prejudice

Sometimes a program just decides to misbehave. At least things are better in Windows 7 than they were in Windows 98 or Me, where one locked program was likely to lock the entire machine. In the Big 7, you should be able to force a nonresponsive program to quit without losing any open files or having to restart your PC — although I always save my files in the other applications, just in case!

To force a locked program to terminate, follow these steps:

1. **Right-click any empty spot on the taskbar and choose Start Task Manager from the pop-up menu to display the Task Manager. (Keyboard mavens can press Ctrl+Alt+Delete — the old familiar "Three Finger Salute.")**

2. **Click the Applications tab to display the list shown in Figure 3-15.**

Figure 3-15: Control the Task Manager, and you control Windows 7.

3. **Click the name of the application that's causing the problems.**

   It's usually marked as Not Responding in the Status column.

4. **Click the End Task button to initiate the terminate sequence.**

   Note: It might take several seconds for the terminated program to disappear, or you might need to repeat this step two or three times to force termination.

   Sometimes, Windows 7 displays a dialog box saying that the program will not shut down properly. In this case, move on to Step 5.

5. **Click the End Now button.**

The program disappears from the Applications list.

6. **Click the Close button to close the Task Manager.**

By the way, you can also log off Windows 7 from the Task Manager. Click the Users tab, and you see the Logoff button. Naturally, to see who's logged in to your machine — either locally or remotely — you can click the Users tab, where you can also disconnect any undesirables.

Those interested in performance should eyeball the Performance tab, which allows you to graphically monitor your CPU and memory usage. The Networking tab lets you track your network speeds and the amount of data moving to and from your PC over your LAN connection.

How to Avoid Formatting a Floppy Disk

If you're lucky, your PC won't even have a floppy disk drive. But if it does, here's my message in a nutshell: You really shouldn't use a floppy disk. Ever. *Honestly.*

Why the floppy should be extinct

Let me tell you my story. More than a decade ago, I lost an irreplaceable document that was near and dear to my heart. The floppy it was stored on gave up the ghost, and I was left a broken man (for at least half a day). It was then that I embarked upon a sacred mission to banish the floppy disk from my PC — and from the PCs of all those who would heed my call:

🖊 Those who have also lost valuable data to the vagaries of the Plastic Pretender, where data can be readable one second and unreadable the next

🖊 Those who have realized that practically nothing fits within 1.44MB of space any longer

🖊 Those who have encountered the recalcitrant floppy disk that reads perfectly well on one PC and stubbornly refuses to be read on another

🖊 Those who need compatibility between PCs and Macs

🖊 Those who are sick and tired of that grinding sound and the slow transfer rate of that prehistoric magnetic media

For an entire decade, I have carried on this fight in every book I've written. Here's your chance to join me. Just repeat the following chant: **"Begone, floppy!** Leave my sight! I banish you forever to the Land of Obsolete Technology. *As it is written, so shall it be done."*

Instead, opt for a USB flash drive, which works perfectly on any PC with a Universal Serial Bus (USB) port. And, if the PC is running at least Windows 98SE, you shouldn't need any installation software or drivers. Most of these drives are so small that they fit on your keychain, and they even work with Macintosh and Linux computers. They're sturdy, with no moving parts to wear out. And, because a USB flash drive is Plug and Play, you can connect and disconnect it without having to reboot your PC.

Today's USB 2.0 flash drives really rock, offering transfer rates of up to 480 Mbps! My USB 2.0 flash drive has 16GB of storage space and cost $45, but you can buy a drive with up to 32GB of storage for a mere $100 or so. All hail the new King of Personal Storage!

To sum up, here's a classic Mark's Maxim:

With a flash drive, you'll never lose a document to a floppy again.™

Aw, geez, my editors say I have to tell you how to format a floppy. Something about a contract that I purportedly signed. Okay, it's your data's funeral, not mine. Floppy disks (like Zip disks and hard drives) must be formatted before they can (unreliably) store any data; this task prepares the magnetic surface of the disk to hold stuff.

Load the floppy you want to format. (This process involves locating the goofy drive bay that looks like it could eat a graham cracker and pushing the floppy into it until you hear a satisfying click that sounds like you stepped on a June bug.) Click the Start button and click Computer to display the drives on your system. Right-click the floppy drive (probably named A for Abysmal) and then choose Format.

Chapter 4: Advanced Windows 7

In This Chapter

- ✔ Customizing your desktop background
- ✔ Working with the Sidebar and gadgets
- ✔ Fine-tuning the windows
- ✔ Sharing stuff on your network
- ✔ Using a HomeGroup
- ✔ Understanding multiuser computing
- ✔ Sending and receiving faxes in Windows 7
- ✔ Playing MP3 files in Media Player
- ✔ Viewing and downloading digital photographs
- ✔ Recording your own data CDs in Windows 7
- ✔ Watching a DVD movie

*I*f you're following along in this minibook, you've been a slave to the Microsoft default settings. That might be the status quo for novice Windows 7 users, but if you want to mold Windows 7 into *your* operating system (and thus become a PC power user), you must master the customization features within Windows 7. Just say "No!" to Icons view or that too-familiar desktop background — add your favorite sound effects from *The Rocky Horror Picture Show* to your Windows 7 experience. (I boot up every morning to the lilting sounds of "The Time Warp," much to the consternation of our family cats.)

This chapter ties together the actions you need to take to transform your PC from a personal computer into a *personal tool* — which, I might add, should be the goal of every hardware manufacturer and software developer, including the Microsoft crowd. In these pages, I do my part: You discover how to optimize your copy of Windows 7 for productivity, share your computer with others in a multiuser environment, and send and receive faxes with your PC's fax modem. I also introduce you to Windows Media Player, which you can use to enjoy all sorts of digital multimedia. And stick around for a brief look at downloading and viewing digital photographs. I even show you how to burn a CD-R with data files from your hard drive — *without* your having to buy an expensive CD recording application!

So, good reader, prepare yourself for the advanced stuff — turn that cookie-cutter machine with its vanilla Windows 7 into your personal, custom-made *muscle PC,* and take it up a notch!

Personalizing Your Desktop

Don't get me wrong — I like the soothing blue-green swirl of the typical Windows 7 desktop. After a few weeks, though, you say to yourself, "Self, you spent two grand on this system. Why not jazz it up a little bit?" In this section, I show you how to take care of spicing up the look and sound of Windows 7.

Changing the background

First up on the makeover tour is the most popular trick — changing your desktop background to something more palatable. Windows 7 prefers JPEG and bitmap images for your background.

Follow these steps to select a new background:

1. **Right-click anywhere on the open space of your current desktop and then choose Personalize from the menu that appears.**

In other words, don't click an icon or a Windows 7 control, such as the Start menu. The Personalization Control Panel window appears.

2. **Click the Desktop Background link to display the settings you see in Figure 4-1.**

3. **Open the Picture Location drop-down list to choose a category of images.**

By default, Windows 7 displays the images in the Windows folder, under the category Windows Desktop Backgrounds. To choose a desktop image from your Windows folder, click the thumbnail image in the list. Windows immediately displays it on your desktop.

You can load your own image by clicking the Browse button and navigating to the location of the image; then just double-click the image file to load it. Windows 7 accepts images in either JPEG or Windows Bitmap formats as desktop backgrounds — personally I use JPEG, because the equivalent image in Bitmap format takes up a honking amount of hard drive space!

4. **To stretch an image that doesn't quite fit across your entire desktop, click the Picture Position pop-up list and select the Fill item.**

If the image is too small to fill the desktop, pick Center to put it in the middle of the desktop, or Fit to increase the size to match the horizontal or vertical dimensions of your screen. Alternatively, you can choose Stretch to increase the size of the image (kind of like pulling taffy); however, the smaller the image, the more likely that Stretch will distort it to an unacceptable degree. (If you choose Stretch or Fit, don't worry: The original image remains pristine.) If the image is a repeating pattern, choose Tile.

Figure 4-1:
The Desktop
Background
screen
offers
many visual
treats.

5. **To set the desktop to a solid color, open the Picture Location drop-down list and choose Solid Colors.**

   Solid white and black are always excellent choices because they help speed up the graphics display on a slower video card.

If you like what you see, click OK. If the result would make Andy Warhol cringe, try again.

 Select an entire folder full of images, and Windows 7 can cycle through them automatically using the delay you choose from the Change Picture Every drop-down list. You can also right-click the desktop and choose Next Desktop Background from the menu that appears to immediately jettison the current background image and load a new one from the folder!

Using themes

A Windows 7 *theme* is a package deal: Selecting a theme gives you a background, a color scheme, a screen saver, and sound effects. Themes are available from Microsoft, or you can download themes (of varying quality) from sites all over the Web. To choose a theme, follow these steps:

1. **Right-click anywhere on the open space of your desktop and choose Personalize from the menu that appears.**

2. **Click the desired theme thumbnail.**

   Windows 7 immediately updates your desktop characteristics with the selected theme.

3. **To create a theme of your own based on the current desktop settings, click the Save Theme link.**

4. **Type a name for the new theme and click Save.**

Changing system sounds

Windows 7 offers a number of events that can be heralded by system sound files in WAV format. Follow these steps to assign sounds:

1. **Right-click anywhere on the open space of your desktop and choose Personalize from the menu that appears.**

2. **Click the Sounds link to display the dialog box you see in Figure 4-2.**

Figure 4-2: The sounds of Windows 7.

3. **To choose an existing sound scheme, open the Sound Scheme drop-down list and choose the scheme you want.**

4. **To assign sounds individually to events, select an event from the Program Events list box and then open the Sound drop-down list to display all sounds installed within Windows 7.**

   To hear a sound, click the Test button. (When you assign a sound to an event, Windows 7 marks that event with a tiny speaker icon.)

5. **You can also use sound files from another folder on your hard drive (as long as they're in WAV format); click the Browse button, navigate to that folder, and then double-click the file to load it.**

If you create your own custom sound scheme, don't forget to click Save As to save it under a unique name so that you can load it in a flash in the future.

6. **When you're ready to rock, click OK to close the Sound dialog box.**

Adding the Sidebar and gadgets

Think of the Windows 7 Sidebar as a collection of "mini-applications" — *gadgets* — that are always available on your desktop. You can pick and choose among a wide selection of gadgets to provide just the information and functions you want within the Sidebar, and they're always on hand.

**Book II
Chapter 4**

**Advanced
Windows 7**

For example, your office PC's Sidebar might include a calendar and the current local weather, while your home PC's Sidebar might feature a stock ticker for your favorite stocks and a TV program listing.

To start Sidebar, click the Start button, type **sidebar** into the Search box, and then click Add Gadgets to the Desktop. The default Sidebar you see in Figure 4-3 appears, complete with three gadgets: an analog clock, a slide show viewer for Windows wallpaper images, and an RSS feed window.

Figure 4-3:
The
Windows 7
Sidebar
feature
brings
gadgets
to your
desktop.

To add a gadget from the Microsoft collection, right-click the desktop and choose Gadgets from the menu that appears. The Add Gadgets dialog box appears, as shown in Figure 4-4 — just click and drag a gadget to a spot on the Sidebar. To remove a gadget, right-click it in the Sidebar and choose Close Gadget.

Figure 4-4: Choose gadgets for your Sidebar.

A gadget typically has options or settings you can adjust. To display any options, right-click the gadget in the Sidebar and choose Options or Settings from the pop-up menu that appears.

To see the latest gadgets available from Microsoft, click the Get More Gadgets Online link at the bottom of the Add Gadgets dialog box.

Switching Views and Sorting Items

Next, allow me to discuss the different views within Windows 7 Explorer — and how you can switch between them in a flash.

To switch between views in the Explorer window, click the arrow button next to the Change Your View button on the toolbar (it looks like a set of tiny icons). The pop-up menu offers these choices, which you can choose by dragging the slider:

✦ **Tiles:** Choose this view to make items appear as icons on well-spaced tiles at regular intervals, thus making it easy to click an item without running something else accidentally.

✦ **Icons:** This view is a traditional favorite, where each item appears as an icon. However, spacing is much tighter than in Tiles view, so longer file-names are often abbreviated (and you must be more careful when click-ing). You can choose four sizes of icons, from small to extra large.

Icon view displays images and video clips as *thumbnails* (pictures), but be warned: Windows 7 can take a significant amount of time to process a folder containing a lot of images, especially on an older machine. In this view, folders contain pictures that are displayed as tiny thumbnails of the images they contain — *sassy* indeed!

✦ **List:** Another long-standing favorite, List view features each item arranged in list format — one entry per line. Depending on the window size and the number of files in the current location, Windows 7 might even see fit to arrange your list in columnar format. Graphically *sassy!*

✦ **Content:** This view is new in Windows 7, and it provides a "sneak peek" at the content within files and folders, along with the item size and cre-ation or modification date.

✦ **Details:** If you like List view but wish you had more information on each item, choose Details view. Again, Details view takes a little more time to display, so expect a delay before you see the statistics — the larger the folder, the longer it takes.

To sort the items in the List or Details views to your particular fancy, click the heading buttons above the contents of the window. (I find that Name, Type, and Size are the most useful.) You can also right-click any open space in the content pane and choose Sort By from the pop-up menu.

You can also elect to group items. Just right-click any open space in the con-tent pane, choose Group By from the menu that appears, and then pick the group criteria.

Don't Forget the Preview Pane!

The default Explorer window displays the Navigation pane, which allows you to jump directly to your favorite locations throughout your system. This classic "tree" display of the folders on your system dates all the way back to Windows 3.1. (Some things are just too good to change!)

From within the Navigation pane, click a drive or folder to immediately dis-play its contents. You can also click a right-facing arrow to expand an item or click the tilted arrow next to an item to collapse it again. The Explorer window is updated automatically with the contents of the drive or folder you're viewing. You can also access network locations and the shared files and printers offered by your HomeGroup. (I'll wax enthusiastic on your HomeGroup later in this chapter.)

You can also add locations to the Navigation pane. Drag a folder from the content pane within any Explorer window to the Favorites heading within the Navigation pane, and you'll see the Create Link in Favorites label appear. Release the mouse button, and suddenly you can hop there in an instant. *Sassy!*

You can also turn on the Preview pane (see Figure 4-5), which I find practically a requirement within Explorer. The Preview pane provides a thumbnail preview and details on the file or folder you've selected in the Content window — and that includes the ability to play audio and video files without opening them up in Windows Media Player. To turn on the Preview pane, click the Organize button on the toolbar, choose Layout, and click the Preview pane item to enable it.

Figure 4-5:
The dependable Folders list is a favorite navigation tool.

Navigation pane

Preview pane

Change your view

What's This Stuff in the My Users Folder?

Windows 7 gives each user a separate account folder (named after your account name), which contains a number of important subfolders, as shown in Figure 4-6. Your account folder appears within the top-level Users folder on your Windows 7 boot drive. For example, it's C:\Users\Mark on my system.

Figure 4-6:
Your
Windows 7
pad: the
Users folder
and its
subfolders.

The default subfolders include

✦ **My Pictures:** Images

✦ **My Videos:** Video clips

✦ **My Music:** Digital audio files

✦ **Contacts:** Your list of contact information

✦ **Documents:** Documents you created with your programs

✦ **Downloads:** Downloaded files

✦ **Saved Games:** Your saved files from your games

Why all the fuss over this standard folder organization? Because the
Redmond Gang wants you to use your account subfolders as your center of
operations, and most software developers respect the Microsoft standard.
Thus, most programs default to saving their documents to the Documents
folder (or another standard subfolder, like My Pictures). In fact, you can see
in Figure 4-6 that I have a number of extra subfolders in my Users folder —
they've been created automatically by the programs I run.

You can reach these locations in a number of different ways:

+ From the Start menu

+ From the Navigation pane in an Explorer window

+ From the Locations list in Save (As) and Open dialog boxes

You can create as many subfolders within your Users folder as you like, and it's a logical place to keep your stuff (at least on your C drive, where Windows 7 is usually installed).

Remember that each user you create in Windows 7 has a separate set of account folders, so the stuff you see in your Documents folder *isn't* the same as the stuff Brother Elroy sees in his Documents folder. (Microsoft makes this easy to remember by prefacing your personal music, pictures, and video collections with the word "My", as in *My Videos*.) What Windows 7 displays is keyed to the active user account.

A Word about Libraries

Check out the new Libraries group, which appear in any Explorer window in your Navigation pane. (See Figure 4-7.) Libraries — new to Windows 7 — represent a new way of accessing documents, music, pictures, and videos. Like a folder, a library contains items, but those items don't necessarily reside in the same place on your system. For example, your Music library might contain MP3 files stored on an external drive, and your Documents library could contain Excel spreadsheets saved on a USB flash drive. So, in other words, a library is a method of organizing and centralizing all sorts of files and folders "under one roof."

You can easily include any folder in a library. Just navigate to the folder's location in an Explorer window, click that folder to select it, and then click the Include in Library button on the toolbar. Windows 7 displays a pop-up menu, from which you can choose from the four default libraries. Note, however, that you can also create your own new library from the selected folder by clicking Create New Library. Windows 7 creates a library with the same name as the selected folder and adds the contents of the selected folder in the new library automatically.

Figure 4-7:
Browse
through
your
Pictures
library.

Share the Documents . . . and Other Stuff

By the way, the contents of your Users account folder are also hidden from other users, so you can't put a document there and expect other users of your PC to be able to reach it. Instead, use the Public folders within the Libraries group. Each of the four default Windows 7 libraries has a separate Public subfolder, like Public Pictures and Public Music.

When you save or copy an item to one of the Public folders, anyone using another account on your PC can open and copy that item. And after you turn on *Public sharing,* anyone on your local network can also access the item.

By default, Windows 7 installs with Public sharing turned off. To turn on the feature and share the contents of these library Public folders among other computers on your network, follow these steps:

1. **In the Explorer Navigation pane, display one of the Public folders inside a library.**

2. **Right-click the Public folder and choose Share With from the menu that appears; then click Advanced Sharing Settings. See Figure 4-8.**

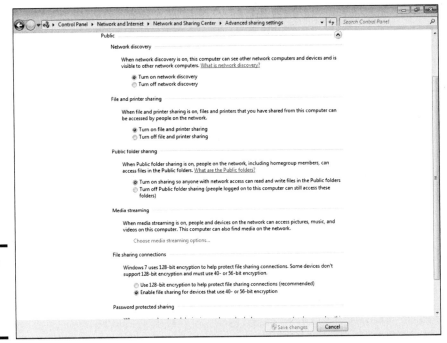

Figure 4-8:
Tell
Windows
to share
libraries.

3. **Under Public Folder Sharing, select the Turn On Sharing so That Anyone with Network Access Can Read and Write Files in the Public Folders radio button.**

4. **Click the Save Changes button.**

Using Your HomeGroup

Speaking of sharing, Windows 7 also introduces a nifty method of sharing files and printers with other computers on your network — a *HomeGroup*. Microsoft designed this new feature to make home networking easier, but it has one somewhat troublesome requirement: Every computer that uses HomeGroup on your network must be running Windows 7, so computers running Windows XP or Vista (or your daughter, the maverick, with her iMac) can't join in the fun. (They can network with Windows 7 using old-fashioned workgroups, just not a HomeGroup.)

When you install the first copy of Windows 7 on a PC on your network, a HomeGroup is automatically created, and any PC running Windows 7 that joins your network afterward will request your permission to join the existing HomeGroup. (Can't get much more automatic than that!) However, you can always add computers or manage the settings within your HomeGroup from the HomeGroup screen within Control Panel, as shown in Figure 4-9.

Book II
Chapter 4

Advanced
Windows 7

Figure 4-9:
Access
everything
HomeGroup
from the
Control
Panel.

"Wait a second, Mark. If I'm part of a HomeGroup, everyone can share everything I have? Where's the security in that?" Fear not! You can select what you share through your HomeGroup. From the HomeGroup screen in Control Panel, click the Choose What You Want to Share link, and Windows 7 opens a wizard that allows you to choose which of the four libraries you want to share. (You can also share your local printer, if you like.) The same wizard provides you with a password which must be entered on all the other computers that join your HomeGroup.

It's important to keep in mind that Windows 7 is referring to your top-level Libraries (and not just the Public subfolders) when you're selecting which Libraries to share. (In other words, others on your HomeGroup can access not just the contents of your Public Pictures subfolder, but also the contents of the Pictures Library itself.) This is different from sharing without a HomeGroup (as I discussed in the previous section), where only the contents of the Public subfolders within each library are shared.

When you join a HomeGroup, all the other user accounts on your PC also join that HomeGroup automatically.

If you're not using HomeGroup to build your home network, I invite you to the comforting confines of Book VIII, Chapter 2, where I describe how to create a network or connect to an existing network.

Creating a Shortcut

In Chapter 2 of this minibook, I introduce you to shortcuts, and now it's time to create them. Here are two ways to create a shortcut. Both ways begin by right-clicking the icon:

+ From the pop-up menu that appears, choose Create Shortcut, and Windows 7 does just that — a new shortcut appears in the same folder as the original icon. You can then copy or move the shortcut to another location on your system. You can also choose Send To➪Desktop (Create Shortcut) to plop a shortcut directly on your desktop.

+ Drag the icon where you want to place the shortcut. When you release the mouse button, choose Create Shortcuts Here from the pop-up menu that appears.

Ever wonder where the shortcut's original file is located? To find out, right-click the shortcut, choose Properties from the resulting pop-up menu, and then click the Shortcut tab to display the Target field (see Figure 4-10). The target path points to the original file.

Figure 4-10: Clearing a path to a shortcut's target (so to speak).

Multiuser Operation For Dummies

Earlier in this chapter, I mention the Public subfolders within each library: where the local users on your PC can share files and folders. That's an example of *multiuser* operation. Unlike a network environment — where multiple computers are connected — a multiuser PC need not be part of a network.

Instead, different people use the same PC; each person has his own user account; and Windows 7 keeps track of everyone's Control Panel preferences, Explorer views, desktop backgrounds, Favorites, and all the other sundry Windows 7 elements that I show you how to customize in this minibook.

In this section, I discuss how multiple folks can share a single workhorse PC.

Windows 7 offers three different user account levels:

✦ **Administrator:** The user has full access to Control Panel, can manage other user accounts, and can install programs and hardware. If you're the only person who will use your PC, Windows 7 sets you up with an Administrator account — as it should.

✦ **Standard:** The user can change the account password, cannot install (or uninstall) hardware and software, and has full control over only those files that she creates. If you're setting up accounts for others and you're less than impressed with their computing skills, by all means give them Standard accounts!

✦ **Guest:** I tell you a tad more about the Guest account in the upcoming section "Be my guest."

Logging in

Your first chore when you sit down to a multiuser PC is to log in. This step identifies you to Windows 7 and allows the operating system to load and apply all your custom settings. You can log in to Windows 7 in a number of ways:

✦ **Boot your PC with multiple users active.** You see the Welcome screen, where you can log on.

✦ **Log off from the Start menu.** Click the Start menu, click the Shut Down button's pop-up menu (the right-facing arrow in the lower-right area of the Start menu), and then click Log Off. Windows 7 displays the Welcome screen.

✦ **Switch users:** If you enabled Fast User Switching, you can allow another person to log on without closing any of your programs. Just make dog-gone sure that the other user knows not to turn off the PC completely! (Windows 7 helps prevent any tragedies by displaying the number of programs that the original user is running on the Welcome screen.) After the switched user completes his session, he should simply log off so that your programs remain running. Click the Start menu, click the Shut Down button pop-up menu, and then click Switch User.

On the Welcome screen, a user must

✦ Click a user account button to select an account.

✦ Type the correct password — and it had better be spelled correctly.

Be my guest

Before I cast off from Multiuser Land, I should elaborate on the third type of user account: The Guest account is perfect for someone who needs to use your PC right this moment but won't need an account in the future. The Guest account

✦ Doesn't require a password.

✦ Can't be duplicated or deleted — there's only one Guest account.

✦ Can be turned on or off in some versions of Windows 7. To toggle the Guest account, choose Start⇨Control Panel⇨User Accounts and click the Manage Another Account link. Click the Guest account and then click Turn On (or Turn Off) as needed.

What exactly can a guest do? Basically, the Guest account has the same abilities as a Standard user account: The guest can use your PC, but Windows 7 prevents that person from abusing it.

Let BitLocker guard your data!

Are you concerned about the security of your data? Although any type of PC could be the target of data theft, laptop owners make the perfect target — it takes only a second for someone to steal an unattended laptop PC, and suddenly your documents and files are in danger. (Even your desktop PC isn't safe, because computers are prime targets during a robbery.) If you're running either the Ultimate or Enterprise version of Windows 7 and you work with sensitive information (or if you just want to keep your Windows Live Mail contacts away from prying eyes), take advantage of Microsoft's BitLocker feature, and encrypt your PC's hard drive! (You can also encrypt a removable drive, such as an external hard drive or a USB flash drive.) With the basic configuration, you must enter a password to unlock your drive and access the contents. Some PCs can also use *transparent encryption* (meaning that once you log on with the correct account password, data is automatically encrypted and decrypted in the background as necessary).

Note that your PC's BIOS must support BitLocker — if your BIOS isn't compatible, Windows 7 will let you know. To encrypt the boot drive (where Windows 7 was installed), you will also need a TPM (short for *Trusted Platform Module*) Security device. The TPM is typically built into a laptop's motherboard, or within the circuitry on a hard drive.

To configure BitLocker, choose Start⇨Control Panel⇨BitLocker Drive Encryption. Click the drive you want to encrypt — remember, Windows 7 will indicate if you can't encrypt a particular drive — then click the Turn On BitLocker link.

If your boot drive supports BitLocker, you can use full transparent mode: Enable only the Automatically Unlock This Drive on This Computer check box (leave the other two disabled). If your boot drive isn't encrypted, enable only the Use a Password to Unlock the Drive check box (and leave the other two disabled).

Fax Me, Please

Yep, I know that many readers are exclaiming, "Hey! I didn't know that Windows 7 could act as a fax machine! That is positively *trick!*" And, indeed it is — all you need is a fax modem, a telephone line, and the instructions in this chapter. (Oh, and you need to be running either Windows 7 Professional Edition or Windows 7 Ultimate Edition. Otherwise, it's time to skip ahead.)

Setting up faxing under Windows 7

You need to configure the fax support within Windows 7 before you tell folks that you're ready to accept calls from their fax machine. Follow these steps to set up your fax-receive service:

1. **Choose Start⇨All Programs⇨Windows Fax and Scan.**

Windows 7 runs the Windows Fax and Scan utility, which you see in Figure 4-11.

2. **Click the Fax button in the lower-left corner of the window to switch to Fax mode.**

3. **Choose Tools⇨Fax Settings.**

Whew. Way to bury this thing, Redmond.

Figure 4-11:
The
Windows
Fax and
Scan
window.

4. **Select the Allow the Device to Receive Fax Calls check box.**

   Of course, if you want to send faxes as well, select the Allow the Device to Send Faxes check box.

   Also specify whether

   - You want the fax modem to pick up automatically (after a certain number of rings).
   - You should manually answer incoming fax calls.

5. **Click OK to save your changes.**

To set up your fax send service, click New Fax on the Windows Fax and Scan toolbar, and the utility displays the Fax Setup Wizard, which you see in Figure 4-12. Click Connect to a Fax Modem and follow the instructions to enter your full name, fax number, and company name, as well as your Transmitting Subscriber Identification (TSID) and Called Subscriber Identification (CSID). Usually both the TSID and CSID are simply a combination of your full name (or company name) and your fax phone number.

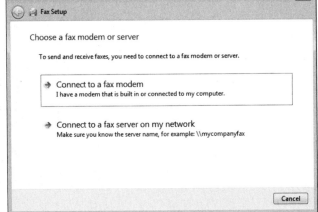

Figure 4-12: Windows 7 sets up your fax-send service with a wizard.

Sending faxes

If you followed along in the previous two sections, you're now Windows 7– fax-sending-empowered. To send a fax, follow these steps:

1. **In its native application, open (or create) the document you want to fax.**

   For example, fax a Word document from within Word.

2. **Press Ctrl+P to display the Print dialog box (or, within applications like Office 2010, the Print pane).**

3. **Choose the fax device.**

Click the Printer Properties link to switch between Normal (200 x 200 dpi) and Draft (200 x 100 dpi) quality. Draft is quicker, but it's, well, draft quality.

4. **Click Print.**

Windows 7 launches the Windows Fax and Scan utility and displays a New Fax window.

5. **Type the name of the recipient and the person's fax number. Or, if she's in your Windows Contacts list, click the Contacts button and choose the contact from there.**

6. **(Optional — but highly recommended) Add a cover page:**

   a. *Choose a cover page template from the drop-down list.*

   b. *If you like, add notes in the Cover Page Notes text field.*

7. **Click the Send button.**

If you configure Windows 7 for automatic reception of incoming faxes after a specified number of rings, you really don't have to do anything to receive faxes other than keep your PC running and stay off that telephone line. (See Step 4 in the previous section for the lowdown on how you want the fax call answered.) However, if you specify manual answering for incoming faxes, you have to follow these steps for each incoming fax:

1. **Choose Start⇨All Programs⇨Windows Fax and Scan to run the program.**

2. **When you hear the phone ring, click the Receive a Fax Now button on the toolbar.**

3. **Verify that the incoming fax has been properly detected by watching the Fax Monitor.**

Doing the Multimedia Thing

The final stop on this customization trip concerns multimedia. Windows 7 can be dead boring without liberal doses of digital audio, digital photographs, and DVD movies! In this section, I show you how to enjoy all sorts of digital entertainment as well as how you can record your own CDs from within Windows 7.

Playing your MP3 files

MP3 files are the modern solution to crystal-clear, high-quality music that's

✦ **Standardized and compatible:** MP3 files are supported within every computer operating system these days, along with countless personal music devices, handheld personal digital assistants (PDAs), and palm PCs.

✦ **Easy to create, copy, and share:** Okay, perhaps the music is *too* easily created, copied, and shared — but I'm just reporting on what you *can* do, not involving myself in the ongoing copyright debate over MP3 distribution. (And, like the bumper sticker on the back of my Jeep used to read, "MP3 is not a crime.")

✦ **Easy to record on CD-Rs:** Same copyright argument, same excuse on my part — but it's currently legal to make "compilation discs" of MP3 songs as long as you own the original audio CDs (or bought and downloaded the songs online).

To play MP3 files within Windows 7, double-click an MP3 file within the Explorer window. Unless you installed an alternative MP3 player, Windows 7 cranks up Windows Media Player, as shown in Figure 4-13, and begins playing the music immediately.

Figure 4-13: My tunes sound great in digital format!

The familiar controls at the bottom of the Media Player window are shown in Figure 4-13 as well. You can click and drag the progress slider to change your current point in the song. You can also mute or pause the playback from the control strip.

For a complete discussion of MP3 files — including how you can "rip" your own digital music from existing audio CDs — see Book VI, Chapter 2.

Viewing and downloading digital photographs

If you have a digital camera, Windows 7 has three features you'll want to try:

✦ **Icon view:** At the beginning of this chapter, I discuss the thumbnail images that appear for images when you're using Icon view within the Explorer window. As I mention there, it's slower than Tiles, List, or Details views, but if you're sifting through a folder full of digital images and you want to move, copy, or delete some, Thumbnails view is the row to hoe. Figure 4-14 illustrates a folder from my digital photograph collection as seen in Large Icons view.

✦ **Preview pane:** Don't forget to use the Preview pane within the Explorer window, as I mention earlier in this chapter. Windows 7 automatically displays a larger preview of a picture when you select it.

Figure 4-14: View thumbnail icons of your digital photograph folder.

✦ **Automatic Import:** The Windows 7 import feature kicks in automatically when you connect your Universal Serial Bus (USB) digital camera to your PC.

You can find much more information on digital cameras and these features in Book VI, Chapter 5.

Recording your own CDs

Most CD and DVD recorders are accompanied by their own recording rograms — like Roxio Creator 2010, from Sonic Solutions (www.sonic.com).

However, you can record a data disc within Windows 7 without a separate commercial CD/DVD-recording application. Grab a blank recordable CD or DVD and follow these steps:

1. **Load the blank disc into your recorder.**

Windows 7 displays a dialog box asking what the heck you want to do with the disc.

2. **Click Burn Files to Disc from the list and then click OK.**

If you're not planning on installing a CD/DVD-recording application any time soon, select the Always Do This for Blank Discs check box before you click OK.

Windows displays the Burn a Disc dialog box.

3. **Click With a CD/DVD player and click Next.**

The Mastered format provides the best compatibility with other computers and older versions of Windows. Windows 7 opens an Explorer window for the recorder.

4. **Select the files you want to record.**

5. **Drag the selected files directly to your optical drive.**

Nothing has been recorded yet, of course, but we're getting close. Note that Windows 7 indicates the drive is ready with the heading Files Ready to Be Written (making it easier to follow what goes where).

6. **Click the Burn to Disc toolbar button within the disc window.**

7. **Sit back and relax — this step can take some time (anywhere from 5 to 30 minutes, depending on the speed of your drive and the type of media you loaded).**

The disk cognoscenti

If you want to avoid looking like an idiot when talking with a PC power user, listen up. The round, shiny object that you load into your CD-ROM or DVD-ROM drive is a *disc,* ending with a *c* — and not a *disk,* ending with a *k.* The latter word more accurately describes your hard disk (or even one of those irritating floppy disks). Think Latin, think Greek, think *disc*us, think *disc*ography — it's just plain round. Anyone who pretends to be a PC power user and talks oh-so-knowingly about a *CD-ROM disk* or *DVD disk* is a dweeb. Shun them like you shun dandruff.

Watching a DVD movie

To watch a DVD movie in Windows 7, just load the disc. Windows 7 should automatically run Media Player — you might have to choose it on the AutoPlay menu first — and then play the movie.

You can also run the program manually by choosing Start➪All Programs➪ Windows Media Player (or click the Windows Media Player button in your Quick Launch icons, if it appears there).

You can switch between the window display and a full-screen display by pressing Alt+Enter.

Plus, you get the same familiar set of control buttons that appear at the bottom of the Media Player window. They work for everything from MP3 files to digital video clips to DVDs. Oh, joy! Rapture!

Chapter 5: Taking Control of the Control Panel

In This Chapter

✓ Configuring the Control Panel the right way

✓ Setting your PC's date and time

✓ Personalizing Windows 7 just so

✓ Configuring AutoPlay options

✓ Fine-tuning power options

✓ Adjusting your keyboard

✓ Changing mouse settings

✓ Setting Internet options

✓ Removing programs the right way

✓ Configuring user accounts

✓ Setting your phone and modem options

*P*icture this: You're the engineer on the bridge of the starship Enterprise — the first one, the real Enterprise — and Captain James T. Kirk suddenly bellows, "I need more power!" in your direction. Where do you turn? Which panel has the right randomly blinking lights and the right fake switches?

In the Windows 7 galaxy, my friend, you (and Scotty) need go no further than the Control Panel — where all the switches are real! Just about all the check boxes, drop-down lists, and buttons that determine how Windows 7 acts are available from this single menu item. And, in this chapter, I show you how to poke a tiny flashlight into the most commonly used Control Panel dialog boxes to fix your starship's shields — whoops — I mean, customize Windows 7 for your needs.

Sorry — like most other first-generation technonerds, I *really* enjoy my *Star Trek*.

First, Put the Control Panel on the Start Menu!

To open the Windows 7 Control Panel the *right* way — at least in this technowizard's opinion — it should be configured as a pop-up menu on the Start menu. The default Windows 7 category view (which opens in a separate window) is about as convenient as a car wash in a monsoon: You *can* use it, but why? A true PC power user jettisons the default Control Panel in a heartbeat.

Follow these steps to configure the Control Panel as a Start menu pop-up:

1. **Right-click the Start button and then choose Properties from the menu that appears.**

2. **In the Properties dialog box that appears, click the Customize button to display the settings you see in Figure 5-1.**

3. **In the Control Panel section, select the Display as a Menu radio button.**

4. **Click OK to save the change to the Start menu.**

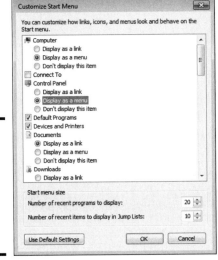

Figure 5-1: Configure your Windows 7 Control Panel as a Start menu pop-up.

Voilà! Now click Start, move your mouse pointer over the Control Panel menu item, and revel in all that pop-up goodness, as shown in Figure 5-2! Now you can access, with just two mouse clicks, any of the Control Panel dialog boxes that I cover in the rest of this chapter — which is faster, more efficient, and just plain satisfying.

Figure 5-2:
That, sir and
madam, is
a power
user Control
Panel.

Note that each Control Panel dialog box sports three spiffy buttons: Apply, OK, and Cancel. You probably already know that clicking Cancel closes the dialog box without making any changes — and if you didn't know that, now you do, so you can safely back out of any Control Panel dialog box by just clicking Cancel. Apply and OK do the same thing — any changes you made are saved — but this list describes their two important differences:

✦ **OK:** When you click OK, the dialog box closes, and you can make no more changes to that dialog box. Because many Control Panel dialog boxes have multiple panels (each of which might have a setting that you want to change), it makes sense to click Apply if you need to hang around.

✦ **Apply:** When you click Apply, Windows 7 makes the setting change immediately. Usually, a setting change doesn't do anything obvious right off the bat, but if you're working in the Personalization Panel dialog box, you usually can see which setting changed (like your background or your screen resolution). If you don't like the effect you just wrought, you can easily choose another setting without the hassle of opening the dialog box again.

Configuring the Date and Time

The first stop on the Control Panel tour is the Date and Time Properties dialog box.

Date and Time tab

Check out its first tab, Date and Time, as shown in Figure 5-3.

Figure 5-3:
Configure
the date and
time.

Click the Change Date and Time button to use

+ **The calendar display:** To select the current day, click it in the calendar display. You can move forward and backward through the months by clicking the arrows on either side of the title.

+ **The Time clock:** Click the hours:minutes:seconds display and then click the up and down arrows to set the time. (In older versions of Windows, you clicked and dragged the hands of the clock. Someone at Microsoft finally put an end to this analog anachronism in a digital world.)

Click the Change Time Zone button to set your current time zone by using the drop-down list. You can also set Windows 7 to automatically adjust for daylight savings time.

Additional Clocks tab

Windows 7 allows you to display as many as two additional clocks — a real boon for the world traveler who needs to keep tabs on different time zones. You can name each display clock to help keep things straight.

To display all your clocks, as well as a convenient calendar, just click the time display once on the taskbar.

The Internet Time tab

If you have an Internet connection that you use every day — either a dialup or an always-on digital subscriber line (DSL) or cable modem connection — you can set Windows 7 to automatically set its own clock by using an Internet time server! Forget about setting the clock manually.

Click the Internet Time tab, and then click the Change Settings button to display the settings you see in Figure 5-4. Select the Synchronize with an Internet Time Server check box and then click the Server drop-down list to select a time server. I prefer the `time.nist.gov` server because the idea of handing over my PC's time to the Redmond Empire is somewhat unsettling. (Sure, Mark — like they don't already control your waking hours through Windows 7?)

Figure 5-4:
Another use
for "that
Internet
thing."

> **Internet Time Settings**
>
> Configure Internet time settings:
>
> ☑ Synchronize with an Internet time server
>
> Server: time.nist.gov ▼ | Update now
>
> The clock was successfully synchronized with time.nist.gov on 3/4/2010 at 5:16 PM.
>
> OK | Cancel

Changing Personalization Settings

Windows 7 groups a number of settings that used to be in separate areas into the Personalization settings, shown in Figure 5-5. Besides using the Control Panel item from the Start menu, you can get to them by right-clicking any open space on your Windows 7 desktop and then choosing Personalize from the pop-up menu that appears. I hit the major stops along the road in this section.

Theme

This list offers a number of different color schemes that apply throughout Windows 7. (The High Contrast schemes may help those who have trouble reading the screen.) Along with a color scheme, most themes also contain one or more desktop backgrounds, a set of sounds, and a screen saver.

Figure 5-5:
The
Personali-
zation
settings are
made for
tweakers.

You can also create your own theme with your own elements — simply choose the desktop background, window color, sound set, and Screen Saver that you want (as I show you in the next sections), then save those elements as a theme for later use! Click the Save Theme link, enter a name for the current theme, and then click Save to seal the deal. You'll see that Windows 7 adds your theme to the My Themes section of the list.

Desktop background

Click Desktop Background to choose a background from the thumbnail list. To display a folder of backgrounds (and optionally cycle through them automatically), click the Picture Location drop-down list. To enable the random background feature, click the Change Picture Every drop-down list and choose the desired delay.

If you want to load your own picture (or a folder of photos), click the Browse button and then navigate to the location of the image or folder. (Windows 7 automatically updates the preview thumbnails.) Although an image with a lower resolution can be stretched to fit across your entire desktop from the Picture Position control, don't be surprised if it loses quality. Instead, pick Center to put the image in the middle of the desktop — or, if the image is a repeating pattern, choose Tile.

Beware some screen savers

It's very easy to write a "bad" screen saver — by that, I mean a screen saver that can slow down or even hang your PC. (Because of their popularity, screen savers are also prime targets for spreading viruses.) Therefore, take care when adding to your system a new screen saver that's not from Microsoft. Your antivirus program should be running (naturally), and you should watch your PC's performance carefully after the screen saver has been running, to make sure that it hasn't caused any problems.

To use a plain-color background, click the Picture Location drop-down list and choose Solid Colors, and then pick your favorite shade.

Sounds

Click Sounds to display the Sound tab within the Sound Control Panel dialog box. You can choose a sound scheme from the drop-down list or create your own scheme by selecting individual programs and events and assigning them your own sound files. Click to select an event in the Program Events list, and then click Browse to locate and select the new sound. You can listen to the selected sound by clicking the Test button.

After you build a new sound scheme, click Save As to save it under a new name, and then you can choose it later from the Sound Scheme drop-down list.

Screen saver

Click Screen Saver to configure these settings:

+ **The screen saver:** Click this drop-down list to choose a Microsoft screen saver or a screen saver that you installed yourself.

+ **Settings:** If the screen saver has any configuration options (like toggling sound effects on or off or increasing the number of flying small appliances on the screen), you can set them by clicking the Settings button.

+ **Preview:** Click this button to see how the selected screen saver will look. To return to the Display dialog box, move your mouse.

Click the up and down arrows to choose the delay period before the screen saver kicks in. You can optionally require your user password to be entered before the screen saver returns you to Windows 7.

Click the Change Power Settings link to display the Power Options settings, which I describe later in this chapter.

Adjusting Display Settings

Choose Control Panel⇨Display to choose from the following smorgasbord:

✦ **Adjust Resolution:** Click this slider and drag it to set a new screen resolution, and then click OK to accept the change.

✦ **Colors:** Click Change Display Settings, and then click the Advanced Settings link. From the Display Properties dialog box that appears (see Figure 5-6), click the Monitor tab to choose the number of colors your PC will display. Whenever possible, leave this value set to 24-bit or 32-bit color. However, if you have an older video card, you might not be able to display higher resolutions at these color-quality levels — 16-bit color might allow you to work with higher resolutions.

Figure 5-6: Display properties are available on a Windows 7 desktop near you.

If you're having trouble reading smaller text on your desktop — like icon labels or menu titles — choose Control Panel⇨Display and choose the Medium or Larger setting. (Alternatively, you can choose Control Panel⇨ Fonts and then click the Change Font Size link.) To fine-tune the ClearType text-smoothing feature — which might make text easier to read — choose Control Panel⇨Display⇨Adjust ClearType Text and follow the ClearType Wizard instructions.

Choosing AutoPlay Options

If you need Windows 7 to automatically run a program when you open a certain file, connect a certain device, or load a certain type of media, you can configure that program from the Control Panel. For example, you might like to run your favorite DVD recording program on your PC every time you load a blank disc.

Many Windows programs can automatically set the AutoPlay options for specific media, files, and devices for you — but if a program stubbornly refuses to snap to attention when it should, click the AutoPlay Options item in the Control Panel. The window shown in Figure 5-7 enables you to choose a default program for just about any type of file or media, and if any devices (like a digital camera or portable audio player) are registered within Windows 7, they show up at the bottom of the list.

Click the drop-down list for the desired media, file type, or device, and choose the option you prefer (including Take No Action, for those moments when you want your PC to remain passive, and Ask Me Every Time, if you often use more than one program for a specific purpose).

**Book II
Chapter 5**

**Taking Control of
the Control Panel**

Figure 5-7:
You can easily specify which programs run when you open or load stuff.

Adjusting the Power Options

From the Control Panel menu, choose Power Options to display the window you see in Figure 5-8.

The radio buttons in this dialog box allow you to choose a default *power plan,* which controls the steps that your PC takes to conserve power. Power conservation is a handy trick for laptop PC owners but still important for desktop PC owners. Each of the three preferred plans — Balanced (the default), High Performance, and Power Saver — is rated according to its energy savings and the overall performance of your PC while using the plan.

To create a completely new power plan for your PC, click the Create a Power Plan link at the left side of the Power Options window. Windows 7 opens a wizard to lead you through the process.

However, you don't have to settle for the default settings! After you decide which of the preferred plans is closest to your needs, click the radio button to select it, and then click the Change Plan Settings link next to the plan to tweak the power options.

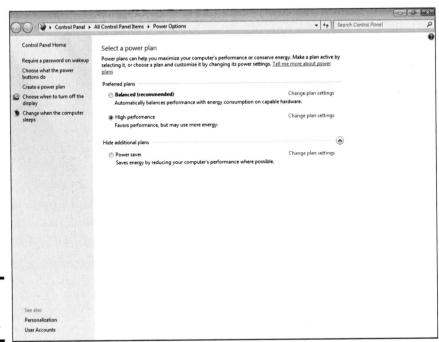

Figure 5-8:
Select a
power plan.

Hibernating For Dummies

As I explain earlier in this minibook, your PC can hibernate rather than enter sleep mode. The difference is one of security for your data. In *hibernation mode,* the contents of your PC's memory are saved to your hard drive; thus, if a power failure occurs, you don't lose any work. "Waking up" from sleep mode is quicker than hibernating because the data doesn't have to

be reloaded from disk, but you run the risk of losing your files.

Click the Hibernate After option (under the Sleep heading in the Advanced Power Options dialog box) to specify the amount of inactivity that should pass before your PC enters Hibernation mode.

The settings include

+ **Turn Off the Display:** Select the amount of inactivity that Windows 7 waits before switching your monitor to *Standby* mode (where the screen goes blank and the power light usually flashes or turns a different color). The monitor is automatically turned back on when you move your mouse or press a key.

Liquid crystal display (LCD) monitors use less power than traditional cathode ray tube (CRT) models, but you save a surprising amount of money when *any* monitor is switched to standby. In fact, your monitor probably uses more electricity than your PC! Therefore, I always set this value to the smallest amount of time that I can (without the feature becoming a hassle or an inconvenience, where I'm continually having to awaken my screen). For me, this setting is typically 30 Minutes.

+ **Put the Computer to Sleep:** Most PCs made in the past several years support *sleep mode,* in which the entire PC (rather than just your monitor and hard drives) switches to low-power mode. Click this drop-down list to select the period of inactivity required to activate sleep mode. Again, mouse activity or the press of a key on your keyboard should return your PC to life, with all programs and files intact. However, some older PCs might require you to press a button on the PC's case to return to full power.

If you need to tweak the operation of your power plan even further, click the Change Plan Settings link, then click the Change Advanced Power Settings link. The settings on this list include

+ **Turn Off Hard Disk After:** This setting determines the period of inactivity Windows 7 waits before powering-down your hard drive. I know that it sounds dangerous, but this harmless feature saves energy because your hard drives are no longer kept spinning unnecessarily. Like your monitor in sleep mode, a mouse movement or a key press returns your hard drives to active duty.

✦ **Require a Password on Wakeup:** This security feature (shown in the Advanced Settings tab in Figure 5-9) is similar to the screen saver password check box. You can require Windows 7 to prompt for your user password before you're allowed to return from sleep mode.

Figure 5-9:
Tweak
your power
options
"just so."

✦ **Power Button/Sleep Button Action:** PCs made in the past several years allow you to specify which action Windows 7 should take when you press the power button on your computer: You can opt to shut down the PC, do nothing (think of the wandering fingers of a three-year-old), prompt for the action to take, or switch immediately to sleep or hibernate mode.

After you choose your advanced power settings, click OK to save the new settings.

Tweaking the Keyboard

Click Control Panel and choose Keyboard to display the Keyboard Properties dialog box, as shown in Figure 5-10. (Note that your keyboard manufacturer's driver may include different tabs that allow you to configure extra buttons.)

The Speed tab

You can use the settings on this tab to customize your keyboard to fit your preferences:

✦ **Repeat Delay:** Drag this slider to specify how long Windows 7 waits before repeating a character when you hold down a key. (If you're a slower typist and your keys keep repeating, set this slider closer to Long.)

✦ **Repeat Rate:** Drag this slider to set the rate at which characters are repeated when you hold down a key.

Figure 5-10: Customize your keyboard settings.

To test the repeat delay and repeat rate, click in the test box and hold down a key. You can also specify the rate at which your cursor blinks within programs like Word or Notepad.

The Hardware tab

If you have multiple keyboards (or an input device configured as a keyboard, like some specialized game controllers), you can display the properties of that device (including information about any driver software it requires) or troubleshoot it from this tab.

Adjusting Thy Mouse

The settings you see when you choose Control Panel➪Mouse vary according to the manufacturer of your mouse. For example, my Logitech trackball displays a completely different Mouse Properties dialog box than does a Microsoft mouse because Logitech supplies its own mouse driver.

No matter which pointing device you own, however, you're likely to find the following settings. They might be named slightly differently, but they should be there nonetheless:

✦ **Middle button function:** You can specify which action is produced when you click the middle button on a three-button pointing device. Possibilities include double-clicking, cutting or copying, maximizing or minimizing the active window, or even running a program you specify. (I have mine set as a double-click because it prevents accidental double-clicking with the left button, which sometimes happens when you want to click the left button only once.)

✦ **Pointers:** You can usually either choose a Windows 7 pointer scheme or assign your own pointer symbols. You can also choose graphics directly from your hard drive: Click the pointer action you want to change, and then click the Browse button to "go shopping." (Remember, however, that selecting a picture of your significant other likely does *not* result in a workable mouse pointer! For this reason, most cursor graphics are especially designed for rodent work, and some are even animated.) If you created a new pointer scheme of your own, click Save As to add it to the Scheme drop-down list.

✦ **Mouse trails:** This feature adds a number of trailing pointers when you move your mouse. This trick is quite helpful when you're using a laptop because the mouse pointer is often hard to find on a laptop screen. Visually impaired PC owners might also find this option helpful.

✦ **Scrolling:** If your mouse has a wheel, you can specify how much screen real estate should scroll whenever you move the wheel a notch. (Heck, some mouse wheels even have a vertical scrolling function *and* a horizontal function. Old-timers like me remember when a mouse had just one button, and you *liked* it. You had no choice.)

✦ **Acceleration:** If you enable acceleration, your mouse pointer moves faster the farther you move it. This setting is a good idea if you're running your desktop at a whopping 1600 x 1200 resolution, where the mouse can seem to take forever to get anywhere!

Configuring Internet Options

Next on the Control Panel hit parade is the always fascinating world of Internet Properties — which, for some strange reason, is titled Internet Options in the Control Panel. (Figure 5-11 bares all.) Sit back for the ride, folks, 'cuz this is gonna be a big 'un. (And that's partly because many of the settings that should be tucked away in Internet Explorer are instead dumped here.)

The General tab

This tab allows you to set these items:

✦ **Your home page:** In the interest of brevity, you can find a complete discussion of this setting in Book III, Chapter 4.

✦ **Browsing history:** Internet Explorer (IE) uses these cache files to speed up the display of pages you've already seen, but after a while, the files can become true hard drive hogs. You can specify which temporary files to delete by clicking the Delete button or simply clicking the Settings button and dragging the file folder disk space slider to 5 or 10MB. (That amount prevents too much waste, and you no longer have to use the Delete button.)

Book II
Chapter 5

Taking Control of the Control Panel

Figure 5-11:
My heavens, what a dialog box! The Internet is a Complex Thing.

You might be wondering what cookies are doing in the Delete pane. The name has nothing to do with baked goods in this context. Instead, *Web cookies* are small files that are saved to your hard drive by your Web browser to allow Web sites to automatically determine who you are. (Ever wonder how Amazon.com always knows that it's you who is visiting? That's because of a cookie.) Most cookies are innocuous (and some sites even require them), but they can be used to store information about you, the sites you visit, and the type of Web browser you use. So, if you like, you can click the Delete Cookies button and wipe 'em out.

The Delete pane also allows you to delete the History file, and the Settings pane includes the option to select the number of days to keep in your History file. Again, a lot of this stuff applies only to IE. (And no, I don't know why this stuff is in Control Panel rather than in Internet Explorer, where it belongs! To wit: You can get to the same dialog box if you choose Tools⇨Internet Options within Internet Explorer.) I discuss the History file in detail in Book III, Chapter 4.

If you'd simply rather allow IE to delete your browsing history automatically when you close the IE window, select the Delete Browsing History on Exit check box.

+ **Search:** Click this button to select a new default search provider within Internet Explorer. The default is Bing (go figgah), but you can add Google or Yahoo! by clicking the Find More Search Providers link, at the bottom of the dialog box.

+ **Tabs:** (Sigh.) Yep, you guessed it, The IE tabbed window display can be configured from this setting. You can enable tabbed browsing and set IE behavior when clicking links, displaying pop-ups, and working with multiple tabs.

+ **Colors:** Specify the colors you want to use for links (both visited and new), the default text color on Web pages, and the default background color on Web pages.

+ **Languages:** Internet Explorer can display text in multiple languages. Click here to select which languages you need or to add extra language packs that you downloaded.

+ **Fonts:** Specify which fonts are used when a Web page doesn't include its own font definition.

+ **Accessibility:** To force IE to use your preferred font style, font color, and font size — no matter what the page is designed to do — click this button. (These features help folks with limited eyesight who have customized their browser font settings.)

The Security tab

You see the settings shown in Figure 5-12 on the Security tab:

Figure 5-12:
Set your browser security level.

✦ **The Web content zone:** Betcha didn't know that you can specify different security sites for the Internet as a whole, your local company intranet, and the Web sites you trust (*and* those you want to restrict). Click an icon to set the security level for that zone. To add sites to the zone you selected, click the Sites button.

✦ **The security level:** Drag the slider in this section to specify a security level, and Windows 7 displays the actions it will take based on the security level you choose. You can build your own, custom security level by clicking the Custom Level button, or you can return this zone to what Microsoft feels is appropriate by clicking the Default Level button.

The Privacy tab

The Privacy tab is another "slider" tab, as you see in Figure 5-13. However, the settings you find affect only the Internet zone:

✦ **The privacy level:** Drag the slider to choose an overall privacy setting for the Web sites you visit. *Note:* This setting also controls the cookies that I mention a bit earlier in this section. Each privacy level is described next to the slider. To import an existing IE privacy preferences file — something that your company might ask you to do — click the Import button. Click the Advanced button to override the cookie handling at the privacy level you chose; you can specify your own cookie handling here.

Figure 5-13:
Privacy
is easy to
set — or
override, as
necessary.

✦ **Web site privacy:** Heck, if you're *really* interested in security, you can even click the Sites button to specify the cookie handling for individual Web sites! This setting might be just the ticket if a site you like to visit requires you to use its cookies but you eschew cookies otherwise. (Man, that is one ridiculous sentence. Who *named* these things, anyway? Pee Wee Herman?)

✦ **The pop-up blocker:** I hate pop-ups — any red-blooded PC user hates them, too. Pop-up banners and advertisements litter the Web like confetti on the fair streets of New Orleans after Mardi Gras; if you select the Turn on Pop-up Blocker check box, however, Windows 7 does a commendable job of blocking these pop-up pests. (Instead, you can choose to display the Information Bar in Internet Explorer. From the Settings button, you can choose to selectively allow the pop-ups you want — some Web sites use pop-ups to display honest-to-goodness information.) To view your list of sites where pop-ups are allowed (and to change the notification and filter settings), click the Settings button.

✦ **InPrivate:** These two check boxes control how Internet Explorer operates while you're using InPrivate browsing, a feature that doesn't leave any indications of the sites you visit or your activities. No cookies, no history storage, nada. Disable the Do Not Collect Data for Use by InPrivate Filtering check box to reduce the information used during InPrivate browsing to an absolute minimum. To prevent add-ons from using information during an InPrivate session, select the Disable Toolbars and Extensions check box as well.

The Content tab

Here's a tab that will interest every parent who's concerned about kids surfing the Web (hang ten on Figure 5-14). The Content tab settings include

✦ **Parental Controls:** If you want to limit the amount of hours a user account is on the Internet, where that user is allowed to go on the Web, or even which games and programs that user can run, click the Parental Controls button and choose a Standard-level user account that you want to control. (You need an Administrator-level account with a password to assign parental controls to another account.)

✦ **Content Advisor:** You can enable Content Advisor to protect your kids, but be aware that it's nowhere near perfect — although, to be honest, no Web content filter really is perfect, including the expensive commercial programs. Why? Well, some sites rate themselves incorrectly. And other sites include valuable medical and artistic information that might inadvertently trigger alarms — for example, if you're searching for information on the human body for a science project. Anyway, to choose a level of content safety, just click the Enable button and drag the "offensive" slider on the Ratings pane, and then click OK.

Figure 5-14:
Control,
filter, and
certify
content to
your heart's,
well,
content.

Enable this feature only if you feel that it's absolutely necessary — and that you *don't* rely on it as a foolproof solution. (Instead, many parents simply use Parental Controls to limit Internet access to certain hours and approved Web sites. This idea isn't foolproof, either, but in my opinion, it's better than relying on imperfect software.)

✦ **Certificates:** These controls allow you to verify your identity to a Web site; many companies use certificates to ensure the privacy of their intranet data. Certificates can get complex, which is why most normal human beings don't bother with them.

✦ **AutoComplete:** With AutoComplete enabled, IE automatically fills out online forms, Web addresses, and username-and-password combinations that you previously entered on a site. Click the AutoComplete Settings button to specify which types of data you want filled out. You can also clear your AutoComplete history or clear the passwords in the history.

✦ **Feeds and Web Slices:** Click this button to set an automatic update schedule for your RSS feeds and Web Slices within Internet Explorer.

The Connections tab

The settings on this tab can be used to set up a virtual private networking (VPN) connection or a special proxy server configuration; you can also modify your local area network (LAN) Internet connection. Again, this ground is covered in other chapters, so I don't repeat myself here. To wit

♦ Setting up a VPN connection is covered in Book VIII, Chapter 5.

♦ Setting up a LAN connection to the Internet is covered in Book VIII, Chapter 2.

To set up a proxy configuration, you need several pieces of information from your network system administrator or your Internet service provider's (ISP) technical support department. And, you should set up and use a proxy server only at the ISP's specific request because configuring or using one incorrectly can seriously mess around with your dialup and VPN connections. Therefore, leave any proxy settings alone unless you're told to change them. (I do the same thing, so don't feel bad.)

The Programs tab

Figure 5-15 illustrates the Programs tab; from here, you can choose which programs handle your Internet functions, including

♦ The program that runs when you edit a Web page

♦ The default Web browsing application within Windows 7

♦ The default e-mail application within Windows 7

♦ The default programs that Windows 7 uses for different Internet applications, such as reading and posting Usenet newsgroup messages or talking with someone using a Voice over IP (VoIP) connection

♦ The add-on applications used within IE

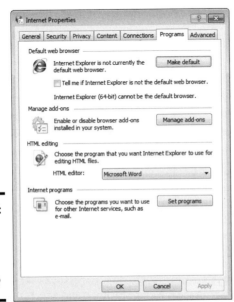

Figure 5-15:
So, like, which Internet program does what?

Note that a program you install might overwrite these settings.

Click the Manage Add-Ons button to display, manage, and update the add-on programs that add extra functionality to Internet Explorer. Most add-ons are offered by third-party companies (such as Symantec's AntiVirus "helper" add-on that appears in the Internet Explorer window), but some add-ons are even bestowed upon us by Microsoft itself. You can selectively enable and disable add-ons, or you can update them from the Manage Add-Ons dialog box.

If you use both IE and another browser (such as Firefox), you've probably been nagged about whether Internet Explorer should be rightfully returned to its spot as the default browser. To get rid of this irritating dialog box, make sure the Tell Me If Internet Explorer Is Not the Default Web Browser check box is disabled.

The Advanced tab

The final tab on the Internet Properties dialog box is chock-full of dozens of individual features that you can enable and disable. These settings affect both Internet Explorer and many other Internet applications, so they're often mentioned in program manuals (and in hushed tones around late-night campfires). The options are divided into eight rather nebulous categories; some are a little more self-explanatory than others — like those in the Browsing and Multimedia categories — but most are cryptic.

Because it would take an entire chapter just to explain each setting — and you won't use 90 percent of them unless you're asked to by your ISP, network administrator, or clergy member — I recommend that you check the Windows 7 Help system for information on individual options.

Click OK to save your settings.

Uninstalling and Repairing Programs and Features

Every Windows 7 user should be familiar with the Control Panel window shown in Figure 5-16, because the Programs and Features window is the one truly safe method of uninstalling applications from your system. (Alternatively, some programs add an Uninstall menu item in their All Programs folder; this is fine, too, because it's basically just a different way of starting the same procedure.)

Let me reiterate: *Never uninstall an application by simply deleting the program and its folder!* This action can raise all sorts of havoc within Windows 7 — your Windows 7 Registry file (which holds most of the configuration settings for your programs) eventually ends up looking like an army munitions testing ground after a day's work. (And that's A Bad Thing.) In the worst-case scenario, deleting a program folder willy-nilly can even lead to lockups and affect other programs that you didn't even know were distant cousins to the original application.

Book II
Chapter 5

Taking Control of
the Control Panel

Figure 5-16:
You want
to uninstall
a program?
You talk
to me.

Follow these steps to remove a program safely:

1. **Click Control Panel from the Start menu and then choose Programs and Features.**

After a few seconds, the Programs and Features window appears. You see a list of the programs you installed within Windows 7.

2. **Click the application entry in the list.**

3. **Click the Uninstall button.**

This step launches the application's uninstall procedure, which varies according to application and manufacturer.

If you want to keep an application on your PC but it's acting screwy (displaying error messages about missing files or not running when you try to open an associated document), you can try the Repair function from the Programs and Features window. (If repairing the application doesn't seem to fix it, you probably have to uninstall the program and reinstall it again.) Note that the Repair button doesn't appear for every program.

4. **Follow the onscreen instructions to complete the uninstall process.**

Unfortunately, some uninstall procedures don't remove all files associated with a program. Games, for example, are famous for leaving orphan folders with Save files. Also, if you relocate a shortcut that was placed on your desktop, that shortcut isn't deleted because it's in a different place. Therefore, I always take a moment to check to make sure that a program folder has been completely dusted after running the uninstall procedure. After you officially uninstall the application, you can indeed delete any orphan folders left on your drive, without fear of toasting your system.

To close the Programs and Features window, click the Close button in the upper-right corner.

Fine-Tuning User Accounts

The User Accounts Control Panel window isn't really a typical window. As you can see in Figure 5-17, it's a classy and helpful collection of wizards that features full onscreen instructions for everything you do. (Way to go, Big M!) Therefore, I don't go into step-by-step detail concerning each function, but I do take a moment to list what can be done from the wizard because everyone who shares a machine with others likely needs to perform some type of magic with a user account.

Figure 5-17:
The truly magnificent User Accounts Control Panel Wizard.

From the wizard, you can

✦ Manage an existing account or create a new account.

✦ Change your account name.

✦ Change a pesky password.

✦ Change the picture associated with an account.

✦ Turn the Guest account on or off (from the Manage Another Account link).

✦ Enable and configure Parental Controls (which I discuss earlier in this chapter) from the Manage Another Account link.

Configuring Phone and Modem Options

The last commonly used Control Panel dialog box is the Phone and Modem dialog box, shown in Figure 5-18. Note that these settings affect only a dialup (analog) modem that uses a standard telephone line.

Figure 5-18: Setting up locations is easy in Windows 7.

The Dialing Rules tab

From the Dialing Rules tab, you can create or switch locations. Whoops — you haven't been properly introduced: A *location* holds a single dialing configuration for your PC's modem. This configuration includes

- ✦ The local area code

- ✦ Any dialing prefixes or numbers necessary to access an outside line

- ✦ Any codes required by your long distance or international carrier

- ✦ The ability to disable call waiting

- ✦ The choice of whether the PC should use tone or pulse dialing (if anyone still uses pulse)

Of course, locations are a helpful feature for those who travel extensively with laptop PCs because you can set up a different location for each town that you visit often. Are you in old Madrid one day and in Berlin the next? No problem: Just change locations and — bam! — you can make a call or connect to a local dialup provider without any fuss. Click the New button to set up a new location, or click the Edit button to change the rules for the selected location.

To switch to a new location, just click it in the list.

The Modems tab

If you have more than one modem connected to your PC — or if you're using a laptop and a Personal Computer Memory Card International Association (PCMCIA) modem — you can add or remove the modem from your system from this tab or modify its properties (like turning down or turning off that doggone speaker).

Click Add to run the Add Hardware Wizard, which helps you install a new modem. Click a modem to select it from the list, and then click Remove; you can then unplug an external modem safely (or shut down your PC and remove an internal modem).

The Advanced tab

This tab definitely isn't one to mess around with unless you have specific instructions from your ISP or modem manufacturer's technical support department. These telephony providers are software drivers and sundry pieces of your operating system that control how Windows 7 handles your modem. (If that description sounds scary, I meant it that way.)

However, if you have instructions to install a new provider, click Add to select it from the Add Provider list. To delete a provider, select it from the Provider list and then click Remove. Select a provider from the Provider list and click Configure to change its properties.

Book III

The Internet

Contents at a Glance

Chapter 1: Making Sense of the Internet **155**

Exactly What Is the Internet, Anyway? 156
Exploring the Potential of the Web 158
Understanding Internet Connections 164
"What Exactly Do I Need?"..167

Chapter 2: Adding an Internet Connection to Windows 7 . . . .**169**

Gathering the Account Incantations 169
Making the Physical Connection 171
Creating a New Dialup Connection in Windows 7 171
Creating a New DSL, Satellite, or Cable Connection in Windows 7 173
"Is My Connection Alive?" 175
"My Connection Appears to Be Dead" 175

Chapter 3: Protecting Your Internet Privacy **177**

What Can Really Happen?...177
Common Sense Goes a Long Way...179
Using the Built-in Windows 7 Firewall 183
Using Antivirus Software 186

Chapter 4: Cruising the Web with Internet Explorer **187**

Running Internet Explorer 187
The Explorer Window and Basic Controls 188
Navigating the Web 193
Downloading Files 199
Keeping Track of Where You've Been...201
Printing and Saving Web Pages..202

Chapter 5: Harnessing Your E-Mail **205**

Introducing the Mail Window...206
Setting Up Your Mailbox..208
The Three R's: Receiving, Reading, and Replying 211
Creating and Sending E-Mail...216
Sending and Receiving File Attachments......................................220
Spam: I Hate It — Truly I Do!...222
Working with Your Contacts..223

Chapter 6: Instant Messaging Done Right **227**

Selecting a Chat Client 227
Running Windows Live Messenger..229
Configuring Windows Live Messenger..230
Keeping Track of Friends and Family...232
Chatting with Your Brethren..233
Selecting a Status 235
Squelching the Unwelcome Few 236

Chapter 1: Making Sense of the Internet

In This Chapter

✔ **Defining the Internet**

✔ **Exploring Internet technologies**

✔ **Comparing Internet connection methods**

✔ **Checking your PC's minimum hardware and software requirements**

*A*lthough the Internet continues to grow and change before our eyes, it seems to be getting more complex rather than simpler to use. Ancient search tools (such as Archie and Gopher) once used to locate stuff before the arrival of the new millennium are practically extinct now, and more everyday uses for the Internet become less exotic seemingly every month: instant messaging, webcams, streaming Internet radio stations, social networking and blogs. Some folks have told me that they're ready to throw their modems out the window and return to the blissfully ignorant days when we all wrote letters with (gasp) paper stamps affixed.

If you're somewhat wary of the Internet, however, don't give up hope. In this chapter, I explain what's available online, using actual English words of fewer than five letters. (Usually. I might have to hyphenate some of the technonerd terms, however.) If all you do online now is visit sites on the Web and communicate through e-mail, you're missing out on a ton of cool activities, and you're likely several years behind the latest Internet technologies. Hey, I live for this stuff.

So, stick with me here to gain a good grasp of what you can do via the Internet and which types of Internet connections are, well, hip and happening. You can then jump to the other chapters within this minibook for in-depth coverage of major Internet applications, such as your Web browser and e-mail program.

Exactly What Is the Internet, Anyway?

Many of the PC owners I talk to are convinced that the Internet is a real substance. They're not quite sure whether it's animal, vegetable, or mineral, but they're sure that they either *have it* or *want it* inside their computers. (It's probably a tiny, glowing ball: a cross between Tinker Bell and St. Elmo's fire.)

Seriously, though, you don't need to know what the Internet is in order to use it. From a PC owner's standpoint, you would be correct (in a way) if you said that the Internet begins at the phone connection or the cable modem coaxial cable. Therefore, if you want to skip to the next section and avoid a glance underneath the hood (or if you already read my description of the Internet in another book), be my guest.

Still here? Good. To help you find out a little more about how your PC connects to the online world, Figure 1-1 illustrates the process.

Figure 1-1:
An eagle-
eye view of
the Internet.

Your PC

Local connection over
phone lines or cable

The ISP's server

Long distance connection
over the major network
trunk lines that service
Internet traffic

The Web server
where the site's
pages are stored

Here's a brief description of what happens when you connect to the Internet and visit a Web site via a Web browser:

1. Your PC connects to an ISP. *ISP* is the techie slang for *Internet service provider,* a company which gives you access to the Internet proper. (Note that your ISP is not the same as a *Web browser* like Internet Explorer — the former is a company that makes money from providing you with an Internet connection, while the latter is a program on your PC that uses your Internet connection to display Web sites.) Your ISP account usually includes reserved space on its computers for your own Web site as well as one or two e-mail addresses. This arrangement is analogous to your dialing the telephone for a voice call, using a specific number that connects you to the other party.

What's in an address?

So, how does your ISP know where that particular Web server is on the network? I don't go into any crush-depth detail here, but here's the quick version. Every computer on the Internet is assigned an address — an *Internet Protocol address,* or IP address — that identifies it to other computers. (This address is technically a Transmission Control Protocol/Internet Protocol [TCP/IP] address. No glazing over of the eyes yet.) This IP address takes the form of four groups of numbers separated by periods, like this example: `192.168.1.100`. (Sophisticated computers keep track of who has which IP address and also which English-language Web address, like `www.microsoft.com`, is tied to which IP address.)

See? Like I said, it's beautifully organized chaos, and I'm proud to say that my Web server adds three or four additional Web sites to the billions on the planet!

2. Your ISP locates the Web site across the Internet. You might hear techie types talk about *pipelines* when they discuss the Internet. Although no physical pipes are involved, the term makes a certain warped sense. In this case, you request a specific Web site, and your ISP uses its name (its Universal Resource Locator, or URL) to locate the computer it resides on (a *Web server*) and then creates a pipeline between your PC and the server. (For example, the URL `www.mlcbooks.com` leads to my Web site, which runs on my coal-driven Celeron server in my office.) Here's another example: If you're using an *e-mail client* (a program that sends and receives electronic mail), that client connects to a certain electronic mail server computer across the Internet to transfer your e-mail.

3. Your computer communicates with the Web server. After you make a connection with a Web site, a Web page is displayed in which you can click links and images to send commands to the Web server, which loads other pages or even sends your PC packing to other Web servers. (How rude!) This process is much like the result of a voice telephone call: You converse with the other party, using a language that you both understand.

This is the essence of everything you do on the Internet: Computers connect with other computers (no matter where on the planet they might be) and exchange information of various types (e-mail messages, Web pages, or real-time video signals).

Keep reading to see what you can do when your PC is connected to the Internet. You have the Web to explore; you can host your own site and keep journals online; you can keep in touch by e-mail; and more.

**Book III
Chapter 1**

**Making Sense
of the Internet**

Exploring the Potential of the Web

Start with the familiar. When it comes to the wonders of the modern Internet, you just can't get any more mundane and humdrum than the World Wide Web. Heck, my kids don't even remember the days when a TV commercial didn't list a company's Web site or when schoolwork didn't involve an online search. (The endless cycle continues: What did we do before the Web? Or microwave ovens? Or air conditioning? Or the telephone? Or a sharpened stick?)

Surf the Web

Visiting Web sites is as simple as starting your browser (in this case, Internet Explorer, as shown in Figure 1-2), typing a Web site address in the Address field, and pressing Enter. Boom. (That's my company Web site, MLC Books Online, which you're welcome to visit at `www.mlcbooks.com`.) Folks surf for all sorts of reasons, including online shopping, research, banking, and various types of fun.

Address field

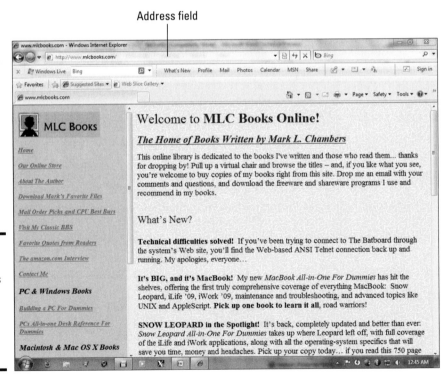

Figure 1-2:
Web
browsing is
as easy as
typing an
address or
clicking a
link.

If you're running Windows 7, Internet Explorer 8 is your default browser, and it's already installed! I discuss Internet Explorer (IE) in all its exquisite design in Chapter 4 of this minibook.

A Web site's *extension* (the three-character suffix behind the period) can help you keep track of the major categories of sites. Some common ones are

✦ `.com`: A commercial or business site

✦ `.org`: Usually a club, organization, or nonprofit group

✦ `.gov`: A federal or state government Web site

Build a Web site

A-ha! Here are more interesting waters. Despite the somewhat magical tech-nowizard reputation of webmasters and Web designers, you can run your own Web site to support your needs whether it concerns your hobby, your business, or your grandchildren. You need

✦ **A little creative work**

✦ **The proper type of Internet connection,** whether it's an always-on connection (such as cable), a digital subscriber line (DSL), or a network

✦ **The right software,** such as Microsoft Word 2010

Unfortunately, all the intricacies of designing and building Web pages and running a Web site are beyond the scope of this minibook, but a short stroll through the shelves of your local bookstore provides you with dozens of books devoted completely to the subjects of Web design and Web server setup. I can personally recommend the excellent books *Building Web Sites All-in-One For Dummies,* 2nd Edition (Doug Sahlin and Claudia Snell) and *Creating Web Pages All-in-One Desk Reference For Dummies*, 3rd Edition (Richard Wagner and Richard Mansfield; both books from Wiley).

Blogging

Until a few years ago, I would have thought that blogging was a bread pudding that has gone bad or a B-movie monster. However, now that I run my own Web log — *blog,* for short — I'm much more sophisticated. (Can't you tell?)

Blogs, the latest cutting-edge Internet technology in writing a diary, are Web sites that are updated fairly continually by individuals and crammed full of daily entries, like a journal. Rather than keep your journal private, however, the idea behind a blog is to share your thoughts with anyone who's inter-ested — family members, co-workers, or fellow hobbyists. Blogs usually include the books and music that the person is enjoying as well as links to other sites that the person favors. To create your own site, try Blogger at `www.blogger.com`.

Book III
Chapter 1

Making Sense of the Internet

E-mail and instant messaging

Long before the arrival of the Web, the Internet provided a number of truly valuable services — and Internet e-mail is still the most important thing I do online. Avoiding spam like a bullfighter, I can converse with folks planetwide and send them all sorts of stuff as attachments: Microsoft Office documents, programs, Web links, and photos, as you can see in Figure 1-3.

Figure 1-3:
Sending files as e-mail attachments is a breeze.

Anyone can use Windows Live Mail (under Windows 7, Vista, and XP) to send, receive, and manage e-mail. I think that Windows Live Mail is one of the best free programs that Microsoft has ever produced — and to that end, Chapter 5 of this minibook is dedicated to that program.

If you travel often or you need to check your e-mail on any computer with a Web browser, you can use a Web-based e-mail account like those offered by Google (www.gmail.com) and Yahoo! Mail (http://mail.yahoo.com). Most Web-based e-mail services are free, but you may have to put up with advertisements.

You can also use applications that allow you to run your own *mailing list,* which is an automated e-mail discussion group, usually concentrating on a specific topic or supporting a specific company or product. Check out the Arrow Mailing List Server at www.jadebox.com/arrow for a good example of a shareware mailing list server.

And e-mail is great, but what if you want to share that gossip *now?* With Windows Live Messenger, you can chat with others by typing your messages in real-time — as long as your family and friends are online and available, you can now communicate with them in seconds (as shown in Figure 1-4). Unlike e-mail, with instant messaging you're sending and receiving messages instantly, in real time, just like texting back and forth on cellphones. (Most folks call this real-time conversation *chatting*, to keep things straight.)

For the full details on Live Messenger (and other instant messaging programs from folks other than Microsoft), check out Chapter 6 of this minibook.

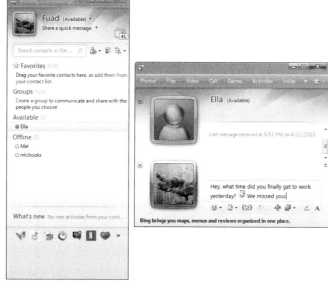

Figure 1-4:
Instant
messaging
allows
instant
gossip.

FTP file transfer

File Transfer Protocol (FTP) is one of the bona fide pillars of the Internet; unlike other antique Internet applications, however, FTP is still alive and doing very well, thank you. You can use FTP to transfer files to and from remote computers; the computer you connect to runs (you guessed it!) an *FTP server.* FTP is great for sending honkin' big files (like 5GB DVD videos) or large numbers of files at a single session.

Internet Explorer provides built-in support for FTP transfers, but the IE list of features is definitely on the Spartan side. If you're planning on using FTP often, I recommend that you use a separate application to transfer files. Figure 1-5 illustrates AceFTP 3 Pro, my FTP program of choice. It's a shareware bargain at only $30 US when you download your copy; you can register at the Visicom Media Web site, `www.visicommedia.com`.

Figure 1-5:
Do the FTP
thing with
AceFTP Pro.

Newsgroups

Think of *newsgroups* as huge discussion boards. Most aren't moderated, and virtually all participants choose to remain anonymous, so opinions and arguments abound.

With that understood, I absolutely *adore* newsgroups! Each newsgroup is dedicated to a certain topic, whether it's Elvis, World War II fighter planes, *The Simpsons,* or something in between. Your ISP usually provides you with access to its newsgroup server when you sign up.

Newsgroups offer more than just the chance to discuss a topic: Many groups are dedicated to certain types of file downloads, so you can share images, sounds, movies, and even programs with others.

As a first stop before you join the group scene, pick up a copy of my favorite freeware newsreader: Xnews, written by Luu Tran, and available on his Web site at http://Xnews.newsguy.com. You can also try Google Groups at http://groups.google.com — it's all Web based, so no additional software is necessary.

Webcams and Web videoconferencing

I shouldn't forget one of the cornerstones of Web technology that has been "right around the corner" for several years: the ability to send video from one computer to another by using a special type of minimal digital video (DV) camera: a *webcam*. For some time now, early adopters have been trumpeting the idea of Web *videoconferencing* (where several folks can get together over the Net for a real-time video meeting).

Is the widespread use of video on the Web still so far away? Large corporations that have nationwide or global offices have been using Web videoconferencing for some time, but they have the superfast T1 connections to the Internet that can easily handle video data. Regular folks with dialup modem connections, however, simply didn't have the bandwidth for decent video streaming.

Now, if you have a high-speed broadband connection such as DSL or cable, it's much more likely that you can offer a video feed that's larger than a postage stamp. Who knows? Maybe the large-scale acceptance of Web videoconferencing really *is* just over the next techno-logical hill.

Enjoy digital media over the Internet

If you enjoy music and video as much as I do, this stuff is exciting — streaming Internet radio offers FM-quality (or even CD-quality) stereo music broadcasts that you can tune into with your Web browser or MP3 software.

Although you can't capture the music as separate MP3 files, I find Internet radio to be a wonderful resource that I can tune into wherever an Internet connection is handy. Like a video feed, a high-speed Internet connection is a must if you're interested in listening to the higher-quality stations.

In fact, I've run my own station for years! It's MLC Radio, specializing in music from The Era That Will Never Come Again: the 1970s! With a broadband connection, you hear hundreds of classic 1970s hits in 128 Kbps CD-quality stereo; to tune into MLC Radio, visit my Web site at www. mlcbooks.com.

And it's not just your ears that will benefit! Online providers like Netflix (www.netflix.com) and Hulu (www.hulu.com) make it easy to watch streaming video on your PC (either for a low subscription fee for commercial-free viewing, or for free if you don't mind an advertisement or two). Talk about *sassy!*

Understanding Internet Connections

If you're wondering what DSL stands for or how the speed of a cable modem connection stacks up against your old phone modem, here I discuss each of the common connection types in addition to their pros and cons.

Dialup connections

Once the single most common type of Internet connection, the hoary dialup modem dates back to the days of the early 1980s. Dialup connections use standard telephone lines. In fact, you can consider a dialup connection to be a telephone call between two computers.

✦ **Dialup pros**

- *Simple equipment:* Only a standard voice telephone line and an inexpensive modem

- *Easy access:* Access available anywhere telephone service exists

- *Minimal cost:* A minimal amount for access ($10–$25 US per month: that is, as long as you're calling a local access number — not a long distance toll call)

✦ **Dialup cons**

- *Busy signals:* Busy telephone line (depending on the feature set offered by your modem)

- *Slow speed: Much* slower than any other form of Internet access

- *Reconnection hassles:* Must dial your ISP each time to connect

Dialup access still has its merits, but I wouldn't recommend a dialup connection unless your Internet needs are limited to e-mail and five minutes' worth of browsing per day.

DSL connections

A digital subscriber line (DSL) is one of the two most common high-speed connections. As long as you're within the DSL service area of your telephone provider and your ISP, you can move to DSL.

✦ **DSL pros**

- *Always-on connection:* No dialing necessary for Internet access

- *Fast:* True broadband access speeds (although generally not as fast as cable)

- *Basic equipment:* Uses standard telephone wiring, although you'll need a splitter (shown in Figure 1-6) to separate the PC's data connection from your telephone's analog connection

✦ **DSL cons**

- *Cost:* Usually at least double the cost of a dialup Internet account

- *Cost:* Need to rent or buy a DSL modem, which is more expensive than a familiar dialup modem

- *Limited access:* Might not be available in your area

Figure 1-6:
Use a DSL splitter to separate your phone/ Internet connection.

**Book III
Chapter 1**

**Making Sense
of the Internet**

I recommend DSL for anyone who spends more than an hour a night online or who specifically needs faster data transfer.

Cable modem connections

Cable Internet access just plain rocks; it's the other popular broadband connection technology on your block.

✦ **Cable pros**

- *Always-on:* No dialing necessary

- *Very fast:* True broadband access speeds (in most areas, faster than DSL)

- *Simple equipment:* Uses your cable TV coaxial cabling to connect

✦ **Cable cons**

- *Cost:* About twice as expensive as a dialup account

- *More cost:* Need to rent or buy a cable modem

- *ISP limitations:* A limited number of ISP choices accompany cable access (generally, one ISP or none)

Cable access speeds vary according to how many fellow users are connecting to the Internet in your neighborhood: The more people who are connected, the slower your access. (Keep that in mind if you're renting an apartment.) Mind you, the difference might not be significant. I have cable modem access, for example, and because my average connection speed is about one-third faster than the DSL in my area, I still end up with faster surfing and download speeds. Therefore, a bit of checking and speed comparison is in order before you choose between cable and DSL in your area.

I recommend cable for folks who spend more than an hour a night online or who specifically need faster transfers.

Satellite connections

A satellite Internet connection provides transfer speeds comparable with a cable connection, but satellite technology is also (as you might have guessed) usually the most expensive. You usually rent your equipment (an internal adapter card) from your ISP, and the account is also typically more expensive. Bad weather or heavy cloud cover can also slow your connection. However, if you're living in the middle of Alaska and can't get anything other than long distance access to an ISP, the satellite route is likely the way to go.

Here's one possible caveat about satellite service (depending on which type of satellite equipment you install): Don't throw away your dialup modem yet! You see, your Internet data is beamed to your home or office from a satellite overhead — hence the speed — but the data *you* send back to your ISP might be transferred over a standard dialup modem connection.

Normally, this isn't a big deal because you probably send a very small amount of data compared with what you receive: Web page addresses, e-mail, and the like. On the other hand, if you must upload large files to an FTP server or you want to host a Web site, the slow crawl of your dialup connection is likely to drive you batty.

The latest satellite service uses the satellite antenna to send and receive data, so a dialup connection is no longer necessary. Check with your satellite ISP for information about which type of connection is offered and how much it costs before you sign on the dotted line.

"What Exactly Do I Need?"

Here's the list of minimum requirements to achieve an Internet connection from your PC:

✦ **Your PC:** Natch. Windows 7 is preferred in my little chunk of the universe.

✦ **An Internet account from a local ISP:** Most larger ISPs offer at least dialup and DSL. If you choose cable or satellite access, your ISP is the company providing the connection.

✦ **A modem of one sort or another:** Whether you choose a telephone modem, a DSL or cable modem, or a satellite adapter, you can't just connect a cable to your PC and expect it to work.

✦ **A service call (for satellite, cable, or DSL access):** You can connect a telephone modem by yourself, but a service technician has to perform a number of magic tricks if you choose cable or DSL access.

Chapter 2: Adding an Internet Connection to Windows 7

In This Chapter

✔ Obtaining the right account data

✔ Checking your physical connection

✔ Creating a dialup, DSL, or cable connection in Windows 7

✔ Troubleshooting a faulty Internet connection

*A*lbert Einstein once said, "Imagination is more important than knowledge." When it comes to adding an Internet connection, however, our friend Albert is just plain wrong. (No disrespect intended — Albert was truly a genius.)

You'll find that this chapter is definitely a work of nonfiction — and for good reason. For most PC owners, setting up an analog dialup, satellite, DSL, or cable connection (or "installing the Internet," as I've heard it called) seems to be one of the most daunting tasks possible. And that's a shame because adding an Internet connection is really a simple process. It's just full of all sorts of strange and weird numbers and snippets of data.

With more and more PC owners turning to broadband Internet connections (like cable and DSL), the old-fashioned dialup modem is already preparing to join the other antique hardware in the PC Dinosaur Museum. However, until we *all* have access to broadband connections (and those faster connections become more affordable), this chapter continues to remove the mystery behind all flavors of going online, so that you can get — and stay — online!

Gathering the Account Incantations

Unfortunately, setting up an Internet account is still not a plug-and-play operation, but that's not the fault of Windows 7. Rather, blame it on how the Internet works (which I discuss in Chapter 1 of this minibook) and the information that other computers need to know before they can communicate with your PC. Without the proper setup, you can have the fastest network connection on the planet to the Internet, but plugging in your PC provides you with absolutely zip — or, as my dad used to say, "the big diddly-squat."

Don't lose hope! Before you get waist-deep in the Sea of Nervous Tension, let me reassure you that you need to gather only a few MIVs (that's my own abbreviation, short for *Mysterious Internet Values*). Plus, they should all be given to you (for free) by your Internet service provider (ISP) when you sign up for an Internet account!

If you opt for using a dialup connection instead of broadband, you'll definitely save money — unless accessing your ISP means making a toll or long-distance call from your home phone. Watch out for that gotcha. Perhaps dialup is your only option for going online. After all, not everyone has cable or DSL available where they live (a good time to consider a satellite Internet connection if you can afford the premium price tag). However, if at all possible, I heartily and healthily recommend NOT using a dialup connection. You'll be truly disappointed at the speed at which things *don't* download, such as streaming video and the like.

If dialup is your choice, though, here's a list of the required information you need to set up your Internet access in Windows via a dialup modem:

✦ **Your ISP account name and password:** *Note that this information is often different from your e-mail account username and password.* This is the first troubleshooting question that I ask when folks tell me that they can't connect.

✦ **(Dialup connection) The local access number provided by your ISP:** Note that many ISPs offer more than one local access number.

✦ **The name of your ISP:** If you have multiple accounts from the same ISP, use more descriptive names, such as *Business account* and *Personal account.*

Now, of course, that's not all the gobbledygook you get from your ISP, but that's all you need to know to handle the steps in this chapter. If you didn't get that gobbledygook, you need to contact your ISP's technical support or help desk by telephone and request it, because you won't be able to connect to the Internet without it.

The rest of the arcane knowledge you receive from your ISP is required later in this minibook, when I cover Windows Mail in Chapter 5 — but after you read this chapter, you'll be a certified technonerd.

If you're using a DSL, satellite, or cable connection to the Internet, you just need your ISP account name and password. If your broadband connection is professionally installed, just hang on to the information in case you have to manually reconfigure your Internet connection because of a hard drive crash, operating system upgrade, or other major change to your system.

Making the Physical Connection

First, make sure that you're plugged in. You've likely heard the horror stories about a recalcitrant PC that stubbornly fails to accept an Internet connection only to find later that the doggone thing simply wasn't hooked up correctly.

Before you delve into the next section, here's a list of the physical connections necessary for each type of Internet access:

✦ **Dialup connection:** Your modem needs to be connected to the telephone wall jack. Most modems are internal (inside your PC case); if you're using an external modem, make sure that it's connected to either your PC's Universal Serial Bus (USB) or serial port. (See Book I, Chapter 3 for more on ports.)

✦ **Digital subscriber line (DSL) or cable connection:** Your modem needs to be connected to the telephone wall jack or DSL phone line splitter (for a DSL connection) or your cable TV coax connection (if you're using cable access), and your PC's network card must be connected to the modem with an Ethernet cable. As I mention in Chapter 1 of this minibook, both these Internet technologies are typically installed by a professional, so you shouldn't have to worry about your physical connections. (In fact, if you have a DSL or cable connection, you might not need anything in this chapter because most installation technicians are nice individuals who usually set up the entire shootin' match for you. If you *don't* get a professional installation with your DSL or cable service, don't panic. I'm still going to demonstrate things here!)

✦ **Satellite connection:** Your PC's network card must be connected to the satellite dish's signal box with an Ethernet network cable.

If you had an Internet connection that was working on a previous computer, use the Windows Easy Transfer Wizard to transfer it. You find it by choosing Start➪All Programs➪Accessories➪System Tools➪Windows Easy Transfer. (Why Microsoft continues to call these programs "accessories," I will never know. It sounds like this wizard is a vanity mirror in a new BMW.)

Creating a New Dialup Connection in Windows 7

If your ISP provided you with complete instructions for setting up your account in Windows 7 — in fact, I would look sideways at the ISP if it didn't — feel free to follow those instructions rather than the steps in this section. Of course, if you didn't get any instructions, you're still covered. (They don't call me Mister Thorough Author for nothing.)

**Book III
Chapter 2**

Adding an Internet
Connection to
Windows 7

This procedure covers the most common scenario, where

+ You already signed up for an account with a local ISP.

+ Your ISP didn't provide a set of detailed instructions (thanks a *heap*).

+ You're using a dialup modem, and it's connected and turned on.

With that said, take a deep breath and follow these steps:

1. **Choose Start⇨Control Panel⇨Network and Sharing Center.**

2. **Click the Set Up a New Connection or Network link.**

Windows 7 displays the Choose a Connection Option screen, shown in Figure 2-1. Click Next to continue.

Figure 2-1: The friendly face of the Set Up a Connection or Network wizard.

3. **Select the Set Up a Dial-Up Connection option and click Next.**

So far, so good, but the screen shown in upcoming Figure 2-2 is where some people go astray.

4. **In the Dial-Up Phone Number text box, type the local access number provided by your ISP.**

A local number should be in form xxx-xxxx, like 555-1234. If the number is a toll-free call, don't forget to add the *1-xxx* prefix, as in 1-800-555-1234. On the other hand, if your ISP doesn't provide a local access number and you have to call long distance to connect, run (do not walk!) to your telephone and cancel that account! (These days, no one should have to incur long distance charges on top of Internet access. Look for a local ISP instead. Here's a chance to use a telephone book again — remember when they used to be so important?)

Book III
Chapter 2

Figure 2-2:
Set up your
ISP account
name and
password
here.

5. **Type your username and password provided by your ISP into the corresponding boxes.**

   For security, the wizard displays round bullet characters rather than the letters and numbers you type. If you're in a secure location and you prefer to see what you're typing, select the Show Characters check box.

   Security is A Good Thing, as you find out in Chapter 3 of this minibook — therefore, enable the Remember This Password check box *only* if you're not sharing your PC with others and it's in a secure location, like your home. Otherwise, anyone can connect to the Internet using your account, *without* knowing your password!

6. **Type the name of the ISP (or an identifying name that you can remember) into the Connection Name text box and then click Next.**

   If you're sharing your computer with another person and you don't want them to be able to use your account to connect to the Internet, don't select the Allow Other People to Use This Connection check box.

7. **Click Create.**

   That's it! See — I told you it was (practically) painless.

Creating a New DSL, Satellite, or Cable Connection in Windows 7

As I mention earlier in this chapter, a DSL, satellite, or cable modem installation might be performed for you or the equipment is accompanied by a detailed set of instructions. Don't forget this:

If the manufacturer or your ISP gives you more specific instructions than the generic steps that you see here, use those instead!™

It's what I would do. You won't hurt my feelings.

Follow these steps to set up Windows 7 for broadband goodness:

1. **Choose Start⇨Control Panel⇨Network and Sharing Center.**

2. **Click the Set Up a New Connection or Network link.**

   Click Next to continue.

3. **Select the Connect to the Internet option and then click Next.**

4. **Click the Broadband option and then click Next.**

5. **Type your username and password provided by your ISP into the corresponding boxes (see Figure 2-3).**

   Again, I recommend that you enable the Remember This Password check box *only* if you're not sharing your PC with others and it's in a secure location. Why allow some elusive, shady character to connect to the Internet with your account?

6. **Type the name of the ISP into the Connection Name text box and then click Next.**

7. **Click Connect.**

Figure 2-3: Entering data for a broadband connection.

"Is My Connection Alive?"

The final step in your odyssey is the testing: Have you successfully connected your PC to the Internet? The easiest way to test your work is to run Internet Explorer and try loading a popular site, such as CNN.com or Amazon.com. Type the site name in the Address box and press Enter, and your PC should automatically dial out if you're using a modem. You might not hear the dial tone, but Windows 7 should display a progress dialog box to let you know what's going on. Naturally, a DSL or cable modem (or a satellite network card) doesn't need to dial out.

If your browser displays the site, you're online! Or, as pilots say, "You're in the pipe, five by five." (I don't know why.)

"My Connection Appears to Be Dead"

If you don't end up clapping your hands in celebration, here are the common troubleshooting tips that I always offer to my consulting customers:

✦ **Check your physical cable connections.** It's always possible that your external modem simply isn't plugged in, connected to your PC, or connected to the phone jack (for a dialup modem or DSL modem) or the cable connector. An internal modem needs only a cable from the correct port on the PC to the wall phone jack.

Speaking of correct ports, remember that most analog dialup modems have two ports on the back: One is for the cable running to your wall jack, and the other allows you to plug in a regular telephone to the back of the modem so that you can use your telephone line in the old-fashioned, human-powered manner. Make sure that you plug your phone line from the wall socket into the correct port, which is usually decorated with an icon showing a wall jack.

✦ **(Dialup) Verify the telephone number provided by your ISP.** Pick up your phone and dial the old-fashioned way, using the exact sequence of numbers you entered for the ISP's phone number in Step 4 in the previous section. If you hear the familiar screeching banshee wail of a modem on the other side, you know that the number is correct.

✦ **Double-check the account name and password.** If Windows 7 displays a dialog box saying that your account name or password isn't correct, make sure that you typed your ISP account username and password and *not* your e-mail account username and password. If all appears okay, a call to your ISP's technical support is in order.

**Book III
Chapter 2**

Adding an Internet
Connection to
Windows 7

Chapter 3: Protecting Your Internet Privacy

In This Chapter

✔ **Understanding the risks of the Internet**

✔ **Using your common sense online**

✔ **Using the built-in Windows 7 Firewall**

✔ **Protecting your PC from viruses**

"**A**m I *really* taking any risks with my computer or my privacy when I'm online?"

That is one of the most common questions I receive from my readers. I wish that I could assure you that security accompanies the once-unimagined freedom of the Internet — but, unfortunately, the opposite is true. For once, the popular media's perception of computer crime is quite accurate: With your Internet connection comes the possibility of exposure to hackers and con artists.

But just what *can* happen online? How much is hype, and how much is reality? With the right precautions and a little additional hardware and software, you can be reasonably sure that you're well insulated from the bad guys on the Internet! In this chapter, I provide you with everything you need to know — the same recommendations I've made to my clients, friends, and family for more than a decade — to protect *your* privacy online.

What Can Really Happen?

Before I present you with the worst that the Internet can offer, please keep these two important questions in mind:

✦ **Are you a target?** The likely answer is no — and I'm glad to say that's my answer as well. Virtually no private citizen really draws the attention of the serious hackers and other bad guys on the Internet. Hackers would rather attack someone famous, the government, or a corporation than spend their time trying to get a copy of your Word documents, your e-mail, and your Quicken data. (Of course, hackers are getting younger and younger these days, so you might be targeted as a practical joke or juvenile prank. To me, nothing is even remotely humorous about attacking someone else's online personal life — the effect is the same.)

✦ **Are you a tough nut to crack?** Yes! (Or at least you will be after you institute the safeguards in this chapter.) Plenty of "open PCs" are on the Internet, whose owners haven't protected themselves, so (like any car thief) a hacker focuses on the easy mark — or in this case, the "unlocked PC." In fact, with the right protection, it's virtually impossible for a hacker to even detect your presence on the Internet — much less try to invade your privacy — thereby preventing most of the nasty scenarios that I'm about to describe.

Okay, take a deep breath and relax. Here's what *can* happen to you with an Internet connection or a network with a shared Internet connection:

✦ **Someone can try to contact you or the members of your family.** Believe me, there are some truly unpleasant and sleazy individuals who can use all the great communications features of the Internet for the wrong reasons. They can use *Windows Live Messenger* (the instant messaging software provided by Microsoft with Windows 7), Web discussion boards, e-mail, or newsgroups. With common sense and diligence, you can stop these people from communicating with you.

✦ **You can be the target of identity theft.** The con game is alive and well and thriving on the Internet, where your credit card number, address, and personal information should be guarded like the jewels that they are.

✦ **Hackers can turn your PC into an Internet weapon.** If a hacker can gain access to your PC, it can be fooled into participating in attacks against public Web servers and File Transfer Protocol (FTP) servers. Denial-of-service (DoS) attacks can actually shut down Web sites like eBay, Amazon.com, and Yahoo!. In simple English, the hackers manipulate PCs that they have "appropriated" over the Internet to flood these large Web sites with millions of simultaneous connections and cause the Web server to simply "freak out."

✦ **The files on your network can be read or erased.** Woe unto those who run an unprotected network — especially a wireless network, which can be accessed from outside your home or office.

✦ **Your system can be hit with a virus, Trojan, or harmful macro.** Most of us have already heard of the havoc that a virus infection can wreak on your system — deleted files or even empty hard drives.

I told you that it was a grim list — but if all these bad things actually happened to the majority of people who go online, the Internet wouldn't be anywhere as popular and important today as it is. Most of us use our common sense — a most valuable commodity that can help safeguard your Internet presence.

Common Sense Goes a Long Way

Along with common sense comes one of the best of Mark's Maxims, which I hope you immediately commit to memory:

If something seems like a bad idea online, *it probably is.*™

You see it happen all the time on the Internet: People give out sensitive (personal and financial) information and communicate with others on a level that they would never do over the telephone or through the mail. Chalk it up to the siren song of the online world and the charms of technology, I guess.

Take a second to review a number of common sense guidelines that should govern your time online.

Passwords

First, consider the password: It's not an elegant solution to the problem of security, but it has been around since the early days of the online bulletin board systems (or BBSes, for short) in the mid-1980s and early 1990s. No one has found an easier way to protect your identity on the Internet — unless, of course, you want to install fingerprint sensors on everyone's keyboard. (This type of sensor exists right now, but don't hold your breath waiting to see them in common use.)

Here are the guidelines I recommend that you follow when using passwords:

+ **Use random passwords.** I know that using random passwords is a hassle, but they work. Even adding a single number to the end of a word can mean the difference between someone guessing your password and your identity remaining pristine. Some operating systems and online sites recognize the difference between uppercase and lowercase characters, and you can also mix cases to make your passwords even better.

Never use a password that's easily guessed, such as the names of family or friends, or your birthdate.

+ **Use a different password for each site and server.** If you connect to a dozen systems and need a dozen passwords each night when you're online, it probably isn't feasible — I understand that. However, for the majority of the PC owners online, only three or four passwords are used daily; in that case, using multiple passwords helps keep things as secure as possible.

+ **Do not write down your passwords.** If you store that sheet of paper or sticky note in a safe, you're okay. A desk drawer, on the other hand, makes that crib sheet a bad idea.

+ **Don't share passwords.** Or why use them at all? —'Nuff said.

✦ **Don't allow applications to remember your passwords.** Many programs that use the Internet offer the ability to remember the passwords you use online. It's convenient as all get-out, but unless you're guaranteed to be the only person using your account, it's also easy for someone to pose as you within your e-mail or instant messaging applications.

✦ **Use the AutoComplete feature in Internet Explorer sparingly.** Most Web browsers can automatically store your personal data for you, but I don't recommend using this feature. I show you how to turn off this feature within Internet Explorer later in this minibook (in Chapter 4).

Of course, your lifestyle might make it easier to skirt some of these recommendations. For example, if you live by yourself, you're already considerably more secure than an office worker surrounded by fellow employees. Just evaluate your own need for security and follow as many of these guidelines as possible. (See there? I can be reasonable.)

Risky behavior

You have to consider a number of online practices that are, sadly, lacking in (you guessed it) plain, common sense. Although you might find it hard to believe, each of these mistakes is committed countless times every day by intelligent individuals (who really should know better). Be sure never to

✦ **Divulge personal information to strangers during online chat.** Chatting is great fun unless the total stranger whom you're chatting with asks for personal information. (Is the person on the other end of this conversation *really* a 17-year-old cheerleader from Omaha?)

✦ **Offer personal information in Internet newsgroups.** This behavior is especially bad. These newsgroups are public discussion areas, and posting anything personal is asking for trouble. (It's no accident that virtually everyone who participates in a newsgroup uses an alias and a fake e-mail address.) Also, these messages remain on newsgroup servers for years, so a single telephone number or e-mail address that you divulge can come back to haunt you years later. After something is posted on a newsgroup, it's there to stay, in the great pile of searchable data that is the Internet. (Try this experiment: Use www.google.com to search for your name or an alias that you use on Web sites and in newsgroups. See how far back that stuff goes?)

✦ **Reply to spam.** Just delete those irritating junk e-mail messages in your Inbox, even if they claim that by replying, you remove your name from their lists. (Yeah, right, and I've got some great oceanfront property in Kansas for you, too.) By replying to spam, you're *verifying* that your e-mail address is correct, and you get double or triple the number of messages overnight.

✦ **Participate in phishing expeditions.** Maybe you're not familiar with the Internet term *phishing*. It refers to the process of attempting to gain your personal information through a combination of an e-mail message tied to a bogus (but official-looking) Web site. Unfortunately, these criminals are good at creating the impression that you're receiving mail from your bank (or eBay, or Amazon), requesting that you "verify your account information" or "update your user ID and password" by clicking the accompanying link (which opens a page that even looks like the company's Web site). Always remember that *no self-respecting company will ever request personal information from you through e-mail!* If you're unsure, visit the company's Web page (by typing in the bona fide address or using a bookmark) and contact the customer support staff. You may just be able to report an intended crime and help put the bad guys out of the phishing business.

✦ **Allow just *anyone* to access your PC remotely.** Both Windows 7 and Windows Vista include a remote control feature that allows someone on the Internet to use your PC as though they were sitting at your keyboard. *Do not use this feature unless you're absolutely sure of the person who will control your PC* — such as a technical support representative or your Aunt Harriet. Remember that the person controlling your PC can delete files and open your personal documents at will. (Sobering thought, ain't it?)

✦ **Download files from a site you don't trust.** It's up to you to decide which sites are trustworthy. If you do download something, at least make sure that your computer is protected by a good antivirus scanning program when you run the downloaded program.

✦ **Buy something from an online store without a secure connection.** A reputable online store establishes a secure connection between its Web server and your browser. Information is encrypted, so it can't be easily intercepted. (Of course, this statement is especially important when you're entering your credit card information.) If you're using Internet Explorer 8 and a small padlock icon appears on the right side of the address bar at the top of your browser window (and the prefix `https:` appears at the beginning of the site address, as shown in Figure 3-1) then you've got a secure connection. If the connection isn't secure, *don't enter any personal information and don't provide your credit card number* — just find another store that offers a secure connection!

✦ **Open e-mail attachments without using a good antivirus program.** These include executable (or `.exe`) files and Word documents. E-mail attachments are becoming the prime method of distributing viruses. And, because the virus uses the victim's e-mail program to replicate itself, those horrid e-mail booby traps can even originate from your "e-friends and e-family!"

Book III
Chapter 3

Protecting Your Internet Privacy

Dodging those personal questions

I generally don't provide my real name, age, address, or phone number on most Web sites. If a Web site demands this type of personal information and I don't trust the company or organization, I use false information. (Coincidentally, I receive very little spam on my private e-mail account. Go figure.)

I know that providing false information sounds dishonest — and it will anger any webmaster who might be reading this chapter — but why do I have to enter my personal information just to download a demo or use a (supposedly) free service? I'm a webmaster myself, and I don't need that information from casual visitors to my sites! Do some Web sites sell that contact information to other individuals and companies? (I think you already know the answer to *that* one.)

Naturally, if you're registering a piece of hardware or software or contacting a company's technical support department, providing the required information makes sense — but weigh other queries with care!

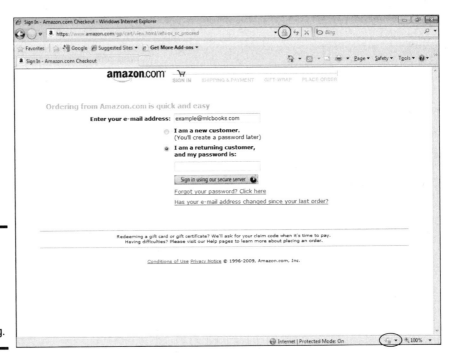

Figure 3-1:
When buying online, a padlock icon is A Good Thing.

E-mail

I mention spam in the previous section. You *can* fight back, you know. Most e-mail applications have their own built-in armor plates, called *filters* or *rules*, which allow you to automatically move junk mail to a separate folder, where it can be quickly perused and tossed at your leisure. I show you how to enable spam protection in Windows Live Mail in Chapter 5 of this minibook.

By the way, get in the habit of at least skimming the Subject lines for probable spam; that way, you can verify that an honest-to-goodness valuable message didn't get accidentally tagged as junk.

Using the Built-in Windows 7 Firewall

Believe me, good people, your firewall *is* your best friend if, for some reason, a serious hacker indeed becomes interested in accessing your PC or your network. A *firewall* is a software application or a separate hardware device (or both) that performs a number of duties:

+ **It masks your PC or network from others on the Internet.** You make it practically impossible for a hacker to locate your PC (much less attack it).

+ **It prevents incoming Internet traffic for the services you specify.** Web and FTP services are two examples, as illustrated so very well by Figure 3-2.

+ **It monitors outgoing traffic and blocks any activity you specify.** Examples are visits to particular Web sites or any Windows Live Messenger communications.

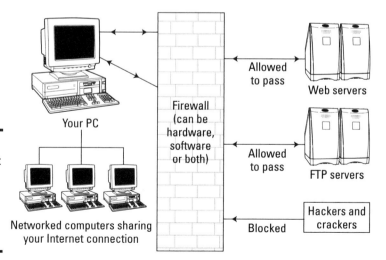

Figure 3-2:
The Internet traffic that you want gets in through a firewall.

Your PC

Networked computers sharing your Internet connection

Firewall (can be hardware, software or both)

Allowed to pass — Web servers

Allowed to pass — FTP servers

Blocked — Hackers and crackers

Which is better — a hardware or software firewall? That depends on the number of PCs on your network — if you have one — and the level of security you need:

✦ **For a single PC (or a shared Internet connection through Windows 7) with typical home or home office security:** The built-in Windows 7 Firewall is all you need.

✦ **For a network of several PCs — or for any environment where you demand the best security:** Turn to a hardware firewall device. For example, Figure 3-3 illustrates some of the port protection features built into my Internet router.

Figure 3-3:
My Internet router can be configured to block just about anything.

Device Administration Settings	
Main Menu	Product Name: XRouter Pro
• OnePage Setup	
Advanced	
• DHCP Settings	Administrator Password
• Access Control	Password Change: •••••
• Virtual Server	Password Confirm: •••••
• Device Admin	External Admin.: ○ Enable ○ Disable
• Status Monitor	Block WAN Port Scanning: ○ Yes ○ No
• Special App	Block WAN Ping Response: ○ Yes ○ No
• DMZ Host	Reset Device: ○ Yes ○ No
• RIP	Factory Defaults: ○ Yes ○ No
• Static Routing	Apply Undo
• PPPoE	

If you're using an Internet-sharing device (such as an Internet router or switch) that includes NAT, celebrate! NAT stands for *Network Address Translation,* which performs the masking that I mention earlier in this section. Most devices with NAT support also include a hardware firewall. Check the device's manual to be sure.

If you peruse Chapter 2 of this minibook, you know that I recommend enabling the built-in firewall in Windows 7 when you create your Internet connection.

You can easily enable the Windows Firewall, but you need a user account with administrator access to do the job. Follow these steps:

1. **Choose Start⇨Control Panel⇨System and Security⇨Windows Firewall.**

2. **Click the Turn Windows Firewall On or Off link to display the Windows Firewall settings shown in Figure 3-4.**

3. **Select both of the Turn On Windows Firewall radio buttons (Home network *and* Public network locations) to enable or disable the firewall as necessary and then click OK.**

Figure 3-4:
Watch your
firewall
there,
friend.

The Windows 7 Firewall is one smart puppy; it shouldn't interfere with any of the Internet activities that a typical home PC owner is likely to try. However, many multiplayer games have trouble sharing your PC with a firewall. If a specific program has problems with the Windows Firewall, check the program's manual to see whether you need to make changes to accommodate a firewall.

Hey, how about a free test of your Windows 7 Firewall? No, pardner, I'm not offering to hack into your system. Instead, I'm inviting you to visit Gibson Research Corporation at www.grc.com, where you can try out ShieldsUP!!. This first-class, *free* online utility checks your Internet connection for a number of entranceways popular with hackers and even gives you advice on how to fine-tune your firewall to close —'em up.

There are third-party firewalls on the market for Windows 7 — for example, Norton Internet Security 2010, from Symantec (www.symantec.com). If you decide to install a new primary firewall, make sure that you follow the instructions provided by the developer carefully to safeguard your PC's security (you may have to disable the Windows 7 Firewall first, for example).

Using Antivirus Software

The last stop on the Internet security tour is a good antivirus program. At the time of this writing, Windows 7 contains no built-in, robust virus protection. Instead, look to McAfee for VirusScan Plus or Symantec for Norton AntiVirus 2010; either program does an excellent job of protecting your computer from viral attack. (If you appreciate a well-written, *free* antivirus application for Windows 7 and Vista, consider the avast! antivirus Home edition, from ALWIL Software. I highly recommend this terrific program! For all the details, visit www.avast.com.)

As I see it, the two most important features of any antivirus program are

✦ **Real-time scanning:** Whatever you run or load, your antivirus program should check it before your PC is exposed. I also appreciate the fact that Norton AntiVirus 2010 checks all my Word and Excel documents for dangerous macro viruses. With real-time scanning, the need to check your entire hard drive for viruses is reduced to once every three months or so rather than once every week.

✦ **Automatic and frequent updates:** The best antivirus protection in the known universe isn't worth a plug nickel the moment you stop applying updates. Without updates that contain the latest virus signatures, your antivirus program becomes vulnerable to the newest strain. (A *signature* is a set of characteristics that your antivirus program can use to spot a particular virus.) Therefore, make sure that the antivirus program you choose is updated often and automatically — ALWIL Software, McAfee, and Symantec excel in providing at least one or two updates a month.

Figure 3-5 illustrates avast! at work.

Figure 3-5: I don't fear viruses with avast! antivirus on the job.

By the way, avast! antivirus works inside most e-mail programs (including Outlook 2010). In fact, the program even checks both the incoming file attachments you receive and the outgoing files you send — just in case.

Chapter 4: Cruising the Web with Internet Explorer

In This Chapter

✔ **Starting Internet Explorer**

✔ **Introducing the browser window and controls**

✔ **Searching for Web sites**

✔ **Adding and using Favorites**

✔ **Using tabs like a pro**

✔ **Working with RSS feeds**

✔ **Downloading files**

✔ **Using the History file**

✔ **Printing and saving Web pages**

*A*nd the answer to the unspoken question is, "Yes, you *still* need this chapter, even if you've been using Internet Explorer for the past several years."

You see, Internet Explorer (or almost any Web browser) is one of the simplest applications on the planet to use, requiring only three or four buttons on the toolbar to operate most of the necessary functions. Many PC owners I've met don't even know that Internet Explorer (IE) offers a ton of additional features to help you organize sites, print pages just-so, and search for the Web content you need. Oh, and don't forget that although you may be using an earlier version of Internet Explorer (like IE6 or IE7), you can upgrade to Internet Explorer 8 for free. Well done, Microsoft!

In this chapter, I show you the power-user side of Internet Explorer 8 — it's time to supercharge your surfing!

Running Internet Explorer

Here are a number of methods you can use to start Internet Explorer 8. (After all, the Web has its tentacles in practically everything, right?)

✦ In Windows Vista or Windows 7, double-click the IE icon on your desktop.

✦ Choose Start➪Internet.

✦ Click the IE button on the Quick Launch portion of the taskbar.

✦ Click an embedded HTML link in many applications and documents, such as Word and Excel documents or e-mail messages. (This automatically opens the Web site corresponding to that link.)

✦ Run Windows Update in Windows XP. (It's weird, but you can surf after you update!)

In Windows XP, don't forget that you can choose Start⇨Run to display the Run dialog box, where you can use your fingers for something other than clicking. Type **iexplore** in the Open box and then press Enter (or click OK, if you absolutely have to click something). This action runs Internet Explorer, but you can get even fancier: Type **iexplore**, followed by a Web site address (like **iexplore mlcbooks.com**), and then press Enter or click OK. The program runs and automatically loads my Web site. (In Vista or Windows 7, type **iexplore** in the Search box on the Start menu.)

The Explorer Window and Basic Controls

After Internet Explorer unveils itself in all its stately grandeur — as you can see in Figure 4-1 — note the following major controls and important spots, in order of appearance from top to bottom:

✦ **The Address bar:** Here's where you type (or paste) the URLs for Web sites. You can click the drop-down list to see the addresses you recently visited. Click a site in the list to return to it with a minimum of fuss.

The all-important Secure Sockets Layer (SSL) encryption icon appears on the Address bar, next to the Web site's address; in the earlier versions of Internet Explorer, the icon appeared on the Status bar. If you do a lot of online shopping, you see this tiny yellow padlock icon whenever you're entering your personal data or credit card number; it indicates that the site you're visiting is *secure,* which means that the encrypted information you're typing can't be intercepted by hackers.

✦ **The Live Search box:** Click in the Live Search box and enter a word or phrase, and Internet Explorer searches the Web for sites containing that text.

By default, IE8 uses Bing as your Web search provider, but you can also switch to other popular providers like Google and Yahoo! Choose Tools⇨Internet Options and click the Settings button in the Search section to display the Manage Add-Ons dialog box; from here, you can add or change search providers.

✦ **The toolbar:** The default toolbar display includes a number of pop-up menu buttons, which I discuss in detail throughout this chapter. The toolbar also displays the Favorites buttons and any tabbed Web pages you might have collected in your travels.

✦ **The Favorites Center:** I don't know why Microsoft calls this huge panel a *Center* — but then again, who gives a flip? Anyway, no matter what you call it, you'll find this configurable panel very convenient. It can be toggled between displaying all sorts of information, including your Favorites, your surfing history, and your RSS feeds. To display the Favorites Center, you can choose the Favorites Center button on the toolbar (it carries a star icon) and then choose the panel you want to see, or you can press the shortcut key combinations that I provide in the following section, "More buttons for your buck"). To banish the Favorites Center from the Internet Explorer window, click the Close button in the upper-right corner of the panel.

Address bar

Content window

Favorites Center Tab

Toolbar Live Search box

Status bar

Figure 4-1: Internet Explorer 8 — what a rush!

Book III Chapter 4

Cruising the Web with Internet Explorer

You can resize the width of the Favorites Center by hovering your mouse pointer over the right edge of the bar until it turns into a double-arrow cursor. Then click and drag the separator to the desired spot.

+ **Content window:** Believe it or not, the IE window shows you Web content, too (among all the other stuff). Clicking an underlined or graphical link in the Content window whisks you somewhere else (either within the same site or on a completely different Web site). Other Windows-style controls, such as drop-down lists and text entry boxes, can also be displayed and used as part of your surfing. It all depends on the webmaster who designed the page you're viewing — or the webmistress, as the case may be.

One of my favorite IE keyboard shortcuts is Ctrl+N, which opens a new Internet Explorer window with the current page loaded. Opening a new window comes in handy when you suddenly need to compare the contents of two Web pages because you can navigate to the second page without disturbing the first. Alternatively, you can open a Web site in a new tab, which I discuss later in this chapter.

+ **Status bar:** Last and smallest — but certainly not the least — the Internet Explorer Status bar displays information about the page you're viewing. If you rest your mouse pointer on a link or photo on a Web page, the status bar displays information about that item, and you can also change your Windows Internet security properties from the Status bar.

You use the Zoom level menu on the right side of the Status bar to zoom out or zoom in on a page within the Content window — a helpful feature if you prefer to zoom in to relieve tired eyes after a long night of Web surfing!

More buttons for your buck

Just in case you were never properly introduced to the default buttons on the Address bar, they include

+ **Back:** With a click of the Back button, Internet Explorer returns to the last page you visited, and each subsequent click of the Back button takes you one more page back. You can also press Alt+← on your keyboard to move backward.

+ **Forward:** If you click Back, you need a way to return, right? Click the Forward button to go to the next page (or pages) where you originally were, in forward order. From the keyboard, you can press Alt+→ to move forward.

If you notice that the Back button is disabled (grayed out), you haven't visited at least two sites yet. If the Forward button is disabled, you haven't used the Back button yet. (Little did we all know that the Internet Explorer toolbar had a PhD in quantum physics.)

✦ **Refresh:** Clicking the Refresh button (the two curly arrows, to the right of the Address field) reloads the contents of the current Web page, which allows the Web server to update the page with any new information. (This button is helpful for connections to news sites, like CNN.com.) You can press F5 to refresh as well.

✦ **Stop:** This option is wonderfully self-explanatory. Click Stop (the X button, to the right of the Refresh button) to cancel a page from loading. Pressing Esc does the same job from the keyboard.

✦ **Live Search:** This text box makes it easy to search for stuff on the Web, which I cover later in this chapter (see the "Navigating the Web" section). Pressing Ctrl+E takes you immediately to the Live Search box.

Now, please shift your attention to the toolbar. The icons on the toolbar include

✦ **Favorites Center:** Click the Favorites button to display the Favorites Center. (Again, I tell you more about this topic later in this chapter.) Press Alt+C from the keyboard to display the Favorites Center.

✦ **Add to Favorites Bar:** Click this button to add the current site to the Favorites Bar (which appears right next to the button).

✦ **Suggested Sites:** Click this button to display suggested sites you might enjoy based upon the sites you visit most often.

✦ **Web Slice Gallery:** This list displays the Web Slices you've selected from Web pages with updated content. (You'll find more about Web Slices in the sidebar titled "What the Heck is a Web Slice?" later in this chapter.)

✦ **Tabs:** These nifty controls make it easy to peruse multiple Web sites — you can click a tab to immediately switch to that site in the Content window. I cover tabs in more detail later in this chapter.

✦ **Home:** Click this button to immediately jump to your home page. Mine is `mlcbooks.com`, for example, which makes a trip to my company home page always one click away. From the keyboard, press Alt+M. (You can click the small arrow next to the Home button to add or change your home page.)

✦ **RSS Feeds:** Clicking this button displays any RSS feeds available from the current site. (If that sounds like Greek, don't worry: I cover RSS feeds later in this chapter, in the sidebar "Lean, fast, and mean — that's RSS.") Click the small arrow next to the RSS Feeds button to display (and choose from) the major feed headings.

✦ **Read Mail:** If you've installed Windows Live Mail on your PC, you can click this button to jump directly to the Mail window.

Book III
Chapter 4

Cruising the Web with Internet Explorer

"The Story of Little URL"

Every Web-touring saga begins with the *URL* — short for Uniform Resource Locator — that identifies every Web site on the planet. It's commonly called a *Web address* because a URL is as unique as a traditional mailing address.

Most URLs begin with the now-oh-so-darn-ubiquitous `www.` prefix. However, Internet Explorer doesn't require that you type the triple-w when you're entering a new Web address to visit. For example, if you just type **cnn.com** on the Address bar and then press Enter, Internet Explorer automatically adds the `www.` prefix for you. You get to visit CNN.com and save four

characters of typing to boot. Also, you never need to type the `http://` portion of the URL because Internet Explorer always tries to load an address as a Web site unless you specifically indicate that you're trying to connect to a File Transfer Protocol (FTP) site by using the `ftp://` prefix.

Also, you might have noticed recently that a number of sites no longer even use the triple-w. Therefore, don't assume that a URL starts with `www.` or else you might not be able to load the page. Instead, always enter the URL exactly as it's given to you.

✦ **Print:** A click of this button (or pressing the Ctrl+P shortcut) prints the contents of the current page. To display the Print Preview window or change the settings for your printed pages, click the small arrow next to the Print button.

✦ **Page:** Click the Page button to display a pop-up menu with different settings that control the appearance of the page: for example, the text size and the page's HTML source listing. You can also find menu items that allow you to save a page or send a page in an e-mail message.

Buried deep within the Page menu is the New Window menu item, which — as you've likely guessed — opens a completely new IE window using the current page as a starting point. I've grown quite attached to the Ctrl+N keyboard shortcut, and use it instead.)

✦ **Safety:** This pop-up menu button is all about security! From here you can delete your history file (which indicates where you've been in past browsing sessions) as well as display a security report for the page you're currently viewing. You can also run Windows Update directly from this menu.

✦ **Tools:** Another pop-up menu button? Yes, indeed — click the Tools button to switch to a full-screen display, view (or hide) the Status bar and Favorites Center pane, and even display an old-fashioned Menu bar (by choosing the Menu Bar item). Then again, Microsoft hides the anachronistic Menu bar by default now!

✦ **Help:** If the Help button (and accompanying menu) doesn't appear on your toolbar, don't panic — just click the double right arrows that appear next to the Tools button, to display "the rest of the toolbar!" (Yep, this is what happens when you have too many buttons in too little space.) Anyway, you find on the Help menu all the high-quality online help you've come to expect from Microsoft.

To display a short one- or two-word description of an Address bar or toolbar button, just leave your mouse pointer motionless over the button for a second or two.

Finding a home page

I always encourage everyone on the planet to choose their own home page. If you're continually returning to the same spot on the Web, you'll find that your home page can significantly speed up your surfing, which is why I use my site mlcbooks.com as my home page. Many PC owners prefer Google or their ISP's home page, or even CNN.com if you're a newshound. From within Internet Explorer 8, follow these steps:

1. **Navigate to the page you want to use as your home page.**

2. **Click the drop-down arrow next to the Home button on the toolbar.**

3. **Choose the Add or Change Home Page menu option to display the dialog box you see in Figure 4-2.**

4. **Select the Use This Webpage as Your Only Home Page radio button.**

5. **Click Yes to save your changes and return to the browser window.**

Book III
Chapter 4

Figure 4-2: There's no place like home (page).

Cruising the Web with Internet Explorer

Navigating the Web

Earlier in this chapter, I talk about how you can visit a site by typing or pasting a URL directly into the Address bar and pressing Enter. Internet Explorer automatically shows you any sites with a matching address while you type the URL. And, if you already visited the site, just press Enter when you see the proper address appear.

What the heck is a Web Slice?

A *Web Slice* is a rather nutty name for a very cool new feature in Internet Explorer 8. Web designers can mark content that updates often as a *Web Slice* — for example, the scores section on your favorite sports site, or the movie listings at your local theater. Instead of manually visiting the same site several times a day to check for new content, you can use a Web Slice to notify you automatically when the page has been updated!

If a Web Slice is available on a specific site, the Web Slice icon appears in your IE toolbar,

and it also pops up when you move your mouse over the "sliceable" section of the page. (The icon looks like a white double-arrow in a green square, at least to me.) You can click the icon in the toolbar to add the content to your Favorites Bar. When IE highlights the Web Slice in the Favorites Bar, you've got new content! Click the button to preview the change, and click the preview pop-up to return to that Web site.

Unfortunately, every time I see the words *Web Slice,* I think of apple pie! Someone at Microsoft needs to consider a new name.

However, here are other methods of navigating to a new site:

✦ **Click a link** within another Web page.

✦ **Click the Home button,** which displays your home page.

✦ **Click a Web link** in a document, an e-mail message, or an application.

✦ **Click an HTML file** from Windows Explorer.

✦ **Click a suggested site** from the Suggested Sites menu.

✦ **Click a Web Slice** from the Web Slice Gallery.

✦ **Click a Favorite** within the Favorites Center or on the Favorites Bar.

✦ **Use the Live Search box** on the Address bar.

In this section, I tell you more about the last two options, Favorites and the Live Search box, and I fill you in on that most pleasant of creatures, the tab.

Simplifying surfing with Favorites

After you select a Web page as a Favorite, you can easily reach that site quickly (and without a forest of sticky notes appearing all over your monitor). To add a Favorite, display the page you want within Internet Explorer and use one of these methods:

✦ **Click the Add to Favorites Bar button on the toolbar.** IE adds the site instantly to the Favorites Bar for easy access.

✦ **Press the Ctrl+D keyboard shortcut.** This method displays the dialog box you see in Figure 4-3. Type a new name (if necessary), click the

Create In drop-down list to select the location or Favorites folder where you want to store the entry, and then click Add.

✦ **Right-click anywhere on a Web page and choose Add to Favorites from the menu that appears.**

Figure 4-3:
Add a Web page as a Favorite.

After you set up your Favorites, using them is simplicity itself:

✦ From the Favorites Center, click the Favorite you want to visit.

✦ From the Favorites bar, click the Favorite you want to visit.

✦ If you displayed the Menu bar (as I discuss earlier in this chapter, in the section "More buttons for your buck"), click the Favorites menu and then click the Favorite you want.

When you add a number of Favorites, you find them easier to use if you spend a moment to organize them. Follow these steps:

1. **Click the Favorites button, click the down arrow next to the Add to Favorites button, and then choose Organize Favorites from the menu to display the Organize Favorites dialog box. (See Figure 4-4.)**

2. **Click the New Folder button to add a new folder, which appears on the Favorites menu on the Menu bar and in the Favorites Center.**

3. **To move a Favorite into a folder, select a Favorite, click the Move button, select the destination folder, and then click OK.**

Alternately, you can just drag the Favorite into the desired folder.

4. **To rename a Favorite, select a Favorite, click the Rename button, type the new name, and then press Enter.**

5. **To delete a Favorite, click to select the offending Favorite and then click the Delete button.**

6. **When you're done organizing your Favorites, click the Close button to return to the browser window.**

**Book III
Chapter 4**

Cruising the Web
with Internet
Explorer

To change the order of the Favorites from the Organize Favorites dialog box, just click and drag a Favorite to its new spot and release the mouse button to drop it.

If the URL for a Favorite changes — because the site moved to another domain and changed addresses, for example — the Favorite will no longer work. However, it's easy to fix! To modify the URL that's connected to a Favorite, right-click the Favorite and then choose Properties (from the contextual menu that appears) to display the Properties dialog box, which you see in Figure 4-5. Click the Web Document tab, type (or paste) the new address into the URL text box, and then click OK to return to the Web.

Searching for the hay in the needlestack

To search for a specific Web site among the billions on the planet, use the Live Search box. Follow these steps:

1. **Click within the Live Search box, or press Ctrl+E to jump directly there.**

2. **Type a complete sentence — as short and lucid as possible — into the box and then press Enter.**

   Any matches that Internet Explorer finds appear in the Content window.

3. **Click a page link to view that page.**

Figure 4-5:
Change a
Favorite's
URL here.

To take a shortcut, you can also search by typing **Find** *whatever* (*whatever* is what you're looking for, like **Find popcorn**) on the Address bar and then pressing Enter. I use this one a lot. Figure 4-6 shows the result of my attempt to find Elvis.

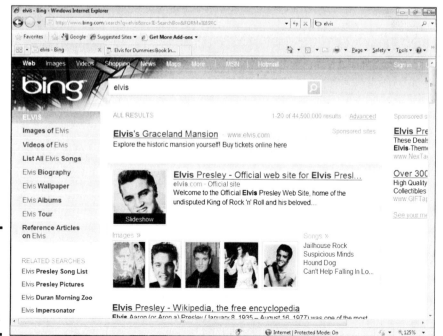

Figure 4-6:
You can
search for
The King
from the
Address bar.

IE8 also includes a new feature called *search suggestions,* which provides you with a list of other possible search terms as you type. If you don't see a matching term in the list, you can keep typing; however, if IE provides the correct term in the suggestions list, click it with your mouse or use your arrow keys to select it. To toggle search suggestions on or off, choose Tools⇨Manage Add-Ons, click the Search Providers entry, click the search engine you're using, and then click Enable/Disable Suggestions.

Doing the Tab thing

It's time to talk about *tabs* — and I don't mean the word processing tab that we've all gotten to know from the ancient typewriter (and the modern word processor). Instead, think of the IE tabs like the familiar tabs on file folders, which make it easier for you to locate a particular folder in a filing cabinet.

The Internet Explorer tabbed browsing system allows you to display (and organize) multiple Web pages at one time. For example, if you're doing a bit of comparison shopping for a new piece of hardware between different online stores, tabs are ideal. Kids of all ages also appreciate tabs while researching because more than one page can remain open — within the same window — while they continue to search the Web.

To open a new, blank tab, click the empty tab on the toolbar or press Ctrl+T. You can also open a link on a Web page on a new tab: Hold down the Ctrl key as you click the link. (If you don't hold down Ctrl, things revert to business as usual, and Internet Explorer replaces the contents of the window with the new page.)

Depending on your mouse button configuration, you may be able to open a link as a new tab by clicking with the mouse wheel button.

Switching between tabs is as easy as clicking to select a tab on the toolbar. However, Internet Explorer provides a cool Quick Tabs button — to the left of the first tab position — that can also be used to switch between tabs. Click the Quick Tabs button to display thumbnail images of tabbed pages; then click the thumbnail you want to display in the Content window. You can also click the arrow button next to the Quick Tabs button to display a menu of your tabs. (Note that the Quick Tabs button appears only when you have multiple Web pages open.)

If you build a group of tabs that you want to return to often — perhaps your favorite stock pages or news pages — click the Favorites button, click the down arrow next to the Add to Favorites button, and choose Add Current Tabs to Favorites. The group is created as a separate folder in the Favorites Center. Click the right-arrow button next to the folder name to load your tab group. *Sweet!*

Lean, fast, and mean — that's RSS

Well, maybe not; RSS isn't *mean* — after all, I don't want you to be afraid of RSS (RDF Site Summary) pages! Internet Explorer 8 supports RSS feeds, which display updated information using a shortened list format, rather like a newspaper headline, without unnecessary graphics or silly advertisements. You can tell when a Web site has an RSS feed available because IE plays a sound and the RSS button on the toolbar changes color. (When you click the RSS icon, the Web address usually switches to an address with an RSS prefix — another indication that you're not in Kansas reading HTML pages any more.)

To display more information about a news item on an RSS page, click the item headline. IE opens the corresponding Web page — yep, once again you're back in the world of HTML — and you can read the full story. To return to the RSS feed, click the Back button on the Address bar. Naturally, RSS feed pages can be saved as Favorites.

You can sort your RSS display from the sort fields on the right side of the page, but IE also provides a number of feed settings within the Internet Options dialog box. Click Tools and choose Internet Options from the menu; then click the Content tab and click the Settings button in the Feed section of the pane. You can set IE to check regularly for updated RSS headlines — and of course, you can also check for updates manually by reloading the RSS page, just like you would check any other Web page. You can also specify that IE mark feed content as Read after you view it to help separate the stuff you've read from the stuff you haven't absorbed yet.

Oh, I shan't forget to mention the RSS feed gadget available from the Vista/Windows 7 Sidebar. It's one of the three default gadgets that appear the first time you invoke the Sidebar.

Book III
Chapter 4

Cruising the Web
with Internet
Explorer

Downloading Files

Downloading files is a simple operation, indeed. When you click a download link within a Web page, Internet Explorer automatically downloads the file to your hard drive.

However, note this catch: Unless you're running an antivirus program that checks your downloaded files, you might be receiving a malignant virus rather than a bona fide treasure. That's why Internet Explorer displays the dialog box you see in Figure 4-7 when you click a download link that includes an executable program.

How best to handle this situation? Here are my recommendations:

✦ **If you're using an antivirus program, such as avast! Antivirus or McAfee VirusScan, go ahead and click Run.** These programs can check the file when you run it.

Figure 4-7:
Internet
Explorer
warns you
of possible
problems
when down-
loading.

+ **If you're not using an antivirus program, click Save.** After you save the file to disk, don't run it until you close any open applications and disconnect from the Internet. However, I *much* prefer that you proceed *immediately* to your closest software store and buy a copy of McAfee VirusScan (or download a free copy of avast! Antivirus Home Edition from www. avast.com)! An unprotected PC is a perfect target for viruses from downloaded files or e-mail attachments.

+ **Do not click Run unless you're downloading a patch or update from the Microsoft Web site (or another well-known site you trust).** Executing the download from your drive is always a better idea than doing it on the fly.

When you click Save, IE prompts you for the location to store the file. You can choose to use the original filename or type a new name. Click Save to begin the download.

Here's a pickle. You see an image that you want to download from a Web site, but it's not really a file that's set up for downloading — instead, it's part of the Web page itself. No problem: Just right-click the image you want and then choose Save Picture As from the menu that appears. Internet Explorer prompts you for the location where you want to save the file. You can also choose Print Picture or instantly make the picture become your Windows desktop background by choosing Set as Background. (Unfortunately, Internet Explorer can't make a small picture look good across your entire desktop — or convert a low-resolution shot into a better-quality background — so use this feature only with larger, high-resolution pictures.) Keep in mind that displaying an image as your background is different from using it in your documents: "Copyrights, people! Copyrights!"

Not all downloaded files can be run immediately. Many sites *compress,* or archive, their download files by using the *Zip* standard, which saves time when downloading (because the compression reduces the file size) and saves hassle (because multiple files are archived into a single file). Zip archives end, predictably enough, with the extension .zip. To *restore* the archive, or decompress it, just double-click it within Windows Explorer.

Keeping Track of Where You've Been

Bet you didn't know that you were building a history when you tour the Web. But what happens if you need to return to a site that you visited an hour ago and you don't remember the URL or how you got there?

Don't worry. The History list of the Favorites Center (see Figure 4-8) makes it easy to retrace your virtual steps. To display the History list, click the Favorites Center button and then click the History tab (or press Ctrl+H). You can immediately return to any page in the list by clicking it.

Note that Internet Explorer keeps track of your history on a site-by-site basis, with all the pages on each site grouped in a single folder. However, you can also display the History list by using other sort criteria. Just click the View by Date drop-down button, and you can specify a sort order based on the date visited, the sites you visited most often, and the sites in the order you visited them today.

You can also search for a specific word or phrase within the History list. Click the View by Date button and then click the Search menu item — now you can type that word or phrase in the Search For text box. Click the Search Now button to display any sites that contain matching text in the page title.

Figure 4-8: Display the history of your recent Web explorations.

If you're somewhat leery of even keeping a history file, click Tools and choose Internet Options from the menu. From the General tab of the Internet Options dialog box, click the Delete button in the Browsing History section. Now you can click the Delete History button to immediately delete the current contents of the History list. To specify how many days IE should keep the History list, return to the General tab and click Settings in the Browsing History section. Set the Days to Keep Pages in History to zero, and Internet Explorer then disables the History list altogether.

Printing and Saving Web Pages

From time to time, you want a printed copy of the content on a Web page. Or, you might want to save the page itself, complete with all its content, graphics, and links, to a set of files on your hard drive. In this section, I serve you these two palatable options.

Putting the Web in print

I *could* say that printing a Web page is as simple as clicking the Print button on the toolbar (or pressing Ctrl+P), and technically, I would be right. But there's really more to it than that — specifically, the Options tab in the Print dialog box, as shown in Figure 4-9.

Figure 4-9: Print a Web site from Internet Explorer.

"Yo, Adrian! Who typed that?"

If Internet Explorer suddenly starts completing Web site addresses and fields within online forms — like your name, your address, or even your password — don't panic. There's no reason to call Ghostbusters. You're seeing the Internet Explorer *AutoComplete* feature, which automatically fills out online forms, Web addresses, and username-and-password combinations that you previously entered on a site.

This feature is all friendly and downright convenient, but what if you're more interested in privacy or security? No problem. You can toggle AutoComplete off for certain types of data, or you can turn it off completely. Click the Tools button and choose Internet Options from the menu to display the Internet Options dialog box, and then click the Content tab. Click the AutoComplete Settings button to specify which types of data you want filled out. If you're already nervous, click the Delete AutoComplete History button to wipe away any AutoComplete data for online forms and passwords.

If the page you're printing uses *frames* — a method of putting different panels on a Web page, each with its own content — you can choose to print the page in three different ways:

✦ **As Laid Out on Screen:** The entire Web page is printed.

✦ **Only the Selected Frame:** Only the contents of the active frame on the page are printed. You can usually activate a frame by clicking within it or by using a scroll bar within the desired frame.

✦ **All Frames Individually:** The contents of each frame are printed separately.

By default, IE prints only the current page. However, you can print the current page and any documents it links to, by selecting the Print All Linked Documents check box. This choice is a good one if you want to print the contents of a Web site with multiple pages.

You can also choose to print an index of links that appear on the page you're printing. This index is a handy tool when the printed page has a large number of links that lead to other documents you might need: Select the Print Table of Links check box.

Saving the best (for last)

Occasionally I run across a page that I want to save in its entirety because I need to view it offline while I'm traveling or when a large number of images accompanies the page. Internet Explorer makes it easy to save a displayed Web page as a set of files on your hard drive. Simply follow these steps:

1. **Click the Page button on the toolbar and choose Save As from the menu to display the special Save Webpage dialog box, which you see in Figure 4-10.**

Figure 4-10: Preparing to save a Web page to disk.

2. **Type a name for the saved page in the File Name text box and then navigate to the desired location on your PC.**

3. **Click the Save as Type drop-down list and choose Web Page, Complete.**

    This is my favorite option, where the program stores the entire kit and caboodle so that you can display the page from the file just as it appeared online.

    Generally, I don't recommend choosing Web Page, HTML Only, or Text File because you're likely to end up with either a partial page of text or a bunch of meaningless HTML commands.

4. **Click Save to begin the download process.**

    Internet Explorer creates an HTML file that you can double-click to display the page, which links to a separate folder that contains all images and documents from the original page.

Chapter 5: Harnessing Your E-Mail

In This Chapter

✔ Touring the Windows Live Mail window

✔ Configuring your e-mail account

✔ Receiving, reading, and replying to mail

✔ Composing and sending a new message

✔ Sending and receiving e-mail attachments

✔ Blocking that dastardly spam

✔ Using the Contacts list

E-mail rules the Internet roost. Sure, the Web gets a lot of attention, but which single service provided by the Internet would cause the most chaos if it were interrupted? That's right — the lowly Internet e-mail message that invites you to lunch or informs you of a new baby (or brings you junk advertising that promises to refinance your home at 2%). Without e-mail, most of today's business world would be left stricken — and you wouldn't get those blonde jokes in your inbox every morning. The mind reels — the soul cries out for more Diet Coke at the very thought.

Because of the mind-boggling importance of e-mail, Microsoft put a lot of work into designing a truly first-class e-mail application for Windows 7. And it's free! You don't get some of the truly powerful features of Outlook 2010, but as an e-mail application, Windows Live Mail can stand proudly on its own. You can download Windows Live Mail as part of the free Windows Live package at `http://download.live.com`.

In this chapter, I describe how you can keep track of your e-mail messages, your contacts, and your identities in Windows Live Mail. You discover how to ward off junk mail messages and how to attach Aunt Gertrude's Big Bang Brownie recipe to the next e-mail you send (for the brownie lovers on your Contacts list).

And even if you use a different e-mail program — meaning, what you see onscreen will look a little different — the concepts are the same.

Introducing the Mail Window

Before you venture into the world of Internet communications, get familiar with the controls of the Live Mail window; catch the hoopla in Figure 5-1.

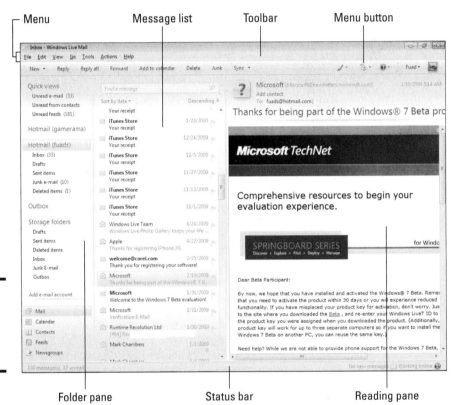

Menu   Message list   Toolbar   Menu button

Figure 5-1:
The Live
Mail
window in
action.

Folder pane   Status bar   Reading pane

These controls include

✦ **Menu:** From this standard Windows 7 application menu, click a menu family to display its items, and then click a menu item to perform that action. Note, however, that the menu system is disabled by default in Live Mail. To turn it on, click the Menu button on the toolbar (which looks like a tiny menu and a mouse pointer) and choose Show Menu Bar.

✦ **Toolbar:** Click a toolbar button to perform the same function as the corresponding menu item. You can customize the toolbar by adding and removing buttons. Just click the Menu button on the toolbar and then choose Customize Toolbar to display the dialog box you see in Figure 5-2. (You can also right-click the toolbar and then choose Customize to display the same dialog box.) Click the menu item (button) that you want to add from the list on the left, and then click the Add button (the right arrow) to add it to the toolbar. Conversely, to remove a toolbar button, click the button name in the list on the right and then click the Remove button (the left arrow).

Figure 5-2:
Make changes to the Windows Live Mail toolbar here.

♦ Folder pane: Click any storage folder link in the tree display to display the contents of that folder. You can also switch between e-mail accounts as well as display your unread e-mail in the blink of an eye by clicking a Quick View.

To add a new folder to the Folder list, right-click any folder in the list and then choose New Folder from the pop-up menu that appears. Live Mail displays the Create Folder dialog box (see Figure 5-3), where you can type a name for your new folder and select the existing folder that will act as its "parent." Click OK, and the new folder appears in the Folder list.

Figure 5-3:
Add a new folder to the Folder list.

✦ **Message list:** Messages in the selected folder are displayed in list form in the Message list.

✦ **Reading pane:** Clicking a message in the Message list displays it in the Reading pane (without the hassle of opening the message in a separate window). After all, we are a people interested in convenience, are we not?

The Message list and Reading pane are highly configurable little beasties. Choose View⇨Layout to display the window layout settings that you see in Figure 5-4. You can hide the Reading pane, or you can display it below or next to the Message list. You can also toggle the display of the messages in the Message list using one or two lines.

Figure 5-4:
Fix your
window
layout
"just so."

✦ **Status bar:** Last — and pretty much least — is our old friend, the humble status bar. Here, you can see basic totals on the number of read and unread messages and also your online/offline status. (The program is typically offline if you're not connected to the Internet.) It also shows you when Windows Live Mail is sending and receiving mail.

You can easily adjust the size of any section of the Live Mail window: Move your mouse pointer over the divider bar that you want to move until it turns into opposing arrows and then drag to relocate the bar.

Setting Up Your Mailbox

Even the mightiest barrage of e-mail begins with a single step. Okay, two steps at first because you have to start Windows Live Mail initially — but then, mind you, you're down to a single step! I'm talking about adding at least one e-mail mailbox account to your Mail configuration because without a mailbox account, you get diddly-squat.

To create a mailbox account, follow these steps:

1. **Choose Tools⇨Accounts to display the Internet Accounts dialog box.**

You must enable the Live Mail menu first. See how in the preceding section.

2. **Click the Add button.**

3. **In the dialog box that appears (see Figure 5-5), click the E-mail Account button. Then click Next to display — tah-dah! — the Add an E-mail Account Wizard.**

No, it's not that Gandalf guy. Even the Dark Lord Gates himself couldn't afford that kind of talent. This is a simple, hard-working Windows Live Mail wizard.

Figure 5-5:
Creating
a new
account
with
zest and
panache.

Book III
Chapter 5

Harnessing Your
E-Mail

4. **In the Add an E-mail Account window (see Figure 5-6), type the e-mail address and password that your Internet service provider (ISP) gave you.**

Make sure that you're entering your *e-mail name* and *password,* which are not necessarily the same as your account logon name and password that you use to connect to the Internet. (If you don't have this information, contact your ISP's technical support or help desk and request it.)

Figure 5-6:
It's time
to enter
some of
that Internet
gibberish.

5. **Type your name as you want it to be displayed when you send messages.**

   Like Outlook 2010, Live Mail can almost always automatically configure your e-mail settings. However, if your ISP or network system administrator requires you to enter your incoming (POP3) server and outgoing (SMTP) server addresses, select the Manually Configure Server Settings for E-Mail Account check box. Check with your ISP.

6. **Click Next.**

   If you have multiple accounts in Live Mail, you can specify this account as the default for sending and receiving mail. Just select the Set This Account as the Default Mail Account check box.

7. **Click Finish.**

   Your new e-mail account appears in the Internet Accounts dialog box. Note that the name of the account refers to the ISP through which the e-mail is received — Hotmail, for example, if you have a Hotmail account.

8. **Click Close to return to Windows Live Mail.**

You can return to the Internet Accounts dialog box at any time to change the settings on your e-mail account. Click the account in the list and then click the Properties button to display the Mail Properties dialog box, which you see in Figure 5-7. Most of this stuff never changes, but occasionally an ISP changes the name of an e-mail server or sets up new security measures that require a change on your end.

Figure 5-7:
Edit mail
account
properties
at any time.

The Three R's: Receiving, Reading, and Replying

Time to get to it! You've got mail! All the fun things (or tedium) that come along with paper snail mail are just the same as in the electronic world. Read along to see how similar they are.

Receiving e-mail

Time to check your e-mail? Windows Live Mail checks automatically each time you run the program, but you can always check manually by clicking the Sync button on the toolbar. Your received e-mail appears in your Inbox, which you can display by clicking the Inbox header in the Folders list.

You have to enable the Live Mail menu first. See how in the earlier section, "Introducing the Mail Window."

Okay, okay — you can press F5 instead. Whoops, I'm being secretive. Here's the chop: Windows Live Mail connects to the Internet (if necessary), and new messages show up as bolded entries in the Message list.

Reading e-mail

To read an e-mail, just double-click a message to open it. (Unread messages display a closed envelope icon, while messages you've read display an open envelope icon.) Mail displays the message in its own, separate window (as shown in Figure 5-8).

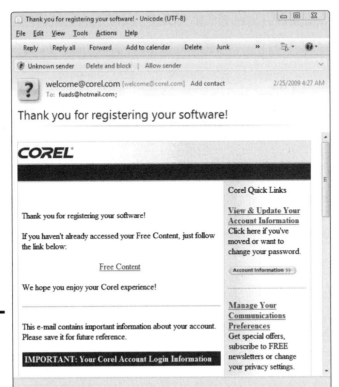

Figure 5-8:
Reading an
incoming
message.

If the Reading pane is active, you can scan a message by clicking it once (or by using the up- and down-arrow keys to move through the Message list). As soon as you scan or read a message, it's marked as read, and the bolding on the message heading in the list disappears. (If you need to restore the Reading pane to its full glory, click the Menu button and choose the Layout menu item.)

If you encounter a message from someone who's not in your Contacts list and you want to add that sender, right-click the message in the Message list and then choose Add Sender to Contacts from the pop-up menu that appears. Read more about the Contacts list in the upcoming section, "Working with Your Contacts."

Replying to and forwarding e-mail

To reply to a message, follow these steps:

1. **Click a message in the Message list to select it, and then click the Reply button on the toolbar.**

If you're reading an open message in its own window, click the Reply button within the window. You can also click the Reply All button to send your reply to others who also received the message (including those who were copied; more on that in a bit).

A Reply window appears (feast on Figure 5-9) with the insertion cursor at the top of the message box. The text of the original message is included under the original header, and Live Mail has already filled in the To field with the name of the person who sent the original e-mail.

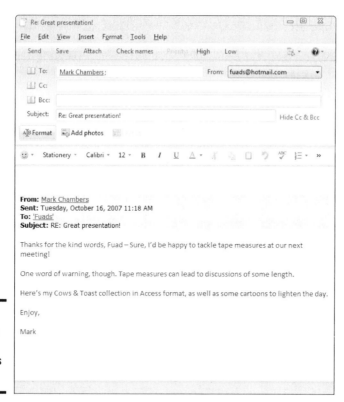

**Book III
Chapter 5**

Harnessing Your E-Mail

Figure 5-9:
Sometimes a simple reply works just fine.

2. **Although Mail has already inserted the prefix Re in front of the original subject line, you can click in the Subject box and type a new subject, if necessary.**

3. **Type your message in the message field.**

4. **Click Send.**

You can also choose to *forward* a message, allowing you to add a comment to the body of the original message before you send it to new recipients. To forward a message, click the Forward button rather than the Reply or Reply All button. Forwarding a message also sends any attachments that accompanied the original message, which doesn't happen when you reply.

Messages you send are deposited in your Sent Items folder. You can peruse them at any time if your memory needs refreshing.

To Bcc, or not to Bcc

When you want to reply to, forward, or even create a new message to more than one person — and you want recipients other than those available from Reply All, if applicable — use the carbon (Cc) or blind carbon (Bcc) copy feature.

If you send standard Cc copies of your message, each recipient can see who else received the message — and even add the e-mail addresses of the other folks to their Windows Contacts lists. A *Bcc* is message sent to more than one person in which the e-mail addresses of some recipients are intentionally hidden.

In some cases, sending regular Cc copies can be a serious breach of privacy. Other than the extra privacy, Bcc addresses are handled in the same manner as Cc addresses.

One look at the new message or reply windows, though, and it's apparent that Windows Live Mail doesn't have carbon copies or blind carbon copies. Tell me that's not true!

All is not lost. Live Mail does indeed offer Cc and Bcc features. To expose the Cc/Bcc Easter egg while creating or replying to a message, click the Show Cc & Bcc link at the right side of the Subject box. Boing! There they are! (You'll have to click the link each time you need to use the Cc or Bcc feature.)

Carbon dating

Talk about your carbon footprint. The "carbon" part of Cc and Bcc harkens back to the previous millennium, when people used typewriters (look it up) and paper with sheets of carbon paper between to create copies. Much less noxious than a ditto machine (look that up, too).

Here's how simple it is to send a Cc or Bcc message:

1. **Click the Show Cc & Bcc link (if necessary), click in the Cc or Bcc box, as appropriate, and then type recipients' addresses manually.**

   Important: Separate recipient names with a semicolon.

   Alternatively, click the Cc button (next to the text field, with a Contact card icon) to choose names from your Windows Contacts list (as shown in Figure 5-10). Then click OK to return to the message window.

Figure 5-10: Extract addresses from your Contacts list.

2. **Click in the message box (if necessary) and type the contents of your message.**

3. **When you're ready to send your message, click the Send button to usher it on its way immediately (or press Alt+S from the keyboard).**

E-mail housekeeping: Deleting and filing

No one likes housework. (Well, maybe some people.) Still, if you don't keep up on keeping things tidy, piles of stuff, well, pile up. Same thing applies to e-mail, which can multiply faster than coat hangers in the hall closet. Take a minute here and there to file away important message as well as throw away the chaff.

To delete a message that you no longer need from any folder, click the message in the Message list and then press Delete or click the Delete button on the toolbar. The messages are deposited in your Deleted Items folder and can be retrieved, if necessary.

To move a message from one folder to another, click the folder where the message currently resides, and then drag the message icon to the new folder.

Creating and Sending E-Mail

Time to create a new e-mail (that is, not reply to or forward a message that came to to you.) Regardless of whether your message is going to someone who's in your Contacts list or not (more on that in a bit), it's a snap.

After you've created a message, it appears in your Outbox in the Folder list at the left of the window.

1. **Click the New button on the toolbar and choose E-Mail Message from the pop-up menu. (Or simply press Ctrl+N.)**

   Live Mail opens the New Message window, which you see in Figure 5-11.

2. **Click in the To box and then type the e-mail address.**

   You can add carbon copy and blind carbon copy recipients by clicking in the Cc and Bcc boxes, respectively. If these fields aren't there, then click the Show Cc & Bcc link next to the Subject line. Read all about this earlier in "To Bcc, or not Bcc." And, of course, you could add the recipient name from your Contacts list; more on that in a bit.

3. **Click in the Subject field, type the subject for this message, and then press Tab to move to the message editing box.**

4. **Type the text of your message; if it's set as an HTML message, apply any formatting you want to the text.**

   Read more about this in the section, "Formatting a message."

**Book III
Chapter 5**

Figure 5-11:
Say, isn't
that a New
Message
window?

5. **Ready to ship it? You have the same options available as you have when replying to a message:**

   - Click Send to send it immediately.
   - Click Save on the toolbar (or press Ctrl+S) to save it in your Drafts folder. (Read about drafts in "Creating and sending a draft.")
   - Move the message to your Outbox by choosing File➪Send Later.

Formatting a message

To spice up your message text, click and drag across it (*select* it) and then apply formatting (such as bold or italic) from the Formatting toolbar. You can also add attachments. (Use the procedure that I outline in the upcoming section "Sending and Receiving File Attachments.")

If the Formatting toolbar isn't present in the reply window — or if the Formatting menu is disabled — you're writing your e-mail message in plain text. Choose Format➪Rich Text (HTML), and all your formatting controls are then available. However, I'm personally not a big fan of rich text messages: Not all e-mail programs handle HyperText Markup Language (HTML)

messages properly, especially older e-mail applications running on Linux or Windows 98. Plus, rich text messages are much larger than plain text messages and can take longer to send and receive.

Creating and sending a draft

If you want to reply to or create a message but delay sending it, save the message in *draft* form.

1. **Reply to, forward, or create a message.**

2. **Click Save on the toolbar and then close the New Message window.**

   The message appears in your Drafts folder.

3. **To send the draft message, click the Drafts folder to open it, double-click the message to open it, and then click Send.**

That's the nub of creating and sending a basic e-mail. Keep reading for the next level of e-mail wizardry.

Windows Live Mail 102

Here are a few more advanced things you can do in Windows Live Mail:

✦ **Add an attachment (or more than one).**

   Find more on this topic in the upcoming section, "Sending and Receiving File Attachments."

✦ **Check the spelling in your message.**

   a. Select the text of your message.

   b. Click the Check Spelling button on the toolbar (which carries the letters ABC and a red check mark).

   Live Mail underlines possible spelling errors automatically. If you get the urge to check for yourself and go the spell-check route, Windows Mail opens the dialog box shown in Figure 5-12.

   • *To substitute the boo-boo word (Not in Dictionary field) to the Change To suggestion:* Click the Change button.

   • *To substitute the wrong word to something in the Suggestions list:* Click the suggestion you want and then click the Change button. If you mangled the word several times in the same message, click the Change All button instead.

Possible misspelling   Check spelling

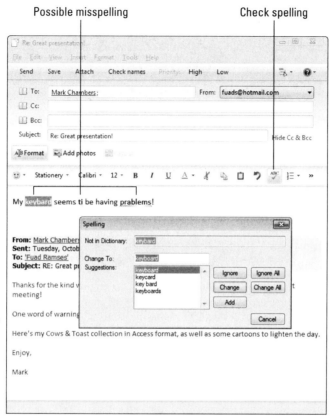

Book III
Chapter 5

Harnessing Your
E-Mail

Figure 5-12:
Speelling
iz ophten
sumwatt
himportunt.

Did you spell *thakamology* correctly? You can always choose to
ignore the flag (click the Ignore button) or ignore all occurrences
(click Ignore All) to avoid further unnecessary nagging during a spell
check. If you use *thakamology* quite a bit in your messages — and
who doesn't? — click Add to add the word to the Windows Live Mail
dictionary, and the program shan't bother you again.

✦ **Flag as high importance.** If the message deserves immediate attention —
"Help, Mom, I'm stuck in Vienna with no cash!" — click High on the
toolbar.

This step doesn't send the message any faster, nor does it travel with
any extra gusto. However, it shows up with a priority flag in the recipient's e-mail application.

+ **Verify that a message has been read.** Choose Tools⇨Request Read Receipt.

   Note: This *does not guarantee* that you receive notice when the message has been read. The recipient is prompted for confirmation beforehand, so a read receipt can be canceled.

Sending and Receiving File Attachments

Why limit your messages to a silly message box? Break out of the box with file attachments! Just about any type of file can be attached to a message, and you can save that file to your hard drive from within the read message window. (Yes, that includes most files sent to you by your friends with those funky Macintosh and Linux computers!)

Unfortunately, some file attachments that you might receive should be *immediately* cast out. I'm speaking, naturally, about e-mail viruses and macros with a homicidal bent, which are becoming as common these days as the generic junk mail messages you receive every day. Luckily, you can use an antivirus program, like avast Free! (from ALWIL, at www.avast.com), that automatically scans attachments for any dangerous programs before you use them. *Never open an attachment without proper antivirus protection!* That includes attached files that you receive from folks whom you know and trust! (They could unknowingly be hosting a virus themselves — some of these bugs are even smart enough to replicate themselves by enclosing copies of themselves in innocuous-looking messages!)

With that stern admonishment in mind, here's how you can add an attachment to your outgoing message:

1. **Reply to a message or compose a new message.**

2. **Click the Attach button on the toolbar to display the Open dialog box, as shown in Figure 5-13.**

3. **Navigate to the location of the file(s) you want to attach; then click the first filename to select it.**

   To add more than one file from the same folder, hold down the Ctrl key while you click.

4. **Click the Open button to add the files to the message.**

   Mail displays attached files in the Attach box within the header area of the message dialog box.

Figure 5-13:
Attaching a
file to your
message.

When you receive an e-mail message with an attachment, a paper clip icon is displayed next to the message entry in the Message list.

To download an attachment from an incoming message

1. **Right-click the file attachment in the header.**

2. **Choose Save As to select a spot on your system to store the file.**

3. **Navigate to the desired location and click Save.**

You can't send the kitchen sink as an e-mail attachment, so don't get carried away trying to send hundreds of photos or the like. It takes a very long time to download big files over a dial-up connection, and all Internet service providers limit the size of a message and all its attachments. This limit usually rejects any message over 2MB or so in total size. (The exact limit is determined by both your Internet e-mail server and the recipient's e-mail server.) Therefore, I recommend limiting your total attachment size to 2MB or less. You can easily tell when your attachments are too doggone big: Either your ISP's mail server or the recipient's mail server sends you an error message saying that your original e-mail is undeliverable.

Spam: I Hate It — Truly I Do!

Is there anyone on the planet who actually opens a message promising instant hair regrowth? Or a once-in-a-lifetime investment opportunity? Or some sort of illicit physical offer that you neither want nor need? Why does junk mail exist? Aren't these spam-slingers just wasting their time?

Good questions, all. For some reason, though, junk mail continues to accumulate on your Internet doorstep. Not even the government can stop it — something about that pesky Bill of Rights — but you can sure doggone reduce the flow of spam to a trickle by using the mail-blocking feature within Windows Live Mail.

When you receive a junk mail message from someone, right-click it in the Message list and then choose Junk E-Mail⇨Add Sender to Blocked Senders List from the pop-up menu that appears. Live Mail displays a confirmation dialog box to let you know that the offending sender has been added to your Blocked Senders list and that the message has been moved to your Junk E-Mail folder.

Use this method to block all messages from a specific e-mail address. Any mail you receive from that source is then dumped directly into your Deleted Items folder. (You can still look at it there, of course, just to verify that the proper trash was picked up.)

However, nefarious junk mail villains can still get around a blocked-sender list by changing their sending addresses: For example, `imajerk@justan example.com` suddenly becomes `hahastillhere@justanexample.com` or something similar.

Does this mean that you have to continue to suffer? Not in the least, good Internet citizen! You can also block an entire *domain name,* which is the part of an e-mail address that follows the @ sign, like `bonehead@spamtwit.com`. That way, no matter which silly username they try, Live Mail still throws straight into the trash anything they send. To block an entire domain name, just right-click the offending message in the Message list and choose Junk E-Mail⇨Add Sender's Domain to Blocked Senders List, to knock them out completely.

If you add an address or an entire domain to your blocked list by accident, you can return that address or domain to good standing. Click the Junk E-Mail folder in the Folder pane to display its contents in the Message list. Then right-click the message and choose Junk E-mail⇨Add Sender to Safe Senders List. To restore the message to your inbox, right-click the message and choose Junk E-Mail⇨Mark as Not Junk. Mail whisks the forgiven message back to the Inbox automatically.

If you get a message from an obvious spam tycoon who includes a line about how you can oh-so-conveniently "unsubscribe" from his mailing list, *don't do it!* This scam is designed to verify that your e-mail address is valid; if you unsubscribe, you end up with a regular tidal wave of junk mail. Better to add his e-mail address (or the entire domain) to the Blocked list.

Working with Your Contacts

The Contacts list in Live Mail is usually all most folks need for 99 percent of their workdays. I explain earlier in this chapter how you can add contacts by simply right-clicking the author's e-mail address in a message; that's the most common action to take.

However, you can reach the Windows Contacts list proper from within Live Mail. Just click the Contacts button at the lower left of the window, and the Windows Live Contacts window appears (behold Figure 5-14).

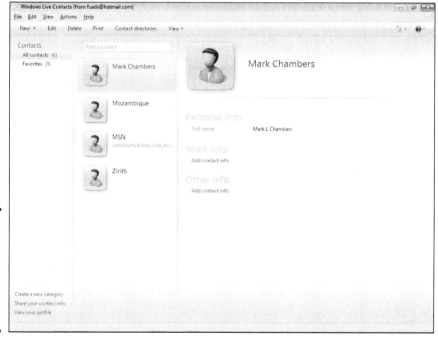

Figure 5-14:
Feel free to open the Windows Contacts list from within Mail.

**Book III
Chapter 5**

Harnessing Your
E-Mail

From this window, you can

✦ **Create a new contact.** Click the New button on the toolbar and choose New Contact; the Contact list displays the Add a Contact dialog box, as shown in Figure 5-15. Click in each field that you need to complete to add the contact's information. To display additional fields for categories (like Personal and Work information), click the corresponding button in the list on the left. To save your new contact, click the Add Contact button.

Figure 5-15:
Add a new
contact.

✦ **Edit an existing contact.** Click the contact name that you want to edit. Then click Edit from the toolbar to display the Edit Contact dialog box, which includes all the fields you originally saw when you created the contact. You can click in any field to either change existing data or add new information. To save your changes, click Save.

✦ **Send an e-mail message.** Select a contact and click the New button on the toolbar; then click New E-Mail on the pop-up menu. You return to the Windows Live Mail window, where you find a brand-new New Message window (already addressed to the contact, naturally).

✦ **Import contact data.** Import vCard information for a contact. A *vCard* is a small text file that contains all the contact information for one or more people in a standard format that you can pass around to others like a virtual business *Card.* (Cute, eh?) Windows Live Mail can also import contacts stored in a Windows Address Book format file (which ends in the .wab extension). To import, click File⇨Import and then click the correct format from the pop-up menu; for example, vCards use vCard (VCF file) format. Windows prompts you for the location of the import file.

✦ **Export a vCard file.** To export one or more contacts in vCard format, select the contact record (or records) that you want to export and then choose File⇨Export. From the pop-up menu that appears, choose Business Card (.VCF), and then navigate to the spot where you want to save the file. Click OK to create the vCard file, which you can then send as an attachment in e-mail messages or place on your Web site for others to download.

Chapter 6: Instant Messaging Done Right

In This Chapter

✔ **Comparing Live Messenger with the competition**

✔ **Running Windows Live Messenger**

✔ **Setting your Live Messenger configuration**

✔ **Building a contact list**

✔ **Chatting with others**

✔ **Changing your Live Messenger status**

✔ **Blocking unwanted communications**

The ability to communicate with someone else halfway across the globe is nothing new. Just ask Benjamin Franklin, who would tell you that the U.S. Postal Service was a civilized and modern convenience. And the ability to communicate by typing to someone via your computer? Heck, any SYSOP *(system operator),* like myself, who was worth the title, offered real-time chatting between users on the *bulletin board systems* (BBSes) that were so popular in the 1980s and '90s, before the Internet took over.

Ah, but *combine* the two — real-time, instant message (IM) chatting over the Internet among an entire group of people — and you have something truly amazing. In this chapter, I show you how to use Windows Live Messenger to communicate in style (as long as you have an Internet connection, that is).

Selecting a Chat Client

Although Windows Live Messenger isn't included in Windows 7, it's a free download. (Read how in the upcoming section, "Running Windows Live Messenger.") In fact, you don't necessarily have to run Microsoft's IM starlet because you have other choices for your IM application. And, before I jump into Live Messenger, I'd like to mention the competition (just in case you like choices).

Like Windows Live Messenger, chatting programs display messages on your screen within a few seconds after they're sent: the very definition of instant messaging. You also find universal support for transferring files and images while you're chatting, adding icons and symbols (*emoticons* or *smileys*), applying text formatting, and displaying a list of your favorite people that you can use to check who's online. However, note this downside: At the time of this writing, each different application has a completely separate membership group, so if you're using AOL Instant Messenger (AIM), you can't communicate with someone using Windows Live Messenger or I Seek You (ICQ). Such is the Tower of Babel (or is that *Babble*?) that results from proprietary software developers. (Sigh.)

AIM

AOL Instant Messenger (AIM, as it's popularly known) is the free messaging application distributed by America Online. And, to debunk a popular myth, you don't have to be a member of America Online to use AIM.

AIM works fine in all popular flavors of Windows. Its features include

+ **Skins,** which you can apply to customize the appearance of your AIM window

+ **Integration with Windows Live Mail,** where you can display your Buddy List and send messages from within Windows Live Mail

+ **Voice support**, for honest-to-goodness verbal communication (among AIM members with the right hardware)

+ **Multiplayer games,** which you can enjoy with your buddies

+ **Integration with Facebook and Twitter** that allows you to handle most of your online social networking from within AIM

To be able to use AIM, you have to set up (register) a screen name, but it's a simple process, and AOL doesn't hound you to join. (At least AOL hasn't hounded me.) You can download the program from www.aim.com.

ICQ

The other well-known alternative to Live Messenger is ICQ — short for I Seek You (which I've always felt is stretching the mechanics of an acronym about as far as possible). You can download the free version from www.icq.com. ICQ 7 runs fine in Windows 7.

ICQ, one of the first IM programs to reach the public, offers a number of powerful options:

✦ **The ability to send SMS messages** (commonly called *texting*) to cell-phones and wireless pagers

✦ **Internet (IP) telephony,** where ICQ members can talk from their PC to an honest-to-goodness standard telephone

✦ **Facebook support** for chatting

✦ **A chat history "miner" feature,** which saves all that important dialog for later perusal and makes that text easy to search

✦ **Multilingual support** so that you can type to friends in any language supported within Windows

ICQ assigns you a unique user number when you join; the number acts as your ID number (much like your unique e-mail address), and others can connect to you by using your user number.

Running Windows Live Messenger

If you decide to follow The Gates Way and use Windows Live Messenger, use the built-in link on the Windows 7 Start menu to install Live Messenger: Just click the menu item, and Windows 7 opens a wizard that leads you through the process. Alternately, you can visit http://download.live.com and download the installation package manually.

If you're already using the Microsoft Hotmail service for Web-based e-mail, Live Messenger not only automatically uses your Hotmail ID but also keeps you updated in the Messenger window with the number of unread Hotmail messages in your inbox. To open Internet Explorer and read any unread mail, just click the Open Your E-Mail Inbox link in the Live Messenger window.

Here are two ways to access the Live Messenger window:

✦ **From the Start menu:** Choose Start➪All Programs➪Windows Live➪ Windows Live Messenger.

✦ **From the taskbar icon:** If you see a Live Messenger icon in the notification area of the taskbar (which looks like a little round-headed person), double-click it. (Clicking the Messenger icon once displays a menu with common Messenger commands, so you don't really have to double-click to send a message.)

**Book III
Chapter 6**

Instant Messaging
Done Right

If you haven't set up a Microsoft Windows Live ID yet, you have to do so before you can use Live Messenger — it's part of the Live Messenger Setup Wizard, so you can't miss it. The *Windows Live ID* is a sort of common "universal" username and password that can act as your logon for all sorts of Microsoft Web sites and online services.

Configuring Windows Live Messenger

The default configuration settings for Live Messenger fly straight for just about everyone, but I specifically cover a handful here just in case you want to fine-tune how the program works. From the Windows Live Messenger window, click the Menu button (which looks like a cursor on top of a tiny menu) and choose Tools⇨Options to display the Options dialog box, which you see in Figure 6-1.

Figure 6-1:
Set your preferences within Live Messenger.

On the Personal pane:

✦ **Display Name:** You can change the name that Live Messenger displays when you chat.

✦ **Personal Message:** Live Messenger displays this line of text next to your name when you're online. (If you like, Windows Media Player can even display what you're listening to at the moment instead of a static message.)

✦ **Display Picture:** Select an image that Live Messenger will display next to your name (click Change Picture to choose one from your collection of photos).

✦ **Public Profile:** Click the Edit Profile button to change your Windows Live user profile, which other people can display or match when using the Member search feature.

✦ **Status:** If you don't type a message or use the Live Messenger window for a specified number of minutes, your account is listed as Away within the Messenger system, and your friends know that you're not immediately available. However, you can alter the inactivity delay period or even deselect the check box to always have your status listed as Online. Personally, I like the five-minute default value for the Away feature.

The Options dialog box offers more ways to tweak Live Messenger by using the tabs along the left side to display the different panes of the dialog box:

✦ **On the Sign In pane:** Use the Sign In options to configure whether Messenger starts automatically when Windows 7 boots and whether the program should sign in automatically whenever your PC is connected to the Internet.

✦ **On the Messages pane:** You can format message text by selecting the font to use in your messages and enabling or disabling emoticons and smileys.

✦ **On the Alerts pane:** Specify when you want Live Messenger to alert you of specific events, like when a person on your contact list comes online or you receive e-mail on your Hotmail account. I recommend leaving the Display Alerts When a Message Is Received check box selected so that you know you have a new message even when you're knee-deep in an Excel worksheet or a Word document.

✦ **On the Privacy pane:** Specify who has access to you online by using the Allow and Block Lists (which I cover later in this chapter). You can also view which Live Messenger members have added you to their contact lists.

Book III
Chapter 6

Instant Messaging Done Right

TIP

Feel free to modify any of the configuration settings as you like, but remember that you can exit without saving any changes to the Live Messenger options by clicking the Cancel button (just in case you decide that you want to back out).

Keeping Track of Friends and Family

Windows Live Messenger allows you to keep a *contact list,* which is essentially a simple address book that you can use to display the Online or Inactive or Not Online status of your friends and family. The contact list appears within the Live Messenger window, grouped by the current status of its members.

To add a contact to Live Messenger by using the person's e-mail address, follow these steps:

1. **Click the Add a Contact button in the Live Messenger window (it carries the familiar Live humanoid with a plus sign) and choose Add a Contact. The program displays the dialog box shown in Figure 6-2.**

Figure 6-2:
Preparing
to add a
contact
to my Live
Messenger
list.

Windows Live Messenger

Enter the person's information

Enter an instant messaging address, mobile device number, or both. When you add someone to Messenger, they also become part of your network on Windows Live.

Instant messaging address:

anexampleaddress@mlcbooks.com

Example: example@live.com or example@yahoo.com

Mobile device number (for sending IMs as text messages):

United States (1)

1 504-555-1234

Favorites

Next   Cancel

2. **Type the person's e-mail address into the Instant Messaging Address text box.**

3. **If you know the person's cellphone or mobile device number, you can add it to the contact record and send SMS or text messages. Click Next to continue.**

4. **(Optional) Send a message to the person letting them know you're on Messenger — or, if the contact isn't on Messenger yet, you can send them an e-mail instead, inviting them to join Windows Live so that you two can "jaw." Then click Send Invitation to continue.**

5. **Click Close to complete the process.**

To remove a person from your contact list, click the entry to highlight it in your list and then press Delete. Live Messenger prompts you for confirmation before removing the contact.

To share your contact list with others — or to copy your work contact list to Live Messenger on your home PC — click the Menu button and choose Contacts➪Save Instant Messaging Contacts. After you save the file to disk and transfer it to the other PC, click the Menu button and choose Contacts➪Import Instant Messaging Contacts.

Even though you add someone to your contact list, you're still not quite home free. The person whom you added sees a dialog box prompting for permission to allow you to chat — and this new contact can also block you from seeing and contacting him or her. This precaution makes it tough for lounge lizards (and worse) to cruise through Live Messenger looking for new victims.

Getting tired of that tiny Menu button? It is rather small and hard to see. No problem — you only have to click it one more time and then choose Show the Menu Bar from the bottom of the pop-up menu. Tah-dah! You see an old-fashioned menu bar at the top of the Live Messenger window — a comfort to old-fashioned technowizards, like me.

Book III
Chapter 6

Instant Messaging
Done Right

Chatting with Your Brethren

After you successfully add folks to your contact list, you're ready to party! Follow these steps to initiate a chat session:

1. **Double-click any name that appears in the Online section of the contact list.**

   Double-clicking a name in the Offline section (see upcoming Figure 6-3) automatically creates a new e-mail message because you obviously cannot chat with that person in real-time if she isn't online at the moment.

   To send a message from the menu system (or the Menu button), choose Actions➪Send an Instant Message. You can also right-click any name in your contact list and choose the same actions from the pop-up menu that appears.

2. **Click in the text box and type your message.**

3. **To insert an emoticon at the current cursor position in the text box, click the Select an Emoticon drop-down list and then select a symbol.**

4. **To change your message font attributes, click the Font button.**

   You can choose a different font, change the size and color of your text, or add italic and bold attributes. Click OK to return to the Messenger window.

5. **When your message is ready to send, press Enter or click the Send button.**

   Figure 6-3 illustrates a message I'm about to send, complete with an emoticon. I am *so* instant!

Figure 6-3: Click Send to whisk your important query to your friend.

You're not limited to a single person when you chat — up to 20 people can join in! Click the Invite button and enter the contact whom you want to invite into your current conversation. Click OK to send the invitation. Again, the other party has the chance to decline if she doesn't like the crowd you're seeing.

Live Messenger also provides support for the following activities (either as entries from the menu that appears when you right-click a contact, or as commands on the File or the Actions menus):

✦ **Watching video:** Click Start a Video Call to use your Web camera to send video to the other person. (Naturally, this activity works best over a broadband connection.)

✦ **Sending files:** To send a file or image to the other person, choose File⇨ Send a Single File. Live Messenger displays the familiar Open dialog box, where you can select a file. ***Note:*** The person on the receiving end must approve the transfer before it can begin, and you're limited to files of less than 3MB.

✦ **Interacting using activities:** You can run approved third-party applications from the Activities menu, like sending news stories to a contact or sharing photos.

✦ **Making phone calls:** You can call a person's computer or their phone. (Note that some connections may require you to use an Internet telephony carrier, like Skype.)

✦ **Launching multiplayer games:** You can launch a multiplayer game from the wide variety offered by Microsoft.

✦ **Using Remote Assistance:** If you're experiencing trouble with Windows 7 or one of your applications, you can "hand over the reins" to a trusted contact and allow that person to control your PC remotely. For example, you can watch while she solves a problem with a Control Panel setting, or demonstrates how to do change margins in Word 2010!

Before you decide to use the Request Remote Assistance feature, make doggone sure that you're talking to a reliable person whom you know and trust — not someone who happens to be sitting at his keyboard — and *definitely not a party you just met!* Remember that Remote Assistance allows the other person to directly manipulate your copy of Windows 7, and nasty (I mean *truly* nasty) things can happen at the hands of an ill-meaning (or just inexperienced) person.

To leave a chat, you simply close the Conversation window.

Book III
Chapter 6

Instant Messaging Done Right

Selecting a Status

As I mention earlier in this chapter, Windows Live Messenger automatically changes your status to Away if you don't use Messenger for 15 minutes (by default).

However, you can change your status at any time, which is a good idea if you step away from your PC for a soda. When you change your status, Live Messenger instantly updates your icon in other people's contact lists.

To change your status, click the My Status drop-down list at the top of the Live Messenger window — it's next to your user name — and then choose a status (as shown in Figure 6-4). Alternatively, you can choose File⇨Status and then choose the status you want from the pop-up menu that appears.

Figure 6-4: Changing your status is a cinch.

To change your status so that you look like you're completely offline, you can choose Appear Offline, which moves you to the Not Online section of the contact list.

Squelching the Unwelcome Few

From time to time, you encounter folks whom you simply would rather not even communicate with. Sorry, but even Microsoft can't produce a program that can turn away the common Internet turkey. Luckily, you can manually take care of turkeys in Live Messenger (when you recognize 'em for what they are, anyway).

✦ **From the Contact list:** If you're mad at an ill-mannered individual — who also happens to be in your Live Messenger Contact list — you can block any further communication with that person by right-clicking her name in your list and then choosing Block Contact from the pop-up menu that appears.

✦ **From the Conversation window:** Click the Block button from within the Conversation window. If you're chatting with multiple folks, you can click the name of the offending person and then click Block to screen out just that person. To unblock the person, click the blocked name again to select it and then click the Unblock button (which toggles between Block and Unblock.)

And if you have a change of heart, you can unblock a person by right-clicking the blocked name and then choosing Unblock Contact from the pop-up menu that appears.

Book III
Chapter 6

Instant Messaging Done Right

Book IV

PC Troubleshooting and Maintenance

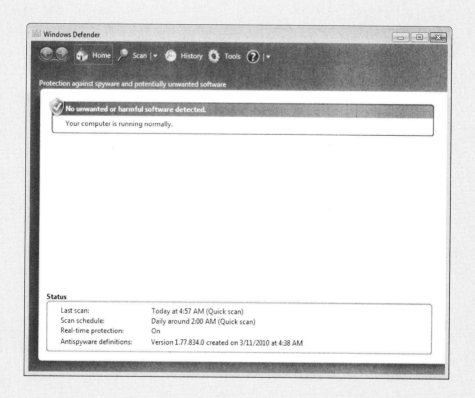

Contents at a Glance

Chapter 1: Easy PC Troubleshooting 241

Relax and Breathe Easy 241
The Troubleshooting Process, Step by Step 243
Drastic Things That You Won't Do Often 249
HELP! Additional Troubleshooting Resources 251

Chapter 2: Maintaining Windows 7 253

Device Manager: The Hardware Tool..................................... 253
Checking Your Hard Drives in Windows 7 256
Defragmenting Just Plain Rocks 258
Be Smart: Back Up Your Stuff... 261
Safeguarding Your System with System Restore...................... 265
Have at Thee, Foul Virus!... 267
Using Windows Defender.. 268
Windows 7 Boot and Recovery Options 269
Using Windows Update... 271

Chapter 3: Maintaining Your Hardware .273

When Should You Move Your PC? 273
Avoiding Dust Bunnies.. 274
Watching Your Cables... 275
Cleaning Monitors and Scanners... 276
Cleaning Your Mouse and Keyboard 277
Cleaning and Maintaining Your Printer 278

Chapter 1: Easy PC Troubleshooting

In This Chapter

✓ Taking a moment to relax

✓ Troubleshooting your hardware and software

✓ Using System Recovery options

✓ Reinstalling Windows 7

✓ Locating troubleshooting help

I *hate* my Rubik's Cube. I've never been able to solve the silly thing, and it just sits on my desk, taunting me and driving me to distraction until I grab it and make another futile attempt to match up all those squares. (Perhaps I'm in need of cube therapy.) What really gets me, though, is how my 18-year-old daughter can pick up that same cube, spend 45 seconds turning it in some wizard way, and then drop the solved puzzle and move on to something different. Geez! Why is such a difficult thing so easy for some people to do?

Troubleshooting Windows 7 has the same frustrating effect on most PC owners. You sit, staring at the keyboard and wondering why your operating system no longer works right and how you can fix it. Often, the solution is to call a friend or family member who can help — or, in the worst case, pack up the entire heap and take it to a computer shop where technotypes smile that mysterious little smile and fix your problem in 45 seconds. And then charge you an arm and a leg.

This chapter is here to help *you* tackle your Windows 7 troubleshooting puzzle. It might take more than 45 seconds, but you'll feel an enormous sense of accomplishment. Plus, you might avoid lightening your wallet.

Relax and Breathe Easy

Here's the first step in Mark's Troubleshooting Procedure: When the going gets tough, the techs relax. That's right, I said *relax*. Even though Windows 7 — or your PC in general — is acting crazy, keep these important points in mind:

✦ **Never blame yourself.** Even the most nimble-fingered computer programmer or hardware technician can make a mistake. (Heck, I've heard that even His Billness makes them every so often.) Accidents eventually happen — and, as with poorly written software or viruses, the fault might not even be yours, anyway. Don't treat yourself to a guilt trip.

✦ **Remember your backup.** As long as you take my advice throughout this book (ahem! *back up your data!*), you won't lose your life's work.

✦ **This, too, shall pass.** Even when hardware and software fail, you *can* find the problem. Remember that the problem is only temporary — and certainly not unsolvable. (Not even my Rubik's cube is impossible to solve.) You *can* get your PC back.

✦ **Help is available.** Besides friends and family, PC user group members, and resources you can find on the Internet, you can always turn to the tech experts at your local computer store for professional help at a price. (But wouldn't it feel gratifying if you could fix it yourself?)

Yes, a Windows Remote Assistance option is available through the Windows 7 Help system — this feature allows a trusted friend or family member to take remote control of your PC to help fix the problem. However, remember these two caveats: First, the person to whom you give remote control over your entire computer had better be *doggone* trustworthy, so this option isn't the one to explore if a neighbor's mischievous kid says "I can fix that, easy." Also, if Windows 7 is the cause of the problem (especially if your network is down or you can't get an Internet connection), Remote Assistance isn't likely to work anyway. With that said, if you have a close friend who's also a technowizard, you find the utility in Start➪All Programs➪Maintenance➪Windows Remote Assistance.

And, a final tip while you're preparing to troubleshoot:

✦ **Your PC is *not* against you.** The troubleshooting process is *not* a battle between you, your hardware, and your software. Many folks tell me that they find it quite easy to personalize the anger they feel and direct it toward that inanimate hunk of metal, plastic, and silicon. Stay calm, and remember this important Mark's Maxim:

Don't take out your frustration on your PC (no matter how uncooperative it seems).™

To illustrate this last point, here's an honest-to-goodness true story that I love to tell. In the days of DOS, before Plug and Play or automatic configurations within Windows, adding a Small Computer System Interface (SCSI) adapter card and even just one SCSI device to your PC was a feat on the order of Hercules cleaning the Augean stables. An old friend of mine — who was quite handy with a screwdriver and normally well versed in PC hardware — spent more than six continuous hours attempting to install a used SCSI card and a SCSI hard drive in his 386 PC. He didn't curse, and he didn't scream. I'll never forget the look of utter peace on his face when he good-naturedly clamped the recalcitrant card in his metal vise and proceeded to melt the SCSI adapter with his portable torch.

He uses Windows these days, of course — but he never has forgiven the SCSI interface standard.

The Troubleshooting Process, Step by Step

It's time for the star of our show: Mark's Step-by-Step Windows 7 Troubleshooting Procedure! Note that this process doesn't center completely on software because it's often hard to tell at the beginning whether the problem at hand is caused by Windows 7 or by your PC's hardware.

Follow these steps:

1. **Simply shut down Windows 7.**

Many folks often don't have to move past this first step. Believe it or not, a simple shutdown solves a good 25 percent of the temporary glitches you might encounter, such as a frozen mouse or a locked-up PC resulting from a power failure. Shutting down works because it resets all your PC's hardware — and Windows 7 itself — and returns everything to normal. (By the way, if you can't reach the Start menu because your PC is locked up tight or the mouse doesn't move anymore, you have every right to get tough with your PC: Either deliver the classic Windows "Three Finger Salute" by pressing the Ctrl+Alt+Del keys simultaneously, or press and hold your power button until your PC turns itself off. Don't unplug your PC directly — always press and hold the power button instead!)

Always check for hard drive errors after you're forced to shut down Windows 7 by simply turning off your PC. For instructions on how to scan your drives for errors, see Chapter 2 of this minibook.

**Book IV
Chapter 1**

2. **If you restart your PC and the problem continues, double-check all cables leading to your PC.**

Yes, I know this sounds ridiculous, but I'll bet you your next paycheck that they do this step on nuclear submarines, too. You might not have problems with your AC power cord, for example, but it's quite easy to accidentally unplug other connectors from your PC — like your keyboard or network or external devices, such as your modem and printer. If you recently moved your PC or bumped against it, loose connections are prime suspects for all sorts of mischief.

**Easy PC
Troubleshooting**

If you just replaced a cable and one of your peripherals (like a printer) is now an expensive doorstop (or your network suddenly no longer recognizes your PC), try a spare cable that you know works. Although bad cables are rare, they do happen. (Bad Ethernet cables have been known to cause insomnia.)

3. **If all your cables are shipshape, your next mission is to sit — and** ***think.***

   Take a moment to consider any software or hardware you recently installed that might be causing (or contributing to) the problem. I always install new hardware or software one piece at a time because then I can easily tell which new addition is wreaking havoc. A PC that was originally chugging along nicely can suddenly turn rogue with one seemingly innocent change. (Note that this also includes any program or operating system updates, patches, or upgrades you might have just applied.)

   I also use System Restore points liberally when installing new stuff. Find more on the System Restore utility in Chapter 2 of this minibook.

4. **Still no go? Time to shut down and remove any offending external devices — such as an external hard drive that's dead in the water — to see whether your PC suddenly returns to normal.**

   If so, that peripheral is your prime suspect, so try it on another PC to determine whether the device is still working. Also try using another cable. If the peripheral works fine on another PC, your problem lies in either the device driver or the device configuration that you set up in Windows 7. Check the manual for the device, reinstall the device driver (make sure to visit the manufacturer's Web site for the latest driver first), and — if all else fails — contact the manufacturer's technical support team.

5. **Uninstall any programs that are misbehaving or locking up Windows 7 and then reinstall them.**

   After you reinstall — but *before* you apply a patch or an upgrade — try using the application to see whether it still exhibits the problem. If not, the software developer has (as Desi so eloquently put it) "some 'splainin' to do." Visit the developer's Web site and check for information about compatibility, especially with Windows 7 and Service Pack patches, which often wreak havoc on unprepared software.

6. **If you recently made changes in the Control Panel, the System Properties dialog box, or any networking dialog boxes, take a moment to revisit those settings and verify that they're still correct.**

   Unfortunately, anyone can easily and accidentally change a setting within one of the Control Panel applets. To make sure that you don't disturb something, just click Cancel if everything looks okay.

7. If you're still having problems, check your hard drives (see Figure 1-1).

Use the procedure I demonstrate in Chapter 2 of this minibook to verify that your drives are free from disk errors.

Figure 1-1:
Check your hard drive often for errors.

8. Scan your hard drives and any removable disks.

I talk about antivirus software throughout this book; on most of my 7 machines, I use avast! Antivirus Home Edition, from ALWIL Software (www.avast.com), as shown in Figure 1-2.

Figure 1-2:
Scan your system with avast! Antivirus.

**Book IV
Chapter 1**

Easy PC
Troubleshooting

Each time you run a scan, take a second to make sure that you're using the latest antivirus signature data file from the developer's Web site. (If you're using avast!, the program automatically checks for updated virus data files.)

9. **Verify that you're still connected to and receiving packets from your home or office network — or, if you're using a broadband connection, your cable modem or digital subscriber line (DSL):**

   a. *Display your network connections by choosing Start⇨Control Panel⇨ Network and Sharing Center.*

   b. *Check to make sure that each connection is displayed, without any red X marks, which indicate disabled broken connections.*

   If your network is down, Windows 7 has a nasty habit of slowing to a crawl when you open files or use Windows Explorer — and many applications that expect a network connection as their divine right can lock up tighter than Fort Knox. Don't forget to berate your network administrator or tech staff — boy, they just *love* it when you do that!

10. **If you're using a shareware or freeware screen saver, realize that a slew of badly written screen savers, readily available for download on the Internet, can take Windows 7 on a permanent vacation.**

    To test whether your favorite Care Bears screen saver is causing those intermittent lockups, follow these steps:

    a. *Right-click your desktop, choose Personalize, and then click the Screen Saver link.*

    b. *Choose None and then click OK.*

    c. *Reboot and use your PC for a day without any screen saver — or choose one of the Windows 7 screen savers provided by Microsoft, which are proven stable.*

11. **Check whether another user with Administrator access might have changed the write-protect status of your applications or your documents.**

    This step is for those who share a PC with other users by taking advantage of the multiuser features built in to Windows 7.

    This is usually the case when Word complains that it doesn't have the rights to open a document you were working on yesterday. Have a user with an Administrator account log in and verify the permissions on your applications and document files. (I tell you more about this topic in Book II, Chapter 4.)

12. **Even if you can boot in Safe mode, first try the Windows 7 System Configuration utility (see Figure 1-3), which can help you diagnose where the trouble lies in your boot process.**

    a. *Run the utility by pressing the Windows key on your keyboard and typing the word **System** in the Start Search box.*

System Configuration should appear at the top of the Search results list, and you can click the entry to run the application. (If you're using an older keyboard without a Windows key, click Start and click in the Start Search box the old-fashioned way.)

Note that you can try a *Diagnostic Startup* (which offers more functionality than Safe mode), or you can choose *Selective Startup* and specify which boot steps to enable.

b.   *After you choose your boot options, click OK and then reboot Windows 7.*

Figure 1-3:
Try a selective startup with the System Configuration utility.

To disable just one startup program, click the Startup tab and deselect the check box alongside the offending application. Then it's a breeze to troubleshoot problems you encounter when installing new software that loads automatically during the boot process. You can repeat this process to disable more than one startup item. If Windows 7 suddenly boots correctly and your problem appears to be solved, immediately uninstall the program that you last disabled and contact the software developer's technical support.

13. **If you're still with me, it's time to get serious with your hardware and display Device Manager (see Figure 1-4), as I describe in Chapter 2 of this minibook.**

Make sure that Windows 7 hasn't flagged any of your hardware devices as either disabled or not working; if a component is flagged with an exclamation point, a little investigation might well turn up the solution to the problem.

Safe mode to the rescue

If your PC is locking up before you even have a chance to click the Start button (or it freezes before your desktop icons even appear), it becomes nearly impossible to get far enough to fix anything. Although you can boot from the Windows 7 installation disc, your choices are severely limited. Even when you know what needs to be done (like a specific driver file needs to be deleted or a device needs removed in Device Manager), the old witticism remains true: "You can't get there from here."

Luckily, Windows 7 maintains an old friend from the days of Windows 95 and Windows 98: *Safe mode,* the alternative boot-up mode where device drivers are disabled (generally a very good thing if your PC is experiencing bad karma) and you again have access to Windows Explorer and basic Windows 7 functionality. Although Safe mode isn't always available — sometimes Windows 7 is so badly obfuscated that even Safe mode doesn't work — it's a valuable addition to your troubleshooting toolbox.

If your PC is in the midst of a breakdown and you can't reach Windows, find in-depth Safe mode coverage in Chapter 2 of this minibook.

Figure 1-4: Device Manager is a handy hardware diagnostic tool.

At this point, you've exhausted most of the easier troubleshooting chores and fixes you can perform. It's time to get drastic.

Drastic Things That You Won't Do Often

As I say at the beginning of this minibook, Windows 7 (like Windows XP and Vista before it) is much harder to crash than previous versions of Windows. In fact, it even attempts to automatically fix system files that are corrupted by other programs, by using the *Windows File Protection* feature. However, the folks in Redmond can do only so much to armor-plate their favorite son. You might end up with a PC that makes even the most dedicated PC technicians shake their heads in defeat — and if that happens, it's time to read this section.

Using System Recovery Options

As I mention earlier in this chapter, I take full advantage of the Windows 7 System Restore utility. But if your PC is in truly bad shape and you can't run the System Restore program, your next step is likely to run the Windows 7 *System Recovery Options*, which you can activate from your Windows 7 installation DVD or during the boot cycle:

✦ If your computer has System Recovery Options preinstalled — as many PCs from major manufacturers do — it's one of the options available when you press and hold F8 just before Windows 7 begins loading.

✦ If the System Recovery Options weren't preinstalled on your PC, you need to use your Windows 7 Installation disc. Load the disc in your DVD drive and reboot, and then press any key during the boot process to start Windows 7 from the DVD.

Besides System Restore, the System Recovery Options include

✦ **Startup Repair:** A basic replacement of critical system files, Startup Repair is helpful if the data on your PC's hard drive was damaged by viruses or your Windows 7 system files have been corrupted by a disk error.

✦ **System Image Recovery:** You can choose to restore your entire hard drive from a backup image, as I discuss in Chapter 2 of this minibook.

✦ **Command Prompt:** For those familiar with the DOS command line, you can perform simple file management and run command-line programs.

✦ **Windows Memory Diagnostic:** This utility checks to make sure that your PC's RAM is glitch-free — a hardware memory problem can wreak havoc within Windows 7.

Each System Recovery Option is fully automated, so just follow the onscreen prompts (and keep your fingers crossed).

Reinstalling Windows 7

If your entire operating system is in serious jeopardy — that is, it doesn't boot or it locks up every single time you use it as soon as your mouse cursor appears — you can reinstall Windows. (Microsoft also calls this remedy a *repair installation*. I find that rather humorous.)

So-called learned people in the world swear up and down that you should never, *never* reinstall Windows 7. Mention such a drastic step to these self-appointed experts, and they immediately start whooping, "There's no reason to do it, and you might possibly launch a thermonuclear warhead at Nepal if you diddle with a single setting. Just suffer! After all, it's Windows 7 — enjoy the eye candy."

Well, good reader, I'm here to tell you the honest truth. You certainly *won't* be reinstalling Windows 7 every weekend, but only as a last resort (after you try the System Recovery Options, attempt to restore from your backup, and consult with the techs at your local computer repair shop). However, in some situations (like the two I just mentioned), reinstalling your operating system might solve your problem.

Back up whatever personal files you can from your system before reinstalling Windows 7. (Perhaps use Safe mode, which I mention earlier in this chapter.) Also, if you want to try to keep the personal files that are on the drive, *do not choose a clean install,* which basically wipes out the existing Windows installation and all files on that drive or partition.

If your PC came equipped with a System Restore disc, note that using a System Restore disc isn't the same as reinstalling just Windows 7! When you use the manufacturer's System Restore disc, your hard drive is probably erased and reformatted and the hard drive restored to the exact condition it was in the first time you booted your PC. All your files, applications, and settings are gone, and you have to set up all your multiuser accounts as well! If there's no other way, and you can't reinstall Windows 7 from a Windows 7 installation disc, please make certain that every file you want to save has been safely stored on a CD-R or DVD-R (or a much roomier external hard drive backup unit) before you use the System Restore disc. (Oh, and don't trust floppy disks with the backup job. They're far too unreliable, and they don't hold squat.)

If you received (or bought) a bona fide Windows 7 installation disc, follow the instructions that accompanied the disc to install Windows 7. However, here are a few tricks that I want to mention first:

+ **You might have to reinstall some applications.** Although the information that most programs place in the Windows Registry (and in their own `.ini` files) isn't affected by a reinstall, some applications might no longer work after you reinstall Windows 7. (If you're reinstalling Windows 7, you're dangling from the end of your rope anyway, so you might as well go for the gusto and take the chance of having to reinstall a few applications.)

In general, most folks should stay as far away from the Windows Registry as possible. Think of the Registry as Bigfoot with a flame-thrower. *Never* try to edit the Registry unless told to do so by a Microsoft technical support person.

✦ **You need the same product key.** If Windows 7 came preinstalled on your PC, you should find the product key on an official-looking sticker somewhere on the PC's case.

✦ **You have to reactivate Windows 7.** Remember how you had to activate Windows 7 when you first installed it or first started your new PC? *Activation* is the Microsoft antipiracy protection scheme; luckily, the folks in Redmond have made allowances for catastrophe and allow you to reactivate a legitimate copy of Windows 7.

✦ **You lose all your System Restore points.** Of course, if you can't get to them, they don't do much good — but I wanted to mention the loss, anyway.

Once again, the best-laid plans of mice and trackballs (sorry about that) can go awry, but as long as you backed up your personal files and important documents, you *will* persevere (even if you have to perform that clean install and manually reload your files and applications)!

HELP! Additional Troubleshooting Resources

If you have a Windows 7 troubleshooting question, you might be able to make a phone call to your local computer shop for a quick answer — even after the warranty expires — but most folks I know turn more often to the source. After all, Microsoft built the doggone thing.

In this final section, I discuss the three troubleshooting resources offered by Mother Bill. (And one option doesn't even require the Internet.)

The Windows 7 Help system

I show you how to use the Help system in the first chapter of Book II. (See, I told you I like to plan ahead.) But I also want to point out that the Microsoft Knowledge Base entries you find in Help (which, to no one's surprise, are pulled directly from the Microsoft Knowledge Base Web site) are particularly valuable when you're troubleshooting problems with Windows 7.

**Book IV
Chapter 1**

Easy PC
Troubleshooting

Microsoft tech support

Microsoft offers both online and telephone technical support, using real human beings. This type of support is probably the most valuable trouble-shooting resource around, along with the technical support you receive from the manufacturer when you buy your PC. Because all Microsoft products have different telephone support numbers, check your Windows 7 documentation for the proper number to call.

The Microsoft Web site

Of course, you can also always find Microsoft online (if you can still get online with the trouble you're encountering) at www.microsoft.com. The Microsoft Web site is stuffed full of information, and each product typically has its own home page. For example, you can visit the Windows 7 site at www.microsoft.com/windows/windows-7 and download that Sidebar gadget you wanted so badly. (Yeah, right.)

Those unsupported newsgroups

You can indeed find plenty of free help in Usenet newsgroup discussions (within Windows Live Mail) — however, these forums aren't moderated or monitored by Microsoft in any way. Therefore, you receive plenty of opinions (and what passes for wit) if you post a troubleshooting question here, but there's a chance that someone else will recognize the trouble you're having and volunteer a solution. Take any solution you're handed, however, with a whopping big grain of salt.

Don't provide anyone with any personal information within these newsgroups because the individuals with whom you're talking *do not* work for Microsoft. (This is a common sense Internet thing.)

Chapter 2: Maintaining Windows 7

In This Chapter

✔ Scanning your hard drives for errors

✔ Defragmenting to speed up your PC

✔ Backing up your files in Windows 7

✔ Using System Restore

✔ Using boot and recovery options in Windows 7

✔ Taking Windows Update for a ride

*M*aintenance. It's important, and you've got to do it — so why not make it *exciting?* Rather than consider it dull preventive care, think of the pit crew around an Indy car, and, well, on second thought, that might be a stretch. Anyway, you gotta do it.

You might not find this chapter overly exciting, but if you regularly follow the procedures you find here, I guarantee that you'll be happy with the performance and stability of your PC running Windows 7. And, who knows? Maybe that Indy pit crew job will materialize someday. (Even if it doesn't, you'll have the smoothest-running PC on the block, and that counts for a lot.)

Device Manager: The Hardware Tool

The first stop on your maintenance tour is the Windows 7 Device Manager, which I recommend that you check at least once per month. *Device Manager* is essentially a status window that displays the operating status of each of the hardware devices in your PC as well as the peripherals connected to it. With one glance, you can see any hardware device that Windows has marked as a troublemaker, and locating trouble is the first step in solving it.

Now, don't panic at the idea of rooting around in your hardware. In fact, the idea of a hardware conflict is easy to understand. Just about every hardware device in your PC needs a unique pathway to be able to communicate with the CPU and other devices. For instance, your Ethernet network card must be able to send and receive data to and from the Internet without getting spurious stuff that's meant for your printer. (Imagine the fun you would have if your hard drive and your DVD-ROM drive kept exchanging data by accident. Harrumph.)

Luckily, Windows 7 does an excellent job of allocating hardware resources and routing data betwixt everything, especially if you're using Universal Serial Bus (USB) and FireWire peripherals. However, sharing problems still crop up from time to time with older hardware that might not have up-to-date drivers. (A *driver* is a program that tells Windows 7 how to communicate with and use a specific hardware device.) Device Manager can not only display which devices are causing trouble but also help you update the drivers for that device.

Follow these steps to use Device Manager in Windows 7:

1. **Click Start and then right-click the Computer menu item. Choose Properties from the pop-up menu that appears, which displays the System Control Panel window.**

2. **Click the Device Manager link on the Task pane button to open the Device Manager window, which you see in Figure 2-1.**

   If a device in the Device Manager window is marked with a yellow exclamation point or a red check mark, it might be in conflict with another device, which in turn might also be marked by a yellow exclamation point.

Disabling a device (in effect, turning it off temporarily) marks that device with a gray arrow pointing down — PC techs sometimes disable devices while troubleshooting to help them track down a problem. To enable a device again within Device Manager, right-click on it and click Enable from the menu that appears.

Figure 2-1:
Check for
possible
problems
in Device
Manager.

If nothing is flagged, skip to Step 5 — Windows 7 has given your hardware the all-clear!

You might also find helpful information in the Device Status display:

- *If a Driver tab appears in the device's Properties dialog box:* Try updating your system with the latest driver for the device. (Go to Step 4.) This strategy often fixes things right away.

- *If no Driver tab exists:* Scurry on to Step 5.

3. **To check for possible conflicts with a particular piece of hardware, right-click the marked device and then choose Properties from the pop-up menu that appears to display its settings.**

Figure 2-2 shows properties for my graphics card.

Figure 2-2:
Display the settings for a specific hardware device.

4. **Click the Driver tab and then click the Update Driver button to run the Update Driver Software Wizard.**

The wizard leads you through the process of checking for a new driver online or from a CD-ROM supplied by the manufacturer.

Don't forget to check the manufacturer's Web site for drivers.

5. **Click OK to return to the Device Manager dialog box and then click the Close button in the Device Manager window.**

If you made changes, Windows 7 prompts you for confirmation before rebooting your PC.

Book IV
Chapter 2

Maintaining
Windows 7

If updating the driver doesn't do the trick, choose Start⇨Help and Support to display the Help system, and then click the Troubleshooting link. The Help system leads you through possible solutions to the problem.

Checking Your Hard Drives in Windows 7

Let me clear up two common misconceptions concerning hard drives:

✦ **Hard drives don't malfunction.** Oh, yes, they do. Even if you've never had a hard drive crash, you've likely heard about them. Even so, today's hard drives are generally so reliable and so long lasting that folks often forget. Hard drive errors can be *physical* (the drive's hardware malfunctions) or *logical* (the error is in the format or the data stored on the drive). If your PC is caught by a power failure and file corruption occurs, you're the victim of a logical file error.

✦ **Errors are immediately noticeable.** Most logical errors don't cause your PC to crash, and they might not affect files that you're currently using, so they often go unnoticed. (They share this trait with computer viruses, which use stealth to hide themselves.) Over time, logical errors can cause real damage to your files and documents, so catching them quickly is vital.

For these reasons, scanning your PC's hard drives often (both internal and external) for potential problems is important. Microsoft makes this task easy in Windows 7 by providing an error-checking feature that you can reach from a hard drive's Properties panel. (For you crotchety Windows old-timers, think *ScanDisk.*)

Follow these steps to scan a hard drive for errors:

1. **Click Start and click the Computer link to display the hard drives on your system.**

2. **Right-click the hard drive you want to scan, choose Properties from the pop-up menu that appears, and then click the Tools tab to display the buttons you see in Figure 2-3.**

3. **Click the Check Now button to display the Check dialog box, which has the settings shown in Figure 2-4.**

Always select the Automatically Fix File System Errors check box.

Figure 2-3:
Microsoft
hides these
programs
away, but
power users
know where
they are.

Figure 2-4:
Preparing
to check a
hard drive
for errors in
Windows 7.

4. **To check the drive's hardware for physical errors, select the Scan For and Attempt Recovery of Bad Sectors check box and then click Start.**

Note: This process can take a very long time, as in four or five hours, on larger drives (250GB or larger). I recommend that you use this feature once every three or six months because today's drives rarely exhibit bad sectors until the entire drive crashes.

When the scanning program finishes, you see one of two messages:

- *The scan completed without you needing to reboot.* Just click OK to close the scan and return to the desktop.

- *The scan could not complete, and you do need to reboot.* If the scanning program determines that you need to reboot Windows 7 to finish the error checking, click Schedule Disk Check to close the scan

**Book IV
Chapter 2**

**Maintaining
Windows 7**

dialog box. You need to reboot manually. (The scan is automatically scheduled to run the next time you boot Windows 7.) Shut down any other programs that might be running and choose Start➪Restart.

Windows 7 automatically completes the checkup during the boot process.

Commercial utilities on the market can also check your hard drive for errors; the most popular and best-known is Symantec's Norton Utilities (www.symantec.com), which includes Norton Disk Doctor. I usually recommend the Norton line of programs, but in this case, Disk Doctor really doesn't do much more than Windows 7's built-in error-checking feature.

Defragmenting Just Plain Rocks

Another program that you can reach from any hard drive's Properties dialog box is Disk Defragmenter. I admit that it's a strange name, but returning file fragments to their proper places can significantly increase your hard drive's performance. (Technonerds call it "running a defrag." *Très* nerd.)

So, what the heck are fragmented files? Here's the straight skinny: Each time you delete or move files from one spot on your PC to the other, you open up sections of your hard drive so that new files can be stored there. When you're ready to save a file, however, it might not fit into any single open area on your hard drive, so Windows 7 saves the file in pieces, or *segments,* across several open sections.

Suppose that you're downloading a 300MB game demo, but your hard drive doesn't have 300MB of contiguous open space handy. Windows 7 decides to save 50MB in one spot, 120MB in another, and the rest in a third open space. When you decide to install the demo and run the file, Windows 7 automatically pulls the right data from these different spots on your hard drive and reassembles the pieces into the original file. (I bet you didn't know all that was happening when that little green light blinks on and off, but then the Seven can be a mysterious beast.)

Of course, this assembly process takes more time if the file has been broken into more pieces. And, when your drive is extremely fragmented with little segments of thousands of files that Windows 7 has to keep track of, your hard drive performance really starts to suffer. Fragmentation slows down everything, and Windows 7 has to work harder every time you open or save a file.

The Windows 7 Disk Defragmenter restores the files on your drive to smooth, unbroken data storage territory. (Think of the *Bonanza* spread, but with ones and zeroes rather than cattle.) Figure 2-5 illustrates your drive before you run Disk Defragmenter, and Figure 2-6 shows your drive afterward. The program reads fragmented files, combines those nomadic segments, and then saves the defragmented file back to the disk. Outstanding!

Figure 2-5: Fragmented files sap performance from your hard drive.

Figure 2-6: Wow! Check out the contiguous sectors on that platter!

I recommend defragmenting your hard drives about once a month, and that you defragment when you're not using your PC (because the process takes much less time to finish that way). Most PC owners defragment at nights or on weekends. Shutting down programs that are running in the background also helps. Just display the taskbar; in the notification area to the right, right-click each icon for programs you don't need, and then click Exit or Close to shut them down.

To run Disk Defragmenter, follow these steps:

1. **Choose Start⇨Computer.**

2. **Right-click the hard drive you want to defragment, choose Properties from the pop-up menu that appears, and then click the Tools tab (refer to Figure 2-3).**

3. **Click the Defragment Now button to open Disk Defragmenter, which you see in Figure 2-7.**

Figure 2-7: Defragmentation is like a bowl of granola for your PC.

4. **(Optional) To schedule Disk Defragmenter to run automatically, click the Turn on Schedule button, and then select the Run on a Schedule (Recommended) check box. Click the drop-down lists to set the schedule and then click OK to save your schedule.**

5. **To run a defragment manually, click the drive you want to defragment in the list and then click Defragment Now.**

Defragmenting a hard drive takes time, and the larger the drive the longer the process will take — a 500GB drive will require at least two to three hours to complete a defragment session, and perhaps even longer depending on how badly the drive is fragmented.

Are you using a hi-tech SSD for storage? (That's short for *solid-state drive*, a super-fast hard drive that actually has no moving parts and uses memory much like a USB flash drive.) If so, don't bother defragmenting your SSD because the drive won't benefit from a defragmenting operation like a standard hard drive will!

Be Smart: Back Up Your Stuff

In this third part of your hard drive triple-header, I talk about how you can back up your hard drive to safeguard your data against future calamity. I don't lecture you here — oh, what the heck, yes I *will* — *DO IT*. All smart PC owners take the trouble to save their stuff. Back up regularly, and someday (maybe years from now) you'll send me an e-mail message at mark@ mlcbooks.com with the subject "Thanks, Mark, My Backup Saved My Tail!" Then we can both celebrate that you did the smart thing. I've received literally hundreds of those messages — so *DO IT*.

How often is often enough when it comes to backing up your data? Like defragmenting, the answer depends completely on how often your data changes. The idea is to back up often enough so that you always have a recent copy of your important files close by. If you wait too long to freshen your backup, you find that you spend far too much time restoring the changes you made between backups. For example, a small business or home office with a large, continually changing database might back up anywhere from every night to every three days. (If you decide that you have to back up every night, you might want to consider a commercial backup solution that can be automated.) On the other hand, a typical home PC might require a backup only once per month.

If you would rather not use the Windows 7 backup features, either buy a commercial backup application or consider copying your most important files to a CD-RW or DVD-RW disc regularly — including the contents of your Documents folder. You still have to reinstall Windows 7 and your major applications if you have a crash or your computer is stolen, but at least the irreplaceable stuff is safe. *Do not use floppy disks* for this important job!

If you use DVD media, I recommend that you use rewriteable DVDs as your backup media. Sure, you can always use CD-RWs, but you need several more discs.

Book IV
Chapter 2

Maintaining Windows 7

Along with CDs or DVDs, you can back up to

+ **A tape drive supported by Windows 7.**

+ **External cartridge media.**

+ **Online backup sites like Carbonite (www.carbonite.com).**

+ **A network folder.** This uses space on your network's file server or another PC's hard drive.

+ **A USB 2.0 or FireWire external hard drive that's especially made for backups.** Nothing works as fast as another hard drive!

To back up your files with the Windows 7 Backup and Restore Center, follow these steps:

1. **Choose Start⇨Control Panel⇨Backup and Restore.**

Depending on the version of Windows 7 you're using, you may not see the Create a System Image feature within the Windows 7 Backup and Restore window. If this option isn't available, you should back up files instead, as I demonstrate in this section. A full image allows you to restore your entire system rather than just documents and files. Click the Create a System Image link to create an image file, and the wizard leads you through the process. It's important to note, however, that a full image backup takes far longer and uses many more discs (or a larger chunk of hard drive or network real estate).

2. **Click the Set Up Backup link to display the first screen of the Set Up Backup Wizard, shown in Figure 2-8.**

3. **Select the destination media for your backup (either a hard drive, CD/DVD/Blu-Ray drive you select from the drop-down list, or a network location you choose with the Save on a Network button), and then click Next to continue.**

4. **Click Let Windows Choose to allow Windows to select which files to back up, or Let Me Choose to specify the target files yourself. Click Next to continue.**

The default setting is Let Windows Choose, and it normally results in the fastest backup (using the fewest discs, if you're using your optical drive).

Windows 7 will set up a regular backup schedule for you, no matter which type of backup you choose.

If you do decide to select your own files, you'll see the dialog box shown in Figure 2-9. Decisions, decisions. To expand the tree and show subfolders, click the triangle to the left of an entry. To choose a file or folder, click the check box next to it. When you've selected all the files and folders you want to include, click Next.

Figure 2-8:
I'm in good
hands with
the Back
Up Files
Wizard.

If you have enough space on your backup device, you can also choose to create a system image as well by selecting the Include a System Image check box. This virtually guarantees that you'll be able to restore either individual files and folders (in case something's deleted by accident, or erased by a virus) or the entire contents of the target drive (in case your hard drive fails completely).

5. **Windows 7 chooses a default schedule time for future backups. If necessary, click the Change Schedule link and specify a different schedule using the three drop-down lists you see in Figure 2-10. Then click OK to return to the confirmation screen.**

    It's easy to change the date and time for your backup if they aren't acceptable — for instance, if your PC is in an office environment and won't be turned on at the default time.

    Your PC must be turned on for a scheduled backup to run, and the appropriate media must be present (or connected and powered on)!

6. **Click Save Settings and Run Backup.**

    Sit back and enjoy the peace of mind as the backup process begins — but don't forget to feed your PC the media it needs during the backup process.

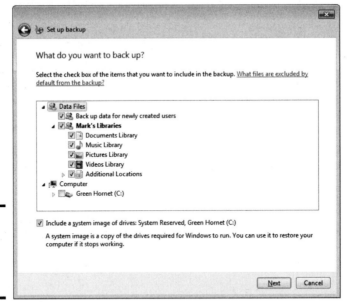

Figure 2-9:
Choose the files you want to back up.

Figure 2-10:
Creating an automated backup schedule.
You rock!

If you scheduled an *unattended* backup, you have to choose either a hard drive with enough capacity to store all your stuff or a network location to store your backup. Why? Well, no one will be around to load more media if your backup takes more than one blank disc!

To restore from a backup you made, load the backup media, choose Start⇨ Control Panel⇨Backup and Restore, and then click either Restore Files and Folders (if you used the Let Windows Choose option) or Restore System Settings or Your Computer (if you created a system image). The wizard leads you through the restore process — don't forget to breathe a sigh of relief!

Safeguarding Your System with System Restore

Remember when you were a kid and you held your fingers crossed behind your back when you made a promise? A "take-back" was a big deal back then. And even though you're all grown now, Windows 7 gives you the chance to say "I take it back!" if an installation goes awry.

This helpful feature is *System Restore*. It lets you set *restore points* (think of them as snapshots of your important system files), which you can return to whenever the Big Seven experiences problems. Most folks turn to System Restore if the installation of new hardware or software causes instability in Windows 7; I also used it when a system file was accidentally erased or altered. Note that System Restore can recover only your Windows 7 *system* files, so if you accidentally trash Aunt Harriet's prized family brownie recipe, you're still out of luck — it's time to turn to your backup.

Windows 7 automatically saves restore points regularly, but you can follow these steps to manually create a restore point as a safety net — for example, if you're about to install a new device.

After you apply a restore point, Windows 7 must reboot. Therefore, I recommend closing down any applications that you have running with open documents *before* you run the System Restore Wizard.

Follow these steps to create a new restore point:

1. **Click Start, right-click the Computer item, and choose Properties from the menu that appears.**

2. **Click the System Protection link to display the settings you see in Figure 2-11.**

3. **Click the Create button.**

4. **In the following wizard window, type a name in the Description box — something like** Windows 7 before adding new video card **— and then click the Create button.**

   Windows 7 displays a confirmation message indicating that the restore point has been successfully saved. Click OK to acknowledge your success.

5. **Click OK to return to your desktop.**

Book IV
Chapter 2

Maintaining
Windows 7

Figure 2-11:
You can
create a
system
restore
point at any
time.

If you need to use a restore point to recover from a calamity, follow these steps:

1. **Choose Start⮡All Programs⮡Accessories⮡System Tools⮡System Restore to run the System Restore Wizard. Click Next on the introductory screen.**

2. **Click to select a restore point from the list (see Figure 2-12) — before you encountered your current problem, naturally — and click Next to continue.**

Figure 2-12:
Selecting
a restore
point
from my
"collection."

Windows 7 displays a confirmation message with information about the point you chose.

3. **Click Finish to apply the restore point.**

Have at Thee, Foul Virus!

One of the first book chapters I ever wrote concerned viruses — that was way back in 1992. I recommended a number of antivirus applications (only one has survived to this day: McAfee VirusScan) and a number of guidelines to help readers avoid viral infection. Unfortunately, many folks ignored viruses back then and paid the price later.

Viruses are much harder to ignore these days. The number of viruses now circulating has jumped dramatically, and you read about viral attacks continually in your newspaper and on your favorite news Web sites. Luckily, antivirus software has stayed current with "infection technology." In fact, the good guys are now out in front, and I'm happy to report that it's now child's play to surround Windows 7 with a protective antiviral wall.

How easy? Just install either the latest version of avast! AntiVirus Home Edition (free; www.avast.com), shown in Figure 2-13, or McAfee AntiVirus Plus 2010 (US$40; www.mcafee.com), and then sit back and watch the viruses beat themselves to deletion trying to reach your system. Unlike the antivirus software of 1992, when you had to scan for viruses from the DOS command line once a day, everything now works in real time. Although you can (and should) still scan your entire system manually once every six months or so, your antivirus program monitors every document you open and every program you run in the interim. It's *fun* to open your e-mail and see viral-laden spam identified and killed *before* you even open the message.

Figure 2-13:
avast!
Antivirus
does an
outstanding
job of
kicking viral
butt.

These packages cover the entry points used by viruses to reach your PC, including

+ Your e-mail

+ Programs you download or receive on disk or CD from others

+ Office documents that might contain dangerous macros

However, here's one important task that you must never take for granted, and it's definitely a Mark's Maxim:

Keep your antivirus data files up to date, or you're toast.™

This step is so important that antivirus programs can now automatically update their data files without your help! (As long as your PC can connect to the Internet, anyway.) Why? Well, without the latest data files, your antivirus software is out of date, and the latest viruses can attack your system undetected.

Using Windows Defender

Microsoft dislikes the word *malicious* as much as you do — hence the folks in Redmond included Windows Defender to help you eliminate spyware throughout your system. (If you're not familiar with the term, *spyware* is software that is designed to collect personal information that you enter through your browser, e-mail, and even IM applications. It's Nasty Stuff, and if your PC is afflicted with a number of them you'll actually see your computer's performance drop significantly. They should be terminated quickly, and with prejudice.)

Windows Defender *doesn't* protect against viruses like a dedicated antivirus program does — only spyware. *Your PC needs full-time antivirus protection, and at the time of this writing, that means installing a third-party application.*

You can run Windows Defender at any time from the All Programs list on the Start menu — or just click Start and type **Windows Defender** into the Search box. From the Windows Defender screen (shown in Figure 2-14), click the Scan button in the program's toolbar to start a manual scan. However, Windows Defender works best when it's set to automatically run in real time and on a regular schedule. To make sure that Windows Defender is working full-time for you, follow these steps:

1. **Choose Start➪All Programs➪Windows Defender to display the screen you see in Figure 2-14.**

2. **Click Tools on the toolbar, and then click the Options link.**

3. **Click Automatic Scanning in the list to the left, and then select the Automatically Scan My Computer check box.**

4. **Choose Daily frequency and a time when your PC is usually both turned on and idle.**

5. **Choose Quick Scan.**

6. **Click Real-Time Protection in the list to the left, and then click the Use Real-Time Protection check box to enable it.**

7. **Click Save to save your changes.**

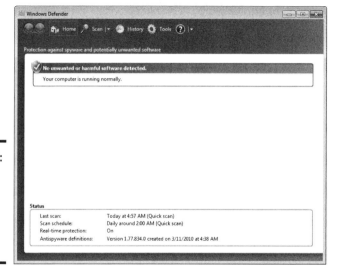

Figure 2-14:
Windows Defender is your weapon against spyware.

If Windows Defender does recognize a spyware attack, it asks for confirmation before deleting the malicious intruder. (I think Microsoft does this so that you can share in the visceral pleasure of zapping spyware!)

Windows 7 Boot and Recovery Options

Ninety-nine percent of the time when you boot Windows 7, you're talking on the phone or pouring another Diet Coke or looking through your (paper) junk mail. That's because 7 requires no help when it's running normally. You just press your PC's power button and wait.

However, if your PC isn't working correctly, you might need one of the options available during the Windows 7 boot process. In this section, I take you on a tour of what you can do in Windows 7 before your attractive desktop appears.

Book IV
Chapter 2

Maintaining
Windows 7

Using Safe mode

Think of Safe mode as generic Windows 7. If a hardware device conflict is locking up your PC, or if a driver that you recently installed or updated is causing Windows to crash, you can use Safe mode to run Windows 7 in a stripped-down mode.

In Safe mode, external devices can't be used, and much of the functionality that's available with your internal hardware is also disabled. For example, you immediately notice that your fancy video card is using the lowest resolution possible at 640 x 480 — but at least you can move or delete files and use Windows Explorer.

To use Safe mode, reboot your PC and hold down the F8 key right after you see text on the screen. (This is before the Windows banner screen appears, so you have only a second or two.) Then choose Safe Mode from the Advanced Boot Options menu and press Enter.

You also notice two other specialized forms of Safe mode:

+ **Safe mode with networking:** Windows 7 loads network drivers and services so that you can log on to your network. If you need to copy files from a network server or copy your latest documents to a network drive for safekeeping (just in case), this Safe mode is the one to use.

+ **Safe mode with command prompt:** Windows 7 loads in Safe mode but reverts to that cryptic DOS-like command prompt. This option should be used only at the request of a tech support person — unless, of course, you're an ancient DOS-using dinosaur like I am.

Using the last known good configuration

Here's another boot option that's a favorite with anyone who's facing severe problems with Windows: Windows 7 automatically stores the last-known, working system configuration — including drivers that were loaded successfully and system settings that worked — and offers that setup as a choice on the Advanced Boot Options menu. By choosing this option, you effectively reset your Windows 7 configuration to how it was before your problem cropped up. It doesn't work every time — for example, it doesn't restore missing system files — but it's a much better choice than reinstalling Windows, using ASR (see the following section), or enduring the hassle of restoring from your backup (see the earlier section "Safeguarding Your System with System Restore").

To use this feature, reboot your PC and hold down the F8 key before Windows 7 begins to boot. From the Advanced Options menu, choose Last Known Good Configuration and then press Enter.

Using Windows Update

Windows Update is a gas. It automatically searches for Windows 7 patches and upgrades from Microsoft and then applies them while you relax. This feature is A Good Thing because any piece of software as complex and powerful as Windows 7 needs frequent patching (especially because every hacker on the planet wants a piece of His Billness). The two methods of using Update are to either leave it completely to Windows 7 or run Windows Update manually.

The fully automatic way

The Big 7 can take care of virtually the entire update process in the background so that you're not bothered with it. To configure Windows Update to run automatically, you must be logged in as an Administrator user. Follow these steps:

1. **Choose Start⇨Control Panel⇨Windows Update.**

2. **Click the Change Settings link in the task pane, which displays the settings you see in Figure 2-15.**

3. **Click the Important Updates drop-down list and select the Install Updates Automatically (Recommended) entry.**

4. **Click the first drop-down list to select the day for installing, and then click the second drop-down list to choose the time.**

5. **Click OK to return to Windows Update.**

Figure 2-15: Set Windows Update for automatic operation.

Note that Windows Update also has three other settings for important updates. Using the drop-down list box in the Important Updates section, you can set Windows 7 to

✦ **Download updates automatically but let you choose whether to install them:** You can decide whether to install each update. (A Notify icon appears in the notification area on the taskbar.) To install the updates that Windows 7 has downloaded, click the Notify icon.

✦ **Check for Updates without automatically downloading or installing them:** (Again, Windows 7 displays an icon in the notification area.) To download and install the updates, click the Notify icon.

✦ **Turn off Automatic Updating completely.**

Naturally, I recommend setting Windows 7 to Install Updates Automatically — however, if you're running an older PC and you would rather not slow it down with all that hidden background activity (or if you're using a dialup connection), you can follow The Manual Path.

The (somewhat) manual way

You can also run Windows Update at any time. Perhaps you've heard of an important patch that Microsoft has just released or you just want to impress your spouse. For whatever reason, choose Start⇨All Programs⇨Windows Update to display the Windows Update Control Panel window, and then click the Check for Updates link in the task pane. Whoosh! Update carries on in manual mode, displaying the number of updates available (both required and optional) and allowing you to begin the downloading process.

If Windows 7 must reboot to install a critical update, you might have to rerun Windows Update to install any other update items.

Chapter 3: Maintaining Your Hardware

In This Chapter

✔ Moving your PC the right way

✔ Dusting your PC

✔ Keeping cables under control

✔ Cleaning your monitor and scanner

✔ Freshening your mouse and keyboard

✔ Practicing printer maintenance

*W*ith the right credit card balance, anyone can buy a supercharged $4,000 (US) PC — but *maintaining* that expensive equipment is another kettle of fish altogether. Although your PC's case might appear to be a closed environment, its fans draw in dust while they're cooling things — and what about peripherals, such as your printer and scanner, which are always more exposed to dust, dirt, and contaminants? The only PC I've encountered that doesn't need regular maintenance is the model that you can buy in *The Sims* franchise.

In this chapter, I cover the basic cleaning and maintenance necessary to keep your hardware in top shape — long enough for it to become a seriously outdated antique! (And that's coming from the proud owner of antique computers, two Radio Shack and three Atari.)

When Should You Move Your PC?

Counter to popular myth, even a desktop PC can go mobile whenever it wants. Of course, you can't stow it with your other carry-on items on a plane, but if you've been challenged to a LAN game at someone's apartment or you're moving to a new home, you'll find that your PC *enjoys* chaperoned trips (rather like a dog, without the tongue out the window).

Ready for one of my Maxims? (Get your highlighter out, if you like.) When you're ready, consider these guidelines that you should follow when moving your PC:

+ **Never move your PC until it's completely powered down.** In this case, *move* means any movement whatsoever (even nudging your PC's case a few inches across your desktop to dust). Hearken to this particularly important Mark's Maxim:

  Never move your desktop PC if it is running.™

  Even laptop computers and external hard drives shouldn't be jolted or jerked around while they're running. Many PCs have only a handful of moving parts, such as fans, DVD recorders, and hard drives — but, brother, any movement while the latter two are still spinning carries the possibility that you can shorten the drive's operational life. Always give your PC at least ten seconds after it shuts down before you pick it up.

+ **Never set your PC upright in a seat or on the floor of your car.** We've all seen the videos of crash test dummies — and your beloved digital friend doesn't have a car seat in case you come to a sudden stop. You can use seatbelts to secure your PC in a vehicle, but I think it's just easier to lay your PC's case flat on the floor of your vehicle. The same also goes for your monitor, which is also dangerous (for itself and your head) when airborne for short distances.

+ **Use your towel.** If your PC has to ride on top of a surface that might scratch your case, wrap your PC in a towel or blanket to protect its finish. (Fans of the *Hitchhiker's Guide to the Galaxy* series know what I'm on about.)

Avoiding Dust Bunnies

Think I'm kidding? Dust bunnies are real — and they seem to reproduce as fast as their namesakes, too. Thanks to your trusty can of techno-nerd compressed air, however, you can banish that dust from your PC and get back to work or play.

Here's a checklist of what to do:

+ **Open and dust your PC at least once a year.** Consider it a birthday present for your computer. Unscrew or unlatch your PC's case and use a can of compressed air (available at any office supply store) to blow any accumulated dust from the motherboard, adapter cards, and cables. If allowed to accumulate, that dust can act as a comfy heat-retaining blanket over your PC's circuitry, and overheated components have a significantly shorter lifespan. (For proof, check out the fans at the back of your PC's case and the fan on top of the processor. Heat is the enemy.)

✦ **Remove dust that's settled on the fan blades.** Speaking of fans, use your compressed air to get rid of any additional dust on fan blades and within air intake holes. To properly ventilate and cool your PC, these openings need to be free of dust bunnies.

✦ **Wipe down your PC case and your monitor with a clean, dry cloth every few months.** Don't *ever* use household solvents to clean your PC's case; instead, use special antistatic cleaning solutions and cloths made just for cleaning computer hardware. You can readily find these at your local computer shop or office supply store.

If you have a stain that won't come off your PC's case, even when you use an antistatic cleaning cloth, try my secret weapon: Armor All protectant (which you've probably been using on your car's rubber and vinyl for years!). Apply a small amount of Armor All to that cloth and try again.

✦ **Avoid eating near your PC.** I know; it's difficult not to snack while you're on the Internet, but at least be diligent about cleaning up afterward — and *never* park anything liquid anywhere near your computer!

✦ **Keep your workspace clean and open.** Surrounding your PC with papers and knickknacks might optimize your desktop space (or at least help you feel more human around an inhuman boss), but you contribute to the accumulation of dust inside your computer. And, in the worst case, you block the flow of air. I try to leave at least six inches of free space around the base of my PC at all times.

If your PC must be located in a dusty environment, consider using an air cleaner and ionizer unit. I use one in my office, and I find significantly less dust to clean from my PC every year.

Watching Your Cables

With the popularity of external Universal Serial Bus (USB), eSATA, and FireWire peripherals these days, the forest of cables sprouting from the back of your PC can look like Medusa on a bad hair day. Normally, this isn't a problem — until you decide to move your PC or you want to repair or upgrade an internal component. Talk about the Gordian knot!

Here's a list of tips for keeping your cables under control:

✦ **Use ties to combine and route cables.** I'm a big fan of the reusable Velcro cable tie strips that you can find at your local office supply store. With these ties, you can easily combine cables that are heading in the same direction into a more manageable group. You can also fasten these cable ties to the underside of your desk or behind furniture to keep network and power cables hidden and out of danger.

Book IV
Chapter 3

Maintaining Your
Hardware

✦ **Label your cables!** Sure, you can determine the source and destination of some cables at a glance (for example, network cables are pretty easy to spot), but what about your USB printer and scanner, which both use the same type of cable? If you must move your PC or unplug cables regularly, avoid the ritual of tracking each cable to its source by doing what techs and computer shops do: Use a label machine to identify the tip of each cable with the peripheral name.

✦ **Tighten those connectors.** "Gee, my monitor was working last night. What gives?" If you didn't use the knobs on either side of the video cable connector to tighten things down, small shifts in position over time could make cables work loose.

✦ **Check your cables for damage periodically.** I have two cats — or, I should say, they have me. Does a cat have you? How about a dog? If so, don't be surprised to find a chewed cable one morning — and pray that it isn't a power cable. (I keep all animals away from my office for this reason — not to mention the mess that a shedding dog can leave around your PC.) Of course, cables can also be damaged by bending or stretching them, so I recommend checking each cable at least once a year; I combine this ritual with my PC's yearly cleaning.

Cleaning Monitors and Scanners

Most PC owners are aware that they should keep the viewing surfaces of their monitors and scanners clean — but beware, because you can do more harm than good if you don't know what you're doing. Here are the guidelines that I recommend you follow when working with monitor screens and scanner glass:

✦ **Abrasives are taboo!** Even some household glass cleaners — which you might think could be trusted — can scratch the glass in your monitor or flatbed scanner when used with a rag or paper towel. With a scanner, small scratches can mean real trouble because a scratch can easily show up in your images at higher resolutions. Therefore, I recommend that you use only a dry, soft photographer's lens cloth (which doesn't scratch) or lens cloths with alcohol that are made specifically for monitors and scanners.

✦ **Never spray liquids onto a flatbed scanner or an LCD monitor.** If liquid gets under the surface, you could end up with condensation on the inside of the scanner when you use it. Again, a dry, photographer's lens cloth is a good choice, or a premoistened lens cloth, which doesn't carry enough alcohol to do any harm. (I launch into scanners full-scale in Book VI, Chapter 1.)

+ **Monitors should never be opened.** *Never* take the cover off any type of monitor, even if it needs cleaning. Why? Well, your PC's monitor is one of the two components of your system that carry enough voltage to seriously hurt you. (The other one is your PC's power supply.) If your monitor needs to be serviced or cleaned on the inside, take it to your local computer shop. (Find more about monitors in Chapter 1 of this minibook.)

+ **Use a cover for your scanner.** Scanners are somewhat different from most external peripherals. They don't generate any heat while they're on (unlike an external hard drive), and most of us use a scanner only once or twice a week. Therefore, your scanner is a perfect candidate for a cover that keeps it clean and dustfree — and, by no small coincidence, you can find this type of cover at your local office supply store.

Cleaning Your Mouse and Keyboard

"Natasha, why we must clean Moose and Squirrel?" (Sorry, I couldn't help it.) Mice and keyboards get *grimy* — *fast* — because your PC's keyboard and pointing device are continually in use, and they get pawed by human hands. (Of course, you could always wear surgical gloves, but what about your kids?)

Never fear. Here's a list of guidelines that help you keep your pointing device and keyboard clean and working:

+ **Buy an optical mouse or trackball.** (You'll thank me.) If you're still using an old-style mouse with a ball — how very 1980s — clean it once a month as well. Unscrew the retaining ring on the bottom, remove the mouse ball, and use a cotton-tipped swab dipped in tape-cleaning alcohol (which is 90+ proof and leaves no residue) to clean the rollers inside. Also, make sure that your mousepad is clean and dustfree to prolong the life of your rodent. (Chapter 1 of this minibook talks trackball.)

An optical mouse or a trackball doesn't need to be cleaned anywhere near as often (if ever) — that's why I keep crowing about them.

+ **Do the Keyboard Shake!** No, it's not a new dance craze, but it is the best method of cleaning accumulated gunk from your keyboard, and I recommend doing it at least once per month. Turn your keyboard upside down and shake it vigorously back and forth; prepare to be amazed (or grossed out, especially if the whole family uses your PC).

A number of manufacturers sell swabs pre-moistened with alcohol that work great for cleaning keys, and there are dusting contrivances especially made for keyboards that can help keep your keyboard pristine.

+ **Find *another* use for your compressed air.** Your keyboard can collect debris that can't be shaken free. If so, using compressed air will likely blow it free (unless it's alive and well dug-in, but I haven't encountered anything like that in my travels so far).

**Book IV
Chapter 3**

Maintaining Your
Hardware

Cleaning and Maintaining Your Printer

It's time to consider a peripheral that not only needs cleaning but can also contribute mightily to its own mess. If you've ever had to clean up spilled laser printer toner, I think you know what I mean. Printers have all the necessary features that make them prime targets for regular maintenance:

+ They're open to the outside world.

+ They're stuffed full of complex moving parts.

+ They're continually running out of ink or toner.

+ They act as magnets for dust.

In this section, I show you how to clean and maintain yon printing instrument.

Cleaning laser printers

Your laser printer contains a mortal enemy — *toner,* the insidious stuff that seems to have a diabolical mind of its own. Luckily, most cartridges are at least partially sealed, and only older models of laser printers can produce a really nasty Three Mile Island-level spill. If any toner escapes, however, you quickly find that the very fine powder is sensitive to static charges and immediately heads to every corner of your printer. Those nooks and crannies can be a real pain to clean. And, because toner can permanently stain clothing and carpet — *and* it's harmful to pets and kids — you should be doubly careful to keep toner inside the cartridge, where it belongs.

Therefore, please take the time to completely read the instructions for your specific laser printer before you install that first toner cartridge. Also, avoid shaking the cartridge unless the manufacturer recommends a particular motion to help distribute the toner evenly.

If you spill toner, head to your local office supply store for toner clean-up cloths. These handy wipes contain a chemical that attracts toner and keeps it on the cloth. Oh, and don't use warm or hot water to wash toner off your hands — toner can literally melt and adhere to your skin!

Never attempt to clean the interior of your laser printer while it's on! Laser technology uses very high temperatures to bond toner to paper, so you could be subject to serious burns if you're not careful. I always make sure that a laser printer has been off for at least 30 minutes before I clean or service it. For the same reasons, you should *always* follow the specific instructions for your brand and model of laser printer while cleaning its interior!

Changing inkjet cartridges

Here are two methods of determining when you need to change the cartridges in your inkjet printer:

✦ **The automatic route:** Most inkjet printers now on the market have onscreen alerts that appear whenever the ink level of the cartridge is low. Or, like you see in Figure 3-1, your printer might display the amount of ink remaining in a cartridge. (This trick is very valuable indeed, especially with a large print job looming.)

Figure 3-1: Checking the ink levels on late-model inkjet printers is a cinch.

✦ **The "Man, I can barely read this page!" method:** If you have an older inkjet printer, you might not receive any warning about the ink levels in your cartridges — but when they're empty, pardner, you'll know.

After you know that you need to change your cartridges, however, the general procedure is the same for virtually every inkjet printer I've ever encountered:

1. **Open the top of your printer.**

This step causes most printer models to politely center the carriage, to provide you with access to the cartridges. Or, there might be a button to press that centers the carriage.

2. **After you have access to the cartridges, turn off your printer.**

Never try to change the cartridges in a printer that's still powered on! Your fingers will thank me.

3. **Lift or turn the latches holding the ink cartridge in place.**

Most inkjet printers have at least two cartridges — one for black and one for color — so make sure that you're working with the right cartridge before you remove it.

4. **Remove the used cartridge.**

At this point, you can opt to refill the cartridge (I discuss the pros and cons of refilling later in this chapter) or replace with new.

5. **Load the full cartridge and fasten the latch to hold it down.**

6. **Turn your printer back on and close the lid.**

Before you count the job done, choose Start➪Control Panel and choose Devices and Printers, and then right-click on the printer and choose Printer Properties. You should see a Print Test Page button on the General tab of the Properties dialog box — it's always a good idea to run a test page to make sure that the cartridge swap went well!

Windows 7 offers a pretty comprehensive printer troubleshooting wizard from the Devices and Printers window as well. If you're having problems printing at any time, right-click on the printer and choose Troubleshoot to start the wizard.

Calibrating your printer

This maintenance task is reserved only for inkjet printer owners. (My, aren't we lucky?) *Calibration* refers to the proper alignment of the inkjet cartridge nozzles to both the paper and each other; without a properly calibrated printer, your print quality degrades over time. This is usually the problem when folks complain that lines appear fuzzy in artwork or when colored areas in printed images start or stop before they should.

If you hear a professional photographer or graphic artist talk about color calibration, that's something completely different; *color calibration* is the process of color matching between the colors that appear on your monitor and the colors produced by your printer. Most of us never need that level of precise color, and most inkjet printers now allow you to make changes to the hue and saturation of your prints by simply dragging a slider in a printer's Properties dialog box. But if you need to perform a full color calibration, check your printer's manual for more information about using Windows color profiles.

Your printer automatically calibrates itself when you first load a new cartridge, so I recommend that you calibrate either three months after installing a new cartridge or when you notice that your print quality is suffering — whichever comes first. (Of course, the period varies according to how often you use your printer and the length of your average printed document.)

Although each brand (and sometimes each model) of printer has different onscreen controls for calibrating output, you should be able to access them from the printer's Properties dialog box. (In Windows 7, choose Start⊏>Control Panel, choose Devices and Printers, right-click the printer, and then choose Printer Properties.) If the calibration controls still fail to appear, check your printer manual for the location of the calibration controls; some printer manufacturers provide a separate application that you can run to display your maintenance toolbox.

Follow the onscreen directions for your specific printer, and have a couple of pieces of plain paper handy.

Cleaning inkjet cartridges

Here's another fun task limited to just inkjet owners. I usually clean my inkjet cartridge nozzles about once every three months or whenever the output from my printer suddenly starts showing streaks of horizontal white lines. (As you probably can guess, the nozzles control the placement and amount of each droplet of ink.) The good news is that you don't need a bucket and a scrub brush for this chore; instead, your printer can take care of cleaning its own cartridges (with your approval, of course).

A new inkjet cartridge provides your printer with a brand-new set of nozzles, so you should restart that three-month period when you change cartridges. However, if you refill an inkjet cartridge — which I discuss in the next section — you should clean the cartridge nozzles immediately after the refilled cartridge has been reinstalled.

Like the calibration controls I discuss in the preceding section, the location of your printer's cartridge-cleaning controls is likely buried somewhere within its Properties dialog box, or else it's available when you run the maintenance program supplied by your printer manufacturer. To display the Properties dialog box for your printer, follow the procedure that I cover earlier.

Figure 3-2 illustrates the cleaning controls for my Epson inkjet printer. I just click the Head Cleaning button and wait about a minute, and I'm done.

Figure 3-2:
Preparing
to clean my
inkjet printer
nozzles.

Refilling inkjet cartridges

I'll be honest with you: I don't refill inkjet cartridges, and I don't recommend that you do, either. The only real advantage to refilling cartridges is the money you save over buying a new cartridge. As a fellow inkjet owner myself, I feel your pain when you're standing in the checkout line at Wal-Mart with a $40 cartridge in your hand.

However, here are the reasons why I buy new cartridges — consider these the facts that you *won't* see when that refill-kit TV commercial appears for the umpteenth time:

✦ **Mess:** Even if you're experienced at refilling an ink cartridge, there's a good chance that you'll end up with a toxic spill. Make sure that you cover your work surface with a plastic sheet and don't wear anything formal.

✦ **Substandard ink:** One of the reasons why ink refills are cheaper is that the quality of the ink used in the refill kits is usually never as good as the ink in a new cartridge. That second-rate ink can cause color changes or uneven coverage and might also end up taking longer to dry (resulting in Smear City).

✦ **Nozzle hassle:** I mention cleaning cartridge nozzles in the previous section. Unfortunately, those nozzles aren't meant to be reused, and refilling a cartridge can result in clogs. You have to clean your cartridges far more often, and the quality of your printer's output might drop appreciably over time when you use a refilled cartridge.

Thus, my decision and my recommendation: Let someone else suffer below-par print quality by refilling their used cartridges.

Book V

Office 2010

By Rich Tennant

"I've used several spreadsheet programs, but this is the best one for designing quilt patterns."

Contents at a Glance

Chapter 1: Introducing Office 2010 285

The Components of Office 2010.. 286
Putting the Office Clipboard to Work 292
Using the Office Help System 293

Chapter 2: Using Word. 297

Running Word 298
Typing, Selecting, and Editing Text 303
Finding and Replacing Stuff 306
Adding Bulleted and Numbered Lists 310
Applying Formatting.. 315
Printing Your Document 323

Chapter 3: Putting Excel to Work 325

Running Excel.. 326
Selecting, Entering, and Editing Cell Data 328
Working with Rows and Columns... 334
The Basics of Excel Formulas 340
Adding a Chart 344
Printing Your Worksheets 348

Chapter 4: Performing with PowerPoint 351

Getting Your Bearings in PowerPoint 352
Creating Slides 356
Installing Graphics in Your Slides 363
Using Movies and Sound... 367
Building and Running a Slide Show 369
Using Package for CD 372
Printing Your Document 374

Chapter 5: Doing Database Magic with Access. 377

Running Access.. 378
Creating Access Tables.. 380
Creating a Form with the Wizard... 381
Entering and Editing Fields Manually 385
Printing Your Data... 386

Chapter 6: Staying in Touch with Outlook 387

Running Outlook.. 388
Configuring Your Mail Account 390
Composing and Sending Messages 396
Using the Outlook Calendar 401

Chapter 7: Working with SkyDrive 407

Signing In to SkyDrive 408
Marking Your Own Territory and Adding Files 409

Chapter 1: Introducing Office 2010

In This Chapter

✔ Working with Word

✔ Using Excel

✔ Creating with PowerPoint

✔ Keeping track of data with Access

✔ Managing information with Outlook

✔ Working with the Office Clipboard

✔ Using the Office Help system

*I*ntroducing Microsoft Office 2010 is a little like introducing Beethoven's *Fifth Symphony:* We're all familiar with Office, we all think that it's a true work of art, and we all wish that we had the royalties (or, in Bill's case, the mound of cash generated by licensing).

That familiarity might be your ticket to skipping this chapter. For instance, most PC power users need no overview of Office; they know what it can do, what the different applications are used for, and how to access the Office Help system. Heck, chances are good that you're already using at least Word or Excel every day or that you already rely on Outlook to handle your e-mail and personal contacts.

But, just like the intricacies of Beethoven's masterpiece, there's a ton of substance to absorb within Office 2010 (along with a toolbar interface that's been completely overhauled in recent versions). Perhaps you've used only Word and you want to know what the rest of the stuff you paid for can do. Or, maybe you're brand-new to the PC scene and you just bought Office 2010. For folks who need a formal introduction to the rest of this minibook, I present to you this chapter — it provides a little information on each Office application so that you can pursue the more in-depth information in the later chapters. (**Note:** Although most Office applications changed dramatically in the Office 2007 version, most remain largely unchanged in Office 2010 with the exception of Outlook.)

The Components of Office 2010

Office 2010 is a suite of productivity applications, designed to help you easily produce a wide range of documents, crunch numbers, and communicate online, covering most of the tasks that you need to accomplish in a home or office environment. In this section, I describe each major Office 2010 application and provide you with an idea of what you can accomplish with each.

Note that you may also receive a number of companion applications, depending on the version of Office 2010 that you buy. The following table shows what apps come with which version of Office 2010. These apps include OneNote, Publisher, InfoPath, SharePoint Workspace, and Communicator. For a complete description of everything and all the arcane productivity possibilities within Office 2010, I heartily recommend *Office 2010 All-in-One For Dummies* by Peter Weverka (Wiley). (To prove just how monolithic Office 2010 can be, that book is as big as this one!)

Application	Home and Business	Professional
Word	Yes	Yes
Excel	Yes	Yes
PowerPoint	Yes	Yes
Outlook	Yes	Yes
OneNote	Yes	Yes
Access	No	Yes
Publisher	No	Yes

Word 2010

Microsoft Word, the world's best-selling word processor for Windows, is an institution these days. (You want to know just how ancient I really am? Your author remembers using the first DOS-based version of Word.) Think of Word as the foundation of Office 2010. You can see a typical Word window in Figure 1-1. Word is suitable for creating any kind of document, from a simple one-page letter to a book-length manuscript. Word also includes features designed for creating scientific, academic, and technical documents as well as powerful collaborative tools for workgroups.

Figure 1-1:
Gaze upon
the cultural
phenomenon
that is
Microsoft
Word.

Other important features that set Word apart include

✦ **Complete control over all levels of document formatting:** This includes
the appearance of everything in a Word document, from the character
level to the entire manuscript. (Believe me: Word can handle a book this
size without batting an eyelash.)

✦ **Sophisticated tables:** Gotta have 'em, and Word delivers — complete
with a wide array of sorting, numbering, shading, and border options.

✦ **Collaboration tools:** If you share editing chores on documents with
other people, you'll welcome the ability to highlight or use revision
marks. (This trick enables Word to track any changes with colored text
to show who did what and when. As a writer who works with editors, I
can attest that the "why" factor can prove a bit more nebulous.) You can
also compare two Word documents, add comments, and implement a
basic version-control system. Word documents can be write-protected
as well (to keep unnecessary fingers away from your work).

✦ **Spell-checking:** Whether you use the default spelling dictionary or
create your own custom dictionary, the Word spell-checking feature can
be a lifesaver. And, if you're looking for exactly the right word (or utter-
ance or remark or exclamation), you'll flip over the thesaurus.

✦ **Artwork and graphical tools:** Sure, you can use clip art, but you can also draw your own graphics or even add all sorts of 3D effects to titles, sidebars, and callouts.

✦ **Powerful macros:** Why type the same stuff or format the same text over and over? With Word's macro feature, you can automate all sorts of repetitive tasks — and it's easy to record a macro, too.

✦ **Printing:** Word can zoom or scale your printed pages and even collate longer documents. With plug-ins like Adobe Acrobat, you can also produce PDF files from within Word.

✦ **Advanced search and replace:** You can find and replace just about anything in a Word document. It even has an option to search phonetically, or you can search according to specific formatting. ("Hey, Earl, how can we find every italicized word in this 50-page list?")

For a more complete overview of Word, skip to the next chapter of this minibook.

Excel 2010

Microsoft Excel (see a window example in Figure 1-2) is much more than just a spreadsheet application. It's a regular jack-of-all-trades in the Office 2010 lineup, handling everything from a simple family budget to complex statistical and financial forecasting. Excel really comes into its own when a worksheet is linked with data in other Office documents.

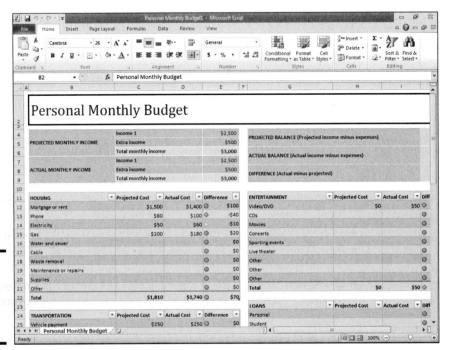

Figure 1-2:
If it's a worksheet, it must be Excel.

Excel offers support for

◆ **Lists:** Excel can generate (and automatically update) lists as you need them, or you can use the complete set of list tools to build your own from scratch.

◆ **Smart tags:** These tags are used to embed and link to all sorts of external data from within your worksheet — contacts, stock quotes, e-mail messages, and more.

◆ **Charts and reports:** If your data needs to be charted or you need to generate reports to your exact specifications, look no further than Excel!

◆ **Forms:** Offices all around the world rely on Excel for building customized forms. You can print them or complete them on-screen and save the worksheet for later use.

◆ **Formulas:** Excel provides task-based examples for common formulas and even includes an error-checking option that checks for potential problems with the formulas you create.

◆ **Functions:** You can use the predefined functions provided by Excel or use the recommendations provided by the Function Wizard. Excel even pops up the arguments for a function when you enter it!

Read through Book V, Chapter 3 for more on this handy application.

PowerPoint 2010

Slide-based and PC-based presentations used to be a business-only proposition, but many schools teach kids how to create their own presentations as part of their class work. PowerPoint, illustrated in Figure 1-3, is the king of the PC presentation applications, with dozens of predesigned templates and styles to help you deliver professional results. Plus, you can easily build a standalone, self-running presentation or a manual presentation. Presentations can be shared online as well.

Highlights of PowerPoint include

◆ **Easy-to-use design tools:** No graphical design experience is necessary when using PowerPoint. Even a normal human being can handle the placement of elements. Master slides make it easy to apply global changes across your entire presentation, too.

◆ **Presentation print preview:** Check out your entire presentation before you print a single slide. And, you can check out different layouts for notes pages and handouts.

◆ **Notes and handouts:** Use PowerPoint to easily produce notes for your reference or handouts that you can print for members of your audience.

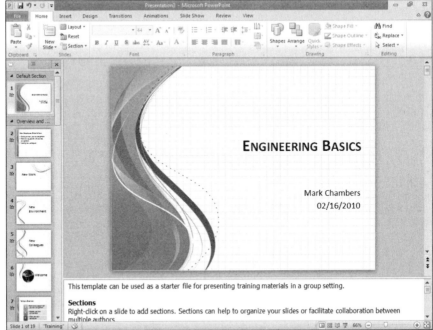

Figure 1-3:
Creating
a class
presentation
with
PowerPoint.

✦ **Support for multiple screens:** With multiple monitors, you can display a special Presenter view during your presentations. This separate display gives you easier control over the sequence of your slides and makes it easy to track the elapsed time.

✦ **Animation and transition effects:** Keep your audience interested in your message with animation on your slides and transitions between major sections.

✦ **Graphics control:** You can rotate or flip images, use the automatic layout feature to adjust the design when you insert objects, and display a grid when aligning elements on your slides.

For more on PowerPoint, see Book V, Chapter 4.

Access 2010

Access is the unsung hero of Office 2010 — if it's included in your edition. (I've encountered a number of experienced Office users who have never even *heard* of Access because they never used the Professional edition of Office.) However, when you tell folks what they can do with Access, they quickly become its most fervent supporters. You can create a database in just a few minutes, complete with reports, charts, and even Web pages that display data on demand. It's a helpful way to store whatever data is important to you — without requiring a degree in software engineering.

Top features of Access include

+ **Sophisticated error checking and validation:** Let Access double-check the data that's entered. You cut down on human error and help ensure the accuracy of your database.

+ **Connection with SQL servers:** If your business uses large-scale, corporate-level Structured Query Language (SQL) database applications, you can use Access to pull that information into your own database projects.

+ **Database encryption:** If you need to keep your databases secure, Access can encrypt the entire file automatically each time you use it.

+ **Customized queries and reports:** What's the use of keeping a database if you can't view that data intelligently? Define relationships that help define trends or predict problems.

+ **Web reports and database access:** Offer data from your Access files to others on your office intranet (or to anyone who connects to your Web site).

+ **Forms:** Build professional-looking data entry and special input dialog boxes that can collect information and act on that data automatically. (Hey, you're a database programmer now!)

Hone your database magic skills with Access in Book V, Chapter 5.

Outlook 2010

Ah, Outlook — no other single application has done so much for so many. (I know it's done a lot for my organization.) Outlook 2010 is a combination of an e-mail manager and a *PIM* (a rather ridiculous acronym that stands for *p*ersonal *i*nformation *m*anager), which keeps track of your contacts and your schedule. The full-blown Outlook 2010 that ships with Office 2010 includes

+ **Contact tracking,** which ties all Office documents and e-mail associated with a contact

+ **An event calendar, complete with daily/weekly/monthly views and an Outlook Today page to sum up today's chores**

+ **Appointment reminders,** which appear onscreen at the time you specify, to ensure that you don't miss The Big Date

Some of the top Outlook features include

✦ **Group scheduling:** Not only can Outlook handle your personal calendar, but you can also participate in a shared common schedule with others in your workgroup.

✦ **A truly awesome Find function:** Imagine being able to search all your e-mail messages, all your appointments, and all your scheduled tasks for the word *pickle* — well, for whatever *you* want, naturally.

✦ **Calendar coloring:** Mom always said, "If it's color coded, it's easier and faster to use." Evidently, the folks in Redmond agree because you can assign colors to appointments.

✦ **Support for Hotmail accounts:** If you use the Microsoft Hotmail Web-based e-mail service, Outlook can retrieve those messages for you.

✦ **Mailbox cleanup options:** It's a messy job, but you've got to do it — or do you? Outlook can automatically archive older messages, or you can manually clean your inbox according to the message date or size.

✦ **Onscreen reminders:** Let Outlook prompt you to attend that meeting or make that phone call. You can set reminders with an audible alarm or keep things quiet with an on-screen notification dialog box.

Discover how to stay in touch (and organized) with Outlook in Book V, Chapter 6.

Putting the Office Clipboard to Work

The *Office Clipboard* (shown in Figure 1-4, as it appears in Word) is essentially a supercharged version of the standard Windows Clipboard. It's specially designed to hold, display, and paste multiple items from one or more Office documents. For example, you can copy a text string from Access, an amount from an Excel spreadsheet, a contact name from Outlook, and even a company logo graphic from PowerPoint — and then copy all those items into a Word document.

You can display the Office Clipboard task pane at any time by choosing the Home tab (or the Message tab in Outlook) and clicking the Clipboard expansion icon. From within the Clipboard task pane, click the Options pop-up menu button.

Figure 1-4:
Collect
items from
several
Office 2010
applications
with the
Office
Clipboard.

When you display the Office Clipboard, anything you copy from the Edit menu (or with the Ctrl+C shortcut) is added to it rather than to the system Clipboard. After the copied material is on the Office Clipboard, you can right-click items to selectively paste or delete them (which you can't do from the other Clipboard). To paste all items at once, click the Paste All button in the task pane; to clear everything in one fell swoop, click the Clear All button.

Note that any items you add to the Office Clipboard stay there until you close all Office applications, and they aren't affected by the single item stored on the Windows 7 Clipboard. Now, *that*, my friends, is handy.

Using the Office Help System

No introduction to Microsoft Office 2010 would be complete without information on the excellent Office Help system, as shown in Figure 1-5. Believe me: The Help system is *especially* helpful in Excel and Access. For example, it can save your derrière when you need assistance with a complex formula or function in Excel!

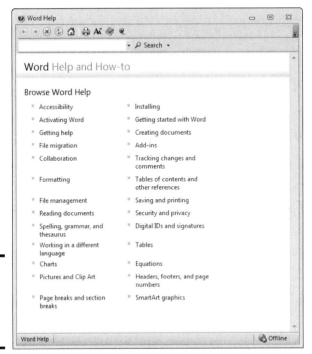

Displaying the Help system

To display the Office Help system for the Office application you're using, you can

- ✦ Click the question mark icon (upper right of the Ribbon; refer to Figure 1-4).
- ✦ Press F1.

The three controls of justice

From within the Help window, you can scroll down to the bottom of a Help screen and click one of the Office Online links to automatically open the Office 2010 Web site within Internet Explorer. There, you can download new clip art and document templates, check on the latest tips from Office experts, and search the Microsoft online Office Knowledge Base for answers to those persnickety questions.

Click in the Type Words to Search For box and type a short, specific question in honest-to-goodness English — or a choice keyword or two — and press

Enter (or click the Search button) to display links to matching Help topics. Yep, you guessed it: Underlined hyperlinks display additional information if you click them. (You can specify the resources to search by clicking the Search pop-up menu button, including Office Online and training courses.)

Click the Show Table of Contents button on the Help window toolbar to display the major topic within the Help system; then you can click a topic to jump to it. This technique is an excellent way to review a subject completely, like paragraph formatting in Word.

Book V
Chapter 1

Introducing
Office 2010

Chapter 2: Using Word

In This Chapter

✔ Starting Word

✔ Changing views in Word

✔ Typing and editing text

✔ Using Find and Replace

✔ Creating tables

✔ Setting tabs and margins

✔ Formatting your document

✔ Printing in Word

✔ Building Web pages in Word

*I*t's time to dive into Word (specifically, Word 2010), which is probably one of the top five most-used applications on the face of this planet. I first used Word when it was a character-based DOS program. (Yes, it's that old. And so am I.) Even then, it was easy to use and produced flawless printed pages — which, in my opinion, are the two all-important requirements for any word processor.

Word is now the cornerstone of most PC-based word processing; it's versatile enough to perform equally well for everything from a kid's homework to the most professional-looking yearly report. Therefore, this chapter starts with the basics — key shortcuts and the different views you can use in Word — and ends up delving into more advanced topics, such as collaborative features and Web page creation. If you're familiar with Word 2007, take heart: You'll be in calm waters, as the program hasn't changed much.

One note about this chapter (and the others in this Office minibook): As Popeye might say, "It ain't quite completes." A casual walk through any computer bookstore will convince you that a dozen 400-page books *completely* concentrate on Word (or Excel or PowerPoint or Access), so you don't find tons o' advanced features or tons o' complex tips in these 30-or-so pages. However, what you *will* find is good, solid coverage of the most commonly used Word features, and that's enough to take care of the vast majority of common documents you might require.

Running Word

Enough talk! To start Word, use one of the following methods:

+ Double-click a Word document within the Explorer window or on your desktop.

This is the only method for opening Word and an existing document at the same time. The next three methods open a new (blank) Word document, cleverly named Document1 (which you rename when you save the file). With Word open, to find an existing document, choose File⇨Open and then use the resulting Open dialog box to browse to the Word document you want.

+ Click Start (or press a Windows key, which looks like the Windows waving flag) and choose All Programs⇨Microsoft Office⇨Microsoft Word 2010.

+ Click Start and choose Microsoft Word 2010 from the Recent Programs list (if you used Word recently, that is) or from the Word 2010 Jump list.

+ Are you ready for a really fast trick? Press Windows key+R, type **winword**, and then press Enter. This sequence opens the Run dialog box, and *winword* is the executable name for Word. Whoosh!

As an author, I use Word more than any other application on the planet — except, perhaps, for *World of Warcraft*. Anyway, if you use Word every hour of your business day, add it to your taskbar, like I did. Choose Start⇨All Programs⇨Microsoft Office and then click and drag the Word icon to the taskbar. When the Pin to Taskbar pop-up appears, release the mouse button. *Voilà!* Now you can summon Word with a single click from the taskbar.

The Elements of Word

If Word isn't open yet, go ahead and run the Grand Dame now. After Word has churned its way onto the screen, you see the program's window, which should look something like the one shown in Figure 2-1. (I say "something like" because I customized my Word interface to my taste, which appears not to match the prevailing thought in Redmond. The default screen looks somewhat different.)

Although you probably know most of the guests invited to the party, you find some surprises if you used previous versions of Word. Here's a quick rundown of who showed up:

File tab

Quick Access toolbar

Tabs

Ruler

Command buttons

Minimize the Ribbon

Expansion icon

Ribbon

Figure 2-1:
One
application
to rule
them all:
the mighty
Microsoft
Word 2010.

Status bar

Editing window

◆ **The File tab:** It's blue and hard to miss, and it was designed that way. (If you're used to Word 2007, the File tab replaces that globe-y Office Button.) Click the File tab to access most of the commands you used to associate with the File menu, like New, Open, Save, and Print. (Some call this the *Backstage* view. Theatrics, I say.) Figure 2-17 at the end of this chapter illustrates the Print pane within the File screen. You also find new headings like Share and Info, each of which offers a subset of commands. The recent files you created and opened appear on the File tab's Recent menu. The Options command allows you to configure global settings within Word.

◆ **The Office Ribbon:** The Ribbon, introduced in Office 2007, is a dynamic, composite, tabbed toolbar. Unlike on an old-fashioned static toolbar, the command buttons you see change according to the group tab you click. (Tabs and command buttons? Read farther down these bullets, please.)

At least you can regain the screen real estate claimed by the Ribbon. Look for the Minimize the Ribbon button (below the Word window's Close button, and to the left of the Help button's question mark icon). When the Ribbon is minimized, all you see are the group names and tabs; if you click a group name, the Ribbon reappears while you're using the command buttons. To restore the Ribbon to its original, pristine state, just click the Minimize the Ribbon menu item again.

✦ **The Quick Access toolbar:** Call it a toolbar if you will (and that's generous), but Microsoft wants you to associate this group of buttons next to the File tab like pinned buttons on the Windows 7 taskbar.

To add or delete buttons from the Quick Access toolbar — which is helpful for often-accessed tools, or to reduce tab-hopping — click the arrow button to the right of the bar to display a pop-up menu. There, you can toggle the display of the most common command buttons. You can choose from a larger selection of command buttons by choosing More Commands from the pop-up menu.

Better yet, give the Quick Access toolbar more real estate by relocating it under the Ribbon (click Show Below the Ribbon).

✦ **The tabs:** Boy, howdy! A lot has changed at the top of the Word window since the early days of Word. Well, at least there's a menu — but wait, *is* that a menu? Actually, the items you see above the Office Ribbon are *group headings,* and each heading corresponds to a *tab* on the Ribbon. To switch to a different group, just click the desired tab, and the Ribbon "morphs" into a new set of command buttons. (In other words, it's kind of like a combination of a menu and a toolbar. For some old-timers, that's like cats and dogs living together.)

✦ **The command buttons:** Clicking a command button on the Ribbon does the same job as a familiar toolbar button or an old-fashioned menu command, by performing a task or displaying a submenu of additional commands.

Hey, did you notice those little down-facing arrows next to some of the command buttons? For example, click the Home tab, and you see arrows next to the font name and next to the Find button. Well, bucko, those aren't there by accident — in fact, they indicate that you can click the arrow to display a drop-down list or pop-up menu of choices. You also notice that many section names (at the bottom of the Ribbon) have tiny, square icons with arrows pointing toward the right corner. Click one of these *expansion icons,* and — *voilà!* — the group is expanded to a separate floating window, making it much easier to see more controls and more choices. (You may not need to expand a group often, because the most common choices are displayed as command buttons, but when you do, it becomes second nature to opt for that window!)

✦ **The editing window:** This window is where all the real work takes place. Type your text here and add graphics, tables, and all sorts of specialized tomfoolery.

✦ **The ruler:** Use the Word ruler to keep track of page dimensions and also to set tabs and margins. (Read more on this in the later section "Adjusting Tabs and Margins.")

✦ **The status bar:** You find all sorts of statistics on the status bar, including the number of pages in your document and the number of words in the document. (To customize the status bar, just right-click it; a pop-up menu appears, allowing you to toggle the display of items on and off.) Also, you can use the buttons to the right side of the status bar to change the view mode and zoom level. Come to think of it. . . .

A Word about Views

Speaking of views, Word can display your document in more than just one mundane way. You can switch between views by clicking the View tab on the Ribbon and then clicking the desired view in the Document Views group, or you can click the view buttons on the right side of the status bar. Take a gander at this selection of views.

Draft view

Draft view is your plain vanilla, default viewing mode (refer to Figure 2-1). However, I find Draft view to be the quickest to use when I'm typing or when I'm editing an existing document. ***Note:*** What you see in Draft view definitely might *not* be what you get when you print, so switch to Web Layout or Print Layout view to edit the appearance of a document. And use Print Preview (choose File⇨Print) to check the appearance of the printed pages before you send them to the Monster of Toner. The last button among the view icons on the status bar selects Draft view.

Outline view

In Outline view (check it out in Figure 2-2), the structure of your document is the important thing, much like the outlining you learned in grade school. Outline view allows you to change and rearrange the sections of your entire document (except that this time, you get to use a click of the mouse rather than that doggone eraser). Click the symbol next to any heading and drag it to a new spot — just release the button to drop the section at the insertion point. Headings and sections of body text can also be reassigned to different levels by clicking the symbol next to the heading and dragging it to the left (to promote it) or to the right (to demote it). You can select Outline view by clicking the fourth button in the view icons on the status bar.

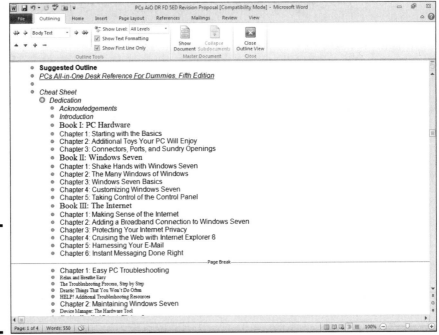

Figure 2-2:
Hey, an
outline
that I really
like, for a
change!

Print Layout view

I recommend switching to Print Layout view when you need to design the
look of your page because you can easily work with page elements, such as
columns and graphics, by clicking and dragging them from place to place.
(You can also click most elements and drag their borders to new locations.)
If you're familiar with desktop publishing programs like Adobe InDesign,
you'll feel right at home in Print Layout view. Click the first tiny button in the
view icons on the status bar to switch to Print Layout view.

Web Layout view

Of course, there's the Internet side of things. In Web Layout view, Word adds
any background you specify, places images where they will appear in a Web
browser, and wraps the text to fit the window size. You can use this view to
design a document that's saved later as a Web page. Click the third button in
the view group on the status bar to use Web Layout view.

Full Screen Reading view

Full Screen Reading view is specially designed to make your document easy
to read onscreen. (Call this view the E-Book Special, if you like.) Pages
appear one at a time, like a book, and the page is automatically sized to fit

virtually the entire application window. (Note that the page does *not* appear this way when it's printed!) Word also turns on Microsoft's ClearType font-smoothing feature, to help make the text easier on the eyes — and personally, I think it works. Because the Highlighter and Comment features are still active in Full Screen Reading view, it's easier to use the Word revision and markup tools, too. Click the second button in the view group on the status bar — which looks like an open book — to use Full Screen Reading view; to return to the previous view, press Esc or click the Close button.

The new Navigation pane offers major convenience for moving quickly through large documents. Just choose View and select the Navigation Pane check box to have Word open a separate pane on the left side of the editing window (as shown in Figure 2-3). To close the Navigation pane, just click the Close button (which bears an X) in the pane's title bar. You can move immediately to any heading within your document by clicking it within the Navigation pane. (Users of earlier versions of Word will recognize Navigation pane as an evolved version of the Document Map feature.)

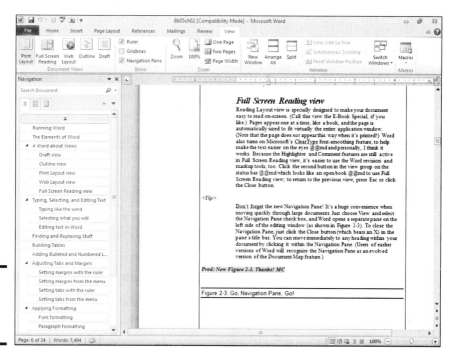

Figure 2-3:
Go,
Navigation
pane, go!

Typing, Selecting, and Editing Text

Ready to start your first foray into the editing window? In this section, I discuss the three all-important things that you do most often during your Word session: type new text, select existing text, and edit existing text.

Typing like the wind

Okay, I know this seems like a no-brainer — and typing in Word is indeed simple. First, locate the insertion cursor (which looks like a blinking bar) where you want in the editing window (by clicking the mouse pointer, which looks like a tiny I-beam, or by using the movement keyboard shortcuts listed in Table 2-1). Tickle the ivories to enter your text.

Press Insert (on the keyboard) to toggle *Overwrite mode,* in which the new characters you type overwrite any existing text; to return to *Insert mode,* in which new characters are inserted at the cursor point, press the Insert key again.

Table 2-1	Movement Shortcut Keys in Word
Key	*Where It Moves the Cursor*
Left arrow (←)	One character to the left
Right arrow (→)	One character to the right
Up arrow (↑)	To the preceding line
Down arrow (↓)	To the next line
Ctrl+←	One word to the left
Ctrl+→	One word to the right
Ctrl+↑	One paragraph up
Ctrl+↓	One paragraph down
Page Up	Up one screen
Page Down	Down one screen
End	To the end of the current line
Home	To the beginning of the current line
Ctrl+Page Up	To the top of the previous page
Ctrl+Page Down	To the top of the next page
Ctrl+Home	To the beginning of the document
Ctrl+End	To the end of the document

Selecting what you will

My father always used to say, "Nothing is perfect the first time around" — and a Word document is no exception. However, don't break out the Liquid

Paper for your screen! Instead, use the mouse to select text or graphics by clicking and dragging the I-beam cursor across the text you want to change or format, or use the selection keyboard shortcuts provided so conveniently by Table 2-2.

To select a word, just double-click it; to select a graphic, click it once. To select a chunk of text (even several pages worth), click to place the insertion cursor at the start of the text you want to highlight and then hold down Shift while you click at the end of the desired text.

Table 2-2	Selection Shortcut Keys in Word
Key	*What It Selects*
Shift+A	Entire document
Shift+←	One character to the left of the cursor
Shift+→	One character to the right of the cursor
Shift+↑	Characters to the previous line
Shift+↓	Characters to the next line
Shift+End	Characters to the end of the current line
Shift+Home	Characters to the beginning of the current line
Shift+Page Down	Characters to the next screen
Shift+Page Up	Characters to the previous screen
Ctrl+Shift+←	Characters to the beginning of the word
Ctrl+Shift+→	Characters to the end of the word
Ctrl+Shift+↑	Characters to the beginning of the current paragraph
Ctrl+Shift+↓	Characters to the end of the current paragraph
Ctrl+Shift+Home	Characters to the beginning of the document
Ctrl+Shift+End	Characters to the end of the document

Editing text in Word

After you select the text and graphics you want to change, you can then pick an action (either from the Ribbon or by right-clicking) or use one of the editing keyboard shortcuts shown in Table 2-3.

Table 2-3	Editing Shortcut Keys in Word
Key	*What It Does*
Any character	Replaces the selected text
Delete	Deletes the selected text and graphics
Ctrl+X	Cuts the selection and adds it to the Clipboard (or the Office Clipboard, if it's displayed)
Ctrl+C	Copies the selection to the Clipboard (or the Office Clipboard, if it's displayed)
Ctrl+V	Replaces the selection with the contents of the Clipboard

If you're not familiar with the Office Clipboard and its features, read more about it in Chapter 1 of this minibook.

Finding and Replacing Stuff

I don't know about you, but manually tracking down every single occurrence of the word *salacious* in my Word documents is not my idea of fun! (Okay, perhaps not *salacious* — substitute your own most common word.) Anyway, Word provides you with the dynamic duo of Find and Replace, which ensures that no word or phrase in your document can escape your all-seeing eye.

To perform a Find or Replace operation, follow these steps:

1. **Click the Home tab and then click Replace (in the Editing group). (From the keyboard, press Ctrl+H.)**

The Find and Replace dialog box appears, which you can see in Figure 2-4. Note that this dialog box floats above the Word window. And, unlike with other active dialog boxes, you can continue to click, select, and type in the Word window while the Find and Replace dialog box is open.

If you opt for Find instead of Replace (also in the Home⇨Editing group), Word eschews the Find and Replace dialog box and displays the Navigation pane instead, complete with a search text box ready for you to enter the text you're looking for.

For this example, I'll stick with the Find and Replace dialog box.

2. **Type the word or phrase that you need to locate or change in the Find What text field.**

If you've already run a search for the same target string earlier, click the down arrow next to the box and select it from the drop-down list.

Figure 2-4:
Substituting
salacious
with *demure*
is child's
play with
Replace.

3. **To replace any matches with something new, type the word or phrase that you want to substitute in the Replace With text field.**

   Again, if you already used the new value to replace something earlier in this writing session, just click the down arrow and choose a value from the drop-down list.

   (Optional) Click the More button, and then click the Special button to display a pop-up menu of special and nonprinting characters that you can insert at the cursor position in the Find What or Replace With boxes. For instance, if you need to search for (or replace using) a graphic, a Tab character, or a caret character, you can pick it from the Special button menu.

4. **To find the next occurrence, click the Find Next button; to replace the next occurrence, click the Replace button.**

   You can also click the Replace All button to locate and replace all occurrences of the word or phrase. However, I recommend clicking Replace one time first, just to make sure that you're indeed matching what you think! If the correct word or phrase is replaced, click Replace All to finish the job.

   You can immediately use Undo after any Word action goes awry. In this case, if you suddenly find that you replaced every *the* in your document with *thee* by accident, choose the Undo button on the Quick Access toolbar or use the Ctrl+Z keyboard shortcut.

5. **If you used Find Next or Replace in Step 4, Word selects the next occurrence.**

   You can continue your Find or Replace activities, or you can click Cancel if you're done.

That's the mundane side of Find and Replace. However, if you click the More button at the bottom of the Find and Replace dialog box (which toggles the More button to Less), you see all sorts of interesting options that can help you fine-tune your search, including

✦ **Match Case:** By default, Find and Replace are case-insensitive toys —
select this check box to make capitalization matter.

✦ **Find Whole Words Only:** When this check box is deselected, Word
matches portions of a word, which comes in handy when changing
tenses, prefixes, or suffixes. To force Word to match only the exact
string you entered, select this check box.

✦ **Use Wildcards:** A throwback to the days of DOS, *wildcards* allow you to
search for specific combinations of letters or numbers in your target
strings. Unix folks call this *pattern matching.* (Check the Word Help
system for a complete list of wildcards.)

✦ **Sounds Like:** If you know what the target word sounds like but you can't
spell it, select the Sounds Like check box, and Word locates matching
words that sound the same. For example, *role* matches *roll.*

✦ **Find All Word Forms:** Select this check box to locate all forms of the
target noun or verb — tenses, plurals, and such. Trick, indeed!

To perform a search based on any sort of formatting (such as character or
paragraph formatting or a specific language within your document), click the
Format button and then select the appropriate type of formatting from the
pop-up menu that appears.

Building Tables

Tables are great for displaying, well, tabular information. (Stunning stuff,
Mark.) But that information need not be uniform, and you can add all sorts
of eye candy (like shading and different types of borders).

Follow these steps to add a standard table to your Word document:

1. **Click within your document to place the insertion cursor in the
   desired spot for the table.**

2. **Choose Insert⊅Table to display the pop-up menu you see in Figure 2-5.**

   For a simple table, just move your mouse pointer over the grid to "mark"
   the number of rows and columns to insert, and then press the mouse
   button. Now you can skip to Step 5.

   If you need more control over your table characteristics, choose Insert
   Table from the same pop-up menu to display the Insert Table dialog box.
   Click in the Number of Columns text box and type the number of columns you need in the table, and then click in the Number of Rows text
   box and type the number of rows you need in the table.

Figure 2-5:
Inserting a
table into
a Word
document,
using the
grid.

3. **Select the AutoFit Behavior option that you prefer from the Insert Table dialog box.**

   The default, Fixed Column Width, is fine if all the values that the table will hold will be uniform in length; however, I recommend that you choose AutoFit to Contents if you need to save space in your document or if certain values are far longer than others. If you're creating a Web page, select AutoFit to Window.

4. **Click OK in the Insert Table dialog box to create the basic table structure, as shown in Figure 2-6.**

5. **Click in each cell and type the value.**

   You can apply the same formatting attributes to the text in a table cell, too. For example, I select the top row of a table and then press Ctrl+B to create bold column headings.

This procedure provides you with a basic table. Select the table itself and right-click it, and then choose Borders and Shading from the pop-up menu that appears. You'll be amazed at all the fun fashions you can use to decorate that simple frame! You can change the type, width, and color of the border, for instance; or click the Shading tab and choose your own colors, shading, and patterns (either for the entire table or just for the cells you select). In fact, you'll notice that Word adds the Table Tool tabs to the Ribbon after you've created a table, where you can tinker with table specifics — I'm all for convenience!

Figure 2-6:
A new table,
ready for
your values.

Adding Bulleted and Numbered Lists

Creating bullets and numbered lists automatically in Word is a cinch. Follow these steps:

1. **Click anywhere within the paragraph you want to format.**

2. **Click the Home tab.**

3. **In the Paragraph group, click the drop-down arrow button next to the Bullets button to view the available bullet formats, or the drop-down arrow button next to the Numbering button to view the available numbering formats.**

   Figure 2-7 illustrates the Bullet Library pop-up menu.

4. **Click the type of bullet or number formatting you want to apply to the paragraph.**

   To apply the same format again to another paragraph, simply click the Bullets or Numbering button — no need to choose the same format again!

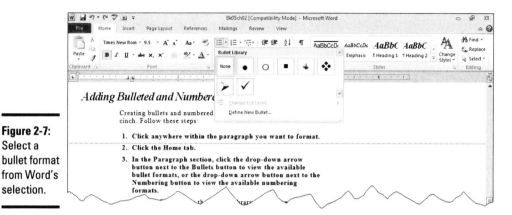

To use your own bullet graphic, change the text positions, or use a character from a favorite font, click the Define New Bullet item at the bottom of the Bullets pop-up menu. (Naturally, the same goes for the Define New Number Format item at the bottom of the Numbering pop-up menu.) Figure 2-8 illustrates the Define New Bullet dialog box that appears.

You can also use the Multilevel List button and corresponding pop-up Library menu in the Paragraph section to create lists, and the Decrease Indent and Increase Indent buttons (which hang out in the same area) to alter the position of the text by a tab stop each time you click them.

Adjusting Tabs and Margins

Call them throwbacks to your typewriter days, but tabs and margins are still with us. After all, these two settings are largely responsible for the appearance of your pages — and how much text and graphics each page can hold.

Word respects these two elders by providing multiple methods of setting tabs and margins; in this section, I show you how to configure tabs and margins by using both your mouse and your keyboard.

Setting margins with the ruler

Follow these steps to set up margins by using Word's horizontal and vertical rulers:

1. **Change to Print Layout view (click the Print Layout button on the status bar or click the View tab and choose Print Layout).**

2. **Move your mouse cursor over the end of either of the shaded bars on the ruler.**

   These bars indicate the current margin, and the mouse pointer turns into a twin-arrow cursor to indicate that the bar can be moved (as shown with the right margin in Figure 2-9).

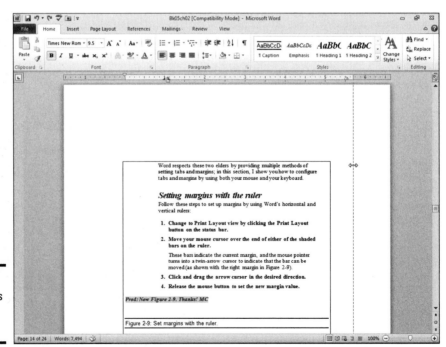

Figure 2-9:
Set margins with the ruler.

3. **Click and drag the arrow cursor in the desired direction.**

4. **Release the mouse button to set the new margin value.**

Setting margins from the Ribbon

Follow these steps to set margins from the Page Layout tab of the Ribbon:

1. **Click the Page Layout tab on the Ribbon, and then click the expansion icon of the Page Setup group to display the Page Setup dialog box, which you see in Figure 2-10.**

Figure 2-10:
Setting
margins
from the
Ribbon.

2. **Click in the appropriate Margins text box (for the margin you want to change) and then type the desired value in inches.**

3. **Click the arrow of the Apply To drop-down list and then select Whole Document.**

   To apply margin changes to just a part of the document, select some text before opening the Page Setup dialog box and then choose Selected Text from the Apply To drop-down list. If you want the margin change to apply to the remainder of the document starting at the current position of the insertion cursor, choose This Point Forward instead.

4. **Click OK to save your changes and return to your document.**

Setting tabs with the ruler

Word offers several different types of tabs, including left, center, right, and decimal- or bar-aligned. To add a tab stop with the ruler, follow these steps:

1. **Click anywhere within the paragraph where you want to place the tab.**

2. **Click the Tab button in the upper-left corner of the editing window. The button appears on the left side of the ruler (looks like a capital L in a square) — until you select the type of tab you need.**

   To check the current tab type, just leave your mouse pointer hovering on top of the Tab button until the tooltip description appears.

3. **Click the spot on the ruler where you want to place the tab.**

To help you keep track of your tab, Word automatically adds a tab stop mark (it looks like the old-fashioned tab pointer on your trusty manual Olivet type-writer) on the ruler.

Setting tabs from the Ribbon

Follow these steps to set a tab stop from the Page Layout tab of the Ribbon:

1. **Click the Page Layout tab on the Ribbon.**

2. **Click the Paragraph group expansion icon, and then click the Tabs button at the bottom of the Paragraph dialog box to open the Tabs dialog box, shown in Figure 2-11.**

Figure 2-11: Hey, isn't Tab an antique diet cola?

3. **Click in the Tab Stop Position field and then type the position of the new tab stop in inches.**

4. **Select an Alignment option.**

5. **To add a leader to the new tab stop, select one of the Leader selections.**

   A *leader* is a character that's used to fill the open space that normally appears when you press the Tab key. Leader characters are often used in a table of contents, telephone list, or restaurant menu.

   Word sets the default tab stops to every half inch; to choose a new default value for tab stops, click in the Default Tab Stops field and type the new value (in inches).

6. **Click the Set button to set the new tab.**

7. **To clear a tab stop, click the tab stop that you want to remove within the list on the left and then click Clear.**

   Or you can clear all tab stops in one fell swoop by clicking the Clear All button.

8. **Click OK to return to your document.**

Applying Formatting

Word offers a number of different formatting commands. At its lowest level, you can manually format individual characters by changing their attributes. At its highest level, you can set Word to automatically format your document while you type! In this section, I describe how to fine-tune your formatting.

Font formatting

You probably already know the trio of attributes that I like to call The Big Three:

+ **Bold:** Press Ctrl+B to add emphasis to the selected text.

+ *Italic:* Press Ctrl+I to italicize the selected text.

+ <u>Underline:</u> Press Ctrl+U to underline the selected text.

Of course, each of The Big Three is represented by a separate button on the Ribbon — specifically, the Font group of the Home tab (**B**, *I*, and <u>U</u>). But there's a heck of a lot more font formatting where that came from — you can also add these attributes to selected text:

+ **The font family:** (No relation to the Addams Family.) Click the expansion icon for the Font group to display the Font dialog box, which you see in Figure 2-12; then click the font name you want to use. (Alternatively, click the Font drop-down list in the Font section. This way, you're treated to a visual preview of each font installed on your PC.)

Figure 2-12:
The Font
dialog box
is a busy
metropolitan
location.

✦ **The size:** Click to select a font size (in points) from the Size list or type the size you want directly into the Size text box.

✦ **The color:** You can click the Font Color drop-down list to choose the latest fashion color for your text.

✦ **The standard effects:** Select check boxes in the Effects section to enable effects, and Word automatically updates the Preview window with the results.

✦ **The spacing:** Click the Advanced tab and then choose the amount of space between characters, or you can raise or lower the characters by the amount that you specify. Word shows you the fruit of your labor in the Preview window.

Note that you don't need to select text to use font formatting. If no text is specifically selected, Word simply applies your font changes to any new text you type at the current location of the insertion cursor.

Paragraph formatting

Word is a consistent machine. And, as you might expect, formatting a paragraph is quite similar to formatting individual characters. Note, however, that not every separate text element on a page is a true paragraph; to qualify, the text block must end with a paragraph mark, which is represented by that weird backward *P* symbol, our friend, the pilcrow (¶).

Because Word normally hides formatting marks (like pilcrows), you probably don't see any paragraph marks in your document unless you specifically tell Word to display them. You can do this by clicking the Home tab and clicking the Show/Hide command button (which brazenly carries that same funky backward-P paragraph mark). Personally, I like to be able to see where my paragraphs come to a halt because I do quite a bit of formatting on manuscripts (and it makes a great difference whether you select a paragraph *with* or *without* the paragraph mark)!

Commonly used paragraph formatting attributes include

✦ **Alignment:** Click the Home tab, and then click the expansion icon of the Paragraph group to display the Paragraph dialog box, which you see in Figure 2-13. Click the Alignment drop-down list box, and you see that Word can align text to the left or right margin or center the paragraph on the page. You can also choose to *justify* a paragraph, which adds extra spacing to stretch each full line in the paragraph from the left to the right margin.

✦ **Indentation:** As I show you in the earlier section "Adding Bulleted and Numbered Lists," you can automatically add bullets and line numbers to your text. From the Paragraph dialog box, you can specify the amount to indent the selected paragraph as well as which kind of indent to use.

✦ **Spacing:** Click the Line Spacing drop-down list box in the Paragraph dialog box to choose double spacing or to specify a precise line spacing of your own choosing. This is also the place where you can add extra space before or after a paragraph.

Figure 2-13:
Need to
format a
paragraph?

These commands are also conveniently located as command buttons in the Paragraph group of the Home tab.

AutoFormatting

Before I leave the fair shores of formatting, I want to mention a well-known "either you love it or you hate it" feature. I'm talking about the Word *AutoFormat* feature, which — true to its name — automatically recognizes what it feels should be formatted and then takes care of the task for you — whether you want it to or not. To illustrate: If you type an asterisk at the beginning of a line and press Enter at the end, AutoFormat figures, "Oh, that crazy human actually wants a bulleted list item" and thus formats the paragraph with an indent and a bullet character and then adds another bullet for your next item. The same thing happens with numbered lists, too. Try typing **1.** at the beginning of the line and pressing Enter, just to see the results.

Don't get me wrong: If you're a newcomer to Word or you don't need precise control over the formatting in your document, AutoFormat can be a true timesaver and a big help. (Pause.) However, if you *do* need that precise formatting control, AutoFormat suddenly becomes a nightmare when you're forced to helplessly watch Word do what it *thinks* is right.

Therefore, here's how to disable AutoFormat — which is on by default — just in case you find it nerve-wracking rather than helpful:

1. **Click the File tab and then click the Word Options button at the bottom of the menu.**

2. **Click the Proofing heading on the left, and then click the AutoCorrect Options button.**

3. **Click the AutoFormat as You Type tab to display the settings shown in Figure 2-14.**

4. **To completely disable AutoFormatting while you type, deselect all check boxes and then click OK.**

   Note that you can still run AutoFormat on your entire document at once at any time — it just takes a little work because you have to add an AutoFormat button to the Quick Access Toolbar (as I discuss at the beginning of this chapter).

5. **Click OK to save your changes.**

(You can bet that I didn't use AutoFormat to create this numbered list, either. Harrumph.)

Figure 2-14:
No, Word!
Bad
AutoFormat!
No biscuit!

Adding Graphics

You have a number of different ways to add graphics to your Word document. After you click in the desired spot (which moves the insertion cursor to that point in your document), use one of the following methods:

+ **Paste it from the Clipboard.** If you copied a graphic to your Windows or the Office Clipboard (which I discuss in Chapter 1 of this minibook), you can paste it to the current cursor location.

+ **Insert it from a file.** If the graphic is stored on your hard drive, click the Insert tab and click the Picture command button in the Illustrations section. Word displays the familiar Insert Picture dialog box, from where you can navigate to the location of the image. Click once on the filename to select it and then click the Insert button.

+ **Insert a clip art image.** Click the Insert tab and click the Clip Art command button in the Illustrations section to display the Insert Clip Art panel. Type a keyword in the Search For text box, click the Search In drop-down list, and then choose All Collections. Click the Search button to display thumbnail images of any matching clip art. As you can see in Figure 2-15, I'm not the only person who loves Halloween!

Doing the Collaboration Thing

Word includes several features for managing collaborative documents — keeping things straight about who revised what or perhaps adding comments and highlighting to indicate where changes are necessary.

Need to share the information in your Word document with data-mining or database applications? You'll be happy to learn that Word 2010 can save a document in Word XML (Extensible Markup Language) format using the standard Save As command (on the File tab). Choose Word XML Document from the Save as Type drop-down list.

Using revision marks

If several editors have their hands in a single document, revision marks are the only way to go. Everyone can make changes (Word assigns different colors to each editor), and those changes can be reviewed and applied (or discarded) individually, or you can accept or revert all changes at once.

To use revision marks, click the Review tab and click the Track Changes command button. Now you've told Word to track anything that anyone does within the document. Nothing appears to happen — at least, that is, until you make any change to the document. Continue typing or editing as you like. Word formats with a unique color the changes you make, underlining them to make things easier to see. Deleted text and graphics are shown with the strikethrough attribute.

When you're ready to review the revision marks in a document, click the Review tab again to display all your revision tools. Click either the Accept Change button (which carries a blue check mark) or Reject Change button (which bears a red X), and you move through your document. (For just a second, you feel like you have the ol' Caesar thumb — you know, the one that Caesar gets to use in any gladiator movie.)

Just in case you don't quite have the power of Caesar, you can always save the revised document under another filename before you decide for or against the edits. (Even a Roman emperor could use a little insurance.)

To accept in one fell swoop all changes made with revision marks, click the down arrow under the Accept button to display the drop-down list and then click Accept All Changes in Document. To toss out all those silly edits, click the arrow underneath the Reject Change button and then choose Reject All Changes in Document. The *nerve* of some people, tampering with perfection!

Using comments

In this section, take a look at *comments,* which allow anyone to flag a document without directly changing its contents. To add a Comment, select the text you want to comment on, and then click the New Comment button on that now-familiar Reviewing tab.

In Print Layout view, Word displays a color marker at the word or point where you made the comment and displays a comment bubble, which you see on the right side of Figure 2-16 in the markup area. The insertion cursor is also automatically relocated in the Comment bubble, so you can type your comment text, which is marked with the name of who added the comment as well as when (date and time). When you're done, click anywhere in the editing window to continue.

When you're ready to review comments, you can

✦ Review the comments in a document by using the Next Comment and Previous Comment buttons in the Comments group of the Review tab. (They appear next to the New Comment button.)

✦ Hover your mouse pointer on top of the highlighted comment marker in the text.

✦ Double-click the shaded header in the markup area, which automatically switches Word into Print Layout view and displays the comment.

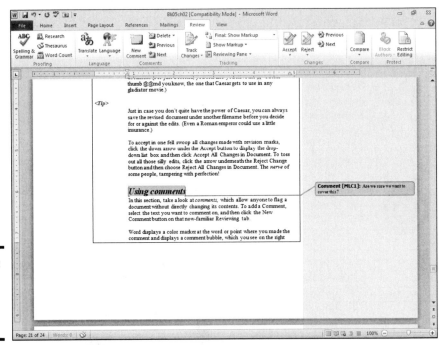

Figure 2-16:
Editors just
love that
Comment
bubble.

Of course, you can't "apply" a comment, but you can delete those that
offend. Just click anywhere in the commented text and then click the Delete
Comment button — which bears a red X — on the Review tab (or just right-
click the Comment marker in the text and then choose Delete Comment from
the pop-up menu that appears).

Using highlighting

Ever wish that you could turn back the editing clock to paper and those
classy neon yellow highlighter markers you used in school? Fear not: Word
can take you there. Follow these steps to highlight text in your documents:

1. **Click the Home tab on the Ribbon, and then click the Text Highlight
Color button (in the Font group). (It looks like a fat, smelly marker
with the letters *a* and *b* perched on top.)**

   - *To select a color:* Click the down arrow next to the Highlight button
   and then click a color.

   - *To erase previous highlighting:* Click None.

2. **Select the text to highlight.**

3. **When you're done highlighting, turn off the feature by clicking the
Highlight button again.**

Alternatively, you can first select the text that you want to be highlighted and then click the Highlight button. The Highlight button also appears on the pop-up menu when you right-click selected text.

Printing Your Document

Word offers you two different ways to print an open document:

✦ **Choose File➪Print.** The Print pane, which you see in Figure 2-17, gives you full control over what gets printed and which printer you use — including the number of copies and the option to print only part of the document. (To display the printer-specific options supported by the printer's Windows 7 software driver, click the Properties button.)

✦ **Press Ctrl+P.** This method also displays the Print pane.

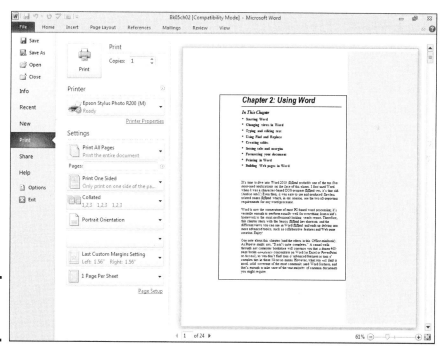

Figure 2-17:
The Word
Print pane.

Creating Web Pages with Word

In a pinch, Word even can step in as a serviceable Web page creation tool! After you create a document, follow these steps to turn that document into a Web page:

1. **Choose File➪Save As➪Web Page.**

2. **Click the Change Title button, type a title for this page, and click OK.**

3. **Navigate to the spot where you want to save the file and then type a new filename for the page.**

   You don't need to. add a HyperText Markup Language (HTML) extension because Word does it automatically.

4. **Click Save.**

   Word creates an HTML page and a separate folder that contains any graphics necessary to display the page; all you have to do is move both to your Web server.

Because some of the advanced formatting you can use in Word doesn't translate at all to a Web page, the application does the best job it can. But at least you can rely on Word to produce a Web page that loads in virtually every browser on the planet.

Chapter 3: Putting Excel to Work

In This Chapter

✔ Running Excel

✔ Presenting the Excel window

✔ Typing, selecting, and editing cell text

✔ Handling numbers and dates

✔ Manipulating rows and columns

✔ Formatting cells in Excel

✔ Understanding Excel formulas

✔ Inserting graphics and charts

✔ Linking cell values

✔ Adding headers and footers

✔ Printing worksheets

xcel is *scary*.

There, I said it. Most Office 2010 users know that Excel is one doggone powerful and versatile tool, but it has a reputation for being difficult to learn. (Not to mention all those strange, foreign-looking formulas and functions — heck, I can barely remember my long division. And don't even get me started on my kid's math homework.)

In this chapter, however, I can help you with that common Excel-phobia that grips the novice who runs Excel for the first time. I show you the basics of selecting cells and entering cell values, manipulating rows and columns, formatting numbers and dates, and adding graphics. And yes — believe it or not — I get you started on the road to understanding and using formulas to calculate the values you need. After all, that's the real power behind Excel — plugging in values to see what happens.

As Thomas Edison, a personal hero of mine, never said, "After Excel formulas are your friends, the world is your oyster." (Then again, he certainly *could* have said it, and perhaps no one was around to write it down. Yeah, that's it.)

Running Excel

You can start the number-cruncher that is Excel in any of the following ways:

✦ Choose Start (or press a Windows key)⇨All Programs⇨Microsoft Office⇨ Microsoft Office Excel 2010.

✦ Click Start and choose Microsoft Office Excel 2010 from the Recent Programs list (assuming that you had Excel open recently).

✦ Double-click an Excel document in Windows Explorer or on your desktop.

✦ If you added an Excel icon to your Windows 7 taskbar, click it.

✦ Press Win+R, type **excel** in the Run dialog box that appears, and then press Enter. (That's assuming that your keyboard is equipped with Windows keys, which look like the waving Windows flags and are located on either side of the spacebar.)

Waltzing Around the Excel Window

The Excel main window (as shown in Figure 3-1) has one immediate drawback, and Microsoft has never really been able to address it: Excel simply looks complex from the moment you start it! However, don't be intimidated by all those cells. When you take a second look, the familiar Office controls are still there.

Although you know most of the screen controls by heart, here's a refresher:

✦ **File tab:** The File tab is the proud replacement for the short-lived Office Button of Office 2007, with many menu items you'll recognize. Recent documents you created and opened appear on the File tab menu, and you find an Excel Options button that leads to global settings you can change that affect all of Excel.

✦ **Quick Access toolbar:** By default, this group of buttons next to the File tab includes Save, Undo, and Redo commands, but you can click the Customize button next to the Quick Access toolbar to add or remove command buttons.

✦ **Office Ribbon:** No, it's not a toolbar, but it does have buttons — and they change when you click a group tab at the top of the Ribbon.

Note that the Excel Office Ribbon includes a unique field called the *Formula bar,* where you can type a formula for a cell or view a formula that's already associated with the selected cell. (More on formulas later in this chapter.)

✦ **Sheet tabs:** These nifty tabs allow you to jump among worksheets and charts in the Excel window. Just click a tab to switch to that worksheet.

Figure 3-1:
The Excel
2010 main
window.
Glorious!

File tab

Quick Access toolbar

Tabs

Command buttons

Ribbon

Sheet tabs

Active cell   Formula bar

Editing window   Status bar

View buttons

Zoom control

✦ **Editing window:** Each individual square in the editing window is a *cell*, which can hold text, numbers, tables, and graphics.

✦ **Status bar:** The Excel status bar displays information about calculations and the contents of cells.

Before I launch into a discussion of cells, however, let me clear up a common misunderstanding among novice Excel users concerning the difference between a workbook and a worksheet:

✦ **Workbook:** A *workbook* acts just like a file folder in a filing cabinet, storing all the worksheets required for a single project. Because a workbook acts as the container for worksheets, it's the file you're working with when you create a new project or when you load and save in Excel (and is featured in the task pane for that reason).

✦ **Worksheet:** A *worksheet* is what you use to enter data, graphics, and charts. You can create a new worksheet inside the current workbook at any time. To switch worksheets in the current workbook, use the sheet tabs.

Selecting, Entering, and Editing Cell Data

As I mention earlier, a *cell* is one individual block within a worksheet, and it can hold a number of elements:

✦ Numeric values

✦ Text

✦ Graphics

✦ Formulas and functions (used to calculate new values)

In this section, I show you how to select one or more cells, enter data into a cell, and edit existing cell data.

Filling a cell to the top

To enter data in a cell, just click it and begin typing. The cell changes into a data entry box, as shown in Figure 3-2. After you're done entering data, press Enter (to move one cell down) or Tab (to move one cell to the right). See there — I told you it was easier than it looks, didn't I?

Later in this chapter, I discuss the Formula bar, which is another method of entering stuff — in this case, a formula — in a cell.

Moving around the worksheet

An Excel worksheet can grow to absolutely momentous proportions. And, even at the highest screen resolutions, you're still limited to using the same onscreen space as in any other Office document. Therefore, your scroll bars are *very* important controls in Excel; use them often and in good health.

You can also use a number of keys and keyboard shortcuts to get to the right place in your worksheet, as shown in Table 3-1.

Figure 3-2:
To enter
data into
a cell, just
click and
type.

Table 3-1	Movement Shortcut Keys in Excel
Key	*Movement*
Left arrow (←)	Moves the cursor one cell to the left
Right arrow (→)	Moves the cursor one cell to the right
Up arrow (↑)	Moves the cursor one cell up
Down arrow (↓)	Moves the cursor one cell down
Home	Moves the cursor to the beginning of the current row
Ctrl+Home	Moves the cursor to the beginning of the active worksheet
Ctrl+End	Moves the cursor to the last cell in the worksheet with a value
Page Down	Moves down one screen
Page Up	Moves up one screen
Alt+Page Down	Moves one screen to the right
Alt+Page Up	Moves one screen to the left

(continued)

Table 3-1 *(continued)*

Key	Movement
Enter	Moves the cursor one cell down (also works within a selection)
Tab	Moves the cursor one cell to the right (also works within a selection)
Shift+Enter	Moves the cursor one cell up (also works within a selection)
Shift+Tab	Moves the cursor one cell to the left (also works within a selection)
Ctrl+arrow key	Moves the cursor to the corresponding edge of any range containing data

Selecting cells the easy way

This section talks about selecting one or more cells, which you do before performing an action on the entire group. You can use the following mouse actions to select cells in Excel:

- ✦ **To select a *single* cell:** Just click it.

- ✦ **To select a *range* of multiple adjacent cells:** Click a cell at any corner of the desired cells and then drag the mouse in the desired direction.

- ✦ **To select *multiple nonadjacent* cells:** Hold down Ctrl while you click them.

- ✦ **To select a *column* of cells:** Click the alphabetic heading button at the top of the column.

- ✦ **To select a *row* of cells:** Click the numeric heading button to the left of the row, or press and hold Shift while pressing the arrow keys.

You can also select a graphic by clicking it once. Table 3-2 illustrates how to select cells from the keyboard.

Table 3-2	Cell Selection Shortcut Keys in Excel
Key	What It Selects
Ctrl+spacebar	All cells in the current column
Shift+spacebar	All cells in the current row

Key	What It Selects
Ctrl+A	All cells in a worksheet
Shift+←	One cell or column to the left (depending on the current selection)
Shift+→	One cell or column to the right (depending on the current selection)
Shift+↑	One cell or row above (depending on the current selection)
Shift+↓	One cell or row below (depending on the current selection)

Of course, you can also use your mouse or keyboard to select existing data in a cell:

+ **With your mouse, double-click the cell, and it again changes into a text-editing box.** You can then click and drag to select characters for editing, just like you do in Word.

+ **With your mouse, click to select the cell and then click on the Formula bar to edit the contents.** I discuss the Formula bar in more detail later in the chapter.

+ **From the keyboard, select a cell and then press F2.** You can use the keys and shortcuts shown in Table 3-2 to select the contents for editing.

Editing cell contents

After you select some data, you can choose an action from the toolbars or the menu system or use one of the editing keyboard shortcuts (also shown in Table 3-3).

Table 3-3	Cell Editing Shortcut Keys in Excel
Key	What It Does
Shift+←	Selects one character to the left of the cursor
Shift+→	Selects one character to the right of the cursor
Shift+End	Selects characters to the end of the text
Shift+Home	Selects characters to the beginning of the text
Any character	Replaces the selected text
Alt+Enter	Starts a new line within the same cell

(continued)

Table 3-3 *(continued)*

Key	What It Does
Delete	Deletes the selected text or the character to the right of the insertion cursor
Ctrl+Delete	Deletes the text to the end of the line
Ctrl+X	Cuts the selection and adds it in the Clipboard (or the Office Clipboard)
Ctrl+C	Copies the selection to the Clipboard (or the Office Clipboard)
Ctrl+V	Replaces the selection with the contents of the Clipboard
Esc	Cancels the edits made to a cell

Working with Numbers and Dates

Excel includes the font formatting basics on the Office Ribbon Home tab — which I cover in a bit — but you also need to familiarize yourself with a different type of formatting that's unique to spreadsheet, statistical, and financial applications. It's called *number formatting,* and it controls the appearance of all sorts of numbers, including

+ Dollar amounts
+ Dates
+ Times
+ Telephone numbers
+ Zip codes
+ Social Security numbers

The characteristics that specify a particular number format include

+ The number of decimal places that appear
+ The notation that represents negative numbers (a minus sign or parentheses)
+ Whether a comma placeholder separator appears in the numbers
+ Whether a number carries a dollar sign or a percent sign

Excel provides a whopping 11 different number-formatting categories. Or, if you like, you can go a little wild and create your own custom format that can be applied whenever necessary.

To specify a number format, follow these steps:

1. **Select the cells that you want to format.**

2. **Click the *expansion icon* — the little square with an arrow emerging from the lower-right corner — next to the Number group heading of the Home tab.**

Alternatively, keyboard types can simply press Ctrl+1 (the number 1). Either way, you see the Format Cells dialog box, which you see in Figure 3-3.

By default, Excel uses the General format for cells, which basically means that they have no specialized number format.

Figure 3-3:
Apply number formats to selected cells.

3. **On the Number tab, click the formatting category you need. For example, if you're working with dates, click Date.**

Excel displays the different format types for the category you select as well as a sample of how the formatted numbers will appear.

4. **If you need number formatting for a specific geographic location, click the Locale drop-down list (if applicable) and pick the right spot on the planet.**

This field only appears with the Date, Time, and Special categories.

5. **Click the type of formatting you need from the Type list.**

   Again, this field might not appear for some format types.

6. **Click OK to apply the formatting and return to your worksheet.**

By the way, the General number format often works for a simple whole number. Excel displays up to 11 digits, but a decimal counts as a digit; for example, the numeral *11.11* counts as five digits. Excel then uses scientific notation for values more than 11 digits (or those too big to fit in the cell). I don't know about you, but my puny budget doesn't even *begin* to strain 11 digits.

Working with Rows and Columns

I won't lie to you: Every Excel worksheet is a haven for rows and columns. (No big surprise there.) However, you're definitely not constrained to the default arrangement of cells, and you can even insert rows and columns in an existing worksheet, if necessary. In this section, I show you how to take charge of your troops.

Resizing rows and columns

Changing the dimensions of any row or column is easy — and often a requirement when adding a longer line of text or when you need to display multiple lines of text in a cell.

To resize, follow these steps:

1. **Move the mouse pointer on top of either divider line at the desired row or column heading.**

   The mouse pointer turns into a bar with opposing arrows to indicate that you're in the right spot.

2. **Click and drag to reposition the dividing line (see how this looks in Figure 3-4).**

   To make the job easier, Excel displays a pop-up menu that tells you the new height (for rows) or width (for columns).

3. **Release the mouse button when the row or column is at the desired dimension.**

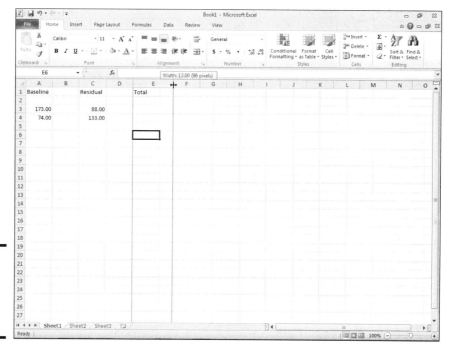

Figure 3-4:
Resizing
rows and
columns is
a cinch.

Inserting blank cells

You can plug new blank cells into a worksheet at any point. Follow these steps:

1. **Select a range of cells.**

   Note: You have to select the same number of cells that you want to insert. For example, if you want to insert two cells at a point in your worksheet, you should select two cells at that location.

2. **Click the Home tab on the Ribbon, click the Insert button in the Cells group, and choose Insert Cells.**

   Excel displays the Insert dialog box, as shown in Figure 3-5.

3. **Choose which direction the selected cells move by selecting either the Shift Cells Right or the Shift Cells Down radio button.**

   Alternatively, select the Entire Row or the Entire Column radio button to shift the row or column, respectively, containing the selected cells.

4. **Click OK.**

Figure 3-5:
Preparing
to insert a
passel o'
cells.

Inserting cells from the Clipboard

You can also insert cells with what you cut or copied from another spot.
Follow these steps:

1. **Cut or copy the desired cells by using the keyboard shortcuts Ctrl+X or Ctrl+C, respectively.**

2. **Select the cell in the upper-left corner of the desired location.**

3. **Click the Home tab on the Ribbon, click the Insert button in the Cells group, and choose Insert Cut (or Copied) Cells.**

   These menu items appear immediately after you cut or copy cells.

   Excel displays the Insert Paste dialog box (see Figure 3-6).

4. **Select either the Shift Cells Right or the Shift Cells Down radio button to determine in which direction Excel moves the adjoining cells.**

5. **Click OK.**

Figure 3-6:
Inserting
cells that I
copied.

Inserting rows and columns

To insert one or more rows or columns in your worksheet, follow these
steps:

1. **Click any cell in the row below (or the column to the right) of the desired spot.**

   Inserting multiple rows or columns works just like inserting multiple
   cells: You need to select the same number of rows or columns that you
   want to insert.

   2. **To insert rows, click the Home tab on the Ribbon, click the Insert button in the Cells group, and then choose Insert Sheet Rows.**

   3. **To insert columns, click the Insert button in the Cells group and choose Insert Sheet Columns.**

Formatting in Excel

Excel includes the standard font formatting that you expect from an Office application, but you also find that you can modify a number of unique attributes for cells, rows, and columns. In this section, I explore the basic formatting tricks you can pull.

Font formatting

Like in Word, you can easily apply the Big Three font attributes from either the toolbar or a keyboard shortcut:

   ✦ **Bold:** Press Ctrl+B to add emphasis to a selected cell's contents.

   ✦ *Italic:* Press Ctrl+I to italicize a selected cell's contents.

   ✦ <u>Underline:</u> Press Ctrl+U to underline a selected cell's contents.

To apply other font attributes to selected cells, click the expansion icon next to the Font section heading of the Home tab to display the Format Cells dialog box. Excel displays the standard font settings you see in Figure 3-7 — they include the font family, size, color, and standard effects.

Figure 3-7:
Excel provides all sorts of font fun.

Cell alignment

Click the Alignment tab of the Format Cells dialog box, and you see the settings shown in Figure 3-8.

Figure 3-8:
Modify the alignment attributes of selected cells here.

In this dialog box, you can

✦ Change the horizontal and vertical alignment of the characters in selected cells.

✦ Specify the indent for the contents of a cell.

✦ Modify the orientation of cells by clicking and dragging the Orientation control. (Hey, dig those crazy angles!)

✦ Choose to wrap text to fit cell dimensions or shrink the text to fit the size of the cell.

✦ Change the right-to-left or left-to-right direction of text in the cell.

Unless you specify otherwise, Excel always aligns numbers, dates, and times to the right edge of a cell. Negative numbers are preceded by a minus sign or are enclosed with parentheses; a single period is recognized as a decimal point. By default, text is displayed as left aligned within a cell.

Changing borders and shading

Need to add a kick to certain cells to make them stand out, like a heading or a total? Click the Border tab of the Format Cells dialog box to display the settings shown in Figure 3-9.

Figure 3-9:
Doggone
it. That cell
needs a
border.

From this tab, you can

✦ Choose a line style and color.

✦ Specify no border, a standard outline border, or an inside grid.

✦ Design a custom border by using the buttons. (Excel displays the effects
of your work in the Border preview window.)

Open the Colors drop-down list to display the familiar color selector you see
in Figure 3-10. You can choose a color from the palette, or click More Colors
and go a little wild by creating your own custom color.

Figure 3-10:
Selecting a
border color
is child's
play.

To quickly and easily change the appearance of a selection, click the Home tab and click one of the predefined Style command buttons in the Styles group. To display all the available styles at once, click the More button at the lower-right corner of the Styles group. You'll find titles, headings, and all sorts of common styles like my two favorites: Bad and Good!

The Basics of Excel Formulas

Okay, talking about spreadsheet formulas might give you the creeps. (I know that it's not a favorite topic around my dinner table.) However, it's important to understand how to enter formulas correctly in Excel, or else you end up with a lot of cells stuffed full of data and nothing else.

A single cell in a worksheet can hold

+ **Constants:** Text or numbers that you type into a cell yourself
+ **Formulas:** Calculations based on the contents of specific cells and ranges of cells

Formulas in Excel start with an equal sign (=), so they're easy to spot. Also, a formula typically includes a cell reference, like F3 (which stands for the current value in the cell located at column F, row 3).

Examples of simple formulas include

+ **=A1–125** instructs Excel to subtract 125 from the value in cell A1.
+ **=C9/B4** instructs Excel to divide the value in cell C9 by the value in cell B4.

See? All that math you studied was worth it! Formulas always include at least one operator, which in the previous examples are the minus sign (–) and the division sign (/).

Excel calculates formulas in sequence from left to right, following the equal sign (just like you and I were taught in school). However, you might need to force a calculation to be performed out of order within a formula, and you can do it with parentheses. To illustrate, I expand on the original example:

$$=50*(A1-125)$$

Without the parentheses, the contents of cell A1 would be multiplied by 50 first, and then 125 would be subtracted from that total. With the parentheses, however, Excel first subtracts 125 from the value in A1 and then multiplies that total by 50.

To insert a formula in a cell, follow these steps:

1. **Click in the cell that should hold the formula.**

It also displays the calculated value, so this is usually the cell that displays a total or the final value.

2. **Type an equal sign (=) to alert Excel that you're going to enter a formula.**

3. **Type the remainder of the formula and then press Enter.**

You can also click your mouse pointer in the Formula bar and enter the formula there. As you can see in Figure 3-11, the Formula bar always displays any formula that you enter in the selected cell.

Figure 3-11:
You can
enter or
check a
formula
in the
Formula
Bar.

If you change a number in a cell that's used in a formula, the value of the cell containing the formula is automatically changed to reflect the new number. Suppose that I add the formula

=A1+B1

in cell C1 of my trusty worksheet. If I put the number 1 in cell A1 and the number 5 in cell B1, cell C1 shows — anyone? Yes, you there — that's right! Cell C1 contains the number 6. However, if I change the number in A1 to 3, C1 is automatically updated with the number 8 because the formula now calculates 3 + 5 and returns the number 8.

With just the simple basics I outline in this section, you can build a home budget or a mortgage calculator. But then again, why not use the built-in templates provided by Excel? Click the File tab and then click New to open the window you see in Figure 3-12.

Help

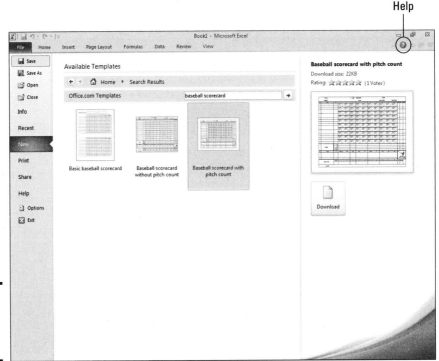

Figure 3-12:
Save time
with Excel
templates.

Click one of the categories under the Microsoft Office Online heading. (You need an Internet connection, of course.) You can choose from dozens of templates for all sorts of Excel projects online — all free, ready for your downloading pleasure. After you locate the apple of your template eye, double-click the template thumbnail to create a new worksheet, complete with snappy formatting, predesigned formulas, and built-in instructions!

For example, you find all sorts of task-oriented Excel templates that were specifically created to help with chores, such as

✦ Remodeling your kitchen

✦ Maintaining a checkbook register

✦ Tracking stock values and quotes

✦ Billing clients and customers

✦ Keeping an allergy log

✦ Planning a baby shower

✦ Generating a grocery list

I told you that this program was versatile!

To search for a specific template — did someone say *baseball scorecard?* — click in the search box and type a keyword or phrase to match. (Refer to Figure 3-12.)

 Excel also offers another important resource that you can use when pondering formulas: the Excel Help system. It's but a click away, compliments of the question mark icon in the upper-right corner of the window. To search for a specific need — such as calculating the days remaining before a date — type a short question or phrase into the Search box, like **budget totals**, and then press Enter. To see the list of commonly used formulas, click the Formula and Name Basics link on the top-level category list.

Of course, formulas (and their siblings, *functions,* which are predefined formulas that use arguments taken from cell values) can get *very* hairy *very* quickly. (There's a lot more to do with a powerful spreadsheet than just add two numbers.) Because I have limited elbowroom here, I must move on. However, I can recommend the best-selling and oh-so-very complete *Excel 2010 Bible*, by John Walkenbach (Wiley), for an all-out tour of everything Excel.

Working with Graphics in Excel

Your worksheets aren't limited to text. As in any other Office 2010 application, you can import pictures with aplomb. Click the cell at the upper-left corner of where the graphic should be located, and then

✦ **Paste it from the Clipboard.** After you copy an image into the Clipboard by pressing Ctrl+C, you can press Ctrl+V to paste the graphic into your worksheet from your Windows or Office Clipboard.

✦ **Insert it from a file.** To insert a graphic file from your hard drive, click the Insert tab on the Ribbon and click the Picture button. Navigate to the location of the image and click the filename once to select it, and then click the Insert button.

✦ **Insert a clip art image.** Click the Insert tab on the Ribbon and click the Clip Art button to display the Clip Art task pane. Type a keyword in the Search For text box and click the Include Office.com content check box to enable it. Click Go to display thumbnail images of any matching clip art. When you find the image you're looking for, click it to insert it into your worksheet.

As you can see in Figure 3-13, Excel doesn't give a hoot about limiting an inserted graphic to specific cells, rows, or columns. Just use the resizing handles around the border of the image (also visible in Figure 3-13) to change the dimensions of the image. Click and drag a handle to expand or contract the image. To move the image, click in the middle of the image and drag it any which-way.

Figure 3-13:
No rows or
columns
can hold
this tiger!

Adding a Chart

Another hit among the Excel crowd is the *chart,* which can present your precious data in the easy-to-digest fashion that we all crave in our digi-frenetic, Internet-straddled, talking-head world. (Easy, Mark. Sorry about that.)

Social commentary aside, you have two choices for displaying charts:

✦ **A separate *chart sheet* within the current workbook:** Your chart gets its own fantabulous tab — pun gleefully intended, seeing as how I'm strung out on Diet Coke — and you can display it at any time, just like any other worksheet.

✦ **An *embedded object* within a worksheet:** The chart acts like a picture to be relocated and resized, just like any other graphic.

No matter which type of chart you decide to use, your journey begins with the Excel Chart Wizard. Follow these steps to add a chart:

1. **Select the cells containing the data you want to include in the chart (with column and row labels, if you created any).**

2. **Click the Insert tab, and then click the expansion icon of the Charts group. Excel displays the Insert Chart dialog box, which you see in Figure 3-14.**

Figure 3-14:
The Insert
Chart dialog
box struts
its stuff.

3. **Click the desired chart type from the list on the left.**

   The wizard updates the subtype thumbnails on the right. (No need to stick with the boring column, bar, or line chart — try a cone or pyramid or even a doughnut chart! Mmm . . . doughnuts.)

   You can always change the chart type at any time — just right-click the chart and choose Change Chart Type from the pop-up menu.

4. **Click OK to embed the chart as a graphic in your worksheet.**

   Whoa! Check out what happened to the Ribbon: Excel adds three new tabs, grouped under the Chart Tools "super" tab. (See upcoming Figure 3-16.)

   • *Design tab:* Click to select a color scheme using the thumbnails here.

   If you want to create a chart sheet rather than an embedded chart, click the Move Chart button on the Design tab to display the Move Chart dialog box (Figure 3-15). You can name your chart sheet, or even switch a chart sheet back into an embedded chart.

Figure 3-15:
Will that
chart be
embedded
or on a
separate
chart sheet?

- *Layout tab:* Add labels and a legend to your chart.

  You can also customize the axis for your chart, and add gridlines if necessary.

- *Format tab:* Adjust the shapes of your chart elements.

  You can use fills and effects to jazz up elements as well.

5. **When the chart is finished, click outside the chart to return to your worksheet.**

Figure 3-16 illustrates an embedded sheet I created within a worksheet.

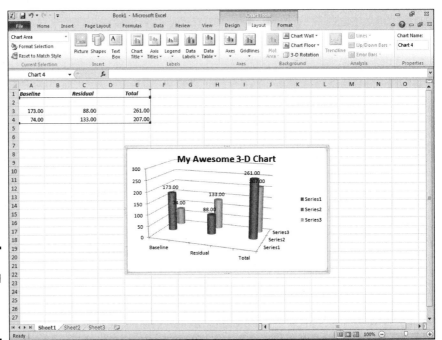

Figure 3-16: A completed chart in embedded form.

Linking Cells

Another powerful feature that's a big favorite with Excel power users is the ability to link values. That is, when one value changes in one of the cells, it's automatically updated when you display the other cell! For example, if cell A1 is linked to cell E3 on the same worksheet, whatever value you place in cell A1 automatically appears in cell E3.

To create a link between cells on the same worksheet, follow these steps:

1. **Select the cell that contains the data you want to link to another cell.**

2. **Press Ctrl+C.**

3. **Click the cell that you want to link to and then press Ctrl+V to paste the value.**

Excel displays a pop-up icon next to the cell when you press Ctrl+V.

4. **Click the pop-up icon to display the menu you see in Figure 3-17 and then select the Paste Link button.**

Figure 3-17:
Link cells
from the
Paste
pop-up
menu.

Paste Link

Adding Headers and Footers

When printing a worksheet, headers and footers can contain quite a bit of valuable identifying information. And that's from someone who has waded through a year's supply of printed personnel worksheets from a midsize company.

To add headers and footers to the active worksheet, follow these steps:

1. **Click the Page Layout tab, and then click the expansion icon of the Sheet Options group.**

2. **Click the Header/Footer tab of the Page Setup dialog box to display the settings you see in Figure 3-18.**

3. **Click the Header drop-down list and choose a predesigned header.**

4. **Click the Footer drop-down list and choose a footer.**

5. **Click OK to save your changes and return to the worksheet.**

Figure 3-18:
Add standard headers and footers to a worksheet.

Click the Custom Header or the Custom Footer button to get all artistic and design your own header or footer format. (Check it out in Figure 3-19.) Click to place the insertion cursor in the proper section — the left, center, or right section of the design — and then click the template buttons to insert the preformatted elements that you want to add, like the time or date. (You can also type your own text rather than use a template.) When your header or footer is set up as you like, click OK to return to the Page Setup dialog box.

Figure 3-19:
Create a custom header and footer here.

Printing Your Worksheets

When you're ready to print the active worksheet in Excel, click the File Tab and click Print for a preview. From there, you can select from multiple printers, print multiple copies, or print only specific pages from the worksheet. Click the Printer Properties link to set any printer-specific options supported by the printer's Windows 7 software driver.

To print with the cell grid, click the Page Layout tab — under the Sheet Options section, and select the Print Gridlines check box. (You can also choose to turn off the row and column headings from this section.)

To print just the contents of certain cells in your worksheet, select the cells first before you display the Print settings and then click the Print Active Sheets button. Click the Print Selection entry in the pop-up menu that appears.

After you're satisfied that you'll get what you expect, use one of these methods to start the printing process:

+ **Choose File➪Print➪Print.**

+ **Press Ctrl+P.** This method also displays the Print settings, just as if you had chosen Print from the File tab.

Book V
Chapter 3

Putting Excel to Work

Chapter 4: Performing with PowerPoint

In This Chapter

✔ Working with the PowerPoint window

✔ Changing views in PowerPoint

✔ Importing and inserting slides

✔ Adding text and graphics

✔ Using templates and schemes

✔ Adding movies and sound to slides

✔ Creating a slide show

✔ Choosing transitions between slides

✔ Using Package for CD

✔ Printing in PowerPoint

*N*eed a slide show? How about a set of professional-looking transparencies for that overhead projector? Have no fear; Microsoft Office PowerPoint 2010 is here! PowerPoint has always been easy to use — including a slew of graphically gorgeous templates to use, and the ability to add movies, and transitions, and CD-quality audio, and — whoops, I'm getting a little ahead of myself.

In this chapter, I provide you with the basics of PowerPoint to show you how to accomplish the most common tasks. If you're brand-spanking-new to the program, you see how to spice up that blank slide with text and graphics, and I also show you the power-user keyboard shortcuts to use in PowerPoint. If you're already familiar with the PowerPoint window, you also find out how to create a package for CD and add all sorts of spiffy transitions to your slide shows.

Naturally, I can't provide The Last Word on PowerPoint 2010 in the space I have — there's too much power to cover in a few dozen pages, if you'll forgive my pun — but I can heartily recommend *PowerPoint 2010 For Dummies,* by Doug Lowe (Wiley), if you need a comprehensive guide.

Getting Your Bearings in PowerPoint

You can run PowerPoint in a number of different ways:

✦ Choose Start⇨All Programs⇨Microsoft Office⇨Microsoft PowerPoint 2010.

✦ Click the shortcut on your Windows 7 taskbar, if you pinned the program there.

✦ Click Start and choose Microsoft PowerPoint 2010 from the Recent Programs list (if you've used PowerPoint 2010 lately).

✦ Double-click a PowerPoint project file.

✦ Press Win+R, type **powerpnt** in the Run dialog box that appears, and then press Enter. (This assumes that your keyboard is equipped with Windows keys, which look like waving Windows flags and are located on either side of the spacebar.)

When you first run PowerPoint, the application's main window looks remarkably simple (as shown in Figure 4-1), especially when you contrast it with the rather frightening appearance of Excel 2010. You quickly find, however, that this program is no pushover. The digital-and-silicon equivalent of a '05 Dodge Magnum is lurking behind the curtain! (Yep, I'm extremely proud of my family muscle car.)

In lieu of formal introductions, here's a quick guide to what you see onscreen:

✦ **File tab:** Like in the other Office 2010 programs, the PowerPoint File tab holds most of the commands you associate with that outdated File menu. It also displays the recent documents you created and opened, as well as an Options button (where you can make changes to the global settings that dictate how PowerPoint behaves).

✦ **Quick Access toolbar:** Another now-familiar old friend, the Quick Access toolbar sports Save, Undo, and Repeat buttons. To tweak the bar, click the Customize button next to the Quick Access bar — you can add or remove command buttons to your heart's content.

✦ **Office Ribbon:** The Office Ribbon replaces the toolbars you probably remember from PowerPoint 2003 and earlier. The command buttons that you see change when you click a group tab at the top of the Ribbon.

✦ **Editing window:** You design your slides here, adding graphics and text and moving slide elements around the layout guide. The editing window also does double duty in other view modes, which I discuss in a bit.

File tab

Quick Access toolbar

Tabs

Command buttons

Ribbon

Figure 4-1:
PowerPoint
is a
graphical
muscle
car —
really!

Outline pane   Editing window   Status bar

Slide pane

Normal View | Slide Show

Reading View

Slide Sorter View

+ **Ruler:** Get a grip on dimensions. You can also use the ruler as a guide when placing objects on your slides. The Ruler check box appears on the View tab.

+ **Slide and Outline panes:** Click either tab to switch between a numbered thumbnail display of the slides in your presentation (the Slide pane) or a display of the text on each slide in outline format (the Outline pane). The Slide pane helps you navigate quickly — you can simply click a thumbnail to jump to that slide. The Outline pane helps you organize your presentation.

You can also click the vertical scroll bar in the editing window to move through the slides in your presentation.

+ **Status bar:** Like other Office applications, PowerPoint has one of these, too. It displays information about your current view as well as information relating to the selected slide or pane.

Each pane within the PowerPoint window can be adjusted. For example, if you don't need the Slide pane at the moment, move the mouse pointer over the border between the Slide pane and the editing window until it turns into those nifty opposing arrows, and then click and drag to enlarge the editing window.

Changing Views

You can view the PowerPoint application window in a number of different views. In this section, I give you the details on the ones you use most often.

Normal view

Normal view, which is the default in PowerPoint, is the best view for adding and editing text and graphic objects. You can display your slides in Normal view by clicking the View tab on the Ribbon and clicking the Normal button. (Alternatively, click the Normal View button on the right side of the PowerPoint status bar. 'Nuff said.

Need to see what your elegant color slides will look like when printed on a monochrome laser printer? Click that very same View tab, and then click the Grayscale command button in the Color/Grayscale group (or go monochrome crazy and click the stark Black and White command button). When you and Toto are done, return to the Land of Oz by choosing the Color command button from the same group.

Slide Sorter view

Figure 4-2 illustrates Slide Sorter view, where the slides in your presentation are arranged in a larger, easier-to-see format. It's not just the scenery that's important, however: You can also click and drag thumbnails to move them and reorder the flow of your presentation. You can also right-click a slide to delete it or to add a completely new slide (a helpful feature when you've forgotten to include something).

To switch to Slide Sorter view, click the View tab on the Ribbon and then click the Slide Sorter button in the Presentation Views group. From the status bar, click the Slide Sorter View button.

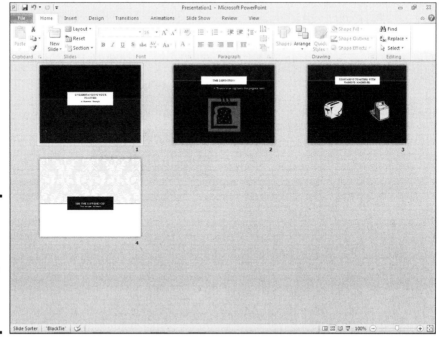

Figure 4-2:
Watch
closely,
folks. The
Slide Sorter
is quicker
than the
eye.

Notes Page view

Click the View tab and then click the Notes Page button to view a full-size layout for your Notes pages (which I discuss later in this chapter), as shown in Figure 4-3. The top portion of the Notes page contains the corresponding slide from your presentation. From this view, you can edit the text in your Notes pages just like you edit the text boxes in your slides (as opposed to the Notes pane, which is somewhat cramped if you have a large number of notes to enter for a slide).

Note that you can't select Notes Page view from the status bar. (Rather an insult to a perfectly fine view mode, wouldn't you say?)

Reading view

Reading view is a good choice for presenting on your laptop's screen, instead of on a projector or larger display. You'll see the presentation in a window rather than full-screen. Previous and Next buttons appear on the status bar, allowing you to page through your presentation quickly.

To use Reading view, click the View tab and then click the Reading button, or click the Reading button at the right side of the status bar.

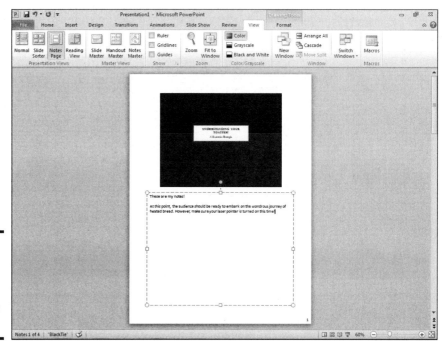

Figure 4-3:
Use Notes
Page view
to put the
spotlight on
your notes.

Slide Show view

Oh, no — this is not your Aunt Harriet's idea of a slide show. ("Enough with the beach pictures, Harry!") Instead, this one displays a PowerPoint slide show using the slides from the open presentation. I cover slide shows later in this chapter, in the section "Building and Running a Slide Show," so hang tight.

To activate Slide Show view, click the Slide Show View button on the status bar. (Note that this runs the show from the current slide, so you don't see any preceding slides.) You can also click the Slide Show tab and choose to start the slide show at the current slide or from the beginning of the presentation.

Creating Slides

As a personal favor to you, PowerPoint creates a new, blank first slide each time you start the program (or each time you create a new presentation by choosing File⇨New).

To add a new slide to a presentation, follow these steps:

1. **If you already have a number of slides in the presentation, click an existing slide in the Slide pane.**

The new slide is inserted after the selected slide.

If you have only one slide, the new slide is appended at the end. Go figure.

2. **Click the Home tab and click the New Slide button to display the pop-up menu, which displays the various types of slides you can add.**

I prefer this method because you can click a layout that most closely fits your needs for the new slide. Heck, you can also press Ctrl+M. (Geez, Microsoft, do you think we have enough options here?)

PowerPoint adds the new slide to the Slide pane and displays it in the editing window.

Note: Each slide is given a sequential number as you add it, which comes in handy, such as when you want to print only certain slides.

Do you have existing slides in your presentation that you want to use as the model for new slides? No problem! Rather than create blank slides from scratch, PowerPoint allows you to duplicate one or more existing slides. Click the slide(s) you want to duplicate in the Slide pane (hold down Ctrl while clicking to select multiple slides), right-click them, and then choose the Duplicate Slide menu item. After the new slides appear, you can move them individually within the Outline or Slide panes by dragging them to their new home. (And when the slides are moved, they're automatically renumbered. *Sweet.*)

If you need to axe a slide, right-click it in the Slide pane and then choose Delete Slide from the contextual menu that appears. It's a goner. Again, renumbering is automatic.

Inserting slides

If you have another PowerPoint presentation with one or more slides that you need for your current project, you can insert them by following these steps:

1. **Click a slide in the Slide pane where the inserted slides should appear.**

An inserted slide appears *after* the slide you click in the Slide pane.

2. **Click the Home tab and choose New Slide⇨Reuse Slides to display the Reuse Slides pane, which you see in Figure 4-4.**

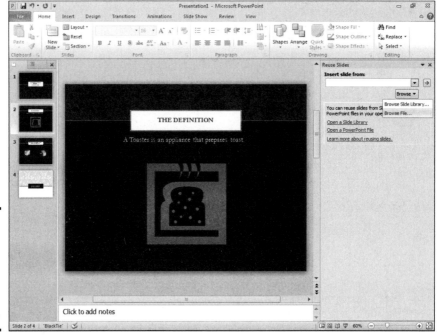

Figure 4-4:
You can
easily
import
slides from
another
presentation.

3. **Click the Browse button and choose Browse File.**

   PowerPoint displays a standard Windows Browse dialog box.

4. **Navigate to the folder containing the existing PowerPoint presentation, click the file to select it, and then click Open.**

   Thumbnails of the slides in the existing presentation appear in the Reuse Slides pane.

5. **Click Insert All to insert all the slides in the file.**

6. **To pick a single slide, click the thumbnail representing the desired slide.**

7. **Click the Close button in the Reuse Slides pane to return to your presentation.**

Inserting a document

You can also insert the contents of a Word document directly into your slides as an outline. This option is useful for those who need to pull the text for a presentation from an existing document, like a student who needs to provide both a written assignment and a PowerPoint presentation on the same material.

Follow these steps to insert a document:

1. **Click a slide in the Outline pane where the inserted text should appear.**

2. **Click the Home tab and choose New Slide⇨Slides from Outline.**

3. **Navigate to the location of the document and then click the filename to highlight it.**

4. **Click the Insert button.**

Naturally, you get the best results if the document you're inserting is formatted in outline form (with a hierarchy of headings), but I find that PowerPoint does a surprisingly good job importing just about any kind of Word document.

Typing, Selecting, and Editing Text

After you create a blank slide — or insert slides from an existing PowerPoint presentation or perhaps insert text from a Word document — you're ready to type and edit text. Luckily, this section is about exactly that topic.

Adding text

You probably already noticed the huge Click to Add XX prompts all over your slides. Reminds me a little of *Alice in Wonderland*, with little slides running around your feet bearing signs that read "Click Me!" Anyway, things couldn't get much easier. Just click the text, and PowerPoint erases it and displays an insertion cursor just like the one in Microsoft Word (see Figure 4-5).

While you type, the text is updated on the thumbnail in the Slide pane, and the text is also displayed in the Outline pane.

You can also edit text in a slide directly from the Outline pane. Just click and drag to select the text you want to change and then type to replace it.

Moving within text fields

Table 4-1 provides the movement shortcuts you can use while typing text in a PowerPoint field.

Table 4-1	Text Field Movement Keys in PowerPoint
Key	*Where It Moves the Cursor*
Left arrow (←)	One character to the left
Right arrow (→)	One character to the right
Up arrow (↑)	To the preceding line
Down arrow (↓)	To the next line
End	To the end of the current line
Home	To the beginning of the current line
Ctrl+←	One word to the left
Ctrl+→	One word to the right
Ctrl+↑	One paragraph up

Key	*Where It Moves the Cursor*
Ctrl+↓	One paragraph down
Ctrl+Home	To the beginning of the text box
Ctrl+End	To the end of the text box
Ctrl+Return	To the next title or body text entry box

To switch between titles or body text entry boxes with your mouse, click once on the box you want to edit. You can add a text box by clicking the Insert tab on the Ribbon and choosing the Text Box command button from the Text group.

Selecting text and objects

After you enter text-editing mode, you have a number of keyboard shortcuts at your disposal for selecting text that needs to be changed. Table 4-2 provides these selection keys as well as selection shortcuts for slide objects.

Table 4-2   Text Field and Object Selection Keys in PowerPoint

Key	*What It Selects*
Shift+←	One character to the left of the cursor
Shift+→	One character to the right of the cursor
Shift+↑	Characters to the previous line
Shift+↓	Characters to the next line
Ctrl+Shift+←	Characters to the beginning of the word
Ctrl+Shift+→	Characters to the end of the word
Tab	The next object
Shift+Tab	The previous object
Ctrl+A	All objects, slides, or text (depending on your view)

You can also get the mouse into the selection act: Double-click a word in a text box to select it, and you can select multiple objects on a slide by holding down Shift and then clicking each object.

Editing text

From the keyboard, you can use the shortcuts shown in Table 4-3 to play Frankenstein with the contents of a text box.

Table 4-3	Text Field Selection Keys in PowerPoint
Key	*What It Does*
Any character	Replaces the selected text
Enter	Starts a new line
Delete	Deletes the selected text or object
Ctrl+X	Deletes the selection and adds it in the Clipboard (or the Office Clipboard)
Ctrl+C	Copies the selection to the Clipboard (or the Office Clipboard)
Ctrl+V	Replaces the selection with contents of the Clipboard (or the Office Clipboard)

You can click the Home tab and click the expansion icon next to the Font group name (it looks like a square with a tiny arrow in the lower-right corner) to display the Font dialog box, as shown in Figure 4-6). From there, you can add all sorts of attributes, change the font family or font size, and determine the color of the text. The Font section of the Home tab provides many of these same commands in convenient mouse-click form.

Figure 4-6: Change font attributes in PowerPoint.

Moving slide elements

Naturally, the elements on your slide — text boxes and graphics — aren't embedded in cement. You can use your mouse or the keyboard to move these elements to a different location around the slide:

✦ **To move an element with the mouse:** Click the object to select it (you get that funky, four-direction cursor again) and then drag it to the desired spot. (For text boxes, click the frame. For graphics, click in the center of the image.)

✦ **To move an element with the keyboard:** Press the Tab key to cycle through the elements on the slide. After an item is selected, press the arrow keys to move it. This feature is useful when you need fine control over the placement of an object, but remember *not* to click a text object. That puts you in Edit mode, and as you can read in earlier parts of this section, the cursor keys have different uses when you're editing.

Installing Graphics in Your Slides

No good presentation is complete without a dog or a pony. Don't ask me why — I just work here. Add graphics to your slides to capture (and securely hold) your audience's attention. From my personal experience of watching many a boring presentation (thankfully, not my own), I can tell you that a pure-text presentation will have your audience heading for a restroom break in less than five minutes.

Follow these steps to add a graphic from your hard drive to a slide (or, if you're using Notes Page view, to your Notes page for the slide):

1. **Click to select a slide in the Slide pane.**

2. **Click the Insert tab and click Picture in the Images group.**

PowerPoint displays — you guessed it — the Insert Picture dialog box.

3. **Navigate to the folder where the image is stored and click that file to select it.**

4. **Click the Insert button.**

The image can be resized by clicking and dragging any of the circular handles arranged around the edges (check out the toaster graphic in Figure 4-7), or you can drag the entire image by clicking in its center and dragging the graphic to its new home.

If you're inserting an image that might be updated later — for example, a graphic of your company's stock price — click the down arrow next to the Insert button and then click Link to File instead, which automatically reloads the image from disk each time you display the slide in PowerPoint.

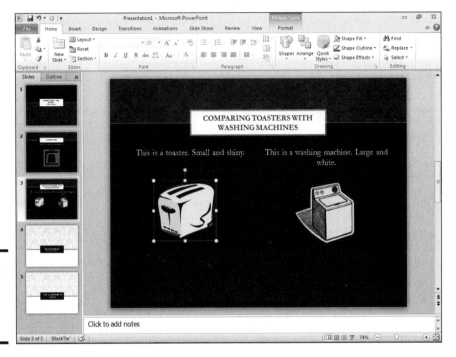

Figure 4-7:
A picture
adds
interest to
a slide.

As always, an image can be pasted into your slide from either the Windows Clipboard or the Office Clipboard. And yes, our old friend, the Clip Art task pane, is also available in PowerPoint! (Again, this is the beauty of an application suite.) To insert clip art, click the Insert tab and click the Clip Art command button, which displays the Clip Art task pane. Click in the Search For box and type a word or phrase, and then click Go. Double-click the thumbnail to insert the desired graphic.

Applying a Theme

Repeat after me: "Themes in PowerPoint are *sassy* things." That's because a theme can change the entire appearance of your slides with just a click or two of the mouse. Themes can control

✦ The position of the objects on your slides

✦ The background design

✦ The fonts and formatting used in text objects

✦ Animation effects

✦ The color scheme

Plus, a theme can be used at any time — even when you have an entire presentation's worth of slides already built!

To apply a theme, follow these steps:

1. **Select the slides that will use your theme in the Slides pane.**

2. **Click the Design tab.**

   PowerPoint opens the Ribbon group you see in Figure 4-8.

Figure 4-8:
The Themes group dominates the Design tab.

3. **Choose the type of theme you want to apply from the thumbnails in the Themes group.**

   To make a change to the theme's colors, fonts, or graphical effects, click its command button (noted in Figure 4-8) to the right of the thumbnail list.

4. **Apply the theme.**

   • *To apply the template or scheme to all slides in your presentation:* Right-click the theme thumbnail and choose Apply to All Slides.

   • *To apply the template or scheme to only the selected slides in your presentation:* Right-click the theme thumbnail and choose Apply to Selected Slides.

PowerPoint immediately updates your presentation with the new theme (like the spiffy one shown in Figure 4-9), so you can either approve or disapprove on the spot. Feel free to try on all sorts of new looks. Microsoft doesn't charge you for the privilege (at least for now).

Figure 4-9:
I must have gone to art school to produce this, right?

Entering Notes

Notes are a handy tool, allowing you to jot down reminders and information about a slide (without those notes appearing on the slide itself). Many folks also print the contents of the Notes pane as handouts; I show you how to print them later in this chapter.

Although PowerPoint has support for more formal handouts, I find that the printed Notes pages (which, as I mention earlier, also boast the images of the slides in your presentation) work just fine for distribution to your audience.

To enter notes, just click in the Notes pane and begin typing (check out Figure 4-10). Or, you can paste text directly into the pane. If you like, you can also edit the notes for a slide from Notes Page view, as I describe earlier in this chapter. To add graphics to your Notes page, you must use Notes Page view — and note that any graphics you add in Notes Page view aren't visible in Normal view. To enlarge the Notes pane, as I did in Figure 4-10, click the divider at the top of the Notes pane and drag it upward.

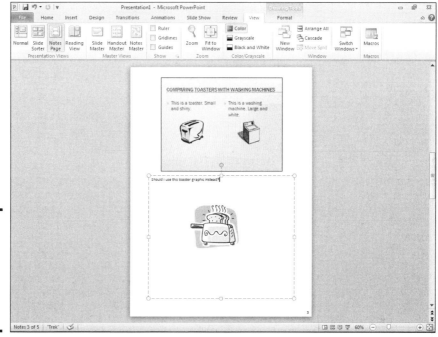

Figure 4-10:
Use the Notes pane to hold those last-minute reminders.

Using Movies and Sound

PowerPoint allows you to add video clips and audio to your slides. Naturally, these don't work well with presentations that use transparencies (no surprise there), but you'll like the effect if you use a laptop screen, monitor, or a projector!

To add multimedia to a slide, follow these steps:

1. **Click to select a slide in the Slide pane.**

2. **Click the Insert tab on the Ribbon and click either the Audio or Video pop-up menu.**

3. **Click either Video from File or Audio from File to display the ubiquitous, all-knowing Insert Video (see Figure 4-11) or Insert Audio dialog box, respectively.**

4. **Navigate to the folder where the media is stored and then click the file to select it.**

5. **Click the Insert button.**

Figure 4-11:
PowerPoint
can play a
clip or sound
automatically
or by your
leave.

Figure 4-12 illustrates both a video and an audio clip inserted into a slide. The video or sound icon appears on your slide like any other object. To play the video or audio clip within the editing window, click the clip and click the Play button in the frame. You can pause the clip by clicking the Pause button.

Although a video object can be moved and resized just like a graphic, don't be surprised if expanding it by a large amount causes it to turn *jaggy* (rough-edged). Video clips (and even images in JPEG, bitmap, or TIFF format) are created at a fixed dimension, and they might not look that good when stretched like taffy.

What's that, Bunkie? You say you have no video or audio handy to use in your presentation? No problem! Click the Insert tab, and then click the Clip Art button on the Ribbon to display the Clip Art pane. Click the Include Office.com Content check box to enable it, and then click the Results drop-down list and enable the Video and Audio check boxes. Finally, click in the Search For text box, type what you're looking for, and click Go. There's your multimedia goodness, ready for adding to your presentation!

Figure 4-12:
A movie
clip and a
sound, hard
at work in a
PowerPoint
slide.

Building and Running a Slide Show

As I mention earlier in this chapter, you can choose to view your presentation as a slide show whenever you like. Follow these steps to run your own show:

1. **Choose Slide Show⇨Start Slide Show⇨From Beginning, click the Slide Show View button on the status bar, or press F5.**

PowerPoint takes control, switches to a full-screen display, and shows the current slide in the presentation.

2. **Click the mouse button or press N (or Enter, or the right-arrow key) to move to the next slide.**

To move backward to the previous slide, press P (or Backspace or the left-arrow key).

3. **Click the mouse button on the final screen in your presentation to return to the PowerPoint window, or press Esc at any time to exit.**

That's the basic method of running a slide show. However, PowerPoint also allows you to build a self-running show that needs no intervention — and you can even choose to limit user input, which is a good feature in case strange fingers hit the keyboard.

To create a self-running show from the open presentation, follow these steps:

1. **Click the Slide Show tab and click Set Up Slide Show to display the Set Up Show dialog box, which you see in Figure 4-13.**

Figure 4-13:
Preparing a
self-running
slide show.

2. **Select the Browsed at a Kiosk (Full Screen) radio button.**

In *kiosk mode,* there are no controls or visible windows, and the slide show fills the entire screen.

3. **Choose the slides you want to display.**

- *To show them all:* Select the All radio button.

- *To show a selection of slides:* Select the From/To radio button and then enter the starting and ending slide numbers in the appropriate fields; you can type the numbers directly in the boxes or use the up and down buttons next to each box.

4. **Select the Using Timings, If Present radio button.**

This step sets the slide show to advance slides automatically. Viewers can also click the mouse button to advance to the next slide, but everything else is disabled in Kiosk mode except the Esc key, which closes the show.

5. **Select the Loop Continuously Until 'Esc' check box.**

Your slide show repeats endlessly until the Esc key is pressed. (Sorry, gotta have *some* way of ending the show, but you can always hide the keyboard.)

6. **Click OK to save your changes.**

To run your show, click the Slide Show tab and click the From Beginning command button in the Start Slide Show section. I list in Table 4-4 the basic slide show control keys that you can use during a presentation.

Table 4-4	Slide Show Control Keys in PowerPoint
Key	*What It Does*
slide number+Enter	Jumps to a specific slide
W	Toggles the display of a white screen
B	Toggles the display of a black screen
S	Stops or restarts an automatic slide show
Shift+F10	Displays a shortcut menu
Ctrl+Shift+B	Starts the slide show from the current slide
Ctrl+U	Hides onscreen controls and pointer in 15 seconds
Ctrl+H	Hides on-screen controls and pointer immediately
F1	Displays the slide show control list

Making a Transition 'twixt Slides

One way that you can add a little life to a long slide show is with the inclusion of *transitions,* which are animated effects that occur between slides. However, remember that a little goes a long way when it comes to transitions. You want your audience to pay attention to the content in your presentation and not gawk at the visual spectacle of your transitions. Less is more.

To add transitions to your slide show, follow these steps:

1. **Switch to either Normal or Slide Sorter view.**

    I find this task much easier in Slide Sorter view.

2. **If you want to apply a transition to selected slides, highlight all the slides to be preceded by the same transition.**

3. **Click the Transitions tab to select a transition from the scrolling list.**

    PowerPoint plays a quick preview of the transition, allowing you to choose another if your director's instincts weren't right the first time.

4. **Click the Duration list box to choose the speed of the effect in seconds.**

   PowerPoint again previews the animation when you select a different speed.

5. **To add sound to the transition, click the Sound drop-down list to see your choices.**

   (I gotta admit that the typewriter and the applause sounds are favorites of mine, but you have to address the audience — the CEO of your company might not approve.) To play the sound continuously until the next slide that has another sound is ready, select the Loop Until Next Sound item at the end of the Transition Sound menu. Click the transition thumbnail again to hear the sound.

6. **Decide whether the slide should advance with a mouse click (the default) or advance automatically after a delay period you set.**

   Enable both, and you get the best of both worlds: A click works; otherwise, the slide advances automatically.

7. **To apply the same transition to all slides in your show, click the Apply to All Slides command button.**

Using Package for CD

I know, I know — "Using Package for CD" sounds *really* weird. (Even the professionals in Redmond can shrug their shoulders from time to time.) Anyway, you can use the PowerPoint *Package for CD* feature to package a PowerPoint presentation to run on another Windows PC.

"But what if my good friend doesn't have a copy of Microsoft PowerPoint installed?" Good question, and Microsoft has the answer: By default, a copy of the free PowerPoint Viewer is included in your packaged presentation!

To create a Package for CD, follow these steps:

1. **Open the presentation file you want to package.**

2. **If you want to save the file to removable media (like a USB flash drive or a blank CD) rather than to a folder on your system, load the media into the drive.**

3. **From the File tab, choose Share⇨Package Presentation for CD. Then click the Package Presentation for CD button to display the dialog box you see in Figure 4-14.**

Figure 4-14:
Preparing
to package
things up.

4. **Type a descriptive name in the Name the CD field.**

5. **If you need to add multiple presentations to a single CD, click the Add button.**

   This step opens an Open dialog box, allowing you to locate and select the other presentations.

6. **If you included any even slightly unusual fonts in your package, click Options and select the Embedded TrueType fonts check box to include them in your package.**

   I mention linked graphics earlier, in the section "Installing Graphics in Your Slides." If you package a presentation that displays linked graphics, those images either have to be on the destination PC (and in the same exact folder structure) or you have to include them in your package file. Otherwise, the graphics don't show up in those slides.

   Take it from someone who has done a lot of work with printing shops and publication houses of all sizes: Assume nothing, and *always* include linked files! (That's why both check boxes are selected by default.) However, you're also assuming that the destination PC has the same fonts. To make absolutely sure that your presentation can be viewed on any PC running Windows, I recommend that you also select the Embed TrueType Fonts check box.

7. **Click the Copy to Folder button to specify the target location on your hard drive or an external drive for the package. Or, click the Copy to CD button to burn the files to a CD-R or CD-RW disc.**

   If you update your presentation, you must repeat this process again to repackage it. However, you can save it on the same CD-RW disc or in the same folder, and PowerPoint prompts you for permission to overwrite the original package.

Printing Your Document

The final stop on the PowerPoint tour is the Print function. In addition to printing slides, you can print several other types of documents, including your Notes pages and any handouts you created.

Don't forget that PowerPoint displays Print Preview to verify how things look before you print. (Click that looming File tab, and then choose Print.)

To print the slides from the entire presentation by using the default settings, you can simply choose File⇨Print⇨Print. However, if you press Ctrl+P (or pause on the Print screen first), PowerPoint offers you quite a bit of control over what gets printed and how it looks, as you can see in Figure 4-15.

Figure 4-15:
Preparing to print in PowerPoint 2010.

From the Print screen, you can choose

✦ The printer to use

✦ The number of copies

✦ The documents to print (from the Full Page Slides drop-down list)

✦ Color, black and white, or grayscale (from the Color drop-down list)

✦ Whether to surround your slides and Notes pages with a frame (the Frame Slides item at the bottom of the Full Page Slides list)

✦ Whether to print the entire presentation, specific slides, or a range of slides (from the Print All Slides drop-down list)

As I mention in other Office chapters in this minibook, your printer's software driver might offer additional settings. To display these settings, click the Printer Properties link next to the Printer drop-down list.

Chapter 5: Doing Database Magic with Access

In This Chapter

✔ Starting Access

✔ Touring the Access window

✔ Creating tables

✔ Creating forms

✔ Using templates in Access

✔ Printing your data

What? You never used Access? Don't sweat it: There's a good reason why Microsoft Office Access 2010 isn't everyone's bag of potato chips. Much like Excel, Access can be more complex and harder than the average application for the novice to use — hence, the relative obscurity of Access compared with Office applications like Word and PowerPoint. (Based on what I see in my appearances at user group meetings and in mail from my readers, Access has far less of a following than the "superstars" of Office.)

However, Microsoft has done its best to help bring Access to the home PC owner. Wizards abound, and the Access Help system is one of the most extensive in the Office 2010 suite. (It's no coincidence that the other stand-out in the Help system is Microsoft Excel.) I'm happy to report that you can now take care of basic Access chores — like building tables and forms — without having to have a degree in particle physics. In this chapter, I introduce you to those basics and show you how to keep track of really important data — like your collection of porcelain chicken planters.

If you're interested in taking the plunge and trying everything that Access has to offer, I can heartily recommend the more comprehensive book *Access 2010 For Dummies,* by Laurie Ulrich Fuller and Ken Cook (Wiley). They have the elbowroom to cover Access from one end of the Ribbon to the other.

Running Access

You can use any of the following methods to start Access:

✦ Choose Start (or press a Windows key) and then choose All Programs➪ Microsoft Office➪Microsoft Office Access 2010. (The Windows keys, if you're so blessed, lurk on either side of the Alt keys on your keyboard.)

✦ Double-click an Access database or project file.

✦ Press and hold a Windows key on your keyboard while pressing R to bring up the Run dialog box. Type **msaccess** in the Open text box and then press Enter.

If you're opening the program for the first time, Access automatically displays the New screen (which you normally reach from the File tab). Figure 5-1 illustrates the settings on the New screen.

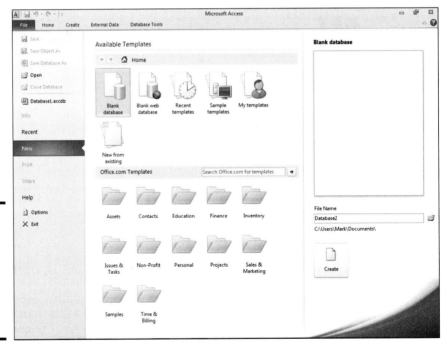

Figure 5-1: You can create a new, blank database from the New screen.

A Quick Tour of the Access Window

After you click Create to open a new, blank database, the initial Access 2010 window, shown in Figure 5-2, looks somewhat empty. That's because the idea behind Access is to accept, store, display, and edit information in a free-form manner — and you can create your own look-and-feel for the program.

File tab

Quick Access toolbar

Tabs   Command buttons   Ribbon

Navigation pane   Editing window   Status bar

Figure 5-2:
A brand-new, empty database in Microsoft Access.

Here's a quick rundown of the elements within the Access window:

✦ **File tab:** Click the showy File tab to access file and global commands, like New, Open, Save, and Print. The recent databases you created and opened appear on the Recent menu, and the Access Options button takes you to your global Access program settings.

✦ **Ribbon:** The Ribbon might look like a toolbar, but it changes to offer different command buttons when you click a tab. (Access is somewhat lean on tabs compared with the other Office 2010 programs, but there's plenty of power there.)

✦ **Quick Access toolbar:** This group of buttons next to the Office Button acts like the Quick Launch buttons on the Windows 7 taskbar, and they can be customized easily.

To add or delete buttons from the Quick Access bar, click the arrow button to the right of the bar to display a pop-up menu from which you can toggle the display of the most common command buttons. You can choose from a larger selection of command buttons by choosing More Commands from the pop-up menu, or even relocate the Quick Access toolbar under the Ribbon by clicking Show below the Ribbon.

✦ **Editing window:** In Access, the editing window is more of a container for the tables you create as well as other windows and displays. However, I used that name already for Word, Excel, and PowerPoint, and I'm not going to stop now.

✦ **Navigation pane:** Although the Navigation pane can be collapsed (by clicking on the double-arrow button), it never completely disappears, and it hangs out on the left side of the editing window. Look to the Navigation pane when you want to create and edit database objects (such as tables, queries, and forms, which I discuss in a bit).

✦ **Status bar:** In Access, the status bar allows you to switch between Datasheet and Design views. In addition, it displays the current status of your Num Lock, Caps Lock, and Scroll Lock keys, and also provides simple help messages and information about database fields. It's not exciting stuff, but such is the life of a status bar.

Creating Access Tables

Tables in Access are interesting database beasties: They look like the tables that I discuss in the earlier Word chapter of this minibook, but they store information as *fields* (or individual pieces of data, like your telephone number) within *records* (each record contains all the fields describing one person, place, or thing). Tables are the building blocks of an Access database. A name and an address of a customer, for example, might make up a record; the customer's first and last name, street address, city, state, and Zip code are all fields within that record.

A table uses Datasheet view, which organizes fields as columns. Records appear as rows.

Note that the database you created already has one blank table — you can switch between tables in a database by clicking the table tabs at the top of the editing window.

To open an existing database that you recently used, click the File tab and then click Recent to select a database file in the list.

To create a new table, just click the Create tab on the Ribbon and then click the Table button. Access adds another blank table to your database file.

The new table you created now shows up in the Navigation pane as a second item. (Check it out in Figure 5-3.) You can open it to enter additional records (or view or edit existing records) at any time by clicking it within the Navigation pane.

Figure 5-3:
Admiring my new table in the Navigation pane.

To delete a table, you must first close it by clicking the Close button (X) in the upper-right corner of the editing window. If you decide not to save the changes made to the table, it disappears immediately. If you saved the table earlier, however, just right-click it in the Navigation pane and then click Delete. Access prompts you for confirmation before trashing the table. (It had better. That confirmation dialog box has saved my rump many, many times.)

I describe how to enter data directly into a table a little later in this chapter. First, I delve into creating a form with the Form Wizard.

Creating a Form with the Wizard

Creating your own form is important because it simplifies your database for normal human beings. By using forms, anyone can enter data into your database, even if they're not familiar with the database creation process or if they have little experience with Access.

By default, all forms are saved as separate tabs in the Datasheet window, and they also appear in the Navigation pane, under the corresponding Table entry. You can enter data into a table by clicking the corresponding Datasheet tab or by clicking the form entry in the Navigation pane. Forms are also used to display existing data in a table. For example, if I only want to find out the length of the film *Alien* from my DVD database, I can just display the record for that film within the form.

You can easily create a custom form for a database table by using the Form Wizard. Follow these steps to build your own form:

1. **Click the Create tab and click Form Wizard.**

The first screen of the Form Wizard appears, as illustrated in Figure 5-4.

Figure 5-4:
You can build a new form easily with the Form Wizard.

2. **From the Tables/Queries drop-down list, choose the table that will be linked to this form.**

To specify the fields that appear in the form — not all need be included, of course — click in the Available Fields list each field you want to include in the form, and then click the single right arrow. (You can click the double right arrow to add all fields in the table.) When you click each field, it moves to the Selected Fields box.

To remove a field from the Selected Fields list, click the field name you don't want and then click the single left arrow; to empty your field list and start all over again, click the double left arrow.

3. **When the Selected Fields list on the right has the fields you need, click Next to continue.**

From the wizard screen shown in Figure 5-5, you can select from a number of predesigned formats, including the Datasheet layout (which looks quite similar to Excel) and the standard Columnar layout that Access uses when it generates a form automatically.

Figure 5-5:
It's time to choose a layout for your new form.

4. **Select the layout you need and then click Next to continue.**

   The final Form Wizard screen, as shown in Figure 5-6, prompts you for a descriptive title for your new form. You can choose to open the form immediately to add records or view existing records, or you can edit the design of the form.

Figure 5-6:
You're nearly finished building your Access form.

5. **Click Finish to close the wizard.**

To delete a form you no longer need, first click the Close button in the upper-right corner of the Editing window to close the form, click the form in the Navigation pane, and then press Delete. You're prompted for confirmation before the file is deleted. *Note:* Deleting a form doesn't delete any data from your tables.

So how do you use a form? Entering data is probably more intuitive within a form than any other method in Access because a form looks so doggone much like an online form that you would encounter on a Web site. The instructions you need to use a form are just this simple:

✦ **To enter data:** Click your mouse pointer in the desired field and then type.

✦ **To move to the next field:** Press Tab.

✦ **To move to the previous field:** Press Shift+Tab.

✦ **To close the form and save your data:** Click the Close button in the upper-right corner of the form.

If a field has the value (AutoNumber), it indicates that the field is automatically incremented when you close the form. For example, if the previous record had a 5 in that field, the next record you add automatically uses a value of 6 in the field.

Access uses the Record box for moving between records — it's in the lower-left corner of the editing window, which displays the current record number. To navigate between records, use the navigation buttons around the Record box, as shown in Figure 5-7:

✦ Click the arrow pointing to the bar at the left to move to the first record in the table.

✦ Click the arrow pointing to the left to move to the previous record.

✦ Click the arrow pointing to the right to move to the next completed record.

✦ Click the arrow pointing to the bar at the right to move to the last completed record in the table.

✦ Click the far right arrow to move to the end of the table and add a new record.

Figure 5-7:
Display a
specific
record
using these
controls.

First Record
Previous Record | Last Record
New Record
Next Record

Entering and Editing Fields Manually

I admit that I get pretty enthusiastic about forms: They're easy for computer
novices to use, and they look quite professional. However, you can view,
enter, and edit your data directly from the table itself, using Datasheet view.
And, because the table displays many records at a time in rows, it's often
faster than using a form.

Follow these steps to enter or edit a field value in a table:

1. **Select the record that you want to enter or change by either clicking
    it with the mouse or pressing the Tab/Shift+Tab combination to move
    to it.**

2. **Type the new data value; depending on the data format, you might
    have to select the contents with your mouse (or the Shift+arrow keys)
    and the original value first.**

    Access displays a pencil icon to the far left of the record to indicate that
    you made a change to the record.

3. **If you're entering data in a new record, press Tab to move to the next field.**

4. **Click within any other record to save the new values.**

5. **To edit another record, begin again at Step 1.**

Each time you enter a value in the empty record at the bottom of the window, Access automatically adds a new, empty record; however, if you create a new record by mistake, just press Esc to cancel your edits.

Using Access Templates

Although most folks tend to design their own databases for specific purposes, Access comes with both a number of built-in templates and a rather bodacious number of templates that are online at `www.office.com`.

To use a general template, click the File tab and choose New. Click a category, and click a template icon to select it. Type a descriptive filename, and click Create (for local templates stored on your hard drive) or Download (for online templates offered by Microsoft).

Yep, free stuff! You'll find an abundance of high-quality, predesigned templates grouped by category available from Microsoft. To search for a specific keyword, click in the Search Office.com text box and then click the arrow button.

Printing Your Data

Before you decide to put your data on paper, I always recommend that you use the Print Preview feature. Just click the File tab and then choose Print. Many times I've been thankful that I checked first to verify that what I expected to print was actually what was going to appear on the hard copy!

Access can print from just about any view, whether the active window is displaying a table, a form, or a query. When you're ready to print, choose one of these two methods:

✦ **Click the File tab, choose Print, and then click the Print button.** The contents of the active window are immediately printed with the current settings. Alternatively, you can elect to print just selected pages (or the selected records in a datasheet window). You can also select from multiple printers or specify multiple copies from the Print screen. If you need to change any printer-specific options supported by the printer's Windows 7 software driver, click the Printer Properties link. When you're ready, click OK.

✦ **Press Ctrl+P.** This method also displays the Print screen.

Chapter 6: Staying in Touch with Outlook

In This Chapter

- Running Outlook
- Introducing the Outlook window
- Setting up your Outlook e-mail account
- Reading and replying to incoming mail
- Sending messages
- Adding file attachments to messages
- Entering contacts
- Creating appointments
- Using the Outlook Today screen
- Printing within Outlook

*I*f you didn't install Outlook 2010, *run* — do not dawdle — to your book-shelf and grab your Office 2010 DVD. You see, you need it in order to install Outlook. It's that good, and — in my opinion — using just about anything else is strictly second best. (No offense to those other electronic mail applications; it's just that Outlook can organize just about everything in your life better than any other program I've ever used — without becoming confusing or complex.) In Office 2007, the design of the Outlook window hadn't "caught up" with the rest of the Office applications — but I'm happy to say that Outlook now has the same look and feel as the rest of its Office 2010 brethren.

In this chapter, I provide you with the basics you need to use Outlook as your comprehensive e-mail, address book, and calendar application. You attach files, read messages, make appointments, and send blind carbon copies in no time at all. I also mention a number of tips that I've found help-ful in my experience with Outlook.

For a complete discussion of everything that Outlook 2010 can do and store, you obviously need more than just a single chapter. And I can't recommend a better book than *Outlook 2010 For Dummies,* by Bill Dyszel (Wiley).

Running Outlook

You can start Outlook by using any of the following methods:

✦ If you added Outlook to your Quick Launch bar (which I definitely recommend), click the icon on the taskbar.

✦ Choose Start➪All Programs➪Microsoft Office➪Microsoft Outlook 2010.

✦ Press a Windows key while holding down R (Win+R) to bring up the Run dialog box; type **outlook** in the Open text box and then press Enter.

Look for the two Windows keys on your keyboard; they reside in the same stratosphere as your spacebar and Alt keys. If ya got 'em (and you probably do), they bear the waving Windows flag.

Elements of the Outlook Window

Figure 6-1 illustrates the Outlook window in all its glory.

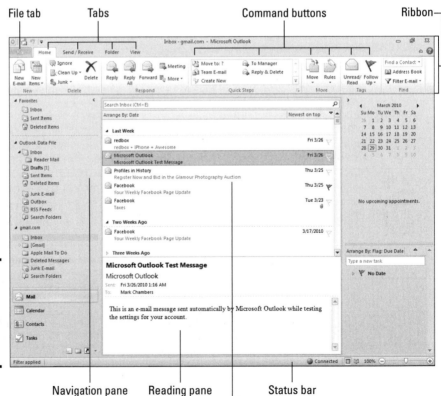

Figure 6-1: The king of e-mail applications is in the house.

Navigation pane   Reading pane   Status bar

Message list

Here's a quick rundown of the elements within the Outlook window:

✦ **File tab:** The File tab is your direct connection to the functions that used to appear on the File menu in previous versions of Outlook. From here, you can open files, import data from other programs, print data, and edit your account settings.

✦ **Ribbon:** For the first time, Outlook sports a Ribbon across the top of the window, just like the other Office programs. The contents of this Ribbon change with the tab you select.

✦ **Tabs:** Clicking a tab changes the content of the Outlook Ribbon, displaying command buttons specific for that tab.

✦ **Command buttons:** Like the toolbars of old, a click on one of these buttons performs a function within Outlook. You'll notice that some of these buttons also have a downward or sideways-facing arrow, which you can click to display a pop-up menu of choices corresponding to the button.

✦ **Navigation pane:** The top of this pane includes a tree display, where you can select an Outlook folder. Just click to select a folder, and the contents are displayed in the Message list. You can use the buttons at the bottom of the Navigation pane to jump between different views and functions within Outlook. For example, you can immediately switch to your Outlook Calendar view, or you can click the Contacts button to check a telephone number from your Address Book.

✦ **Message list:** Here are displayed messages of the current folder; however, in other views (like Contacts or Tasks view), the contents change to match the data you're displaying.

✦ **Reading pane:** If you click a message in the Message list, the contents are displayed in the Reading pane. This is a neat way to see what's contained in the message without opening the message in a separate window.

If the Reading pane doesn't appear on your screen, click the View tab and click the arrow next to the Reading Pane button. Then click either Bottom or Right to specify where the Reading pane should appear.

Virtually any pane can be resized in Outlook. Move your mouse pointer over the divider bar until it turns into opposing arrows and then drag to relocate the bar.

✦ **Status bar:** The Outlook status bar typically displays the total number of messages in a folder or the total number of contacts in your Contacts list — you get the idea. (Don't get me wrong: I appreciate the totals. The status bar is a good soldier in the fight to hold down RIE, or runaway inbox expansion — but that's about it.)

Configuring Your Mail Account

First things first. When you initially launch Outlook 2010, you see an Outlook 2010 Startup Wizard. The prompts and onscreen help are self explanatory, but the information you're asked for is also covered in this section (because the Startup Wizard sets up your first mail account). With that in mind, I recommend that you refer to this section if you need a dash of clarity while running the Startup Wizard.

"But Mark, I have more than one e-mail account!" No worries, good reader. Adding a mail account within Outlook involves — surprise! — a wizard. (I think that someone in Redmond got the message that wizards are A Good Thing.)

Although Outlook 2010 and Windows Live Mail both handle your e-mail, Outlook 2010 is far superior in features and functionality. If you have both on your PC, take my advice and use Outlook 2010 . . . you'll thank me later!

Follow these steps to add an Internet e-mail account within Outlook:

1. **From the File tab, click Info. Then click the Account Settings button and choose Account Settings from the pop-up menu. (Whew!)**

Outlook displays the dialog box you see in Figure 6-2.

2. **Click the New button on the E-Mail tab toolbar.**

Figure 6-2:
The
Account
Settings
dialog box.

The Add New Account wizard appears, as shown in Figure 6-3. (Note that you can also change an existing account from the toolbar.)

Outlook 2010 can automatically set up most e-mail accounts for you. For virtually all home PC owners, that's a POP3 server, which is the common choice with most dialup and digital subscriber line (DSL) or cable Internet service providers (ISPs). (Enough abbreviations for one sentence?) You can also set up a separate account for a Web-based HyperText Transfer Protocol (HTTP) server (like Hotmail). For this automatic luxury, click the E-Mail Account radio button.

If you're connecting to an office e-mail server, check with your network administrator to determine the manual settings you'll need to enter, and make sure you select the Manually Configure Server Settings or Additional Server Types radio button.

Figure 6-3:
Provide
Outlook 2010
with your
account
information,
and it does
the rest!

3. **Type your name into the Your Name box and then type the e-mail address supplied by your ISP into the E-mail Address box. Finally, type your e-mail account password into the Password box, and then retype it to confirm your spelling.**

   Check the documentation provided by your ISP for information like your e-mail address and password — if you can't find it, a call to your ISP's technical support line is in order.

4. **Click Next.**

   Outlook attempts to connect to the specified server and download a sample message.

   Any errors are reported at the bottom of the dialog box. If you misspelled your password, you can correct it and retry the connection. The wizard reports success after the connection has been made and the message downloaded.

5. **Click Finish to close the wizard.**

   Note that your new account has been added to the list in the Account Settings dialog box.

To remove an account or to specify a new account as the default, click the account in the list to select it, and then click the Remove or Set as Default buttons on the E-Mail tab's toolbar.

If you rely heavily on Outlook to store all your important information, I beseech you — even more than usual — to *back up your doggone hard drive!* You might be able to re-create most of your résumé, but how about every single telephone number that you ever stored in Contacts or every single e-mail message you ever received? Do it. *Back up. Do it!*

Reading and Replying to E-Mail

Naturally, receiving and reading your incoming mail is the primary thrust behind Outlook, and you can easily check all your accounts at once. Click the Send/Receive tab and click Send/Receive All Folders — or press F9. (To send and receive from just a specific account, click the Send/Receive tab, click Send/Receive Groups and then choose the desired account from the resulting pop-up menu.)

Oh, joy! "You've got mail" — and it's not a chunk of worthless spam that you want to immediately delete. (Read more on eradicating spam later in this chapter.) New messages appear as bolded entries in the Message pane; double-click the message to open it in a message window (as shown in Figure 6-4).

Wait a second! There are our friends, the File tab and the Ribbon! Yep, they appear within the Reading and Replying windows. Note, however, that the Ribbon is limited to one tab in the Reading window (and five in the Reply window), and the File tab is really necessary only for file functions, such saving a draft message and printing message contents.

If you would rather scan your mail, click the message once, and it's shown in the Reading pane. (If the Reading pane is missing, click View and click the Reading Pane button, then select the location where the Reading pane should appear. If you're not interested in previewing your mail, this option is a good one to toggle off because you see much more of the Message list that way.)

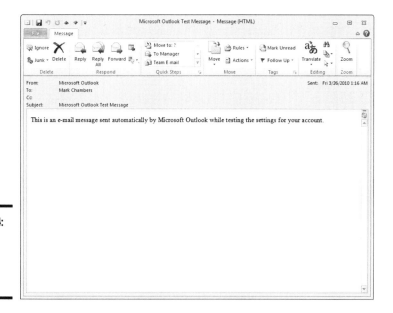

Figure 6-4:
Read a
message
in its own
window.

By default, Outlook uses a Usenet or newsgroup format, where the messages
are arranged in a conversational style rather than by the date you received
them. (This style of display is also called *threading,* where a message is followed by all its replies in linear order.) You can disable this format:

1. **Click the View tab.**
2. **Clicking the Conversations command button,**
3. **Click Show Messages in Conversations.**

To add the author of an incoming message to your Contacts list, right-click
the person's e-mail address in the From field (while the message is displayed
in a message window) and then choose Add to Outlook Contacts from the
contextual menu that appears. (More about adding Outlook contacts later in
this chapter.)

Does one of your incoming messages deserve a pithy reply? (Otherwise
called "returning a piece of flaming e-mail" — all in fun, of course.) If so,
follow these steps to reply to it:

1. **Click to select a message in the Message pane list, click the Home tab,
   and then click the Reply button.**

   If the message is already open in its own window, click the Reply button
   within the message window.

Was the original message addressed to additional folks besides yourself? If so, you can send your reply to everyone who received a carbon copy of the original message by clicking the Reply All button (rather than Reply) button on either the Home tab or the message window Ribbon.

Outlook opens the Reply window, as shown in Figure 6-5, with the insertion cursor already hanging out at the top of the message. Outlook includes the text of the original message, too — just look underneath the separator line to see the original message. The To field is already completed, filled with the name of the person who sent the original e-mail.

Notice that Outlook automatically adds the prefix RE: to the beginning of the original subject line, but feel free to click in the Subject box and type a new subject if you like.

2. **(Optional) To send copies of the reply to other individuals, click once in the Cc box and enter addresses manually (separated by semicolons) or click the Cc button to select names from your Outlook Contacts list. See Figure 6-6.**

The text of the original message is included. If necessary, you can delete it manually to preserve that all-important privacy.

Figure 6-5: Preparing to reply to a message.

Figure 6-6:
Selecting
names from
my Outlook
Contacts list
for carbon
copies.

"Hey, can't I send *blind* carbon copies too?" (That's where the recipients of copies don't see the others who have also received a copy.) You surely can, but for some strange reason, Outlook hides the Bcc field in the Reply header unless there's already a Bcc recipient. To add a Bcc recipient, click the To or Cc button to display the Select Names dialog box. Click the contacts you want to include and click the Bcc button to add them directly into the Bcc box. (You can also type or paste addresses into the Bcc box.)

3. **Go ahead — type like the wind! After you enter the text of your message (and format it, if you like, by using the familiar formatting controls in the Basic Text group of the Message tab), you can add attachments.**

   I cover attachments later in this chapter, in the section wittily titled, "Using File Attachments."

4. **When all is in readiness, click the Send button to send your message immediately.**

To save a draft of the message without sending it immediately, click the File tab, click Save, and then close the Reply window. The message appears in your Drafts folder; to send it later, click the Drafts folder to show a list of the documents in it, double-click the message to open it, and then click Send.

To save a copy of a message or reply in text or HTML format, click the File tab and click Save As.

You can also forward a message, allowing you to add a comment to the body of the original message before you send it to the new recipient. To forward a message, click the Forward button rather than the Reply button. Then sally forth, following the instructions I detail within this section.

Could you use some help prioritizing the messages that need replies? That's where the Outlook Follow Up feature comes in handy. Check out the column at the far right of the Message list that contains a ghostly outline of a pennant. Right-click the Flag column for a particular message to indicate the importance of a timely reply. When you need to prioritize your inbox, click the Flag column heading button. When you're done with a message, you can right-click the Flag column again and choose Clear Flag from the pop-up menu. *Sublime!*

Composing and Sending Messages

Sometimes a reply just isn't enough; instead, you need to stir up trouble by initiating the e-mail conversation. To compose and send a new message, follow these steps:

1. **Click the New E-mail command button on the Home tab, or press Ctrl+N.**

Outlook displays the new message window you see in Figure 6-7.

Figure 6-7:
Creating
a new
message
begins here.

2. **Address your message.**

   • *If the recipient for this message isn't in your Contacts list:* Click in the To box and type the e-mail address. (Or, if it's on the Clipboard, you can paste the address by using the Ctrl+V shortcut.)

   • *If you have the recipient for this message in your Contacts list:* Click the To button and then choose the person from the Select Names dialog box that appears. You can also add carbon copies and blind carbon copies from this dialog box.

   Click OK to return to the new message window.

3. **Click in the Subject field, type the subject for this message, and then press Tab to move to the message editing box.**

4. **Type the text of your message and apply any desired formatting to the text.**

5. **Add any attachments.**

   Use the procedure that I show you in the next section.

6. **Send the message.**

   • *Now:* Click the Send button to send the message immediately.

   • *Later:* Alternatively, click the File tab inside the new message window and then click Save to save the message in your Drafts folder, as I explain in the preceding section.

   The ability to save your e-mail messages is a truly neat feature, especially if you're composing messages offline on your laptop without an Internet connection. You can turn that idle time spent waiting in the airport into productive time. When you get back to your home or office and your Internet connection, send each message as I describe earlier.

Using File Attachments

Turn your attention to file attachments. You can include all sorts of files with your e-mail messages, such as

✦ Office documents

✦ Pictures, sound clips, and *short* video clips

✦ Programs and data files

If the recipient of your message is using Outlook (or another popular e-mail application), she should be able to save and use the files you send just as though they had been stored on a USB flash drive or a CD-ROM.

Attaching files and sending them to your friends with Macintosh and Linux computers is a useful way to swap documents that can be read on multiple platforms (like a Word document, for example).

ISPs place a ceiling on the size of an individual message — and that includes any attachments. How much is too much? The typical limit is under 2MB for a single message, but the exact limit is determined by both your Internet e-mail server and the recipient's e-mail server. With this in mind, another Mark's Maxim appears:

Never send a 300MB video clip to your best friend as an e-mail attachment and expect it to arrive in one piece.™

You know that you exceeded the maximum message size if you receive an error message from either server that declares your original e-mail to be undeliverable. The *noive* of some people! Nyuk.

Here's how to send an attachment:

1. **Reply to a message or compose a new message.**

2. **Click the Message tab on the reply or new message window Ribbon and then click the Attach File button in the Include group.**

   Outlook displays the Insert File dialog box.

3. **Navigate to the location of the files you want to attach and then click each one.**

   For multiple files, hold down Ctrl while you click.

4. **Click the down arrow next to the Insert button and then click Insert to add the files to the message.**

   Attached files appear in the Attached header area of the message dialog box (see Figure 6-8).

If someone sends you an attached file, right-click the file attachment in the header and choose Save As from the pop-up menu that appears; then browse to select a spot on your system where the file will be stored.

Repeat after me: "Mark, I promise never to run an attached file unless I manually scan it — or unless my anti-virus scanning software has already scanned it automatically!" E-mail viruses and malicious macros are widespread these days, and running any attachment (even one from someone you know) without protection is just asking for trouble.

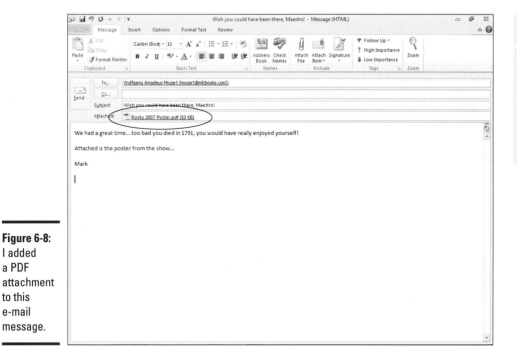

Figure 6-8:
I added
a PDF
attachment
to this
e-mail
message.

Keeping Track of Your Contacts

Enough with the e-mail! Outlook can also take care of your contacts, like
any other good personal information manager (PIM). To display your contacts, click the Contacts button on the Navigation pane or press Ctrl+3. The
Contacts window appears, as shown in Figure 6-9, with each contact presented as a business card!

To jump directly to a specific first letter of a contact's last name, click the
desired letter on the button strip down the right side of the Contacts screen.

So what can one do with a contact? Of course, half the value of the Contacts
window is the ability to simply store your address book information in an
organized central location, but you can also

✦ Create a new e-mail message to that contact.

✦ Set up an appointment or a meeting request with that contact.

✦ Set a new task or journal entry for that contact.

All these sundry actions are available when you right-click any contact entry
displayed in the Contacts window.

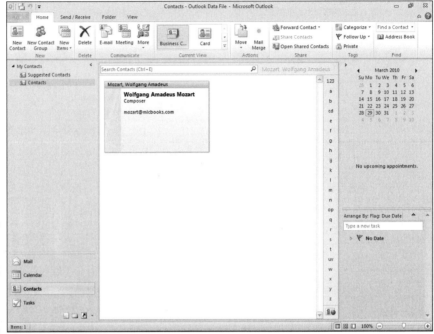

Figure 6-9:
Maintain
your Outlook
Contacts
information
here.

Entering a contact

To enter a new contact from the Contacts window, follow these steps:

1. **Press Ctrl+N or choose New Contact from the Home tab.**

Outlook displays the Contact window, which you see in Figure 6-10, complete with File tab and Ribbon.

2. **Click in the appropriate field to enter information such as the person's telephone numbers, job title, address, and Web page address.**

Entry is completely free-form; the only fields that you should always enter are the person's name and e-mail address. Click in the Notes box at the right side of the window and type any comments or notes that you want to save for this contact.

To add a photo of the contact from your hard drive, click the Picture button and choose Add Picture.

If a field has a down-arrow button next to it, you can click the button to display additional fields of the same type. For example, click the down arrow next to the Business Phone field, and you can click to display the person's pager or home fax machine number.

Figure 6-10:
Enter a new
contact
here.

3. **To display additional fields, click the Details button on the Contact tab; from this panel, you can enter the person's birthday and anniversary, spouse's name, and other such data.**

4. **After you enter all the data for a contact, click the Contact tab and then click Save & Close.**

Editing a contact

You can easily add new information to an existing contact or even edit the data you already entered: Just double-click a contact entry in the Contacts window. Outlook opens the same window that you used to enter the contact information. Of course, the data that you already added to the contact is still there, but everything can be edited if necessary, and you can add new data.

To close the window and save the updated information, click the Save & Close button again.

Using the Outlook Calendar

If I told you that Outlook is also a full-featured calendar program, would you believe me? Yep, this program is a regular Swiss Army knife! To display

the Calendar, click the Calendar button from the Navigation pane or press
Ctrl+2. Figure 6-11 illustrates the Calendar window.

Figure 6-11:
The Outlook
2010
Calendar
window.

Click the Home tab and then the appropriate button at the top of the Editing
window to display the different Calendar periods, which are highlighted
within the Calendar window. From these views, you can set appointments
that will appear on your Calendar:

✦ **Day:** A single day.

✦ **Work Week:** A five-day work week.

✦ **Week:** A full, seven-day week, beginning on Sunday and ending on
   Saturday.

✦ **Month:** An entire month.

✦ **Schedule:** Your current calendar view is presented in a horizontal
   arrangement, making it easier to schedule appointments that don't over-
   lap (like mine always seem to do).

Creating an appointment

To create a new appointment for your Calendar from the Calendar window, follow these steps:

1. Press Ctrl+N or choose New Appointment from the Home tab.

Outlook displays the Appointment window, as shown in Figure 6-12.

Figure 6-12:
It's time to add a new Outlook appointment.

2. Type a descriptive subject for the appointment, press Tab, and then type the location for the meeting.

To use a location you used previously, open the Location drop-down list and select it from the list.

3. Set the start and end times for the meeting.

a. *Start:* Click the Start Time drop-down list, choose the date for the appointment, and then click the start time.

b. *End:* Likewise, click the End Time drop-down lists and set the ending date and time for the appointment.

c. *All day:* If the appointment lasts all day, select the All Day Event check box, and Outlook disables the End Date and Time fields.

4. **(Optional) If you need a reminder from Outlook before the appointment, click the Reminder drop-down list in the Options group of the Appointment tab. Choose the length of time you need to reach your appointment after the reminder appears.**

   You can also set an audible reminder from the Reminder Sound item at the bottom of the Reminder drop-down list, choosing an alarm sound to play as a little added "encouragement."

5. **From the Show As list in the Options group, choose a status for the appointment.**

   The appointment status shows up in your Calendar as a shaded or colored block.

   By default, Outlook uses Busy as the status for a new appointment.

6. **Click in the Notes box at the bottom half of the Appointment window and type any free-form comments or notes that you want to associate with this meeting.**

7. **Click the Categorize button on the Appointment tab to assign a category to this appointment.**

   Click the All Categories item at the bottom of the list to display the Color Categories dialog box, as shown in Figure 6-13.

   You can assign multiple categories to an appointment.

8. **After everything is set, click the Save & Close button on the Ribbon to add the appointment to your Calendar.**

Figure 6-13: Categories help you organize your appointments.

Displaying appointments in Outlook Today

To view your daily appointments and summarize your entire existence each morning — pretty cool when you think about it — click the Today button on the Home tab. Outlook displays everything that's happening today arranged on a single screen. This, folks, is a neat trick, and I use this view throughout my workday.

To display the specifics about an appointment or task, double-click the item.

Printing within Outlook

Believe it or not, you can print just about any data from Outlook in its native form — and considering the wide variety of information stored within Outlook's copious environs, that's quite a feat. Depending on the current view and the selected item (items), you can print anything from the contents of an e-mail message to your appointment schedule and your Contacts list — the printed output varies according to the module you're currently using, like Contacts or Calendar.

Like with the other Office 2010 applications, I strongly recommend that you pause long enough to preview the printed copy. When you're displaying the view you need within Outlook (and you've selected any specific items to print), you can view how things will look by clicking the File tab and clicking Print.

Remember how I just finished crowing about how great the Today view is? And here we are talking about printing. Hmmm . . . what better way to print a reminder of what you need to do during the day than by printing the Today screen? It's your entire day on one sheet of paper.

So you're satisfied with the preview — but don't forget the powerful settings available from the Print screen! From here, you can set the page style, print multiple copies, select the target printer (including network printers), and select a range of pages to print. Figure 6-14 illustrates the Print screen when you print from within the Calendar screen. To set any printer-specific options provided by your printer's driver, click the Printer Options button. After you set the printer options you need, click Print.

From anywhere within Outlook, you can jump directly to the Print screen by pressing Ctrl+P.

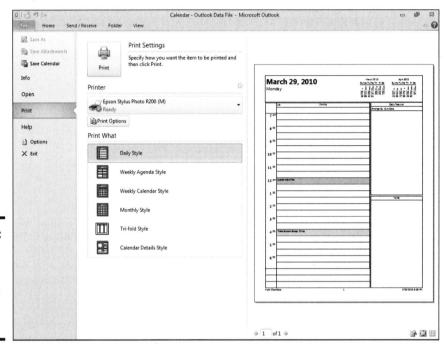

Figure 6-14:
Preparing
to print a
Calendar
page within
Outlook
2010.

Chapter 7: Working with SkyDrive

In This Chapter

⮡ **Creating a SkyDrive**

⮡ **Adding your own folders**

⮡ **Saving and loading documents from your SkyDrive**

*I*n the ancient days at the turn of this century, Microsoft Office stayed put on your hard drive. Sure, you could share documents with others through e-mail, or scoot documents around on your office network, but you *certainly* didn't create or save stuff online!

Enter the neatest innovation that I've seen in many years for Office users: the new Microsoft SkyDrive online storage system, which offers anyone with a Windows Live account a whopping 25GB of space. Oh, and did I mention that you can access the files stored on your SkyDrive anywhere in the world? If you have an Internet connection, you're online with SkyDrive — it's that simple.

In this chapter, I demonstrate how you can use SkyDrive to store your Office documents, and how you can customize your online storage for your needs. Get ready to live the carefree life of hardware independence!

Answers to Your Online Storage Queries

Before I delve into creating and using a SkyDrive, I want to answer some common questions I've often received from readers about online storage:

+ **Is my stuff safe?** The answer is a definite yes; Microsoft maintains the servers where your data is stored, and backs them up on a regular basis. In fact, I'd venture to say that the data you store on your SkyDrive is as safe as your physical hard drive. Just locate an Internet connection you can use, and your data is within reach at all times!

+ **What can I store online?** Although SkyDrive is designed for easy use with Office documents, Microsoft allows you to store just about any type of file online (as long as it's legal). This also makes SkyDrive a great choice for simple file backups, allowing you to keep copies of your truly invaluable files online in case of catastrophe. Each SkyDrive account can store up to 25GB of data.

✦ **Is my stuff private?** Again, I'm going to wax enthusiastic about Microsoft's implementation of online storage. The company has taken great pains to ensure that your data remains secure from prying eyes.

✦ **How much will it cost me?** A number of online storage sites on the Web will charge you for territory, but I'm happy to say that SkyDrive is free to all Windows Live members.

✦ **How fast is the transfer?** Online storage is nowhere near as fast as the dedicated hard drive inside your PC. However, most Office documents and photographs of reasonable size should transfer within a few seconds. Naturally, the faster the Internet connection you're using, the faster SkyDrive will work.

So what do you need to use SkyDrive? Here's a list of Microsoft's requirements at this writing:

✦ **Windows XP or later**

✦ **Internet Explorer 6 or later**

✦ **A Windows Live account**

If you're already using the Windows Live suite of online tools (or you have a Hotmail account), you've already set up your account, and you can use that username and password. Otherwise, visit `http://home.live.com` and click Sign Up.

Signing In to SkyDrive

Ready to join the SkyDrive revolution? Good, fire up Internet Explorer and visit `http://skydrive.live.com`. In the Sign In window (as shown in Figure 7-1), type your Windows Live ID and password and then click Sign In.

Here we are with the old battle betwixt security on one hand and convenience on the other. If you'll be using SkyDrive from a secure location (like your home) and you're the only one using the PC, feel free to select the Remember Me and Remember My Password check boxes. If you're in a public place, using a laptop, or sharing your PC with others, however, I **strongly** recommend that you don't enable the Remember My Password check box.

Figure 7-2 illustrates the main SkyDrive screen, with the following important items you should note:

✦ **All Folders link:** Click this link to display all folders within your SkyDrive (whether you used them recently or not).

✦ **Recent Folders list:** This group of folder icons represents the SkyDrive folders you used within the last few sessions.

Figure 7-1:
Sign in for
Microsoft
SkyDrive
online
storage.

✦ **Space remaining:** You can always check the amount of space remaining in your SkyDrive using this meter.

✦ **Options menu:** Open this drop-down list to customize the look of your SkyDrive screens and the language that the site uses. You can also choose to tag people in the photos you store in SkyDrive, allowing anyone viewing the photo to jump directly to your Windows Live profile.

Marking Your Own Territory and Adding Files

The default folder names are essentially self explanatory: The contents of My Documents are for your eyes only, for example, and the Public folder can be accessed by anyone through your Windows Live profile. I'm a customizing kind of guy myself, though, and I'll bet you'd prefer to create your own top-level folders within SkyDrive, with names like "My Krazy Kat Klassics" and "Important Stuff." (I know I did.)

To organize your SkyDrive to your liking, follow these steps from the main SkyDrive screen to create a new folder:

1. **Click Create Folder.**

SkyDrive displays the screen you see in Figure 7-3.

2. **Type a descriptive name into the Name field and press Tab.**

Figure 7-2:
The
SkyDrive
main
screen.

3. **Click the Share With drop-down arrow and choose the desired level of security for your new folder.**

   You can allow everyone to access the contents (Everyone/Public), make the folder private (Just Me), or allow only those in your Windows Live network to access the contents (My Network). You can also click Select People to choose individuals and groups that will have access rights to the folder.

4. **Click Next to continue.**

5. **If you'd like to immediately add files to your new folder — as many as five — click the Choose File buttons and select the desired files using the Upload File dialog box, as shown in Figure 7-4.**

   The maximum size for each file upload is 50MB.

6. **Click Upload to transfer the files.**

   Uploading may take some time, depending on the speed of your Internet connection, so do not close or navigate away from the Upload screen until the completion message appears.

To add files to an existing folder, click the folder from the main SkyDrive screen to open it, and then click the Add Files link. SkyDrive returns you to the Add Files screen, ready for you to specify another five files.

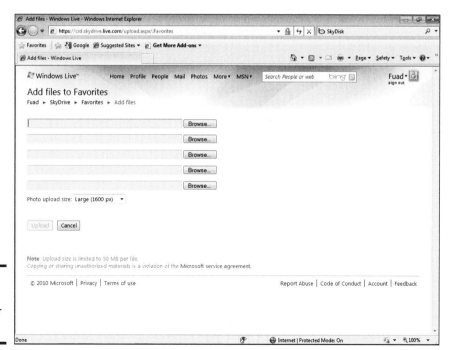

Figure 7-3:
Creating
a new
SkyDrive
folder with
aplomb.

Figure 7-4:
Adding
files to your
SkyDrive.

Office anywhere!

From the folder contents screen, you can also create a new Office document. Click New and choose the document type you want to create, which automatically opens the corresponding Web-based version of Word, Excel, PowerPoint, or OneNote. Whoa, wait a second, *what just happened here?*

Welcome to Microsoft's new direction: Web-based Office applications, which are an integral part of Microsoft's Office Live Workspace on the Web. (Think "cloud computing.") Consider these new applications the "lite" version of the familiar (and far more powerful) hard drive–based Office programs. With these online versions of your Office applications, you can work anywhere there's an Internet connection (even if the PC you're using doesn't have Office installed)! Friends and neighbors, it doesn't get much cooler than that.

If you click a document icon within one of your SkyDrive folders, you'll see an information screen that displays the file's properties, as well as comments that you can add. To open the existing document from this screen using the Web application, click Edit. To retrieve the file and save a local copy on the PC's hard drive, click Download. ***Note:*** At the time of this writing, you can't load a SkyDrive document directly into your full Office applications, so you must download it first before you can edit it on your hard drive.

Although the Web-based Office applications have nowhere near the features and options that I discuss in earlier chapters in this minibook, they do allow basic editing with controls that usually mirror the full version as closely as possible. Plus, the Web-based applications will create, open, and save documents in the standard office formats (.docx for Word, for example), so you can conveniently work with your files on either platform.

Oh, did I mention that Microsoft has made these Web-based Office applications completely free to Windows Live members? Time to celebrate, PC owners!

Saving Files within Office Applications

As I mention in the nearby sidebar, "Office anywhere!," clicking an Office document on your SkyDrive will display the file information screen. From there, click Edit to load the document within the corresponding Web-based application.

"Well that's great, Mark, but I want to save a file to my SkyDrive from within my traditional hard drive-based Office program!" No problem, good reader, just follow these steps:

1. **Click the File tab in Word, Excel, PowerPoint, or OneNote (Microsoft's note-taking and collaboration tool, also part of Office).**

2. **Click Share.**

3. **Click Save to SkyDrive.**

   If you haven't used SkyDrive so far in this computing session, you're prompted to enter your Windows Live login information.

4. **Click the destination SkyDrive folder and then click Save As.**

   After a moment, you see a standard File Save dialog box where you can enter a filename and pick a document format.

5. **Click Save.**

   You might experience a bit of "busy time" as your Office application uploads the file to your SkyDrive.

Book VI

Fun with Movies, Music, and Photos

The 5th Wave · By Rich Tennant

"Hey – let's put scanned photos of ourselves through a ripple filter and see if we can make ourselves look weird."

Contents at a Glance

Chapter 1: Scanning with Gusto 417

What Happens inside a Scanner? 417
Your Friend, the Flatbed 419
Popular Scanner Features 421
Basic Scanning with Windows Live Photo Gallery 422
Scanning Do's and Don'ts 429
Those Irritating (Or Invaluable) Copyrights 430

Chapter 2: Dude, MP3 Rocks! 433

An MP3 Primer 434
Ripping Your Own MP3 Files 435
Listening to Your Stuff 438
Downloading to an MP3 Player 440
Using Other Sound Formats 441
Burning Audio CDs from MP3 Files 443

Chapter 3: Making Movies with Your PC 445

Getting the Lowdown on Windows Live Movie Maker 445
Rounding Up Clips and Images 447
Building Your First Movie 448
Adding Transitions without Breaking a Sweat 450
Adding Special Effects without Paying George Lucas 451
Adding Sound 452
You've Just Gotta Have Titles! 453
Previewing Your Oscar-Winning Work 454
Saving and Sharing Before Traveling to Cannes 455

Chapter 4: I Can Make My Own DVDs? 457

Welcome to Windows DVD Maker 457
Clips 'R Easy! 459
Time to Preview 463
Burning Your DVD and Celebrating Afterward 464

Chapter 5: I'm Okay, You're a Digital Camera 465

How Does a Digital Camera Work? 466
The Pros and Cons of Digital Photography 468
Digital Camera Extras to Covet 471
The Lazy Man's Guide to Composing Photographs 473
Organizing Your Pictures 478
Downloading Your Images 478

Chapter 1: Scanning with Gusto

In This Chapter

- ✔ Understanding scanner technology
- ✔ Shopping for a flatbed scanner
- ✔ Acquiring an image
- ✔ Rotating and cropping your scans
- ✔ Converting and saving scanned images
- ✔ Scanning guidelines to follow
- ✔ Handling copyrighted material

A scanner might rank as one of the most versatile pieces of hardware that you can slap onto your PC. With an investment of anywhere from $75 to $400 (US), you can add the ability to copy and fax printed documents (with a modem and a printer, of course), create digital images from all sorts of materials, and even use optical character recognition (OCR) to read text from documents directly into your PC's word processing application.

What's inexpensive isn't always easy to use, however. You have to choose from different types of scanners that use different types of connections to your PC — and to produce the best results, you need at least an introduction to the basics of scanning. You also need the skinny on cleaning a scanner, deciding on an image format, and handling copyrighted material. In this chapter, I provide you with an introduction to the basics of scanning.

By the way, if you're planning to copy your face — or any other body part — you don't need to read this chapter. Just visit your local copy center or stay a little late at the office. (Oh, and be discreet.)

What Happens inside a Scanner?

I can't say that it's Party Central inside your scanner; in fact, most popular scanners now on the market have very few moving parts, so the entire device is rather boring compared with a digital camera or DVD recorder. Plus, you don't really have to know how your scanner does its job in order to use one, so you can skip to the next section with a clear conscience.

Still with me? Then read on to discover how this magic box can turn a printed document into a digital image. Check out Figure 1-1.

Figure 1-1:
A scanner captures a digital image, line by line.

Here's how it works:

1. The scanner's sensor (an array of photosensitive cells) moves one line across the material you're scanning. (In some scanners, the material moves past a fixed sensor; this concept gets important pretty soon.) The sensor is paired with a strong light source that illuminates whatever you're scanning.

2. As the sensor moves past the original, each cell sends a level of current corresponding to one dot (a *pixel*) of the reflected light from the material. For example, scanning the white part of a printed page results in a far different signal than scanning the black text on the same page.

3. Your scanner's electronic brain (tiny as it is) collects all the signals from each pixel, resulting in a digital picture of one line of the original.

4. The scanner sends the data from the scanned line to your PC.

5. The sensor (or the material) advances one line, and the entire process begins again at Step 1.

I often compare this process with taking a digital photograph of each line of your document and then laboriously pasting those separate images together in an image-editing program. Luckily, you don't have to do the hard work: Your PC collects each line sent by the scanner and builds the document for you, usually while you watch. Technology is grand that way.

Your Friend, the Flatbed

I present the Mark's Maxim for this page:

Buy a *flatbed* scanner.™

Figure 1-2 illustrates a flatbed scanner preparing to do its duty; note that the top lifts up, just like a copy machine. The sensor head moves in a flatbed scanner while the material you're scanning remains motionless on top of the scanning glass. (In a second, you discover why a motionless original is A Good Thing.)

**Book VI
Chapter 1**

Figure 1-2:
Nothing
pleases like
a flatbed
scanner.

Comparatively, with a sheet-fed scanner, the material you're scanning moves through a system of rollers while the sensor remains stationary. Printer manufacturers typically use sheet-fed scanning hardware in all-in-one, or *multifunction,* devices, which combine the functionality of a printer, a scanner, a fax machine, and a copy machine in one svelte case. Gotta be honest, though; I don't recommend sheet-fed scanners. And, before all you owners of sheet-fed scanners out there in PC Land begin reaching critical mass and flooding my e-mail inbox, let me attest to the single major advantage to sheet-fed scanners, like the one you see in Figure 1-3: They take up far less space. (I know this from personal experience because I have both sheet-fed and flatbed scanners in my office.)

"Okay, Mark, I'll 'byte': If I can save valuable desktop space with a sheet-fed scanner, why are you such a diehard supporter of flatbed models?" Dear reader, here are the top three reasons why you should pick a flatbed:

✦ **They deliver a better-quality scan.** Because the original material remains fixed in a flatbed (compared with the moving original in a sheet-fed), you have less chance of shifting, which allows a flatbed to deliver a better scan with more detail.

Figure 1-3:
A sheet-fed scanner looks much like a fax machine.

✦ **They're versatile.** If an original can fit on top of the flatbed's glass, you can scan it — pages from a book, small items such as business cards, or even items such as clothing. With a sheet-fed scanner, you're limited to paper documents, and you have to use a clear plastic sleeve to hold those business cards. (Many sheet-fed scanners don't even accept small items.)

Sheet-fed owners: Keep those documents as pristine as possible meaning no torn edges, no staples, and no brittle or fragile antique documents that could suddenly decompose inside the hard-to-reach areas of your all-in-one unit.

✦ **They have fewer moving parts.** Sheet-fed scanners can easily jam if the original document doesn't feed correctly, and I've found them less reliable over the long run than flatbed models because sheet-fed scanners require more cleaning and adjustment.

If you already invested in a sheet-fed model, don't despair; there's no reason to scrap your hardware. However, you have to limit yourself somewhat in your material — unless, of course, you don't mind cutting pages from books and magazines to scan them.

Other specialized types of scanners are lurking in the shadows these days:

✦ **Negative scanners:** These expensive models are especially designed to produce the best possible scans from film negatives. They do nothing else, so versatility isn't their claim to fame. (Read about how to scan film in a bit.)

✦ **Business card scanners:** Again, the name says it all. These portable scanners capture images and information from standard-size business cards. They're often used in conjunction with laptop computers or palm-top computers.

✦ **Pen scanners:** A pen scanner captures only a single line of text at once, but they're easy to carry around and can be used with a laptop computer and OCR software to read text from documents into a word processing application.

Popular Scanner Features

Here's a list of the minimum features I typically recommend for home or home office use when you're shopping for a flatbed scanner:

**Book VI
Chapter 1**

Scanning with
Gusto

✦ **A flatbed optical resolution of at least 4800 x 9600:** Without delving too deeply into the details of scanner *resolution* — the number of pixels your scanner can capture — you should reject any flatbed scanner that offers less than 4800 x 9600 dots per inch (dpi), and any sheet-fed scanner with less than 600 x 1200 dpi. Note that you should be checking the *optical* (also often called *hardware* or *raw*) resolution and not any resolution figure that's *enhanced* or *interpolated.* Those fancy words just indicate that the scanner's software is adding extra dots in the image. I call them *faux pixels* because they aren't read from the original. Just ignore any enhanced or interpolated resolution figures when shopping for a scanner.

✦ **Single-pass operation:** If a scanner can capture all the color data that it needs in one pass, it takes less time (and introduces less room for registration error) than a scanner that must make three passes across the same original. —'Nuff said.

✦ **One-button operation:** Most scanners now offer one or more buttons that can automatically take care of common tasks. For example, one button might scan the original and create an e-mail message with the scanned image as an attachment, and another might scan the original and automatically print a copy on your system printer. I'm all about convenience.

✦ **A minimum of 42-bit color:** The higher the bit value, the more colors your scanner can capture. Ignore any scanner that can't produce at least 42-bit color; heck, many scanners can now produce up to 96-bit color!

✦ **A film adapter:** Whether it's optional or included with the scanner, the ability to add a film adapter allows you to scan film negatives and slides ("positives") with much better results.

✦ **USB or FireWire connection:** Choose a scanner that uses either a Universal Serial Bus (USB) 2.0 connection or a FireWire connection. Of course, your PC needs the prerequisite ports, as I explain in Book I, Chapter 3.

Basic Scanning with Windows Live Photo Gallery

Scanner manufacturers ship a bewildering number of different capture (or *acquisition*) programs with their hardware, so there's no single proper way to scan an original. However, scanners that comply with the TWAIN standard can be controlled from within popular image editors such as Photoshop. *TWAIN,* for you acronym nuts, is not an acronym — it refers to the line "and never the twain shall meet," from that Kipling guy. (Many folks think that TWAIN means *technology without an interesting name.* It doesn't.)

Now that you've been properly introduced, here's the important part you'll be tested on: Devices that are TWAIN compatible are operating-system-independent, meaning that these devices are interchangeable between Windows and Macintosh. Any TWAIN-compatible hardware device can work with any TWAIN-compatible image editor or software application — pretty *sassy,* no?

Acquiring the image

In this section, I demonstrate how to use a typical USB Hewlett-Packard scanner within Windows Live Photo Gallery, which you can pick up as a free add-on for Windows 7 at `http://download.live.com`. If you follow along with this procedure, you end up with an image that you can edit within a program like Photoshop, convert to another format, or simply save to your hard drive. (Of course, your scanner will also include the manufacturer's software, which likely includes at least a basic image editing program. It's up to you which editing program you choose.)

Assuming that you have the Windows Live suite loaded on your computer, follow these steps:

1. **Choose Start⇨Windows Live⇨Windows Live Photo Gallery.**

The main program window, shown in Figure 1-4, appears.

2. **Choose File⇨Import from a Scanner or Camera.**

3. **Click the entry for your scanner and then click the Import button.**

At this point, Photo Gallery invokes the scanner's TWAIN driver, so if you're using another brand of scanner, the resulting dialog box looks different; however, the same controls should be available if you explore a bit. Figure 1-5 shows the Acquire dialog box for an HP scanner.

4. **Click the Start a New Scan button (or whatever it's called within your scanner's controls).**

Your scanner should rumble to life, and eventually the Acquire dialog box produces a thumbnail image of the original.

Figure 1-4:
The Photo
Gallery main
window.

Figure 1-5:
My HP
scanner is
ready to go.

5. **If you're satisfied with the dimensions of the image and the automatic settings chosen by your scanning software, click the Send the Scan Now button.**

   The result appears as a new image within Photo Gallery, ready for you to edit and experiment to your heart's content.

However, if you need to fine-tune the image before sending it to Photo Gallery in Step 5, here are the common settings that you can change in most scanner drivers, along with what you accomplish. (With my scanner driver, you click the icon buttons under Step 3.)

✦ **Output type:** This setting controls which type of image file the scan produces. Typically, you want a color photograph in 24-bit (or 16.7 million) colors, but other choices might include a Web image at 256 colors, a grayscale image (what most folks think of as "black and white"), a true black-and-white–only drawing, or simple text (optimized for reading with an OCR program). Generally, use JPG format for smaller file sizes, and TIFF format when archival storage and highest quality is important.

✦ **Image boundaries:** Use this feature to click and drag the boundaries of the scanned image. For example, I recommend moving the scanned image border inside any extraneous material on the edges of the original, such as text that surrounds a picture you want from a magazine page. By reducing the size of the actual scan, your image file is smaller and the scanner takes less time to do its job — plus, you can save a step by cropping that extraneous part of the image now instead of later within your image editing program.

   If your scanning program includes an auto-edge detection feature, use that option and you'll likely eliminate most of this fine tuning.

✦ **Image scale:** Figure 1-6 illustrates the scale options for my HP scanner. Note that I can use the original image size, or I can scale the scanned image by a specified percentage. Also, I can set the width or height of the scanned image in inches, and the software automatically calculates the proper proportion change for the other dimension.

✦ **dpi (or resolution):** A setting of 150 to 300 dpi is usually fine for scanning photographs or documents, but if you're planning to enlarge an image with a lot of detail, you might want to specify a higher resolution. However, this significantly increases the size of the finished image file.

Rotating and cropping images

After the scanned image is safely in your image editor (either Windows Live Photo Gallery or the editing software provided by your scanner's manufacturer), you're free to have fun — fixing problems big and small, removing portions of the image that you don't want, or even zooming in to view and change individual pixels.

Figure 1-6:
Adjust the
size of the
scanned
image.

Although a complete discussion of image editing is far too in-depth of a subject for this chapter — in fact, you can find dozens of books on Photoshop and other high-octane image editing programs — I want to cover the two most common procedures required for most scanned images:

✦ **Rotation:** An image that's literally standing on end or displayed upside-down needs to be *rotated* (turned).

✦ **Cropping:** An image with too much extraneous background needs to be *cropped* (trimmed). Cropping an image can significantly cut down its file size.

To rotate an image within Photo Gallery, follow these steps:

1. **Scan an image into Photo Gallery. Or if the image already appears within Photo Gallery, click it to select it.**

Read how in the previous section.

2. **Click the Rotate Clockwise or Rotate Counter-clockwise button.**

Photo Gallery rotates the entire photo in the desired direction by 90 degrees.

If you only to need to straighten a photo — not rotate it a full 90 degrees — use the Straighten Photo feature of the Editing pane, which I discuss next.

To crop a scanned image inside Photo Gallery, follow these steps:

1. **Click the Fix button on the toolbar.**

Photo Gallery displays the Editing pane shown on the right side of Figure 1-7.

Figure 1-7:
Select an
area of
an image
before
cropping it.

Crop box   Handles   Rotate buttons

2. **Click the Crop Photo button in the Editing pane.**

   On your image, Photo Gallery displays a highlighted crop box, as shown
   in Figure 1-7. The edges of the box are marked with tiny boxes called
   handles. The area inside the box is the portion of the photo that will
   remain after the cropping is complete.

3. **Click and drag any handle to resize the crop box to the desired size.**

4. **To select a specific proportion (like 16 x 9 for use in a widescreen
   slideshow), click the Proportion drop-down list and select the desired
   ratio. To set your own proportions for the cropped image, opt for the
   Custom proportion.**

5. **Click the Apply button to remove everything outside the selection
   box; see the results in Figure 1-8.**

Figure 1-8:
The image is cropped.

Book VI
Chapter 1

Scanning with Gusto

Other simplified photo editing tools available here include Auto Adjust, Adjust Exposure, Adjust Color, Fix Red Eye, and Black and White Effects. These are rudimentary tools, though. You'll always have much more control and creativity in a beefy photo editing app like PaintShop Photo Pro X3 or Photoshop.

If you make a mistake, you can always click the Undo button at the bottom of the window to cancel the last action you performed.

Converting and saving the image

When you're finished editing your image, your new work of art is ready to be saved to disk. That leads me to discuss another feature of Photo Gallery: *conversion,* which is the ability to save a copy of the image in a different format that might be more suited to your needs.

Think of a format as the structure of the image file — which, after all, is a data file, just like the programs you run and the documents you save. The *format* is the "road map" used to organize the image data within the file. I don't go into a huge discussion of the different formats in this section; rather, I just indicate which formats are better for certain situations — and which ones you should avoid for those same situations:

✦ **Saving space:** The winner in this first category is definitely the JPEG (or JPG) image format, which can save you several megabytes over image formats such as Windows bitmap (BMP) and TIFF.

✦ **Maintaining image quality:** JPEG images are so small because they use a form of compression (rather like that used in Zip files) to crunch the file size to a minimum. Unfortunately, compression can result in image degradation over time; for example, each time you open and edit a JPEG file, it can lose a tiny bit of detail. If archival image quality is your aim, throw file size limitations to the wind and use TIFF; they're much larger, but they preserve image quality no matter how often you open them.

✦ **Operating systems compatibility:** Folks on the Mac and Linux side of the fence might have problems loading and using an image in the proprietary Windows (BMP) format. For compatibility reasons, consider saving your image in TIFF format, which is well supported on just about every computer in use.

✦ **Better suited for the Web:** Virtually all Web pages use JPEG images, which is the common format recognized by all browsers.

Okay, now that you know whether your image needs converting, follow these steps to save a copy (and optionally convert) your image within Photo Gallery:

1. **Choose File⇨Make a Copy; see Figure 1-9.**

Figure 1-9: Convert image formats in Windows Live Photo Gallery.

   2. **Open the Save as Type drop-down list (at the bottom) and then choose the desired format.**

   3. **Type a filename in the File Name field.**

      Don't worry about adding a file extension. Your choice in Step 2 takes care of that for you.

   4. **Click Save.**

Scanning Do's and Don'ts

Today's scanning software helps make the scanning process easier than it was just a few years ago, but here are some tried-and-true guidelines to follow for the best results from your hardware:

   Do

   ✦ **Work with the largest possible original.** The larger the original, the better-quality image you're likely to get. (Sure, you can scan a postage stamp, but use a higher dpi setting so that you have enough pixels to enlarge the image later.)

   ✦ **Clean your scanner glass with the right material.** Never spray glass cleaner directly on the glass: Too much liquid on the glass can leak under the surface, causing condensation later. Instead, use a soft photographer's lens cloth or a monitor wipe moistened with alcohol, which evaporates quickly. I clean my scanner glass at least once weekly.

   ✦ **Add as much memory to your PC as you can afford.** The more memory you add, the easier and faster your PC can handle larger scans. Remember that some of those scanned images might end up being 50MB (or even more). Also, any image editor performs much better with additional memory. If you're using Photoshop regularly, I recommend a minimum of 2GB. Memory, my friend, is cheap.

   ✦ **Keep your scanner drivers up to date.** Like other hardware devices that I mention throughout this book, check your scanner manufacturer's Web site often for updates to your scanning software and for Windows drivers.

   Don't

   ✦ **Overwrite your original scan.** If you're experimenting with a scanned image — for example, if you're applying filters or changing the color balance for an artistic effect — keep the original as-is but save a *copy* with your changes. After you apply changes in an image editor and save those changes, you usually can't backtrack to the quality of the original image.

✦ **Place heavy objects on your scanner's glass.** Believe it or not, I've heard horror stories of people trying to scan bricks and rocks — usually trying to capture a particular color or pattern for an e-mail attachment or a Web graphic. Besides the possibility of a cracked or a broken scanner glass, rough or pointed objects can cause scratches that show up in your images.

Paper clips and staples are Public Enemy #1 for your scanner. Remove them before you place your original!

✦ **Use outdated or specialized image formats.** PC owners should avoid Microsoft Paint (MSP) images. (I like to call these little-known and less-recognized formats by single collective acronym WIF, which stands for *w*eird *i*mage *f*ormat.) My point is simple: By using one of the major image formats (TIFF, JPEG, or BMP), you give others a better chance to load and work with your scanned images.

Those Irritating (Or Invaluable) Copyrights

Of course, copyrights aren't so doggone irritating if you happen to be the creator of a work of digital art (whether it's a photograph, a painting, or a poem). As an author, I'm personally all for copyrights. However, as a scanner owner, you might find yourself walking a legal tightrope without a pole when you decide to include scanned material in your own documents.

Like I said, I'm an author — *not a lawyer!* (I do know some great lawyer jokes, but that's not the same as a law degree.) Therefore, before I describe some common myths about copyright law, let me say that you should *always* consult with a knowledgeable copyright/intellectual properties lawyer. These guidelines are here to help, but they're not a substitute for bona fide legal advice.

With that well-worded disclaimer in mind, here's a selection of the most common fallacies concerning copyrighted material:

✦ **"I got it off the Internet, so it must be in the public domain."** Wrong. It doesn't matter where you got a creative work — from the Internet, a publication, or even off the wall of a subway tunnel. If you use anything that you didn't create completely by yourself, you need permission from the author.

✦ **"I added a line and some shading to this scanned image, so now it's mine."** Embellishing an original work does *not* make it yours. (After all, I can add an extra line of lyrics to any Beatles song that you can name, but that doesn't give me the copyright to "Eight Days a Week.")

✦ **"This photograph didn't carry a copyright mark, so the scan is my original work."** Nope. An original work, whether a document, a photograph, or a scribble on a napkin, doesn't need any mark (although a copyright mark does reinforce your copyright claim). In the legal world, a copyright is bestowed automatically in most cases as soon as the creator completes the work.

✦ **"This project is not-for-profit, so I can include this artwork."** This one *might* be true, but only if you're using something from a clipart collection or royalty-free photograph archive that gives you specific rights to use intellectual property in your work. Otherwise, it doesn't matter whether your work is for profit or nonprofit — a copyright applies to the original work in either case.

✦ **"Why, the very act of scanning this photograph gives me the copyright."** I don't hear this one often. Evidently, by creating a digital copy, these folks think that they can magically acquire the copyright. (Sound of palm slapping forehead.) Why didn't I think of that strategy before? Oh, yes, now I remember — it's *not true.* Simply changing the form of a work doesn't release the creator's copyright.

✦ **"This artwork was drawn 100 years ago — the copyright doesn't apply to me."** Before you assume that a copyright has expired on a work, check with a copyright lawyer. Descendants of the original copyright owner might now own the rights to the work.

Chapter 2: Dude, MP3 Rocks!

In This Chapter

- ✔ Understanding the MP3 format
- ✔ Ripping MP3 files from an audio CD
- ✔ Playing MP3 files
- ✔ Downloading MP3 music to your MP3 player
- ✔ Comparing other audio formats with MP3
- ✔ Burning audio CDs from MP3 files

Can you name one or two truly revolutionary technologies that have arrived in the past 20 years? Perhaps CD-ROMs and DVD-ROMs, cell-phones, or *Oprah?* (Okay, that last one was a deliberate attempt at humor.) Anyway, historians often claim that no person can accurately point to a world-changing technology in his lifetime because we just don't have the perspective to recognize its importance when it happens.

Well, guess what? MP3 is here in your lifetime; it absolutely rocks, and, my friend, it is *indeed* one of those revolutionary technologies. You can quote me on this, with a Mark's Maxim I coined several years ago that made me a visionary (who wears glasses):

The creation and distribution of digital music will permanently change everything in the recording industry, including the career of every musician on the planet.™

To be honest, that wasn't really such an earth-shattering prediction — in fact, it's already happening! In this chapter, I tell you what's so incredibly cool about MP3 digital music, how you can create your own MP3s, and (here's the spoiler) why the recording industry would love to stop you from using MP3 files altogether.

And yes, MP3 is legal when used correctly. Sorry, Big Brother Music.

An MP3 Primer

First, what is a furshlugginer MP3, anyway? Things can get really technical really fast here, and that's not what this book is about — therefore, here's my definition of the MP3 process for Normal Human Beings:

> When you create (or *rip*) an MP3 (short for MPEG-1 Layer 3) file, you're capturing (or *sampling*) an analog sound recording and saving that audio in digital form.

Clear as mud? Here's another way to think of it: MP3 files store music and audio in the same fashion that music is stored on an audio CD — as a string of *binary* characters. It's all zeroes and ones, but your PC — and Macs and MP3 players and even many personal electronic devices, such as personal digital assistants (PDAs), car CD players, and portable stereos — can decode that binary information and re-create it as the original analog signal.

 Note that just about any CD- or DVD-ROM drive — including the read-only variety — can rip tracks, so you don't need a CD or DVD recorder to do the job. The process is technically called *digital audio extraction,* but you and I call it *ripping.*

Here are more parallels between audio CDs and MP3 files:

+ A typical MP3 file corresponds to a single track on an audio CD (which makes sense because virtually all MP3s are ripped directly from audio CDs).

+ MP3 files offer the same — or even better — audio quality than audio CDs.

+ Like the tracks on an audio CD, MP3 files can contain information about the song title and artist.

+ Like the music on an audio CD, the quality of an MP3 recording stays pristine no matter how many copies of that MP3 file you make. Because an MP3 is digital, it suffers no degradation when you make additional copies of it.

+ A series of MP3 files can be recorded (or burned) onto a blank CD-R, creating a new audio CD. You can even burn MP3 files from many different CDs to produce your own compilation discs.

Because an MP3 file is just another data file to your PC, you can do many of the same things with an MP3 file that you can do with other digital media files (such as an image from your digital camera). For example, you can

+ **Send 'em.** Send smaller MP3s as e-mail attachments — generally, most ISPs allow you to send 2 or 3MB (total) of attachments for a message.

+ **Offer 'em.** Allow MP3 files to be downloaded from your Web site or File Transfer Protocol (FTP) server. (You must have legal ownership of the file to be able to offer it for downloading. A good example would be an independent recording artist allowing others to download her music for free.)

✦ **Save 'em.** Save MP3 files to removable media, like CDs, DVDs, and Universal Serial Bus (USB) Flash drives.

Of course, this very portability is a double-edged sword because it makes MP3 music easy to copy — which, under copyright law, is a synonym for *steal.* I discuss what you can and can't legally do with your MP3 files in a sidebar toward the end of the chapter.

The audio quality of an MP3 file is determined by the *bit rate* at which it's *sampled* (a fancy engineering term for *recorded*). The higher the bit rate, the better the sound file (and the larger the size of the physical MP3 file itself, which makes sense). Table 2-1 lists some common bit rates for different types of MP3 files; anything more than 128 Kbps is actually better than the quality of audio CD tracks.

Table 2-1	Bit Rates for MP3 Files
Quality Level	*Bit Rate*
Audio book	48 Kbps
FM stereo	64 Kbps
Near CD	96 Kbps
Audio CD	128 Kbps
Audiophile	160/192/256/320 Kbps

Ripping Your Own MP3 Files

To demonstrate just how easily you can rip MP3 files from an audio CD, I'll choose one from my collection at random — hmmm, how about music legends Frank Sinatra and Count Basie and their classic 1963 album *Sinatra-Basie?* — and then extract a set of MP3 files that I can listen to with my MP3 player.

For this demonstration, I'll use the Microsoft tool of choice for ripping MP3 files on the PC: Windows Media Player 12, which is built in to Windows 7! PC owners using Windows Vista and XP can run version 11 of Windows Media Player, which you can find at

www.microsoft.com/windows/windowsmedia/player/previousversions.aspx

Here's the first inkling of the copyright controversy, which I wade into at the end of this chapter: You can legally rip MP3 files *only from audio CDs you bought for yourself!* If you rip songs from a friend's CD — or even an audio CD that you borrowed from the public library — you're violating copyright law. (In this case, I own this audio CD, so I can legally create MP3 files from it for my own, personal use. However, I can't give those MP3 files to anyone else, or else I'm in violation of copyright law.)

Now that Perry Mason has had his say, follow these steps to create your own MP3 files from an audio CD:

1. **Click the Windows Media Player icon in the Quick Launch bar, or click Start and type** Windows Media **into the Search box. Media Player displays the main window you see in Figure 2-1.**

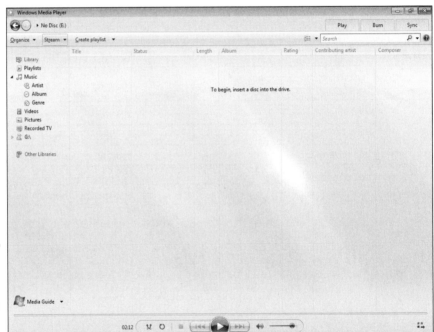

Figure 2-1: Windows Media Player struts its stuff.

2. **Load the audio CD with the music you want to rip into your drive.**

Media Player automatically connects to the Internet and retrieves the track names and album cover. The program displays the CD information in the window (see Figure 2-2) and begins to play the CD. Because I don't want to listen to the disc right now, I click the Stop button (the square) on the control strip at the bottom of the window.

Stop

Figure 2-2:
Media
Player
automati-
cally plays
an audio CD.

3. **Before you extract any tracks, you must configure the MP3 settings within Media Player. Click the Rip Settings button in the toolbar at the top of the window.**

4. **From the menu that opens, choose Format and then choose MP3 Format.**

    In this case, I want my MP3 tracks for my iPod player (instead of the default, which is Microsoft's Windows Media Audio or WMA format).

5. **Click the Rip Settings button again; choose Audio Quality and then choose 128 Kbps from the list.**

    Typically, CD-quality (128 Kbps) is the best choice for ripping MP3 music with Windows Media Player, unless you prefer audiophile sampling rates with higher quality. (Remember, though, that higher bit rates result in larger MP3 files.)

6. **Mark the tracks you want to rip.**

    By default, Media Player automatically rips all tracks on the disc. However, if you don't want to rip all the tracks, you can select individual songs from the track list. Click the check box next to a track to select or deselect it.

7. **Click the Rip CD button on the toolbar.**

The completed MP3 files are placed in a separate folder within your Music folder, complete with the artist name and album title. Media Player also adds the tracks to your Media Player Library, which you can display by clicking the Music entry in the Navigation pane at the left side of the Media Player window.

Listening to Your Stuff

After you're riding the digital wave of the future and rip a number of MP3 files, you're ready to enjoy them. Here are a number of different ways to listen to MP3s on your PC using Windows 7:

✦ **Double-click an MP3 file.** Double-clicking an MP3 file loads the program associated with MP3 audio on your system. By default, this program is Windows Media Player, but if you installed another MP3 player — such as the excellent Apple digital audio player, iTunes (www.apple.com/itunes, shown in Figure 2-3) — Windows plays the file with that program instead.

Figure 2-3: Another MP3 favorite, iTunes from Apple, hard at work.

✦ **Right-click an MP3 file and choose Play from the menu that appears.**

✦ **Run Windows Media Player.** As I mention earlier, you can always display the tracks you added to your collection by clicking the Music entry. To play a specific song, double-click it in the track list. You can also switch between displaying songs by artist, album, and genre.

If Windows 7 is using the wrong application to play MP3 files — for example, you installed iTunes but you want Windows Media Player to run when you double-click an MP3 file — it's time to change the association for the file. Right-click the MP3 file, choose Open With from the menu that appears, and then choose Choose Default Program to display the Open With dialog box, which you see in Figure 2-4. Click the application with which you want to play your MP3 files, make sure that the Always Use the Selected Program to Open This Kind of File check box is selected, and then click OK.

**Book VI
Chapter 2**

Dude, MP3 Rocks!

Figure 2-4:
Change the
association
for an MP3
file.

To skip to the previous and next tracks, click the Previous and Next buttons on the Media Player control strip at the bottom of the window — huge surprise there, right?

MP3s are easy to pause while you're retrieving your toaster pastry from the toaster. Just click the Pause button to pause the audio and click it again to restart the playback.

Internet radio arrives

Wait — there's more! Digital audio players like Windows Media Player and iTunes can now open up an entirely new world of music: broadcasts of Internet radio stations! Computer technomusic jocks call this method of delivery *Internet audio streaming*.

You can tune in to an Internet radio station from a sponsoring Web site (like my favorite, SHOUTcast, at `www.shoutcast.com`) or from the Windows Media Guide Web page (click the Media Guide button at the bottom left corner of the Media Player window).

Just like everything else on the Internet, you enjoy better-quality stations and have less trouble if you have a broadband DSL or cable connection, but even dialup Internet users can take advantage of Internet radio. To try out a station, visit my Web site at `www.mlcbooks.com` and follow the instructions you find there to connect to *MLC Radio*. I specialize in classic hits from 1970–1979, delivered commercial-free (and in CD-quality stereo, if you have a broadband connection).

You can also create a group of songs — a *playlist* — and return to that group at any time in the future (a great feature if you like to match your music to your mood). To create a playlist, click the Create Playlist button on the toolbar. Media Player adds a new unnamed entry under the Playlists heading at the left of the window, ready for you to type a descriptive name. Press Enter to save your name and create the playlist.

Now you can add songs to your new playlist: Click the Music header at the left of the window to display your song collection, and then click and drag track names from your library to the playlist entry in the Navigation pane. You can drag as many tracks as you like, and you can click and drag the track titles within your playlist to rearrange them! To load that playlist in the future, just click the playlist name in the Navigation pane.

Downloading to an MP3 Player

Here's another significantly cool thing that your PC can do for you: Download MP3 files to your personal MP3 player for your portable listening pleasure. For example, I use my iPod, which has 80GB of storage, a built-in 12-hour battery, and a very fast USB 2.0 connection. (Although PC owners might not like it, the iPod is another masterpiece of design from our friends at Apple Computer, `www.apple.com`. Luckily, the iPod works on the PC as well when using the Apple iTunes player.) I heartily recommend the iPod sweet machine as the best MP3 player now on the market. In fact, iTunes automatically downloads and synchronizes your music on both your PC and your iPod, so there's really not much else to say.

But wait — what if you don't have an iPod? If you're using one of the many MP3 player models supported within Windows Media Player, you're still in good shape! However, you may have to install a specific driver or plug-in for your player (these files are supplied by your MP3 player manufacturer, so follow the instructions provided by the installation program to add them to your system).

When any drivers or plug-ins are installed, follow the steps in the previous section to add MP3 tracks to your playlist (or to load an existing playlist).

To download the songs in your current Media Player playlist to your MP3 player, follow these steps:

1. **Plug your MP3 player into the USB or FireWire port.**

   Windows should automatically recognize that you plugged in the device.

2. **Click the Sync tab at the top right of the window.**

   Media Player should recognize your device and display the sync list. Drag and drop individual tracks or complete playlists to the sync list.

3. **Click the Start Sync button.**

4. **After the copying process is complete, unplug your player and jam!**

Using Other Sound Formats

I would be remiss if I didn't mention some of the other sampled sound formats out there on the Internet (and sometimes swapped between PC owners). However, the MP3 format is now so popular for music that these other formats have been reduced to storing Windows sound effects and such. Some sound editors can convert audio between different formats, but if you're working with music, you can't lose with MP3.

WAV format

The Microsoft Windows Audio/Video (WAV) audio format is the standard format used by Windows for playing sound effects, and it's also used in games and on the Web. Your browser should recognize and play WAV audio files like a familiar old friend. Although WAV files can be recorded at audio CD quality — and therefore can be used to record music — MP3 files offer the same (or better) quality and are much smaller (*megabytes* smaller) in comparison. All current versions of Windows include a simple sound recorder that can capture WAV files by using a microphone plugged into your PC.

WMA format

Not to be outdone by MP3, Microsoft has been pushing the WMA (Windows Media Audio) format as a contender for the Best Digital Audio Format crown. Indeed, WMA files are as high in quality as MP3 files, and WMA audio can be recorded in multichannel 5.1 Surround sound. However, I don't see the challenger from Redmond usurping MP3 any time soon. For once, I think that the open standard is stronger than any proprietary standard that Microsoft attempts to enforce. For example, many current MP3 players don't recognize or support WMA tracks — and portable MP3 players sure don't need Surround sound. Plus, the built-in DRM protection (short for Digital Rights Management) severely limits what you can do with your WMA tracks — you may not be able to burn an audio CD with your WMA-format music, for example, or play that track on another PC.

AAC format

Apple's entry into the digital audio format wars is higher in quality and smaller in size than MP3, so they make a good choice for squeezing the largest number of songs into your MP3 player (as long as it supports AAC, like the iPod). Any music you download from the iTunes Store is in AAC format. Note, however, that Windows Media Player doesn't support AAC.

AU format

The Audio Unix (AU) format was introduced by Sun Microsystems, so (as you would expect) it's a popular standard for systems running Unix and Linux. AU audio files are typically of lower quality than MP3 files, but they're even smaller in size, making them popular on many Web sites. Luckily, both Internet Explorer and Firefox can play AU files with ease.

AIFF format

Apple once used the Audio Interchange File Format (AIFF) as standard equipment within its operating systems, including music files. However, these days, the Cupertino Crew has switched wholeheartedly and completely to AAC, so AIFF has already started down the road once taken by the dinosaurs. (Mac OS 9 and Mac OS X still recognize AIFF files for sound effects, but that's about it.) Although AIFF files can be recorded at CD quality, they're simply huge, so don't expect to find them on the Web or on your personal MP3 player.

MIDI format

Musical Instrument Digital Interface (MIDI) files aren't digital audio but instead are directions on how to play a song — kind of like how a program is a set of directions that tells your computer how to accomplish a task. Your PC or a MIDI instrument (like a MIDI keyboard) can read a MIDI file and play back the song. As you might guess, however, MIDI music really doesn't sound like the digitally sampled sound you get from an MP3 or WMA file. I discuss MIDI support when I cover upgrading your sound card in Book VII, Chapter 5.

Burning Audio CDs from MP3 Files

Return with me (or just come along) to the multitalented Windows Media Player so that I can demonstrate how to burn your own audio CDs from your MP3 collection. The resulting disc is a perfect match for any home or car CD player and can also be played in your PC's CD or DVD drive.

To record an audio CD from MP3 files, follow these steps:

1. **Click the Burn tab at the top right of the window.**

2. **Drag tracks and playlists to the burn list.**

Figure 2-5 shows a burn list that I created.

3. **Load a blank CD-R into your recorder.**

Only certain audio CD players can read a CD-RW (rewriteable disc), so always use write-once CD-R media for true compatibility with all audio CD players.

4. **Click the Start Burn button — and sit back and relax while your new disc is recorded.**

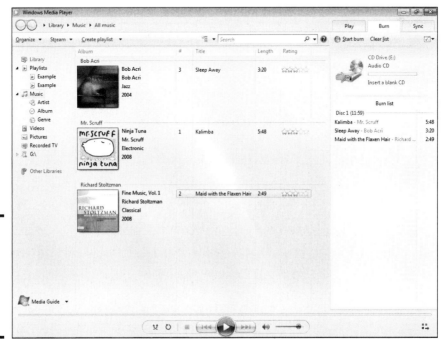

Figure 2-5:
Selecting songs to burn to an audio CD with Media Player.

I got the music in me — illegally?

"Okay Mark, everything that I've read in this chapter is cool beyond belief — now, what's this you're telling me? My MP3 (or WMA, or AAC) collection might be *illegal?*" It's possible — it all depends on where you obtained the original audio CDs! Here's the rule: If you didn't buy the audio CD and you don't own it, you can't legally rip any audio. Period. (Naturally, if you purchase and download music from an online store like Amazon or iTunes, that music is also legal for you to own.)

The reasoning behind this copyright law is similar to the law governing the duplication of computer programs, where only the owner is generally allowed to copy a piece of commercial software. By law, any copy of a program that you make is to be used for backup purposes; you can't give that copy to anyone else, and it can't be loaded on anyone else's PC.

Likewise, you can create all the MP3 files from your own audio CDs that you like, and you can listen to them with your personal MP3 player — but you can't give those MP3 files to anyone else. You also can't distribute them over the Web or Internet newsgroups, and you can't give one of your *Best of Slim Whitman* compilation CDs to your friend.

Music publishers are considering a number of different copy protection–schemes that can help safeguard audio CDs from wanton ripping; as I mention earlier, the WMA and AAC formats include copy protection. Only the future will determine just how successful these schemes will be. You know how tricky those hackers can be, and it's likely that any copy protection will be broken sooner or later.

Of course, not everyone follows these rules to the letter. As a matter of fact, I don't know any folks who spend their nights tossing and turning because they ripped tracks from *Johnny Cash at Folsom Prison*. However, it's my duty to make sure that you know the legal ramifications of The Rip Thing. End of story.

Chapter 3: Making Movies with Your PC

In This Chapter

✔ **Adding and importing clips and photos**

✔ **Assembling a movie**

✔ **Adding transitions**

✔ **Using special effects**

✔ **Adding a soundtrack**

✔ **Using titles**

✔ **Previewing your movie**

✔ **Saving and recording the finished film**

*H*ave you long harbored the urge to make your own film? You pick the subject — from your kid's kindergarten graduation to a science fiction action flick worthy of James Cameron himself. You edit your footage, add professional-looking transitions and special effects, and even set the mood with a custom soundtrack recorded on your aunt's antique Hammond organ. Ladies and gentlemen, this is the definition of *sweet* — and it's all made possible by your PC. (For the full effect, buy a canvas director's chair and a megaphone.)

In this chapter, I demonstrate how you can use footage from your digital video (DV) camcorder — or, with the right equipment, even the footage you recorded on tape — to produce your own film. Your finished work of visual art can be saved to a recordable DVD or stored on your hard drive for use on your Web pages.

Getting the Lowdown on Windows Live Movie Maker

My filmmaking tool of choice is Windows Live Movie Maker, as shown in Figure 3-1. The program is available for free as part of the Windows Live Essentials suite, which you can download at `http://download.live.com`. Live Movie Maker runs like a well-oiled machine under XP, Vista, and Windows 7.

Movie Maker tab

Player window

Storyboard

Ribbon

Figure 3-1:
It's easy
to edit and
enhance
your movies
in Windows
Live Movie
Maker.

After you install Live Movie Maker, you can run it from the Start menu by
choosing Start➪All Programs➪Windows Live➪Windows Live Movie Maker.

Take a moment to examine the Live Movie Maker main window, and you'll
see the three major controls you use:

✦ **Ribbon:** Like the Office 2010 applications, Live Movie Maker includes
this powerful collection of command buttons, which changes to reflect
the tab you select.

✦ **Player window:** It sounds self-explanatory, and (for a change) it is. The
Player window allows you to play back and view your movie within Live
Movie Maker while you're working on it.

✦ **Storyboard:** If you're familiar with the concept of *storyboarding* in cine-
matography — where sketches of scenes are arranged to create a paper
mock-up of the film — you probably already guessed that you use this
section of the window to add and reorder items that you import from
your hard drive. And you're right. These media clips are the building
blocks of your finished movie.

Rounding Up Clips and Images

First things first. Live Movie Maker might not directly import video clips from some camcorders! Instead, depending on the camcorder you're using, you might need to run the software that came with your camcorder to import your video clips to your hard drive.

After you import your clips, however, Live Movie Maker does allow you to import digital photographs and use them anywhere you like within your movie — even directly from your scanner or your digital camera. Digital cameras that also take video might allow you to directly import video clips as well.

To import video clips or photos that are saved to your hard drive, follow these steps:

1. **Open an Explorer window.**

2. **Navigate to the location of the video or photograph that you want to add.**

3. **Drag it to the storyboard pane within the Live Movie Maker window.**

To add video clips and photos from your hard drive via the Ribbon, click the Add Videos and Photos command button to display a standard Open dialog; select the desired items and then click Open. Live Movie Maker supports a very wide range of common video, audio, and image formats — at the time of this writing, however, there's no support for DivX video clips, and any media you add can't be copy-protected with Digital Rights Management (DRM).

Video clips appear as a filmstrip, and photos appear as individual snapshots. (Live Movie Maker can produce slide show movies from photos, so it's not necessary to add video to a project.)

Book VI
Chapter 3

Making Movies
with Your PC

Never the TWAIN shall meet

TWAIN. You're probably saying to yourself, "Self, that's the most ridiculous acronym yet." Well, it sounds silly — many folks think that the acronym stands for *technology without an interesting name.* However, in this case TWAIN is not an acronym at all; it refers to the famous poem by Kipling, *The Ballad of East and West,* which includes the line "and never the twain shall meet." It makes sense, considering that the TWAIN standard helps make sure that your scanner and software, like Live Movie Maker,

can work together. Never let it be said that technotypes don't have occasional flashes of wry literary humor!

By the way, if you're not completely acronym-happy by now, visit VERA, the Virtual Entity of Relevant Acronyms, no less — on the Web at `http://cgi.snafu.de/ohei/user-cgi-bin/veramain-e.cgi`, and you can discover the true meaning of computer-related acronyms to your heart's content.

Besides importing from your hard drive, here are other ways to import video and audio clips:

✦ **Download them.** Any still images or and sample video clips you download from the Web are suitable for use in Live Movie Maker (as long as they're legal for you to use, and video clips are not protected with DRM).

✦ **Acquire clips and photos from your camcorder, scanner, or camera.** If your camcorder, scanner, or digital camera is TWAIN compatible, O Happy Day! (Find out more in the sidebar, "Never the TWAIN shall meet.")

   a. *Connect your hardware.*

   b. *Click the blue Movie Maker tab.*

   c. *Click Import from Device to import items directly.*

   As shown in Figure 3-2, Live Movie Maker prompts you to select the image source from the available TWAIN-compatible hardware devices. Again, the process varies according to the hardware you're using, but if you're experienced with scanning or downloading images, you're in familiar waters.

Figure 3-2:
Putting
TWAIN
to work,
importing
video and
photos.

Building Your First Movie

After you import all the pieces of your new film, it's time to grab your megaphone and start creating. You start by adding items in the linear Storyboard window, which you use to literally assemble your movie, moving from left to right.

I like to map out the general flow of my film on paper — even as a simple list of scenes, titles, and images — before I start creating it. However, Live Movie Maker makes editing so easy that many folks can simply build a film on the fly, following their inspiration where it takes them. Go figure.

Anyway, when you're ready for the real work, add all the video clips and photos you want to use. Figure 3-3 illustrates the first photo and video clip that I added to my film.

When you have multiple items in the Storyboard pane, you can change their order by clicking and dragging an item from one media square to the desired media square.

Figure 3-3: Photos and video clips find a home in the Storyboard pane.

If you decide against using a clip or photo, delete it from the Storyboard pane by right-clicking the item on the strip and then choosing Remove from the pop-up menu that appears.

To trash all the media you added within the Storyboard pane and start completely over, right-click any item on the strip and choose Select All from the menu that appears. Then right-click again and choose Remove from the menu that appears.

Adding Transitions without Breaking a Sweat

Imagine a film that cuts directly from scene to scene with fade-ins, fade-outs, dissolves, or wipes. These are all types of *transitions* — and without transitions, your movie ends up moving at a frantic pace. (I call it *jarring the audience;* most horror films are shot with few transitions.) Of course, this might be your intention with some projects, but it's not likely to be your goal with most films you make. In this section, I demonstrate how to add transitions to your film.

Transitions can be placed within the Storyboard pane only after you add at least one video clip or still image. After the pane contains at least one item, follow these steps:

1. **Click the Animations tab to display the list of transitions, as shown in Figure 3-4. (Click the More drop-down list button, which bears a horizontal line over a downward-facing arrow, to display additional transition effects.)**

2. **Click the item in the Storyboard pane that should follow the transition.**

If you need to place a transition between a photo followed by a video clip, for example, click the video clip to select it.

No Transition

Figure 3-4:
Add transitions to tie your clips and photos together.

3. **Click a transition from the Ribbon to select it.**

   Live Movie Maker has a cool feature to help you decide which transition you want to use: Click a transition in the list, and the item animates in the Player window to demonstrate how the transition will appear onscreen.

   To add the same transition throughout your movie, right-click any item in the Storyboard pane and choose Select All. Then click on the desired transition.

4. **To delete a transition you added to the strip, click the following item again and click the "blank" No Transition button at the far left of the Transition group.**

   Or, to get radical, right-click any item and choose Select All, and then click the No Transition button to remove all transitions in your film with one fell swoop.

As you experiment with transitions, you begin to understand where your movie needs them to link together scenes and still images, as well as where you can simply cut from one item to the next. One cardinal rule of filmmaking is to maintain the focus of your audience on your message: Too many transitions are distracting.

Book VI
Chapter 3

Making Movies with Your PC

Adding Special Effects without Paying George Lucas

Ready to take your creativity up a notch? Click the Visual Effects tab to display the Effects group you see in Figure 3-5. From there, you can add special visual effects throughout your film.

When most of us think about special effects in the movies, *Star Wars* and *Harry Potter* come to mind: light-sabers, flying brooms, and invisibility cloaks. (I really, *really* want one of those cloaks.) However, in the world of video editing, an *effect* is a special visual appearance that you add to the video. For example, Live Movie Maker allows you to

+ Flip your movie's alignment (horizontally or vertically).

+ Change color footage to black and white.

+ Rotate your entire movie 360 degrees.

+ Turn your movie into an animated charcoal drawing.

Maybe these effects aren't appropriate for your sister's wedding video, but when the subject of your movie is fun and games or when you want to create a new film *noir* masterpiece in stark black-and-white, effects are just the ticket. (Horrible pun intended.)

Figure 3-5:
Add all sorts
of visual
bells and
whistles
using
Effects.

To experiment with effects, simply click the desired item in the Storyboard pane to select it. Or, throw caution utterly to the wind: Right-click any item and then click Select All to apply the effect to your entire movie. Now click any effect thumbnail on the Ribbon and gauge the results.

Again, you can delete an effect on an item (or on your entire film) by selecting whatever needs fixing and clicking the "blank" No Effect button at the left side of the Effects group. How 'bout them apples, Mr. Hitchcock?

Adding Sound

What movie is complete without a stirring soundtrack? For example, would the zombies in *Return of the Living Dead* have been anywhere near as scary without that punk rock playing in the background? Or, how about the signature scary chord you heard every time you saw any body part from the monster in *Creature from the Black Lagoon*? With Live Movie Maker, it's easy to add music to your movie.

If a video clip already contains audio, you don't have to add anything. However, you can still overlay — or, as videoheads call it, *dub* — extra music or sound effects, which play along with the audio from the clip.

Live Movie Maker program accepts audio in MP3 and Microsoft WAV formats. (Just don't forget those pesky copyrights, and add only what you're legally allowed to add.)

To add a soundtrack, follow these steps:

1. **Click the Home tab.**
2. **Click the Add Music command button and click Add Music on the pop-up menu.**
3. **Navigate to the desired audio, select it, and then click Open.**

After you add music to your movie, it appears as a named "strip" over the items in the Storyboard. To delete the musical score, just click this strip and press the Delete key.

You've Just Gotta Have Titles!

In movie jargon, *titles* can be anything from the opening titles of your film to the ending credits. With Live Movie Maker, you can open your film with impressive titles that fill the screen, or you can thank your brother for being the best boy, grip, or gaffer. (I have no earthly idea what those exalted individuals do, but they must be pretty important.)

To add a title, click the item that the title should precede, click the Home tab, and click the Title button. As you can see in Figure 3-6, the Player window turns into a text field where you type your title. To save your changes, simply click in any open space within the Storyboard pane.

Heck, Live Movie Maker can end your film with professional-looking credits as well! Choose Home➪Credits, and the program automatically adds a credits item to the end of the movie. The credits item works just like a title item, so it only takes a few seconds to thank your gaffer.

Don't forget to add effects to your titles and credits! When you select your title or credits item, the Ribbon includes a number of different animated effects to choose from — click a button to check out the effect.

Figure 3-6:
No movie
is complete
without
titles.

Previewing Your Oscar-Winning Work

Okay, I know you're itching to see what your next masterpiece looks like.
Lucky for you, Live Movie Maker allows you to preview your work at any
time. Of course, your Storyboard strip must contain at least one video clip
or still image, or else you have nothing to preview.

✦ **To view the entire film from beginning to end:**

 a. *Click the slider under the Player window and drag it all the way to the
 left.*

 b. *Click the familiar Play button.*

✦ **To preview the film from another point:**

 a. *Drag the slider to the desired point*

 b. *Click the Play button.*

When you click Play, Live Movie Maker displays a black vertical line (commonly called a *scrubber bar*) across the items in the Storyboard pane. The program also displays the total duration of the selected clip (or the entire movie) as well as the elapsed time.

Saving and Sharing Before Traveling to Cannes

I think that Cannes is somewhere in France — or perhaps Belgium. Anyway, it's a big thing among filmmaking legends like you and me, so you want at least one copy of your finished masterwork to carry along with you. Luckily, Live Movie Maker allows you to save your films, burn them to DVD, or even share them on YouTube — which I cover in this last section. (You'll see many of these same commands on the Ribbon in the Sharing group.)

You can always save your work in progress. To save a project that you're working on to your hard drive for later, click the Movie Maker tab and choose Save Project. Windows opens the familiar Save As dialog box, where you can specify a location and a filename.

After your project is completed, here are two methods you can use to produce a finished movie.

Creating a digital video file

If you simply want to watch your film on your PC monitor or burn it to a DVD, this option is best. Just don't forget that it can take several hundred megabytes or more of space to store a single movie. Follow these steps:

1. **Click the Movie Maker tab and click Save Movie.**

2. **Choose the quality or destination.**

   You can choose between several different resolutions, including high-definition, widescreen, or standard TV. Note that you can also choose to record the movie to a DVD, or prepare the movie for use with a mobile phone or as an e-mail attachment.

3. **Choose a location and type a name; then click Save.**

If you chose to burn the movie to a DVD, Windows 7 leads you through the process automatically.

Sharing your masterpiece on YouTube

Talk about convenience! Live Movie Maker automatically formats your movie for optimum viewing on YouTube and then sends it there for you. If you have an existing account on YouTube, simply follow these steps:

1. **Click the Movie Maker tab and click Publish Movie.**

2. **Choose Publish on YouTube.**

   Live Movie Maker displays a dialog box where you can enter your YouTube username and password.

3. **Click Sign In.**

   After Movie Maker logs you in, you're given the chance to enter a name and description, and then the film is uploaded for you. See you at the Oscars!

Chapter 4: I Can Make My Own DVDs?

In This Chapter

✔ Adding video clips

✔ Previewing your DVD menu

✔ Recording a finished DVD video

As a PC owner — and as a dedicated movie fan with my own digital video (DV) camcorder — I honestly can't think of a current technology in the world of personal computers that's more exciting than burning my own DVD videos! That's why I chose the title for this chapter: DVD recording is still new enough and sounds so much like rocket science that even many PC power users don't know much about it. (Another large cross section of PC owners knows that recording DVDs is possible on a PC but thinks that it's too complex or far too expensive.)

With the drop in the price of DVD recorders — and the availability of easy-to-use DVD authoring software, such as Windows DVD Maker — recording your own DVD videos is now kid's stuff. Trust me: You *can* do this, and it doesn't cost you an arm and a leg. Your DVD videos will have professional-looking menus, and they'll run on standard DVD players. But rather than watch Arnold Schwarzenegger, you'll watch your family at Walt Disney World. (And, unlike those VHS tapes, your DVD home movies will never wear out!)

In this chapter, I concentrate on showing you how to record DVDs by using existing video clips and multimedia files from your hard drive.

Welcome to Windows DVD Maker

Windows DVD Maker is — wait for it — absolutely free, so you can produce truly professional-looking DVD movies on your own PC on the cheap. To begin your foray into the world of Digital Versatile Discs (or whatever the heck *DVD* means — check out the nearby sidebar), choose Start➪All Programs➪Windows DVD Maker. The program displays the wizard you see in Figure 4-1.

I should know what DVD stands for . . .

. . . and the rest of the civilized world is still scratching its head as well. Normally, I'm pretty sure about what an abbreviation stands for, but in this case, I have two choices!

When the DVD standards were being developed, everyone agreed that the recordable version of the new disc would be useful for all sorts of neat tasks — not just for video storage but also for backups, data, superior audio, and anything else that a PC owner with 4.7GB of free space handy could think of. Therefore, everyone proudly agreed that the new standard should be named DVD, short for Digital Versatile Disc. Everyone went home and celebrated.

However, it took three or four years for recordable DVD technology to arrive at a price point that regular folks could afford. And by that time, DVD had become firmly entrenched in people's minds as a video storage medium. (After all,

DVD movies caught on like wildfire — there was none of that VHS-versus-Betamax waffling that the 50-something crowd remembers. Or even the HD-DVD/Blu-Ray war so recently fought . . . it was over much quicker though.)

During that same time, everyone without a DVD standards book handy took one look at the abbreviation and exclaimed, "That's got to mean *Digital Video Disc*, right?" Now, even most computer books and Web sites claim that Digital Video Disc is the original meaning!

That leaves us with one of the most interesting acronyms this side of TWAIN, which is commonly considered to mean *technology without an interesting name,* but actually *doesn't.* (In fact, it's not even an acronym). And, whether you side with the original translation or the popular meaning, everyone still agrees that DVD technology is the cat's meow. (You can still celebrate, if you like.)

Figure 4-1:
The initial
Windows
DVD Maker
window —
I like things
easy.

From here, you click the Choose Photos and Videos button to select the content for your DVD, which I demonstrate in the next section.

Of the slew of different DVD formats out there, only one is compatible with virtually all DVD players: *DVD-R,* the record-once version of the DVD-RW (rewriteable disc). If you burn a DVD project on a DVD-RW, DVD+R, or DVD+RW, it might not run on an older DVD player. Or, even worse, it might run fine on your player but be useless on your Aunt Betty's machine. The *+R/RW* and *-R/RW* formats are different, too, and they're not compatible! I do believe that a Mark's Maxim is in order:

The only way to be completely sure that a DVD format produced by your recorder will work on a particular DVD player is to actually try it!™

Clips 'R Easy!

DVD authoring programs allow you to build a menu system that can be controlled by a DVD player's remote control. In the past, DVD authoring software was a confusing nest of weird-looking arrows, funky technical terms, and configuration settings that would give a Mensa member a splitting headache — but applications like Windows DVD Maker (and iDVD, in the Mac world) have revolutionized how you construct a DVD video.

In this example, I show you how to build a menu system with multiple video clips and a professional-looking, animated menu! As I mention earlier in this chapter, open Windows DVD Maker, click the Choose Photos and Videos button on the first page of the wizard; then follow these steps:

1. **Click the Add Items button on the toolbar.**

The program displays the Add Items to DVD dialog box, which you see in Figure 4-2, already set to display media files from your Videos Library.

Figure 4-2:
Peruse your
hard drive
for video
clips.

2. **Navigate to a specific clip on your system and double-click the clip to load it.**

   This step displays your first video in the media list, as shown in Figure 4-3. The pie chart in the lower-left corner of the window lets you know how much time remains on a standard DVD after you add your clips.

   You can produce your own video clips and slideshows using Windows Live Movie Maker, which I cover in Chapter 3 of this minibook!

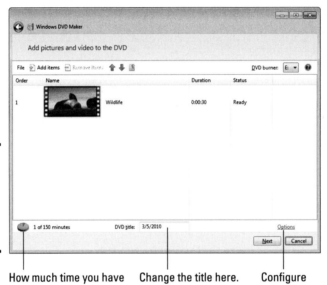

Figure 4-3: Add a video clip, and it shows up in the Media list.

How much time you have   Change the title here.   Configure disc settings.

3. **If you want, change the title for your disc to something more descriptive:**

   a. *Click within the DVD Title text box.*

   b. *Type the new label for your disc and then press Enter to save it.*

4. **Click the Options link to open the DVD Options dialog box, where you configure your disc settings (see Figure 4-4).**

   • *Playback settings:* By default, the DVD you produce opens with a menu, but you can choose to play the video clips first and then show the menu, or even play the video continuously without a menu (a useful feature for those who need a "kiosk" video presentation).

   • *DVD aspect ratio:* For the best compatibility, choose 4:3 DVD aspect ratio (standard TV).

- *Video format:* For the best compatibility, choose NTSC for use in the United States. For compatibility with many DVD players in Europe and Latin America, choose PAL.

- *Burner speed:* Generally, choose the fastest burning speed allowed by your drive — however, if you're working with media with a recording speed slower than the maximum burning speed (or if you're encountering burn errors at maximum speed), you can reduce the burning speed using this drop-down list.

Figure 4-4:
Configure
your disc
properties
from the
DVD Options
dialog box.

5. **Click OK to return to the DVD Maker window.**

6. **Repeat Steps 1 and 2 to add all the desired clips to your DVD.**

   If you want clips to play in a certain order, click and drag them to arrange them "just so."

7. **Click Next to continue to the Ready to Burn DVD screen, as shown in Figure 4-5.**

   Ah, not quite so fast. You have additional chances to customize your menu system before you burn!

8. **Choose a menu style from the list on the right.**

   Microsoft offers an excellent selection of animated and static menus. Just click a menu thumbnail, and the preview screen is automatically updated.

Figure 4-5:
The Ready
to Burn DVD
screen.

9. **Click the Menu Text button on the toolbar to modify your menu titles and button labels.**

From the dialog box that opens, as shown in Figure 4-6, you can change the font, font attributes, disc title, and button names. You can also add notes. As before, just click in a text box and type the new text to update a field. When you're done, click Change Text to save your changes.

Figure 4-6:
Modify DVD
menu text
and buttons
or add notes
here.

10. **Back in the Ready to Burn DVD dialog box, click the Customize Menu button (on the toolbar) to modify your menu's graphics and audio**

track in the Customize the DVD Menu Style dialog box, as shown in Figure 4-7.

Click the Browse button next to each setting to select a custom foreground video, background video, and menu audio track. You can also select a new frame style for your buttons. When you're done, click the Change Style button to continue.

Figure 4-7:
Create a
custom style
here.

You just created your first disc layout — and without the carnage you expected, I'll bet! Keep reading to see how to preview your handiwork — and then burn, baby, burn!

Time to Preview

Would a Hollywood studio release a movie these days without editing it thoroughly first? Not very likely — and Windows DVD Maker allows you to preview your disc before you burn it, so that you can edit and fix the occasional goof. I'm all for avoiding the possibility of wasting a recordable DVD because something was wrong with my videos or my menu system. In Preview mode, the program displays your project just as it will appear in a DVD player. You even get a virtual remote control that you can use to test out your menu system.

To enter Preview mode at any time, click the Preview button on the toolbar. Your menu system appears exactly as it will look onscreen, and the remote control pad appears, ready to use, as shown in Figure 4-8. Click any button to simulate the press of that button on your DVD player's remote control.

Figure 4-8:
Preview
your work
before you
burn your
disc.

Click the Menu button to display the Title menu.

After you check each button and function on your menu, press Esc to exit Preview mode. You can then make any changes that you need to make to your menu, or you can burn your project to disc.

Burning Your DVD and Celebrating Afterward

Here it is — the moment you've been waiting for with such anticipation! To burn a DVD video from your project, follow these steps:

1. **Load a blank disc into your recorder.**

   Again, for the best possible compatibility with older DVD players, I highly recommend that you use DVD+R discs.

2. **Click the Burn button at the bottom of the window.**

3. **Click OK and sit back to watch your recorder do the work. (I wonder whether George Lucas has it this easy.)**

Don't reach for that permanent marker just yet! There are a number of great labeling programs on the market these days that can produce colorful paper labels for your finished DVDs, giving them a more professional look. If your PC's drive includes support for LightScribe labeling technology, you can also use special blank DVD media that will allow you to "burn" a label directly on your finished discs . . . no ink or paper needed!

Chapter 5: I'm Okay, You're a Digital Camera

In This Chapter

- ✔ Understanding digital camera technology
- ✔ Evaluating the advantages of digital photography
- ✔ Buying extras (besides your camera)
- ✔ Composing photographs for better results
- ✔ Organizing your images
- ✔ Downloading your images
- ✔ Using Windows Live Photo Gallery

I'll be the first to assure you that I'm no Ansel Adams, yet I've been capturing moments and memories on film for most of my life, and I've slowly worked my way into what most folks would deem semiprofessional photography. (I can shoot a decent portrait, I take on a commission from time to time, and I have a reasonably well-stuffed camera bag.)

Does that mean I'm loaded down with expensive 35mm cameras and a dozen different varieties of film? Definitely not! I've never been darkroom material, and film photography no longer excites me. These days, I work entirely with *digital* cameras, which don't use traditional film. Why digital? My entire portfolio of digital photos — which would easily fill up at least two dozen traditional bound photo albums — fits comfortably on two DVDs. I can display those photographs on practically any PC or print hard copies that are almost impossible to tell from film prints. I don't spend a dime on film processing, either — and when you take 10 to 20 images per day, that savings really adds up.

I spend this chapter introducing you to the world of digital photography. You discover how a digital camera works, why it's better in many respects than a film camera, and how to move to your PC the images you take with your camera. If you're interested in shooting better pictures, I also cover a number of well-worn basic rules used by professional photographers all over the world. You also discover how to download images from your digital camera (by using the features built into Windows 7) and how to catalog your photographs (thus making it easier to locate a specific image).

How Does a Digital Camera Work?

A common misconception surrounds today's digital cameras: Because these cameras don't use film and because they produce pictures as data files, many folks think that digital cameras must use a radically different method of capturing images. Actually, your family film camera and that power-hungry, battery-munching digital camera you got for Christmas are remarkably similar in most respects.

As you see in Figure 5-1, a film camera has a shutter that opens for a set amount of time (usually a fraction of a second), admitting light into the body of the camera through at least one lens. (Of course, that lens can be adjusted to bring other objects at other distances into focus, or different lenses can be tacked on.) Figure 5-2 illustrates (up to this point, anyway) that your film camera and its digital brethren work exactly the same.

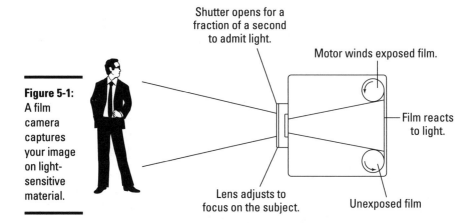

Figure 5-1: A film camera captures your image on light-sensitive material.

Shutter opens for a fraction of a second to admit light.

Motor winds exposed film.

Film reacts to light.

Lens adjusts to focus on the subject.

Unexposed film

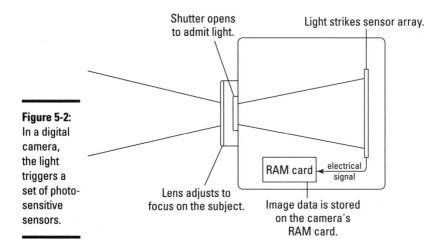

Figure 5-2: In a digital camera, the light triggers a set of photo-sensitive sensors.

Shutter opens to admit light.

Light strikes sensor array.

RAM card ← electrical signal

Lens adjusts to focus on the subject.

Image data is stored on the camera's RAM card.

The big difference is the method that each of these two types of cameras uses to record that incoming light. To wit:

✦ A **film camera** uses a strip of light-sensitive celluloid coated with silver halide, which retains the image. The film must later be developed, and the negatives and positives that are produced can be used (reproduced, usually on photographic paper) to make copies of the photograph.

✦ A **digital camera,** on the other hand, uses a grid (or an *array*) of photo-sensors to record the incoming pattern of light. Each sensor returns an electrical current when it's struck by the incoming light. Because the amount of current that's returned varies with the amount of light, your camera's electronic innards can combine the different current levels into a composite pattern of data that represents the incoming light — in other words, an image in the form of a binary file.

If you've read some of my other books on CD/DVD recording, photography, and scanning, you already know about *binary,* which is the common language shared by all computers. Although your eye can't see any image in the midst of all those ones and zeroes, your computer can display them as a photograph — and print the image, if you like, or send it to your Aunt Harriet in Boise as an e-mail attachment.

"Wait a second, Mark. How does the image file get to my computer?" That's a very good question; naturally, no one wants to carry a PC around just to shoot a photograph. Your digital camera stores the image file until you can *transfer* (download) it to your computer. Different types of cameras use different methods of storing the image files:

✦ **RAM cards:** *Random access memory (RAM) cards* (the most common storage method) are removable memory cards that function much like the memory modules used by your computer. Some memory cards are proprietary, but some cards are interchangeable with personal digital assistants (PDAs) and palm PCs. The most popular types of media include CompactFlash, SmartMedia, and Memory Stick cards, generally ranging from 512MB to 64GB of storage. When the card is full of images, you either download the images from the card (presumably to your PC) to free up space or eject it and "reload" with a spare, empty card.

✦ **Hard drives:** Yep, you read right — some cameras have their own onboard hard drives, and others use tiny removable hard drives that are roughly the same size as RAM cards. Naturally, these little beauties can easily store gigabytes of your images. (Geez, I'm old enough to remember when a full-size computer hard drive couldn't store that much.)

Older storage mediums for digital cameras

Older digital cameras might not use a hard drive or RAM card like the current crop of cameras. You might find a camera that uses one of the following storage methods on eBay or at a garage sale:

✔ **Floppy drives:** Okay, I know that I rant on and on throughout this book about how unreliable floppies can be and how I use them only as a last resort, yet some older digital cameras used floppies to store photos. (Guess what? I don't like those cameras. Go figure.) If your camera uses floppies, make doggone sure that you get your images backed up to your computer's

hard drive as soon as possible. Because of the larger image sizes produced by today's higher-resolution cameras, floppy-based digital cameras have essentially disappeared from the market.

✔ **Recordable CD and DVD drives:** Here's a camera that can burn your digital photographs directly onto a recordable CD or DVD! Although these cameras can be a little bulkier than models that use RAM cards, this type just plain *rocks* (imagine handing a disc of photos to Grandma after your visit).

If you're wondering approximately how many images you can fit onto a specific RAM card, remember that most 10- to 16-megapixel (MP) cameras now produce images of about 2 to 6 megabytes (MB) at their highest-quality mode.

The Pros and Cons of Digital Photography

I mention earlier in this chapter that I switched completely from my 35mm single lens reflex (SLR) cameras to a (rapidly expanding) collection of digital cameras. However, there's a lot more to like about the digital revolution than just cutting the expenses of film and processing. Here are some other advantages:

✦ **Digital photos and prints are versatile.** The digital photographs that you take can be enclosed in e-mail messages, burned as CD or DVD slide shows, or displayed as your PC's Windows desktop and screensaver. Of course, you can also print them; and with today's special inkjet papers, your images can end up on items like greeting cards and T-shirt transfers.

If you're interested in producing prints from your digital photographs in the shortest time possible, check out one of the latest inkjet printers that can directly accept memory cards from your digital camera. Heck, with one of these inkjet marvels, you don't need a PC. Some of these printers can even rotate and resize images.

✦ **Look, Ma, no developing!** With a digital camera, you have practically instant access to your photographs. Save yourself the trip to the photo store — even a one-hour photo lab can't match the three minutes that it takes to connect your camera to your PC (with a Universal Serial Bus [USB] cable) and download your images to your hard drive. (And, you avoid the ravages of a misaligned development machine or a clumsy operator.)

✦ **Editing is easy with your PC.** Imagine everything that can go wrong with a picture: a bad exposure, a case of red eye, or perhaps a tree sprouting from someone's head. With a digital photograph, you can reduce or eliminate these problems altogether; with the proper editing, a bad picture becomes mediocre, and a good picture can become a work of art. *Bonus:* After the images are on your PC, you can edit or print them immediately.

✦ **You can manage your photographs on location.** Imagine being able to review a shot as soon as it's taken. With a traditional film camera, you're stuck with what you take, and you don't see the results until that roll of film has been developed. A digital camera, however, gives you the freedom to *manage* your images. For example, you can view each image on a memory card and delete the ones you don't need, to free up space. Using the camera's liquid crystal diode (LCD) screen also allows you to review a photograph as soon as you take it. Don't like the way a particular photograph turned out? If you review each shot as soon as you snap it — which I always do — you can try to retake most pictures immediately! (Of course, this feature doesn't help you if the UFO has already zipped over the horizon, but it's darned handy on vacation.)

Virtually all digital cameras on the market these days can also do double-duty as simple video camcorders — at least for anywhere from 30 to 240 seconds or more — using the *movie mode* feature. Some cameras can even record audio along with the video; the length of time you can record depends on the amount of storage available, so a digital camera with a 4GB memory card can capture many more seconds of video than a camera with only a 2GB memory card.

However, all is not perfect in the digital world — not yet, at least. Film cameras aren't doomed to share the fate of the dinosaurs because traditional film photography still has these advantages over digital photography:

✦ **Film cameras are still less expensive.** Although digital cameras have dropped considerably in price over the past few years, film cameras still provide better resolution and image quality for a lower initial price. In fact, at the time of this writing, most film cameras less than $40 (US) can still take a better-quality photograph than most digital cameras selling for less than $150. Of course, if you're willing to spend more, you narrow the quality gap, and these days it's much easier to find an 8MP camera that can produce film quality. Although digital camera prices continue to drop, an entry-level digital camera will eventually be able to take a shot that's as good as a film camera.

How can you tell which digital cameras produce better images? While shopping for a digital camera, keep the camera's *megapixel rating* in mind — that's the number of *pixels* (individual dots) in an image that the camera can capture. Here's another Mark's Maxim to keep handy:

> **The higher the megapixel value, the better the image quality, the more expensive the camera, and the larger the photographs that you can print.**™

As a rule, a 6–8MP camera is suitable for most casual photography, but amateur photographers will prefer at least a 10MP camera.

✦ **Film cameras are better at capturing motion.** Older consumer digital cameras in the 3–4MP range still have trouble taking shots of subjects in motion, such as at sporting events. (It's because of the longer delay required for those photosensitive sensors to capture the image.) However, current higher-megapixel digital cameras are much better at *motion* (stop action) photography.

✦ **Man, do those digital cameras use the juice!** Unlike a film camera, a digital camera relies on battery power for *everything,* including that power-hungry LCD display. If you're in the middle of shooting a wedding and you haven't packed a spare set of batteries, you have my condolences. A film camera is far less demanding of its batteries.

As you might have already guessed, many photographers have chosen to carry both traditional film and digital cameras, which allows them to use whatever best fits the circumstances (depending on the subject and the level of control they need on location). For me, the long-term savings and convenience of my digital cameras — and the ability to review my photographs as soon as they're taken — makes them the better choice.

So what can you do with digital photographs? A heck of a lot more than a film print, that's for sure (at least on your PC and in the online world)! Common fun that you can have with digital images includes

✦ **Printing 'em:** Today's inkjet printers can produce a hard copy on all sorts of media (everything from plain paper to blank business cards and CD/DVD labels), but naturally you get the best results on those expensive sheets of glossy photo paper.

✦ **Using them on your personal or business Web site:** Jazz up your Web pages with images from your camera.

✦ **Sending them as e-mail attachments:** I get a big kick out of sending photos through e-mail! As long as you add a total of less than 2 to 3MB of images to an e-mail message, the recipient should receive them with no problem. (And then the attached files can be viewed, printed, or saved to the recipient's hard drive.)

✦ **Creating slide shows:** Check your camera's software documentation to see whether you can create a slide show on your hard drive (or on a CD/DVD disc) to show off your digital photographs. (I also demonstrate how to use Windows Live Movie Maker to create a slide show in Chapter 3 of this very minibook!)

✦ **Using them in craft projects:** Plaster your digital photographs on T-shirt transfers, buttons, greeting cards, and all sorts of crafts.

Book VI
Chapter 5

I'm Okay, You're a Digital Camera

Digital Camera Extras to Covet

No one gets a pizza with just sauce, and the extras are important in photography, too. If you take a large number of photographs or you're interested in producing the best results from your camera, consider adding these extras to your camera bag.

External card readers

As I mention earlier, virtually all modern digital cameras connect to your computer via a USB 2.0 cable to transfer pictures. The downside is that you can't take more shots until the downloading process is complete. If you're in a hurry or if convenience is important, buy an external card reader that takes care of the downloading chores for you. Simply pop the card into the reader (which in turn connects to your PC's USB port), load a backup memory card into your camera, and you're ready to return to the action.

External card readers are also the best solution if you have an older digital camera that connects to a USB 1.*x* port. Because an older USB 1.*x* connection is as slow as watching paint dry, you can speed things up considerably by ejecting the memory card from your camera and pushing those pictures to your PC through a much faster USB 2.0 connection. An external reader is cheap, too, usually running less than $30.

Rechargeable batteries

Gotta have 'em. I'm not kidding. You'll literally end up declaring bankruptcy if you use your digital camera often with single-use batteries. For example, one of my older 3MP cameras can totally exhaust four AA alkaline batteries after one session of 20 photographs.

Here are the three major types of rechargeable batteries to choose from:

✦ **Nickel-cadmium (NiCad):** *NiCad* batteries are the cheapest type and are available in standard sizes, but they drain quickly and take longer to recharge.

✦ **Nickel-metal-hydride (NiMH):** *NiMH* rechargeable batteries provide the middle of the road between higher cost and longer life; they take less time to recharge than NiCad batteries, and they last longer, but they're not as expensive as Li-Ion batteries.

✦ **Lithium-ion (Li-Ion):** These batteries are the best available. They provide more sustained power over a longer period than either of the other types, but they're the most expensive and they're hard to find in standard sizes. Your camera might need an adapter to use them.

Just as I recommend an extra memory card, I also recommend carrying a spare set of charged batteries in your camera bag. The Boy Scouts are right on this one: Be prepared.

Lenses

Like their film brethren, most medium-price and higher-end digital cameras can use external (add-on) lenses. Although your digital camera is likely to have several zoom levels (both digital and optical), photographers use a number of specialized lenses in specific situations. For example, consider these common extra lenses:

✦ **Telephoto:** Using a *telephoto* lens provides you with tremendous, long-distance magnification, but you don't have to be James Bond or a tabloid *paparazzo* to use one. For example, wildlife and sports photographers use telephoto lenses to capture subjects from a distance. (Referees tend to get surly when you stray on the field just to photograph the quarterback.)

✦ **Macro:** These lenses are specially designed for extreme close-up work; with a *macro* lens, you can capture images at a distance of a few inches. (They're great for making your fiancée's engagement ring look much, much bigger.)

✦ **Wide angle:** A *wide angle* lens can capture a larger area — what photographers call the *field of view* — at the expense of detail and the possibility of adding linear distortion. These lenses are often used for scenic or architectural photographs.

Don't forget a decent lens cap and a photographer's lens-cleaning cloth to help prevent scratches on those expensive lenses!

Tripods

When most people think of tripods, they think of unwieldy, 5-foot-tall gantries suitable for launching the Saturn V. Yes, some tripods meet those requirements, but they're absolutely required for low-light, time-lapse, and professional portrait photography.

My camera bag also stows two other platforms that are much smaller:

✦ **Mini-tripod:** My Ambico mini-tripod can hold my cameras anywhere from 2 to 4 inches above the table. I use it in concert with my macro lens for shooting my scale models from a realistic perspective. The Gorillapod (`http://joby.com/gorillapod/original`) is another popular mini-tripod I'd recommend.

✦ **Monopod:** My collapsible monopod (which looks just like a walking stick) can hold the camera steady for quick shots on just about any surface. It also works great when you trip over exposed roots in the forest — but you didn't hear me admit to that. I should also note that many museums (and government buildings and churches) do not allow monopods because of security considerations.

Although a tripod isn't a requirement for the casual photographer, you'll find yourself wishing for one quickly if you move to more serious amateur photography. They sell tripods at your local megamart for a reason.

The Lazy Man's Guide to Composing Photographs

If you want to remain firmly in the point-and-shoot casual photography crowd, you can comfortably skip any discussion of *composition* — that's the process (most call it an art) of aligning your subject and compensating for the available light at your location. Composition isn't a requirement for simple snapshots, but if you're going to create true visual art, you need the time to prepare your subject, your viewing angle, and your lighting.

In fact, what if I told you that composing a shot can result in less cropping and editing time on your computer — and that you end up taking better photographs? If you follow the tips that I provide in this section, I can just about guarantee that you'll discover at least one FRP in every set of images that you download! (*FRP,* coined by my favorite journalism instructor at LSU, means *first-rate photo* — the kind of photograph that you'll be proud to display on your wall.) The photograph examples in this chapter are taken from my personal FRP collection.

And, despite what you might have heard about composing photographs, it takes only a few seconds before each shot to make a difference. Take it from me — with practice, you'll compose your shots automatically!

The rule of thirds

The *rule of thirds* is the foundation of good composition for most photographers. Applying this guideline helps draw the eye toward multiple subjects or to the focus of interest while maintaining balance within the frame. To use the rule of thirds, simply split the frame in your viewfinder into nine equal areas, as shown in Figure 5-3, "Time Tunnel." Align your subject (subjects) and the surroundings (where possible) along either

✦ A line crossing the frame

✦ One of the intersections where two lines meet

Figure 5-3: Divide your photograph by the rule of thirds.

The rule of thirds works exceptionally well when taking photographs of landscapes or architecture, as you can see in Figure 5-4. This photograph, "View from Hoover Dam," uses the rule to draw the viewer's eye along the river until it disappears around the bend. (Bet you never knew that Mother Nature was a shutterbug, right?)

That's all there is to it. If you take a moment to examine the composition of the photographs in your favorite magazines, you see this time-tested classic rule followed over and over.

Figure 5-4: The movement of water flows closely along one line and ends at an intersection.

The rule of asymmetry

The second rule of composition often used in photography, the *rule of asymmetry,* presents the subject against a number of minor subjects as well as the background. Asymmetrical composition revolves around a relationship that you build between the major subject and either one or more minor subjects or the background itself. Following this rule, you merge different combinations of the three basic shapes — the square, the circle, and the triangle — to form a new outline or contour.

To illustrate, take the still life shown in Figure 5-5, "Cultures." Here, I mix a light circular shape (the instrument) with strong rectangles (the skis). I find that an asymmetrical composition works better when you feature a sharp contrast level between light and dark elements or between strong color patterns and shadows.

I always make it a point to experiment with different camera angles — for instance, moving to the side or below the subject, as in "Warbird" (see Figure 5-6). Of course, sometimes you don't have the luxury of extra time to try something different, but I think that you'll like the results. (And remember, you're not wasting any film.)

Figure 5-5:
Add interest with a classic asymmetrical composition.

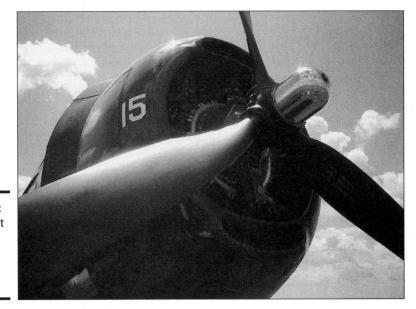

Figure 5-6:
Experiment with unusual camera angles.

Using lighting creatively

Before I finish this quick tour through photo composition, turn your attention to lighting. Virtually every digital camera made these days has an automatic flash feature, and it's usually a good thing to use. However, if your camera allows you to disable the flash, you can take better photographs in many different situations.

Here's a list of exposure do's and don'ts for those who want to compose with light:

Do

+ Make use of existing light when possible, if you can disable your camera's flash. Natural lighting can really "make" the photo.

+ Use a tripod (or brace your camera if possible) when taking photographs without flash, which requires a longer exposure time to capture the image.

+ Use your PC's image editor — such as Photoshop or Paint Shop Pro — to enhance the contrast for underexposed shots. You can also change the hue and saturation levels for the colors in a photograph with your image editor. In Chapter 1 of this minibook, I cover some of the basics within Windows Live Photo Gallery, such as cropping and rotating images, converting images to different formats, and saving them to disk.

Don't

+ Attempt to photograph your subject through a sheet of glass or plastic if you're using a flash. Also don't pose your subject against a reflective background — you create *hotspots* or flash reflections.

+ Use a flash if your subject is illuminated internally or with spotlights, such as a neon sign or a statue at night.

Shadows can add a tremendous visual impact, as shown in a favorite FRP of mine, "French Quarter Staircase," in Figure 5-7. In this case, I needed no additional light, but I'm not above using an isolated spot *flood* (light source) to cast the shadow effect I want. Even a flashlight can do the job in a pinch.

Figure 5-7:
Remember
that
shadows
can be your
friend.

Organizing Your Pictures

If you would rather not stare at a meaningless collection of filenames, here are some tricks you can use to help you locate a photograph that you stored on your hard drive or a DVD full of images. First, organize your photos into folders based on the date, location, or subject of your photographs. Also, use the long filename support in Windows 7 to better describe your photograph. After all, you can more easily visualize `Goats Grazing Outside Nepalese Village.jpg` than `nepgoats.jpg`.

To take your organization a step further, use an image-cataloging program, such as PaintShop Photo Express 2010 from Corel (`www.corel.com`). The contents of your photo collection are shown as *thumbnails* (small images), making it easier to spot the photograph you're looking for. Plus, Photo Express 2010 can create a collage from your images, back up your images easily to DVD, and even perform simple image editing. At $40, this program is an invaluable tool for any amateur photographer.

Downloading Your Images

Before you launch into the downloading process, make sure to take care of those dull prerequisites:

✦ Make sure that you installed any software that came with your digital camera or card reader; this ensures that any drivers are installed before you connect. (It's always a good idea to check the camera manufacturer's Web site to see whether a new set of drivers has been released for Windows 7.)

✦ Connect the cable that came with your camera (or your external card reader) to the corresponding port on your PC — which is very likely your PC's USB port. If you're using a card reader — a special slot on your PC that accepts memory cards from your camera — eject the memory card from your camera and load it into the slot in the card reader (as shown in the card reader's documentation). For more details on ports, visit Book I, Chapter 3.

✦ If you're connecting your digital camera directly to your PC and it has an AC adapter, make sure that you plug the camera in to the AC adapter first; this can save you an hour of recharge time!

Although most digital cameras come with their own software, Windows 7 has its own built-in wizard for downloading (or importing) images. (If your camera comes with its own downloading software, it's a better idea to use that program instead, but at least Windows 7 can likely do the job alone in a pinch.) If your camera or card reader is supported within Windows 7 (check the manufacturer's Web site or the specifications on the side of the box) and you're not using your camera or card reader's software, you'll see the AutoPlay dialog (as shown in Figure 5-8) when you plug in the USB cable from your camera.

**Book VI
Chapter 5**

I'm Okay, You're a
Digital Camera

Figure 5-8:
Let
Windows
7 help you
download
images
from your
camera.

To complete the download process, just click the Import Pictures and Videos using Windows button. (However, don't enable the Always Do This check box, unless you're absolutely certain that this is the only action you'll perform on photos! Bad automation, bad!)

By default, Windows 7 uses the tag you enter to name the images and videos as they're imported. For example, if you enter the tag Fun Photos, the filenames are `Fun Photos 001.jpg`, `Fun Photos 002.jpg`, and so on.

After the download is complete, Windows 7 automatically opens the Windows Live Photo Gallery, shown in Figure 5-9. Photo Gallery selects the Recently Imported heading in the source list at the left for you, so the photos you just downloaded appear in the pane on the right side of the window. To view a larger version of a thumbnail with information about the image, just hover your mouse cursor over the photo.

Figure 5-9:
The new Windows Live Photo Gallery is a great place to organize your imported photos.

Rotate Left

Rotate Right

Delete

Play Slideshow

Resize thumbnails

Follow these steps to manipulate images within Photo Gallery:

✦ **To rotate an image:** Click to highlight a photograph, and then click either of the rotate buttons on the toolbar at the bottom of the window.

Each click on the Rotate Left or Rotate Right button rotates the image 90 degrees in that direction.

✦ **To select a group of images:** Hold down the Ctrl key while you click or drag a selection box around the desired photos. You can also select a thumbnail by clicking the Next and Previous buttons.

✦ **To delete an image from your imported photos:** Click the thumbnail to select it and then click the Delete button.

✦ **To display your imported photos in a full-screen slide show:** Click the Slide Show button.

To exit the slideshow at any time, press the Esc key.

✦ **To view another collection of images:** Click to select an entry in the source list, to the left of the Photo Gallery window.

Entries include all photos (or videos), collections of photos grouped by tags, photos taken within a certain month or year, and photos you assigned a rating (ranging from 1 to 5 stars).

To assign a star rating or change a photo's tag, right-click to select a thumbnail and choose Add Tags from the menu.

After the images are transferred, you can unplug your camera's USB cable. If you're done with your images, you can close the Photo Gallery application — but don't ignore those flashy buttons on the toolbar at the top of the window! You can use these buttons to

✦ Click Fix to edit a selected image by fixing exposure and color levels or by cropping the stuff you don't want.

✦ Click E-mail to send selected images as e-mail attachments, or Publish to publish an online album.

✦ Click Print to send your selections to your system printer.

✦ Click Make to open the selected images in Windows Live Movie Maker so that you can create a slideshow movie.

✦ Click Make to burn the selected images to a CD or DVD.

Book VII

Upgrading and Supercharging

The 5th Wave
By Rich Tennant

©RICHTENNANT

"So I guess you forgot to tell me to strip out the components before drilling for blowholes."

Contents at a Glance

Chapter 1: Determining What to Upgrade 485

Making Performance Upgrades: CPU, Motherboard, and Memory.......486
Expansion Upgrades: eSATA, USB 2.0, and FireWire 488
Making Storage Upgrades: Internal and External Drives.........489
Making Sound and Video Upgrades: Sound and Video Cards 490

Chapter 2: Adding RAM to Your Hot Rod 493

Defining the Different Types of RAM........................493
Figuring Out Which Type of RAM to Buy......................495
Deciding How Much RAM Is Enough 496
Installing Extra RAM.....................................497

Chapter 3: Adding Hard Drive Territory to Your System 499

The Tale of Virtual Memory 499
Recognizing a Well-Dressed Hard Drive 501
Internal versus External Storage 503
Adding a Second Internal Hard Drive.......................504

Chapter 4: Partying with USB, FireWire, and eSATA 509

A Tale of Three Fine Ports................................509
Or Do You Just Need a Hub?................................512
Installing a Port Card 513

Chapter 5: Pumping Up Your Sound and Video. 517

Sound Card Features to Covet 517
Shopping for a Monster Graphics Card 520
Installing Sound and Video Cards 523

Chapter 1: Determining What to Upgrade

In This Chapter

✔ Knowing when to upgrade your CPU and motherboard

✔ Figuring out whether you need additional memory

✔ Determining whether you need extra ports

✔ Considering a hard drive upgrade

✔ Evaluating a CD/DVD recorder or a tape backup drive

✔ Deciding on audio and video improvements

*M*y father always said, "Son, never take a long trip without a road map handy." This is why our old family Plymouth had six metric tons of paper maps for every state in the Union stuffed into the glove compartment, ready to be pulled out just in case we went astray. (Now I just visit MapQuest — progress marches on.)

Consider this introductory chapter a road map to upgrading your PC: what you can do, what you should add or replace, and what your benefits will be after the dust has cleared. After you read this PC upgrade primer, you can easily determine what you need to upgrade, and you can jump to the proper chapter within this minibook to find the specifics.

One note before you jump in: Upgrading your PC is not a difficult job! All it requires is

✦ The courage to remove your computer's case. (Believe me, you'll get used to it.)

✦ The ability to follow step-by-step instructions.

✦ Basic skills with a screwdriver.

With these requirements in mind, read on to determine what you need in order to turn your PC back into a hot rod.

Making Performance Upgrades: CPU, Motherboard, and Memory

I cordoned off the upgrades in this section into a separate category that I call *performance upgrades:* They give your PC an overall performance boost that affects all programs you run, including Windows itself.

Upgrading your CPU and motherboard

Simply put, a *central processing unit (CPU)* is the brain of your PC. A significant upgrade to your CPU usually results in more than just replacing the CPU chip itself. For example, if you decide to upgrade from an older Intel Core 2 Duo processor to the quad-core Intel i7 Extreme, your PC's motherboard almost certainly needs to be replaced as well. The *motherboard* is the largest circuit board in your computer's case, shown in Figure 1-1 — it holds the CPU and memory and all the rest of the electronics — so this is probably one of the most technically demanding upgrades you can make.

Figure 1-1: A typical PC motherboard, exposed for the world to see.

Naturally, replacing your computer's brain with the next generation of chip results in faster performance. How much faster depends on the speed of the chip — which is usually specified in megahertz (MHz) or gigahertz (GHz) — and on whether you're skipping a generation. This list describes two upgrade examples:

✦ **From a Core 2 Duo 2.66 GHz processor to a Core 2 Duo 3.16 GHz processor:** This upgrade results in a speed increase. And, because the chip generation may remain the same, you probably can use your current motherboard. However, the performance increase might not be significant enough to be noticeable in many of your programs. (You're not really advancing very far.)

✦ **From a Celeron 2.2 GHz processor to the same Core 2 Duo 3.16 GHz:** This upgrade, on the other hand, changes your plodding plowhorse into Shadowfax (the uberstallion from Tolkien's *The Lord of the Rings*). You're not only installing a CPU that's much faster but also upgrading from single-core Celeron technology to dual-core technology — and the tasks that you perform now will finish in a fraction of the time.

Hence, this Mark's Maxim:

Upgrade your CPU and motherboard only when you're either moving to a new generation of processor or when you're at least doubling the speed of your current CPU.™

Anything less is a waste of time and effort (unless the CPU fairy dropped a new chip on your pillow for free).

Adding memory

I'll be honest: Adding memory (*random access memory,* or *RAM*) is my favorite performance upgrade, and I recommend adding memory far more often than I recommend upgrading a CPU/motherboard combo. Here's why:

✦ **Memory packs performance punch.** Any PC tech will tell you that dollar for dollar, adding memory results in a far more significant performance boost than simply upgrading your processor by a few megahertz. Windows uses every *bit* of that additional memory (bad techno-nerd pun intended there), and everything your PC does is done faster.

✦ **Memory is cheap.** I'm talkin' really, *really* cheap. Most folks can now afford to max out their memory capacity. (The total that you can add depends on your motherboard, so check with the PC manufacturer or look up the specifications for your motherboard to determine the maximum amount of memory you can add.)

✦ **Memory is easy to install.** Compared with upgrading a motherboard and CPU, adding memory is one of the simplest upgrade tasks you can perform in the bowels of your machine.

**Book VII
Chapter 1**

Determining What
to Upgrade

Here's the prerequisite Mark's Maxim for memory:

Add memory to your PC before embarking on a CPU and motherboard upgrade.™

'Nuff said.

Expansion Upgrades: eSATA, USB 2.0, and FireWire

Consider adding ports to an older PC — what I call *expansion upgrades.* Although adding or upgrading ports doesn't speed up your computer, you can connect a wider range of external devices.

Like the RAM upgrade that I discuss earlier in this chapter, adding Universal Serial Bus (USB 2.0), eSATA, or FireWire ports to your PC is a relatively easy upgrade. All you do is remove the cover from your PC and add an adapter card to one of the open slots on your motherboard (Figure 1-2). Remember, this is how the original cadre of IBM engineers — the ones who designed the architecture of the first PCs and sat in those squeaky nerd-chairs — intended for you to add functionality to your computer, so it's practically a walk in the park.

Figure 1-2:
Adding a port adapter card expands your PC's connectivity.

I discuss eSATA, USB 2.0, and FireWire ports in-depth in Chapter 4 of this minibook.

If you already have USB or FireWire ports on your PC and you simply run out of connections (for example, you have two USB ports and you're using one for your printer and one for your webcam), you don't need to add another set of ports. Instead, you just need a USB or FireWire *hub,* a nifty little device that plugs into one of those ports and turns it into four or eight additional ports! (Think of the familiar AC extension cord, which plugs into one of your wall power sockets and allows you to plug in three or four cords.)

Making Storage Upgrades: Internal and External Drives

Why limit yourself to the sorry patch of digital real estate that originally shipped with your PC? I'm talking about your PC's original hard drive, a creaking tape backup unit, or perhaps a slower, older DVD recorder. Upgrading these devices is a *storage upgrade* because you use these devices to permanently store (or record) data for later use.

Hard drives and DVD/Blu-Ray recorders are both continually dropping in price (and adding extra capacity and features), which is fortuitous because today's operating systems and applications tend to take up more and more hard drive space. Therefore, it's only natural that most serious PC users will eventually decide to add a second drive (or replace their existing drives with new units).

Adding a hard drive

The majority of today's PCs use Integrated Drive Electronics (IDE, sometimes called PATA) hard drives, which can be mounted *internally* (within your PC's case) or *externally* (by connecting to a USB or FireWire port). You'll also encounter Serial ATA (or SATA) hard drives, which are fast becoming the norm — they're significantly faster than IDE drives and easier to configure. Finally, some super-high-performance machines can use external SATA drives by connecting to an eSATA port.

Here's how to tell which type of drive you should choose:

✦ **Internal:** Choose an internal drive if you don't mind opening your PC's case and installing a new drive. (I show you how later, in Chapter 3 within this very minibook.) Internal drives are significantly cheaper than external drives and are somewhat faster than even an external FireWire or USB 2.0 drive. Finally, you won't use any more of your precious desktop space.

✦ **External:** Choose an external drive if you would rather not open your computer or if you have no available hard drive bays left in your computer's case. (Don't laugh — techno-types can fill up even the largest tower case with all sorts of devices.) External hard drives can be shared among computers that have the same ports, and you can simply unplug an external drive and carry it with you. (How's that for security?)

Adding a recorder or a tape drive

DVD recorders and backup tape drives have been around for years, but only with the advent of USB and FireWire have they become attractive to the PC power user as external devices. That's because in years past, hardware manufacturers had to depend on the PC's parallel port to connect these peripherals. The PC's parallel port was never designed for high-speed data transfer, so parallel port drives were as slow as your Aunt Harriet in her '53 Pontiac.

However, today's eSATA, FireWire, and USB 2.0 recorders are almost as blazing fast as their internal brethren! Therefore, as long as you have an eSATA, USB, or FireWire port, you now have the same choice that I describe with hard drives: Either stick it in your machine or leave it outside. It works like a charm either way.

One final word about tape backup drives: They're beginning to disappear from the PC landscape because today's recordable DVD formats can hold 4.7GB (or 8.5GB for a dual-layer drive) on a single disc — and DVD recorders are faster and more reliable than most tape drives. In fact, the new generation of recordable Blu-Ray drives can hold 30 or 50GB on a single disc! Therefore, before you invest in a hideously expensive Digital Audio Tape (DAT) backup drive, consider buying a (comparatively) inexpensive rewriteable DVD or Blu-Ray drive instead and use it for your backups.

Making Sound and Video Upgrades: Sound and Video Cards

To finish my road map of PC upgrades, consider the hottest video and audio cards now on the market. There are more reasons than just gaming to add or upgrade your PC's eyes and ears: For example, maybe you want to move up to a sound card with Dolby Surround sound support or perhaps a video card with video capture capability. Like the addition of high-speed ports, these upgrades are pretty simple: Just take the case off your PC, remove your current sound or video adapter card, and plug the replacement card in its place.

Before I jump into a discussion of these cards, I should note that most motherboards now have built-in sound (and/or video) hardware on the motherboard rather than on separate adapter cards. If your motherboard has either a built-in video card or sound card, you should be able to disable the onboard hardware so that you can add your upgrade card. Typically, you must either display your PC's Basic Input/Output System (BIOS) and disable the onboard hardware from there or move a jumper on the motherboard. Read your motherboard user manual to discover which avenue to take.

Sound cards on parade

A number of specialized sound cards are available for the discriminating audio connoisseur — which, no doubt, you are. Consider these gems:

✦ **An MP3 card:** If you're an MP3 wizard with a hard drive's worth of MP3 digital audio files, you'll appreciate one of these specialized audio cards. An MP3 card contains a hardware encoder/decoder, which speeds up your PC's *ripping* (the process of creating MP3 digital audio files from existing audio CDs) and MP3-playing performance. With one of these cards (which typically cost $35–$50 US), you can listen to (or rip) the Talking Heads while using Photoshop, and the sound quality stays just as good.

✦ **A 24-bit card:** For the absolute best in audio reproduction, pick up a card that can produce 24-bit audio (that's 192 KHz, for you audioheads), which is far superior to the sound produced by virtually all audio CD players. Many high-end sound cards also support DVD audio or feature front-panel controls that fit in an open drive bay (whipped cream and cherry on the sundae). Expect to pay a prime price for one of these cards, usually in the $75–$150 range.

✦ **A Surround sound card:** These cards are specifically designed for 3-D environmental audio within games and for full support for Dolby Surround sound as you watch DVD movies on your PC. Naturally, you need more than two mundane speakers from a discount store to enjoy the full effect — which is why a premium set of speakers is usually included with these cards. Look for these cards to set you back around $75.

Deciding which video card is right for you

Book VII Chapter 1

Determining What to Upgrade

When you think about upgrading a video card, please do not — I repeat, *do not* — just think "gamers only." A number of specialized video cards on the market have nothing to do with games. (Okay, I admit it: Gamers like myself do indeed love video cards.) Here's a cross section of what's available:

✦ **A gamer's card:** The latest 3D video cards (equipped with chipsets from NVIDIA and ATI) simply kick serious tail, no matter whether your favorite games involve mowing down Nazis, building a civilization one stone at a time, or matching wits with your computer over a chess board. If you haven't seen the realistic 3D figures that these cards can produce, visit your local mall's Maze o' Wires store (you know what I mean) and ask a salesperson to crank up the latest game. Of course, Windows displays ho-hum applications faster with one of these cards as well. Many 3D gaming cards also offer dual monitor support so that you can run two monitors side-by-side for a really big desktop.

These high-end, 3D cards run tremendously hot — after all, they're practically separate computers — so they usually have a fan already installed on the card. However, if you're planning to install the card in an older PC, I recommend having at least two fans installed in your case — that's one for the power supply (which is standard equipment) and at least one larger auxiliary fan (to help circulate air to all those hot components). Unfortunately, most "pizza box" and "shoe box" cases don't have the necessary fans on-board to handle a cutting-edge video card.

✦ **An MPEG card:** These cards are specifically designed for encoding and decoding Motion Picture Experts Group (MPEG) digital video (usually from a DVD, but hardware MPEG support is also very useful for doing serious video editing on your PC). Like the MP3 card that I describe in the previous section, on audio cards, the idea is simple: Let the card, rather than your PC's processor, do the video grunt work, and everyone is happier. High-end video cards specially designed for digital video editing are significantly more expensive than video cards meant for home and gamer machines.

✦ **A capture card:** You use this popular video upgrade card to capture an incoming analog video signal and convert it to digital video. For example, you can connect your VCR or older analog VHS-C camcorder to the card, convert the signal to digital video, and then record DVD backups of your home movies. If you can display it on your TV, you should be able to capture it with one of these toys.

Chapter 2: Adding RAM to Your Hot Rod

In This Chapter

✔ Determining which type of memory you need

✔ Understanding the myth behind "minimum RAM"

✔ Installing additional memory

*W*hat's not to like about a memory upgrade? As I discuss in the previous chapter, the *dinero* required for extra random access memory (RAM) is a mere pittance compared with a new CPU (or CPU-and-motherboard combination). Plus, RAM is easy to install, requiring only that you remove your PC's case and plug in the modules. Your PC should recognize additional RAM immediately, with no silly drivers required. Also, additional RAM makes everything run faster in Windows — both the applications you run and the operating system itself.

"Mark," you say, "there's *got* to be a hitch *somewhere*." True: The problem is that you have so many different types of RAM modules to choose from. Read this chapter before you buy RAM modules, and keep these pages handy when you upgrade.

Defining the Different Types of RAM

To begin this primer on memory, review the different types of RAM available for PCs made within the past five years or so.

Before I begin: If you're considering installing a new motherboard and CPU on an older PC, double-check that the new motherboard will use the same RAM type and speed as your current motherboard. (Visit each manufacturer's Web site to compare the specifications for your existing motherboard and the new toy, or refer to the documentation for both motherboards.) If not, the RAM that you add won't do you any good when you upgrade your motherboard. If you have your eye on a significant motherboard/CPU swap in the near future, I definitely recommend upgrading the motherboard, CPU, *and* RAM all at once. For example, the memory modules that work with an older Athlon 64 X2 PC aren't likely to work with a faster AMD Phenom II X4 motherboard. In a case like this, I recommend ordering a *populated* motherboard, complete with a preinstalled CPU and the amount of RAM you specify.

DDR

Double data rate (DDR) modules were the first 168-pin standard Dual Inline Memory Modules (DIMMs) available for PCs; they're commonly used on older Pentium and Athlon computers running Windows XP. The *double* in the DDR name is significant because a DDR module effectively doubles the speed of the module, compared with older Synchronous Dynamic Random Access Memory (SDRAM) memory. Also, DDR memory is assigned a speed rating as part of its name, so it's commonly listed as DDR266 or PC2100 (for the 133 MHz speed versions) and DDR333 or PC2700 (for the 166 MHz version). As you might guess, the faster the access speed, the better the performance. The speed rating that you should choose is determined by the memory speeds that your motherboard supports. DDR memory modules have one notch on the connector and two notches on each side of the module.

DDR2

DDR2 modules doubled the data transfer rate between RAM and motherboard, but they basically look the same. DDR2 modules are the most common type of RAM, and they're used in most machines running Windows Vista and Windows 7.

DDR3

Here's a good question: Which new memory specification is fast replacing DDR2? "Gee, Mark, *could* it be DDR3?" That's right: DDR3 modules provide the best performance around, suitable for PCs running Windows 7. DDR3 modules were once significantly more expensive than their older DDR2 brethren, but prices are dropping at a fast clip.

RDRAM

Rambus (RDRAM) modules are much faster (and also more expensive) than standard DDR modules. In fact, until the arrival of DDR2 and DDR3 memory, RDRAM was the memory standard of choice for high-speed PCs. DDR3 has now crept up from behind and taken the coveted title of First Place Performer, and RDRAM is slowly disappearing from the market.

SDRAM

SDRAM (sometimes called SyncDRAM) took the form of standard 168-pin DIMMs. These modules were standard equipment on most Pentium III and some older Pentium 4 machines. SyncDRAM ran at an access speed of 133 MHz, which is too doggone slow for today's fast processors. SDRAM memory modules sport two notches in the bottom and only one notch on each side.

TIP

If you're planning to add memory to a motherboard that uses SDRAM modules, I strongly urge you to instead upgrade the Big Three: motherboard, CPU, and memory. (I don't intend to offend, but I'll be blunt: Your PC is so far behind the performance of new models that it just isn't worth adding SDRAM memory to your older motherboard. Plus, SDRAM memory is now much harder to find and is getting *more* expensive over time. Just chalk that up to the price of running antique hardware.)

Figuring Out Which Type of RAM to Buy

Here are two methods to determine which type of memory modules your current motherboard requires and which memory speeds it can handle:

✦ **Check the specs.** Refer to the motherboard manual. Or, if you purchased your PC from a manufacturer, check the documentation that accompanied the computer. If you don't have any manuals (think used PC), visit the company's Web site for memory compatibility information or specifications so you don't have to open your PC's case until you're ready to install the new RAM modules.

✦ **Check the existing modules.** If you can't find any documentation, specifications, or data on the Web concerning your PC's RAM modules, it's time to remove the case from your computer. (See how in the step-by-step procedure at the end of this chapter.) Look for the memory slots on your motherboard; DDR, DDR2, and DDR3 modules look like the ones shown in Figure 2-1. (*Note:* You might have more than one module already installed on your PC.) Your RAM modules might also have a descriptive label (which allows you to read the specifics without taking anything out). However, more likely, you'll have to remove one and take it to your local computer shop. Use the instructions later in this chapter to remove a module; then protect the module in an empty CD-ROM jewel case when you take it for identification. The good techs, when presented with the module, should be able to tell you which memory type and speed you're using.

**Book VII
Chapter 2**

Adding RAM to
Your Hot Rod

Figure 2-1:
A DDR/
DDR2/DDR3
DIMM.

Deciding How Much RAM Is Enough

Every motherboard has a maximum amount of memory it can support. You can install the maximum amount by filling up all the motherboard's memory banks (sockets) with modules of the right type.

It's time for another Mark's Maxim:

Whenever possible, buy RAM modules of the same brand at the same time from the same dealer.™

This advice ensures that you're spared any compatibility problems when you install the modules.

Theoretically, any RAM module of the same type and speed should work with any other brand of RAM, but I date back to the earlier days of PCs when using memory chips from different manufacturers resulted in errors and a locked computer. In fact, I still hear tales of compatibility problems, even in our new, improved, fresher-smelling world.

However, not everyone can afford to take their PC's memory to the max — even with today's prices, buying several gigabytes of fast DDR3 RAM modules can set you back. Therefore, the following table illustrates my recommendations for the minimum amount of RAM that you need in order to run the different versions of the Windows operating system comfortably on your PC. ("Comfortably" means *my* opinion of decent performance, perhaps with Microsoft Word running. Of course, memory-hungry applications such as Adobe Photoshop run their best only with plenty of memory elbow room to spare, so consider this the *absolute* minimum.)

Windows XP	*Windows Vista*	*Windows 7*
512MB	1GB	2GB

You might notice that my recommendations sometimes don't jibe with Brother Bill's — that's because the folks in Redmond literally mean *the least you can get away with* when mentioning minimum memory requirements. With 1GB of RAM, Windows 7 is slower to awaken than my kids on a school day. Personally, I like to *use* my computer and not wait half an hour for a scanned image to load.

Using ReadyBoost

Do you happen to have a high-capacity USB 2.0 flash drive — say, a 1GB to 16GB model — lying around doing nothing? If you're running Windows Vista or Windows 7, you can use the ReadyBoost feature to magically use that solid-state external storage to speed up your PC!

To use ReadyBoost, just plug your USB flash drive into one of your PC's USB 2.0 ports. Windows displays a ReadyBoost option in the AutoPlay dialog box that appears; choose the ReadyBoost entry and Windows prompts you for the amount of space on the drive that you

want to allocate to ReadyBoost. (Generally, a minimum of 1GB is a good rule, but if you're not using the rest of the drive, throw caution utterly to the wind and use the entire thing!) Windows keeps ReadyBoost turned on until you eject the USB drive or reboot your PC.

Note that ReadyBoost doesn't run with most older 1.*x* USB flash drives because the memory those drives use is too slow — hence the need for a USB 2.0 flash drive, which uses high-speed memory.

Installing Extra RAM

If you're ready to install your new RAM upgrade, follow these steps to install a typical DDR/DDR2/DDR3 module:

**Book VII
Chapter 2**

1. **Cover your work surface with several sheets of newspaper (to protect your case).**

2. **Power down your PC, unplug it from its power source, and place it on top of the newspaper.**

3. **Remove the PC's case.**

   Most PC cases are held on with two or three screws; just remove the screws and slide the case off. (Don't forget to stash those screws in a safe place.) Other cases are hinged, often with a lock. If you're unsure how to remove your PC's case, check the manual that accompanied your computer.

4. **Touch the metal chassis of your case to dissipate any static electricity on your body.**

   An electrical charge can send your new RAM modules to Frisco — permanently.

5. **Locate the DIMM slots.**

   Check the motherboard manual, which should have a schematic diagram that helps you locate the slots. Typically, the RAM modules are found close to the CPU, in the center or in one corner of the motherboard.

6. **Turn your PC's chassis so that the DIMM slots are facing you (as shown in Figure 2-2) and make sure that the two levers on the side of the socket are extended.**

Figure 2-2:
Align the
DDR/DDR2/
DDR3
module with
its socket.

Note that the notches cut into the connectors on the bottom of the memory module match the spacers in the sockets themselves, so you can't install your modules the wrong way. (Smart thinking there.)

7. **Align the connector on the bottom of the module with the socket and push down with a light pressure to seat the module.**

8. **While you push down, the levers on each side of the socket should move toward the center, as shown in Figure 2-3, until they click in place.**

Figure 2-3:
Hey, those
levers just
clicked into
place!

After you correctly install the module, the two levers should be tightly flush against the sides of the memory module to hold it securely.

9. **Slide the cover back on your PC and secure it.**

10. **Move your PC back to its place of honor and plug it in.**

11. **Restart your computer and prepare to enjoy a faster PC!**

Chapter 3: Adding Hard Drive Territory to Your System

In This Chapter

✔ **Understanding virtual memory**

✔ **Selecting the proper drive**

✔ **Choosing an internal or external drive**

✔ **Adding a second internal drive**

Here's what I call the *Elbowroom Hypothesis:* Both mankind and his computer tools will expand to fill whatever room they're given. If you're bent on becoming a PC power user, I can assure you — in fact, I can downright *guarantee* you — that the largest hard drive you can buy today will eventually be filled in the future. As you discover in this chapter, even Windows 7 itself demands a chunk of hard drive territory — when you install it *and* when it's running. Hence the explosion in hard drive capacities over the past ten years or so.

Luckily, you can upgrade your PC's hard drive with ease by either connecting an external drive or upgrading your current internal hard drive. Alternatively, you can simply cast yourself to the four winds with abandon and keep your current internal drive and add a second drive. This chapter is your road map.

The Tale of Virtual Memory

"Wait a furshlugginer minute here, Mark — you cover memory upgrades in Chapter 2 of this very minibook. Why bring it up now?" Good question, and the answer lies in the fact that the pseudo-RAM called *virtual memory* actually exists on your hard drive rather than as memory modules on your motherboard.

Hard drives in ancient times

I'm old enough to remember when a 1GB hard drive was an unheard-of dream. Heck, I still have the first hard drive I ever owned in my wild single years: a huge RadioShack 15MB (yes, you read it right, *15 whopping megabytes*) disk system that I used with my TRS-80 Model IV. (Oh, did I mention that those 15 megs of storage cost me more than $1,000 US in 1983 and that the drive is about the size of a typical modern PC case?) I use it as a combination monitor stand, conversation piece, and possible proof of past visits by extraterrestrials.

If you're totally confused, here's the explanation: Modern operating systems (Windows 7/Vista/XP, Mac OS X, Unix, and Linux) all use the virtual memory trick to feed your applications the memory they need. Suppose that your PC has only 2GB of random access memory (RAM) installed, but you just ran Photoshop and demanded that it load two 500MB high-resolution digital images. If Windows were limited to using only your computer's *physical* RAM (the memory modules you installed on your PC's motherboard), you would be up a creek because Windows 7 Ultimate requires a minimum of around 500MB of memory itself, and Photoshop takes a significant chunk of memory to run. On top of all that, you'd be loading 1GB of data! Considering the size of today's documents and the amount of RAM needed by memory-hungry mega-applications, your 2GB PC literally couldn't do its job. And, don't forget that you'd probably be running more than one application at a time. What's a computer to do?

As you can see in Figure 3-1, Windows turns to your hard drive for help. It uses a portion of the empty space on your hard drive to temporarily hold the data that would otherwise be held in your computer's memory. In this case, your hardworking silicon warrior uses 2GB of hard drive space, so the total memory available within Windows (using both 2GB of physical memory and 2GB of virtual memory) is now 4GB, providing more elbowroom to work with. Your programs don't know that they're using virtual memory — Windows takes care of everything behind the scenes, so Photoshop thinks that you have 4GB of physical memory.

Now that you understand how virtual memory works, commit this Mark's Maxim to memory:

Always leave enough empty hard drive space for Windows to use as virtual memory!™

How much is enough? I try to leave at least 25GB or 30GB free on the C: drive at all times on my Windows 7 machines. (Your C: drive is typically the hard drive that Windows 7 boots from: To check how much space it has remaining, choose Start⇨My Computer, then right-click the C: drive and choose Properties from the menu.) A PC that runs out of hard drive space is a terrible thing to see; applications start to lock up, you might lose any changes you made to open files, and Windows begins displaying pitiful error messages begging you to close some of your open application windows (or even restart).

Without virtual memory = 2GB system RAM

2GB of RAM

Figure 3-1: Windows creates memory space using the free space on your hard drive.

With virtual memory + = 4GB system RAM

2GB of RAM

2GB of hard drive space

Also, note that virtual memory is always — and I mean *always* — slower than true physical memory. After all, that data has to be written to and read from your hard drive rather than from superfast memory modules. This is why I'm a proponent of adding as much RAM to your PC as possible; the more memory that you add, the less likely that Windows needs to resort to virtual memory.

PC techs call your computer's use of virtual memory *drive thrashing* because Windows must continually write data to, read data from, and erase data from your hard drive. When you run out of physical memory, the hard drive activity light on the front of your machine never seems to go out. And yes, if you're wondering, all that activity shortens the life of your hard drive.

Recognizing a Well-Dressed Hard Drive

When you decide to take the plunge and add storage space, reading this section helps you shop by separating the good specifications from the gobbledygook.

Today's PCs use Enhanced Integrated Drive Electronics (EIDE, also called PATA) or Serial ATA (SATA) hard drives. Although a PC can use an internal Small Computer System Interface (SCSI) hard drive, anyone using expensive and complex SCSI hardware is already a PC power user and can probably skip this chapter without a second glance.

Size definitely matters

Virtually all EIDE and SATA drives on the market today are 3½" format, which means that they can fit within a typical floppy drive/hard drive combo bay of your computer's case. Unfortunately, some mini-tower cases have only one or two of these 3½" bays.

Therefore, if you're planning to park that 3½" drive within a much larger 5¼" bay (the kind used with DVD and Blu-Ray drives), you need a metal framework called a *drive cage kit.* In effect, the hard drive is mounted into the drive cage, which in turn is mounted in the PC's 5¼" bay. Most drives don't come with a drive cage kit (check first, of course), so you need to buy one at your computer shop. (They usually run about $10 US.)

How fast is your access?

When you see a drive's *access* (or *seek*) time listed, that's the amount of time (in milliseconds; ms) that it takes the drive to read or write data. Naturally, a lower access time is desirable — and usually somewhat more expensive. Drives with access times less than 7 ms are usually at the top of their price range, especially when the drive in question has a higher revolutions per minute (rpm) rating.

What does rpm have to do with hard drives?

In the world of personal computers, just like in the world of the Indy 500, the abbreviation *rpm* means *r*evolutions *p*er *m*inute. (However, I'm counting the revolutions that the magnetic disk platter turns inside the drive.) And, with a refreshing constancy, a higher-rpm hard drive means better performance, just like a beefier engine's rpm means greater speed in auto racing.

Most of today's EIDE and SATA drives fall into one of three ranges:

+ **5,400 rpm:** These drives are standard equipment on most older PCs and can also be found on low-cost Intel Celeron and AMD Sempron computers. As reliable as vanilla ice cream, one of these drives gets the job done — but don't expect whipped cream and a cherry.

+ **7,200 rpm:** This is the standard rpm rating for most consumer hard drives on today's market.

✦ **10,000 rpm:** Lucky dog! These "sports car" hard drives are found on today's high-performance PCs. You pay a bit more, but a 10,000 rpm SATA drive can really speed up your disk-intensive applications (and Windows 7 itself).

I heartily recommend that you select a 7,200 rpm or 10,000 rpm drive when upgrading any PC or buying a new one. The significantly faster read/write performance on one of these drives peps up your entire system.

Internal versus External Storage

I address the idea of internal and external peripherals in a number of places elsewhere in this book, so I don't go into a crazy amount of detail here. Suffice it to say that I recommend using an internal hard drive whenever

✦ You don't need to share the drive among multiple computers, or take your drive with you while traveling.

✦ Your PC has an additional open drive bay, or you're willing to upgrade the existing drive.

✦ You want to save money.

As you might expect, with those criteria, I usually push internal hard drives on both my unsuspecting consulting customers and on myself. Figure 3-2 shows the curvaceous rear end of a typical modern hard drive. (Well, at least it *looks* curvaceous to a techno-nerd like me.)

Figure 3-2:
A sweeping
vista — the
connectors
on the back
of an EIDE
hard drive.

Power supply
connector

Ribbon cable
connector

Master/slave
jumper

Don't get me wrong: External drives are neat toys, and they're perfect for back-ups and media storage (like your photo and MP3 music collections). However, they cost significantly more than their internal counterparts, and you lose some of your precious desk space accommodating them. Most external drives also have their own power cords, so you have to pull another AC wall socket out of your magician's hat. If you really do need an external drive and you want to save yourself the hassle, consider a drive that's powered over a Universal Serial Bus (USB) or FireWire connection, which means no additional power cable worries. For under $100 (US), you can pick up one of my favorite external drives, the Western Digital My Book 1TB with USB 2.0 connection, at www.newegg.com.

If someone tries to give you a USB 1.*x* hard drive — or, heaven forbid, you're thinking of buying a used USB 1.*x* hard drive — I beg you *not* to do it! The first generation of USB drives was ridiculously slow. In other words, your kids are likely to graduate from college before you finish transferring a single gigabyte's worth of data from that drive to your PC. Keep a safe distance from that tired drive and call your local antique hardware shelter.

Adding a Second Internal Hard Drive

For most current PC owners, the easiest method of adding more hard drive space is to add a second hard drive to their systems. I cite three very good reasons for this:

✦ **No backup is required.** Of course, *you should be backing up your current hard drive anyway.* (If not, shut this book immediately and back up your drive!) Adding a second drive eliminates the setup that you have to perform if you upgrade your current drive because you don't have to restore the current contents of your old drive to the new drive.

✦ **Most PCs have at least one open drive bay.** Unless your computer is already stuffed to the gills, you should have enough room to add a second hard drive. If it *is* stuffed to the gills, you either have to upgrade the current drive or add an external FireWire, eSATA, (external SATA) or USB 2.0 drive. For more information about these external connections, visit Chapter 4 in this minibook.

✦ **It's like . . . well . . . more for less.** Rather than replace an existing 500GB drive with a 1TB drive — and end up with only 500GB more room — I always find it more attractive to leave the original drive as is and add that second drive, resulting in the full 1TB that you paid for. (***Remember:*** You *will* eventually use that space. Trust me.)

Are you girded and ready for battle? Then follow this procedure to add a second internal EIDE hard drive to your current system:

1. **Cover your work surface with several sheets of newspaper.**

2. **Turn off your PC, unplug it, and place it on top of the newspaper.**

Serial ATA is in the house

Although EIDE is still the most popular hard drive interface for new PCs, serial ATA is rapidly catching up. That's because a SATA connection allows significantly faster data transfer rates (in English: SATA is faster than EIDE) and there are no jumpers for a SATA drive. (Jump to the steps on adding a second internal hard drive for more on jumpers.) The installation of the physical drive is the same as I outline here for an EIDE drive; then simply plug in the data cable from your motherboard (it goes on only one way) and the power cable from your PC's power supply, and the drive is ready for action.

In fact, virtually all the latest motherboards on the market have both EIDE (sometimes called PATA, short for Parallel ATA) and SATA connectors onboard. You can mix and match and use both or work only with the faster SATA connections.

3. **Remove the case screws and slide off the case, putting the screws aside in a glass or wooden bowl or cup.**

   If you're unsure how to remove your PC's case, check the manual that accompanied your computer.

4. **Touch the metal chassis of the computer to dissipate any static electricity.**

5. **Verify the jumper settings on the back of your original drive, as shown in Figure 3-3. If necessary, change the existing drive to *multiple drives, master unit* (or just *master*) by moving the jumper to the indicated pins.**

**Book VII
Chapter 3**

Adding Hard Drive
Territory to Your
System

Figure 3-3:
Change
jumper
settings
on an EIDE
hard drive
when
installing
a second
drive.

Jumpers are the tiny plastic and metal shunts that you use to configure hard drives and CD/DVD drives. (If you're installing a SATA drive, though, you won't need to worry about jumpers: Just skip to Step 7.)

Jumper

 Your jumper configuration is probably different from the one shown in Figure 3-3. Most hard drive manufacturers now print the jumper settings on the tops of hard drives. If the settings aren't printed on the drive, you can refer to the drive's manual or visit the manufacturer's Web site and look up the settings there. If all this seems a little exotic, the terms really aren't risqué; *master* means primary (and if you have at least one drive, there must be a master device), and *slave* means secondary. Other than that, the devices are treated the same way by your PC.

6. Set the jumpers on the back of the new drive for *multiple drives*, *slave unit* (often listed as just *slave*).

7. If your new drive needs a drive cage to fit into the desired bay, use the screws supplied by the drive manufacturer to attach the cage rails to both sides of your drive.

 For more on drive cage kits, see the earlier section "Size definitely matters."

8. Slide the drive into the selected bay from the front of the case, and make sure that the end with the connectors goes in first and that the exposed circuitry of the drive is on the bottom.

9. Slide the hard drive back and forth in the drive bay until the screw holes in the side of the bay are aligned with the screw holes on the side of the drive (or on the drive cage rails).

10. Tighten down the drive to the side of the bay with the screws that came with the drive (or your cage kit), as illustrated in Figure 3-4.

11. Choose an unused power connector and plug it in, and make sure that the connector is firmly seated (see Figure 3-5).

Joyfully, there's only one way to connect a power cable to a hard drive — the right way.

Figure 3-4:
Secure your
new friend
in place.

Figure 3-5:
A drive
without
power is
a paper-
weight.

12. **Plug the other connector from the hard drive cable into the back of
the drive and make sure that the cable is firmly seated.**

Note that both hard drives use the same cable, so you might need to
unplug the original drive from the cable and switch connectors. Don't
worry: It doesn't matter which connector goes to which drive as long as
the jumpers are correctly set.

Check for a blocked hole in the cable connector, which should align with a missing pin on the drive's connector. This alignment trick, called *keying*, helps ensure that you're installing the cable right side up. However, don't panic if the cable isn't keyed: Remember that the wire with the red or black marking on the cable is always Wire 1 and that it should align with Pin 1 on the drive's connector (see Figure 3-6).

Figure 3-6:
Connect the
drive to the
data cable.

13. **Replace the cover on your PC and tighten its screws.**

14. **Plug your PC back in and turn it on.**

15. **Run the drive formatting utility that accompanied your new drive to prepare it for use.**

Chapter 4: Partying with USB, FireWire, and eSATA

In This Chapter

✔ Comparing USB 1.*x* with USB 2.0

✔ Using FireWire for high-end fun

✔ Putting eSATA to work

✔ Extending your system with a hub

✔ Adding a port card

*I*n the days of the early IBM PCs, practically every device that you added was *internal* (in the computer case). Because so few peripherals existed that you could add to your system, this situation really wasn't a problem. Back in the day, the parallel port took care of the printer (if you could afford one), and as the modem grew in importance, it took up residence with the serial port.

Today, however, PC cases have shrunk. When it comes to size, I can't tell the difference between many new desktops and my kid's PlayStation. And, less internal room means more need for external stuff. Also, because of the huge increase in the number of portable devices you can add to your computer, those toys are naturally designed to be external, such as digital cameras, MP3 players, and the like. The days of the PC as a monolith are over.

So what's a poor CPU to do? Enter the star ports of the digital age: Universal Serial Bus (USB) and FireWire, along with the up-and-coming eSATA. Talk about *sassy:* They're fast, they offer plug-and-play convenience, and they don't hassle you with arcane errors or strange settings. Plus, you can use them to connect practically everything but the kitchen sink to your computer simultaneously.

In this chapter, I share the joy as we party together with these three ports.

A Tale of Three Fine Ports

Even the original IBM PC had ports — that's because the designers of that first digital beast knew that not everything would fit inside the computer's case. The first example of a piece of "outside" hardware was the computer printer, but soon others appeared: Modems, mice, joysticks, drawing pads, and an entire pantheon of other toys started demanding ports.

Today's machines typically offer at least one of the Big Three ports (and depending on the price tag, perhaps two or even all three). In this section, we'll compare and contrast USB, FireWire, and eSATA ports.

Comparing USB ports

You might think that all USB ports are the same, but they're not. In the beginning, only USB 1.*x* was available. Sure, USB 1.*x* was a fine little port (easy to use and requiring no configuration) but only a few times faster than an old-fashioned serial connection. (To be honest, a FireWire device wipes the floor with the first generation of USB devices when it comes to speed. You can read more about FireWire shortly.) Around the turn of the millennium, the list of peripherals that really required 400 Mbps of transfer speed was limited to digital video (DV) camcorders and external audio/visual (AV) hard drives used by video professionals. Today, that list has expanded:

+ **Digital cameras:** They produce images with bigger file sizes.

+ **High-resolution scanners:** These items need to churn out images with 500MB of pixels (or, incredibly, more than that).

+ **External, high-speed DVD and Blu-Ray recorders:** Don't even dream of recording a DVD over a USB 1.*x* connection.

+ **MP3 players:** These include my favorite, Apple iPod, which was the first MP3 player to use a FireWire connection. The iPod now uses a USB 2.0 connection for better compatibility with all types of computers.

Enter USB 2.0, the current specification. This generation of port ups the ante, delivering 480 Mbps, which handily tops the original FireWire specification, version A. And because it's backward compatible with older USB 1.1 devices, you don't have to start all over with your USB hardware, and cables will still work no matter which version of the port your PC uses. (Sometimes, change is not A Good Thing.) Of course, only those peripherals that support the USB 2.0 standard can take advantage of the warp speed increase. USB 3.0, which offers yet another huge jump in raw speed, will also be backward compatible with USB 1.1 and 2.0 hardware.

Comparing speeds of popular PC ports

Check out the following table to see just what a dramatic jump that USB, FireWire, and eSATA made in connection speed over the standard PC serial port.

Port	Year Appeared on PCs	Transfer Speed (in Megabits per Second)
PC serial	1981	Less than 1 Mbps
PC parallel	1981	1 Mbps
USB (version 1.1)	1996	12 Mbps
FireWire 400 (version A)	1996	400 Mbps
USB (version 2.0)	2001	480 Mbps
FireWire 800 (version B)	2003	800 Mbps
eSATA	2005	1500 Mbps
USB (version 3.0)	2010	4.8 Gbps

"Hey, Gladys, the external USB drive isn't getting any power. And I've got it plugged in and everything!" Of course, that drive might not be plugged into the wall socket for AC power — an easy troubleshooting task — but if you're using a USB device that's powered through the USB port itself, the problem might be more insidious. Some USB ports don't provide the full power support called for by the USB standard because they're designed only for connecting mice, keyboards, and joysticks. As a workaround, try plugging that USB drive into another PC's USB port to see whether it wakes up. If it does, try plugging it into another USB port in a different location on your PC.

1 vote for FireWire

Not to be outdone, the FireWire 800 version B port — which can pump a whopping 800 Mbps between your PC and an external device — began showing up on Macs in the first months of 2003. This port is now available for any power-user PC. If your PC doesn't have one and you need that kind of performance, you can add a FireWire 800 port to your current machine with a port adapter card. The new version of FireWire is also backward compatible, but the connector is different; to connect a FireWire 400 device to a FireWire 800 port, all you need is an inexpensive go-between adapter. No biggie.

IEEE 1394 is the techie name for FireWire. You might come across this term in your computer and peripheral travels.

Even with the faster USB 2.0 specification, I'm still a FireWire kind of guy, and not just because it has a cooler name. Here are my reasons:

✦ **Device support:** FireWire has been around since 1996 on most DV equipment, so it's a well-recognized standard.

✦ **Control over connection:** Ignore the engineer-speak. Basically, this feature allows you to control your FireWire device from your PC. For example, if you have a DV camcorder with a FireWire port, you can control your camcorder from your keyboard. Just click Play within your editing software, and your camera jumps into action just as though you had pressed the Play button on the DV camcorder itself. Although USB can send a basic signal or two to the device (for instance, a command to erase an image from your digital camera), it's nowhere near as sophisticated as the control over your connection that's possible with a FireWire connection.

The latest power user port: eSATA

This section ends with a bang — and that bang is eSATA, the latest port on the block for connecting external hard drives and other high-performance peripherals. Unfortunately, eSATA hasn't appeared on many consumer-level PCs yet, but that's likely to change in the not-too-distant future. (Of course, if you want to leap into the fray right now, you can add an eSATA adapter card to your existing PC!) You'll find plenty of eSATA peripherals available, waiting for the port to appear on more computers — if that sounds like the state USB was in a decade ago, you'd be correct.

An eSATA connection is about twice the speed of a FireWire 800 connection, making it ideal for external storage (think applications like video editing and high-speed backups). Like USB and FireWire, eSATA is plug and play, and additional eSATA devices can be daisy-chained if necessary (more on daisy-chaining in the next section).

Or Do You Just Need a Hub?

A technician friend of mine has a great T-shirt with the logo "Got ports?" If your PC already has FireWire or USB ports but they're already all taken, you don't need to install an adapter card to provide your computer with additional portage. (Of course, you can eject one of those devices and unplug it each time whenever you want to connect your digital camera, but that might involve turning your PC around and navigating through the nest of cables on the back.)

PC power users eschew such hassles. Instead, buy a *hub,* which is a split-ter box that turns one USB or FireWire port into multiple ports, as shown in Figure 4-1. (***Note:*** Don't confuse a USB/FireWire hub with a *network* hub, which is an entirely different beast.) Although using a hub fills a port, you gain four, six, or eight ports in the bargain (depending on the hub), and everything stays as convenient and plug-and-play as before. (It's engineering that's both simple and *sassy.*)

Figure 4-1:
Power users love USB hubs.

Don't forget to check whether some of your USB/FireWire devices have daisy-chaining ports on the back that will allow you to connect another device. You can tell that a device is designed for daisy-chaining by check-ing whether it sports two ports of the same type (like a scanner that has two USB ports). If so, you should be able to daisy-chain additional devices. A series of daisy-chained devices will likely help you avoid buying a USB or FireWire hub because everything is still linked to one physical USB or FireWire port on your PC.

By using these methods, you can theoretically plug 63 devices into one FireWire port and 127 devices into one USB port. Heck, not even James Bond can stack gadgets that high!

Installing a Port Card

Here's where the original modular design of the IBM PC (all those many, many moons ago) comes in handy. If your computer didn't come with eSATA or FireWire ports, you'll find that adding new ports to your PC is as simple as plugging an adapter card into a slot in the back of your motherboard. A typical FireWire 800 card costs around $75 US and gives you two FireWire 800 ports. Follow these steps to do it the right way — once!

1. **Cover your work surface with several sheets of newspaper.**

2. **Turn off your PC, unplug it, and place it on top of the newspaper.**

3. **Remove the case screws and slide the case off, and put the screws aside in a bowl or cup.**

   If you're unsure how to remove your PC's case, check the manual that accompanied your computer.

4. **To dissipate any static electricity, touch a metal surface before you handle your new adapter card or touch any circuitry inside the case.**

   Yes, I know I keep haranguing you about static electricity — but it's important. I typically touch the metal chassis of the computer.

5. **Locate an adapter card slot of the proper length at the back of your computer case.**

   You want to use a Peripheral Component Interconnect (PCI) slot, which is the standard adapter card connector in today's PCs. See Figure 4-2.

Figure 4-2: Locate the PCI slots on your mother-board.

6. **Remove the screw and the metal slot cover at the back of the case, as shown in Figure 4-3.**

   Because you don't need these items again, put them in your spare parts box.

Figure 4-3:
Remove the
slot cover
and screw
before
installing a
new card.

7. **Pick up your port card by its top corners, and line up the connector on the bottom of the card with the slot on the motherboard.**

   The card's metal bracket should align with the open area created when you remove the slot cover from the back of your PC.

   WARNING!

   Never try to force a connector into a slot designed for another type of card! For example, PCI Express video cards have different types of connectors, and they don't accept PCI cards. If you need help determining the location of your PCI card slots, check your motherboard manual.

8. **After the connector is aligned correctly (as shown in Figure 4-4), apply even pressure to the top of the card and push it down into the slot until the bracket is resting against the case.**

Adapter cards

Empty slot

Make sure all
notches line up

Figure 4-4:
Alignment!
Alignment!

9. Place the screw in the corresponding hole in the bracket and tighten it.

10. Place the cover back on your PC and replace the screws that you saved from Step 3.

11. Plug your PC back in and turn it on.

12. Run the installation disc that came with your port card or load the driver disc when prompted by Windows.

    Don't forget to check the manufacturer's Web site for new Windows 7-specific drivers!

Chapter 5: Pumping Up Your Sound and Video

In This Chapter

✔ Selecting a sound card

✔ Upgrading your video card

✔ Installing your new toys

Technology has advanced so much that at last, we've reached the point where the personal computer lives up to all that personal entertainment hoopla. You know — the idea that your PC is at the center of your gaming, audio, and TV environment. Or, as I've been putting it for the past couple of years (another one of Mark's Maxims):

One box to rule them all and in the den to find them.™

(Man, I *love* that one. That's T-shirt material.)

However, putting your PC at the center of your digital lifestyle is a bit difficult if you're still stuck with a subpar sound card or if your computer's video card is more than two or three years old. Look at what you're missing out on: Closing your eyes and enjoying Dolby Surround sound with better than CD-quality audio, watching TV with TiVo-style control on your PC's crystal-clear LCD monitor, listening to streaming Internet radio and playing online games where you can behead a super-realistic, 3D orc with extreme prejudice. This, ladies and gentlemen, is a good time to be alive!

If your system needs an audiovisual upgrade, you'll find what you need to know right here.

Sound Card Features to Covet

The first stop on your audiovisual upgrade tour is your PC's sound card (naturally). Shoppers, in this section, I show you what to look for when comparing sound cards.

3D spatial imaging

Most PC owners think of 3D sound as purely a gamer's feature, but nothing could be further from the truth. Sure, today's games are even more fun when you can use your ears as well as your eyes to locate your enemy, but 3D sound comes in handy when you're listening to audio CDs, watching movies, or playing digital audio files from your hard drive. With audio files and music, 3D spatial imaging can add an auditorium or concert hall effect, where the stereo separation is enhanced.

Surround sound support

With a Dolby Surround sound card and the right speakers, your PC can deliver Dolby Surround sound while you're listening to audio CDs or watching DVD movies using your PC. (For me, the biggest hassle wasn't the extra cost or upgrading my PC's sound card: It was finding the space for all five speakers around my already crowded computer desk!)

High-end Surround sound cards, such as the X-Fi Xtreme Audio card from Creative Labs, can deliver Dolby Digital 7.1 Surround sound, 24-bit/192 KHz audio playback (far superior in quality than even a commercial audio CD), and 3D imaging for your games — and all for about $50 (US) from most Web stores. Life is truly good.

Figure 5-1 illustrates an old friend to any PC audiophile: A *subwoofer* adds realistic, deep subsonic bass to not only your music but also your games. A subwoofer is an important part of any 5.1 (or better) Surround sound system. Whether you're experiencing the grinding of tank treads or launching a Hellfire missile, a subwoofer provides the necessary sonic punch. Most subwoofers should be placed on the floor, where the vibration isn't a factor.

Figure 5-1:
All hail your subwoofer, King of the PC Speaker System.

MP3 encoding support

Although I discuss MP3 files in detail in Book VI, Chapter 2, I want to mention them here because anyone who's heavily into MP3 digital audio will really appreciate a sound card with built-in MP3 encoding and digital effects. That MP3 hardware feature relieves your PC's processor from the job of ripping and playing MP3 files so that you can rip music while you edit a digital photograph in Photoshop with nary a drop in performance. No stuttering audio or long delays, especially on older PCs.

Many hardware MP3 sound cards also allow you to introduce to the MP3 files you create the same concert hall environmental effect that I mention earlier in this chapter. (Now your garage band can claim to have played Carnegie Hall.)

Game and FireWire ports

Many sound cards are equipped with a little something extra: a FireWire port or a joystick/gamepad port, which was once a dear friend of any PC game player (because it used to be the only way to hook up most joysticks and external game controllers). Lately, most PC controllers have switched to the Universal Serial Bus (USB) port, but it's still a plus for a sound card to include a game port. Older game peripherals — many joysticks and flight throttles — don't work with USB, so it's a legacy thing. (Chapter 4 of this minibook delivers the goods on FireWire.)

MIDI ports

Before I move on, I have to address musicians and their Musical Instrument Digital Interface (MIDI) ports. You can use a sound card with standard MIDI ports to connect synthesizers and many different electronic musical instruments, such as drums and keyboards, to your computer. Most MIDI instruments now feature a USB port as well.

With a MIDI instrument connected, your computer can play MIDI music files on the instrument, or you can play the instrument and record the music as a MIDI file on your computer. Note, however, that most of today's sound cards can play MIDI music files without attaching instruments, so you don't have to buy a card with built-in MIDI ports just to play MIDI music files.

Shopping for a Monster Graphics Card

Having a terrific graphics card isn't all about blasting aliens to kingdom come. A fast 3D video card can speed up the display of digital video and even the operating system eye candy provided by Windows 7. In this section, I clue you in on what to look for when considering a video card upgrade.

Just say, "PCI Express"

Although today's video cards look like any other typical adapter cards, they usually fit only into a dedicated PCI Express video card slot, so check your motherboard manual or PC manual to make sure that your machine will accept a PCI Express video card. However, after you install a PCI Express video card, you enjoy the fastest possible video performance; if you're a hard-core gamer, I strongly recommend that any new machine you build or buy be equipped with a PCI Express video slot! (In fact, most high-performance motherboards now include a second — or even third — PCI Express slot, allowing you to use multiple video cards to catapult your gaming performance through the roof!

Rate the performance of a particular card while you're shopping by checking the box or the manufacturer's Web site for benchmark results that you can use to compare with other cards. Try the popular benchmark program 3DMark Vantage (the Basic edition is $7, from www.futuremark.com). You can also run games like BioShock 2 or Borderlands and compare the maximum frames per second (fps) that the card can display. (The higher the frame rate, the better.) You can also find up-to-date reviews of the latest cards and video chipsets at Tom's Hardware on the Web at www.tomshardware.com.

Exploring the differences between chipsets

You won't find many differences among *chipsets,* which are the separate graphics processing unit (GPU) "brains" that power today's top 3D video cards. Allow me to explain: The two major players in the PC video card chipset battle are

✦ **NVIDIA:** The cutting-edge crew at NVIDIA (www.nvidia.com) has produced some of the fastest video cards for the PC in recent years, including the classics RIVA TNT and TNT2 as well as the GeForce series.

✦ **ATI:** ATI Technologies (www.ati.com) has been producing popular video chipsets for a decade now, including its Rage line. Typically, ATI video cards are somewhat less expensive than NVIDIA cards, and many motherboard manufacturers build ATI video hardware directly onto their products.

Here's the payoff for you, the consumer: The fastest offerings from either company deliver more performance than PC gamers are likely to need for at least six months. However, a powerful video card also appeals to videographers and photographers who demand super–high-resolution images — Photoshop, After Effects, and Premiere Pro are perfect examples of programs that will take everything your card has and then some, especially on multiple-monitor setups.

Other video card features that you'll want

Naturally, you can evaluate more than just chipsets and connectors when comparing video cards. Keep an eye out for these features and specifications while you shop:

✦ **Onboard random access memory (RAM):** Like your motherboard, your video card carries its own supply of memory. Today's cards typically have anywhere from 128MB to 1GB of memory. Again, the general rule is to buy a card with as much onboard RAM as possible. More RAM equals higher resolutions with more colors onscreen.

✦ **Driver and standards support:** Any PC video card should fully support the Microsoft DirectX video standards — now at DirectX 11.0 for Windows 7 (or DirectX 10.0 for Windows Vista). Gamers will also appreciate robust *OpenGL* support (an open video standard that's becoming very popular in 3D action games). Support for these standards should be listed on the product's box.

✦ **Maximum resolution:** The higher the resolution a card can produce, the more your monitor can display at once — and not just in games, but documents, digital photographs, and your Windows desktop. For example, I like to write manuscripts at a resolution of 1152 x 864 rather than 1024 x 768 because I can see more of the page in Microsoft Word without scrolling. Today's cards can reach truly epic resolutions, such as 2560 x 1600; personally, however, I don't work at such stratospheric resolutions often because a few hours of work usually leaves me with eyestrain (and possibly a headache).

The maximum resolution you can display on your system also depends on the monitor you're using. Therefore, if you upgrade to the latest video card but you're still using an old clunker of a monitor with a maximum resolution of 1024 x 768, you're stuck there. (Time to invest in a new display.) For more about your monitor, see Book I, Chapter 1.

**Book VII
Chapter 5**

Pumping Up Your
Sound and Video

✦ **Video capture and TV output:** A card with these features can create digital video footage from an analog TV signal (that's the *video capture* part) and transfer the image you see on your monitor to a TV, VCR, or camcorder (the *TV output* part). If you want to create video CDs or DVDs from your home movies on VHS tape, spend a little extra on a video capture/TV output card.

✦ **TV tuner:** A card with a built-in TV tuner can turn your PC into a TV set, including giving you the ability to pause and replay programs on the fly (like how a TiVo unit works with a regular TV). You can use a traditional antenna or connect the card to your cable or satellite system, as shown in Figure 5-2. Just don't let your boss know that the new video card that the company bought gives you the ability to watch your favorite soaps in a window on your desktop . . . you're supposed to be working.

Figure 5-2:
Watch and record TV shows on your PC with a TV tuner card.

TV tuner card

✦ **Multiple monitor support:** Most new video cards allow you to connect two monitors to one card. This is considered a must-have for video editing and 3D or CAD work, and hardcore gamers crave that extra real estate as well. You can either see two separate desktops or make the two monitors into a seamless desktop. Imagine the size of your Windows workspace when it's spread across two displays!

✦ **MPEG hardware support:** Finally, I describe digital video — which, as you can read about in earlier chapters of this book, is typically stored in MPEG, AVI, or MOV formats. (The most popular is the MPEG format.) Without the *compression* that these video formats offer (which shrinks the size of the digital video file), you would never squeeze a full-length movie on a single DVD. Although your PC can use software to *encode* (create a compressed MPEG file) and *decode* (read a compressed MPEG file) MPEG files on your hard drive or DVDs, a video card with built-in encoding and decoding features can really speed up the process. This hardware support is particularly valuable if you're going to do serious video editing on your PC because you cut down the amount of time required to save your movies to disk.

Installing Sound and Video Cards

Installing a sound card or video card is much like adding any other adapter card to your PC. If you're installing a sound card, make sure that you connect the audio cable from your CD-ROM/DVD-ROM drive (see Step 5 in the following step list); if you're installing a video card, make sure that you pick the right PCI-Express slot (see Step 7).

Follow these steps:

1. **Cover your work surface with several sheets of newspaper.**

2. **Shut down your PC, unplug it from all external connections, and place it on top of the newspaper.**

3. **Remove the screws on the back of the case and slide the case off, saving the screws for later.**

   Find a bowl (glass or wood; not plastic or metal) to sequester your screws. Nothing worse than a runaway, AWOL screw.

4. **To dissipate static electricity, touch a metal surface before handling any cards or touching your PC's motherboard.**

   For example, touch the PC's metal chassis. I shudder to think of what I'll do if anyone develops a fiberglass computer.

   To you, it's just a momentary painful spark. To your PC hardware, however, that static electricity can zap components into oblivion! Always ground yourself by touching a metal surface before handling any hardware, including adapter cards and memory modules!

5. **If you're installing a new sound card, check for a thin audio cable connected from your old sound card (or a connector on the motherboard, if your PC has an integrated sound card) to your CD-ROM or DVD-ROM drive; if your existing sound card has such a cable, disconnect the cable from the old sound card or motherboard connector.**

6. **Remove the screw holding the adapter card you're upgrading, and pull upward to remove it.**

   Don't forget to put the screw in your spare parts box and put the old adapter card in an antistatic bag for safekeeping. (I use the bag left behind by the new card.)

Some video card slots have plastic tabs that act as a locking mechanism. Just bend the tab gently with your finger, and you should be able to remove the existing card.

7. **Locate the adapter card slot that matches the card you're installing.**

A PCI Express video adapter requires a dedicated PCI Express 16 slot. (See Figure 5-3.) On the other hand, a standard PCI sound card should fit in any open PCI slot. Naturally, if the upgrade card uses the same type of slot as the card that it's replacing, use the empty slot you just opened up.

Figure 5-3:
Locate the PCI Express slot.

8. **Pick up the adapter card by its top corners and line up the bottom connector on the card with the slot on the motherboard, as shown in Figure 5-4.**

Make sure that the card's metal bracket aligns properly with the opening in the back of the PC.

Figure 5-4:
Align the card and the slot.

9. **After the card is aligned, apply even pressure to the top of the card and push it down into the slot.**

10. **Place the screw in the corresponding hole in the bracket and tighten it.**

11. **If you're installing a sound card and you disconnected a CD-ROM/ DVD-ROM audio cable from the old card (or a connector on the mother- board), reconnect the cable from your drive to the new card.**

Check the manual for the card to determine where the CD/DVD audio connector is located; this is a standard connector, so it should be easy to track down.

12. **If you've installed a video card with a TV tuner, connect the cable from your satellite or cable box to the card (refer to Figure 5-2).**

13. **Place the cover back on your PC and replace the screws that you saved from Step 3.**

14. **Plug your PC back in, reconnect all those cables, and turn it on.**

For video cards, you should immediately be able to gauge the success of your work — if there's an image on your monitor, the installation was a success! However, don't be alarmed if the resolution is completely wrong, and don't adjust your monitor yet — Windows will likely be able to return to your previous resolution once you install the drivers for your new card.

15. **Run the installation disc that came with your upgrade card or load the driver disc when prompted by Windows.**

For sound cards, you'll likely hear nothing until you install your new card's drivers. Reboot once the installation is complete, and listen for Windows to make sure it greets you with its welcome sound. You can also run Windows Media Player and play an MP3 song to verify things are working. Your sound card should also come with an audio configuration program that you can use to test and fine-tune your new ear candy — check your documenta- tion to see what free stuff you got, and where it was installed!

These steps should do it for you. If you need a little more help, I heartily recommend my profusely illustrated book, *Build Your Own PC Do-It-Yourself For Dummies,* for detailed instructions and even more photos to see this upgrade in process. My book even has a companion DVD with the same steps, so you can see me do this live!

**Book VII
Chapter 5**

**Pumping Up Your
Sound and Video**

Book VIII

Home Networking

Contents at a Glance

Chapter 1: Do I Really Need a Network? 529

Discovering the Advantages of a Network 529
What Can I Connect To? 533
What Hardware Do I Need? 534
What Software Do I Need? 535

Chapter 2: Ethernet to the Rescue 537

A Quickie Ethernet Primer 537
The Hardware You Need 539
Doing the Cable Dance 542
Configuring Windows 7 for Your Network 543
Printing across the Network 550
Using a Standard Switch with a Cable or DSL Modem 550
Troubleshooting Your Network 551

Chapter 3: Going Wireless 555

Understanding Wireless Networking 555
Using Wireless Hardware in Windows 7 563

Chapter 4: Sharing Your Internet Connection 565

Why Share Your Internet Connection? 565
Sharing through Hardware 566
Sharing through Software in Windows 7 571

Chapter 5: Securing Your Home Network 573

Common Sense Tips for Wired Networks 573
Ensuring Security on Your Wireless Network 576
Using Shared Folders (The Right Way) 578
Knowing Why You Need NAT 579
Marveling at the Magic of Virtual Private Networking 580

Chapter 1: Do I Really Need a Network?

In This Chapter

- ✓ Evaluating the advantages of a network
- ✓ Connecting to other computers and devices
- ✓ Selecting networking hardware and software

*N*etworking is neat stuff: The ability to copy or edit a document that's on another computer halfway down the hall is invaluable, whether that hallway is in a business or your own home. (Even a home office like mine, where six computers constantly vie for my attention in the same room, benefits from a network. Although the computers are only a few feet apart, moving 60GB worth of data between them would be no small feat without a common network connection.)

However, not everyone with multiple computers *needs* a network. For example, if you don't often exchange information between your computers, you can get by using a "sneaker net" or a simple USB or FireWire transfer cable. However, if you regularly need to share files, applications, and an Internet connection, you'll want a network. (I think you know which course of action I usually recommend. After all, look at the rest of this chapter and this minibook!)

Here, I cover what a network can do for you, which hardware and software you need, and how much work is involved. Later chapters in this minibook fill in the blanks (and compare the pros and cons of wired versus wireless), but after you read this introduction, you'll know whether a network is worth your effort.

Discovering the Advantages of a Network

If you've never used a network to link multiple computers, you might not realize which applications are network ready. Here's a quick list of the most common uses for a network.

File transfer

There's no faster method of moving files between computers than a network connection. And network file transfers are *transparent* to the person making the transfer, which means that you don't have to do anything special to transfer files between computers on a network. You can just drag and drop files as usual or use your favorite file management application to copy or move files between computers on the network, and Windows acts like you would expect. I like the Total Commander file management tool, as shown in Figure 1-1. To try out this excellent piece of shareware, visit www.ghisler. com. With Total Commander, it's a cinch to compare the contents of two different drives or folders, and the list display format can pack the maximum possible number of filenames onto your monitor. Copying or moving files 'twixt the panes is as simple as selecting and clicking a button.

Figure 1-1:
I use Total Commander to quickly and easily manage files on my network.

However, you certainly don't want just *anyone* transferring files to and from your PC — or, for that matter, even accessing your PC over the network. To help preserve security, Windows 7, Vista, and XP make certain that only the users and PCs with the proper rights can transfer files over your network. I discuss network security in greater detail in Chapter 5 of this very minibook.

If you're running more than one PC with Windows 7 on your network, you can also take advantage of the new HomeGroup feature, which helps automate the configuration of a secure file and printer-sharing network. It takes only a few clicks of the mouse to take advantage of HomeGroup, and I show you how in Book II, Chapter 4.

Sharing that-there Internet

Another popular networking benefit is the ability of one computer to share a single Internet connection with all other computers on a network. Typically, this arrangement works best with a broadband connection technology like a digital subscriber line (DSL) or cable, but it's possible with a dialup connection as well.

You can share a connection by using one of these methods:

+ **Software:** Use the built-in Internet Connection Sharing within Windows 7, as I demonstrate in Chapter 4 of this minibook.

+ **Hardware:** Add an Internet sharing device (such as a network router), which usually comes with other features, such as a built-in firewall.

I cover both these methods in Chapter 4 of this minibook.

One word: Games!

What's that you're saying, Bunky? You're tired of predictable computer opponents in your favorite games? Hordes of enemies in that zombie game that you can handle in your sleep? How about timid enemy monsters that don't attack you or ambush your character in Borderlands (as shown in Figure 1-2)?

Well, forget those lazy "artificial intelligence" tactics because in network *multiplayer mode,* you fight real human beings — the treacherous, backstabbing kind (which, oddly enough, usually turn out to be your best friends). Whenever possible, I try to attend *LAN parties,* get-togethers where multiplayer games are the featured attractions. Your host might have all the PCs and network hardware necessary for 8 or 16 people, but I usually bring my desktop or laptop computer so that I can sit down and plug in with a minimum of effort.

Shared documents and applications

Of course, a document that's handed from person to person on a floppy disk or CD or flash drive is technically shared, but is that really a convenient method of working on a document together? (To this day, PC hardware technicians and software developers call this antiquated kind of floppy-based transfer a *sneakernet*.) Anyway, forget wearing out your shoe leather just to hand off a document for the next person's comments — today's office workgroup relies on the company network to share documents and common applications the *right* way!

After you network your computers, any PC on your network can copy or open a document on another computer: that is, *if* the owner of the PC being accessed has been granted the proper rights to that file or to the folder where it's stored. For example, say you have a Word document that others need to edit, but you want to keep it on your hard drive: You can move that document to a shared folder. Others on the network can open the document within Word from their computers, just as though it were on their local machines.

And, if that's not *sassy* enough, consider the fact that Bob over in accounting (or your daughter in her bedroom) might be using an application that you don't have. If that application has been written for network use, you can run it on your computer remotely over the network! This type of program is a *shared application,* and it's the neatest thing since sliced cheese.

Figure 1-2:
A favorite multiplayer network game, Border-lands.

Read the details on both shared documents and shared applications in Chapter 2 of this minibook.

What Can I Connect To?

A surprising number of objects on the planet have network ports or wireless network cards. Here's a list of the network-savvy stuff I've used:

+ **Other PCs:** The most common connection on a Windows network is to other PCs — some of which are standard desktop and notebook PCs, and others which are specialized network *servers* that perform only one task. (One example is a *file server,* which is used like a mega-hard drive that everyone on the network can access.) A PC running Windows 7 makes a great dedicated media server, storing your digital photographs, music, and video within networked "easy reach" — any other computer on your network can access those files quickly and conveniently.

Although HomeGroup is a great way to configure your network if *all* of your PCs are running Windows 7, other PCs on your network running Windows XP or Windows Vista can still become part of the family! Windows 7 networking is backward-compatible with older versions of Windows.

+ **Macintosh and Linux computers:** Your network need not be a snobby Windows-only country club; invite the neighbors to join in! Macs running Mac OS X can easily plug right in with a minimum of fuss, as can those Linux folks with the beards and suspenders. Of course, you can't run a Mac program on a PC, but — and this is a winner — many applications are available in versions for both operating systems, and they can share the same document! The best example is Microsoft Office, which is available in both Mac and PC versions. Word and Excel on both operating systems can open and edit the same Office documents.

Speaking of Mac OS X, I'm also the proud father of the *Mac OS X Snow Leopard All-in-One For Dummies* (Wiley). And, yes, I really do own both PCs and Macs, and I take advantage of both operating systems' offerings on my same office network. Anyway, if you find this tome helpful and you know a Mac owner who's using Leopard, please drop 'em a line and recommend the MOSXSLAIOFD! (How's *that* for an abbreviation?)

+ **Personal digital assistants (PDAs):** With the right adapter, your Palm handheld or Pocket PC can join in the fun.

+ **Shared network hardware:** Some shared hardware actually resides within a PC on the network (like an internal hard drive or DVD-ROM drive that you selected to be "visible" and accessible on the network); other network hardware devices work as standalone units (like an Internet sharing device, which is a box by itself).

✦ **Network printers:** Finally, a shared network printer can be connected to a PC on the network. Or, if you have enough pocket change, you can buy a standalone network printer that has its own network card.

Of course, this list is incomplete because it's constantly growing, but suffice it to say that a network usually includes more than just a smattering of desktop and laptop PCs.

What Hardware Do I Need?

The hardware basics that you need for a simple network include

✦ **A network adapter card or PC card:** Each computer on your network requires either a network adapter card (for a desktop) or a PC card (for a laptop). These cards can accept either a wired connection or a wireless connection. Naturally, if your desktop or laptop has wired or wireless hardware built in, you don't need to add a card — instead, smile quietly to yourself in a contented and smug manner. If you have to shop for a wired or wireless adapter for your PC, however, I don't leave you stranded: Chapters 2 and 3 in this minibook discuss what you need.

Naturally, the adapter card you buy will come with installation instructions — but if you'd like a hands-on guide while elbow-deep in your computer, my best-selling book *Build Your Own PC Do-It-Yourself For Dummies* (Wiley) illustrates the installation process (along with many other hardware chores you encounter throughout this book)!

✦ **A network router or switch:** I describe these black boxes in depth in Chapter 2 of this minibook. For now, I'll just say that they allow you to connect multiple computers to the same network. Some routers and switches are wireless, so no cables are necessary.

✦ **Cabling:** If you're not going the wireless route, you need an Ethernet cable for each computer you add to the network. Again, more on this in Chapter 2 of this minibook.

The hardware that I list here would be used in a standard Ethernet network, but remember that other types of network technologies might use your home's AC wiring or telephone jacks (which I cover in Chapter 3 of this minibook). You can also network two computers by using special Universal Serial Bus (USB) and FireWire cables although they're no substitute for the convenience and compatibility of an Ethernet network; they're simply for transferring files in a single session.

You might be able to buy all these hardware toys in a single box — *a network kit* — which is a great choice for a home or small-office network with four or fewer PCs. (Plus, the documentation is typically pretty well written.)

What Software Do I Need?

If each of your PCs will be running any version of Windows 98 or later, you have all the operating system software you need for a home network. (Thanks, Microsoft!) However, you might also need

✦ **Drivers for your network adapter card or PC card:** The manufacturer of your network card provides you with the drivers that Windows needs during installation, but don't forget to check the manufacturer's Web site for updated drivers.

✦ **Network management software:** The administrator of a larger network (I consider a network of ten or more computers to be a *larger* network) will likely buy extra software to monitor network traffic and optimize network hardware although the extra software isn't necessary for a simple network.

✦ **Network-ready applications:** As I mention earlier in this chapter, network applications can include productivity suites (such as Office), fax software, and workgroup applications (such as Lotus Notes) that provide a common calendar and e-mail system.

Chapter 2: Ethernet to the Rescue

In This Chapter

✔ Understanding how Ethernet works

✔ Gathering the various pieces o' hardware

✔ Considering cables

✔ Configuring Windows 7 for your network

✔ Putting shared folders to work

✔ Configuring a network printer

✔ Connecting a switch to the Internet

✔ Troubleshooting your network

This is it, my friend: the chapter with the bravado and the chutzpah to show you how to set up a home- or small-office wired network in Windows 7! Setting up a network gives you many benefits, including saving money by sharing resources (such as printers and an Internet connection) and the added convenience of file sharing.

You'll find that a *working* network (note that I stress the word *working*) quickly becomes as essential as Tabasco sauce or [insert name of your favorite condiment here]. By the way, if you find the word *working* to be more elusive than you first expected, I include a section at the end of this chapter that highlights common problems experienced by folks running their own network — as well as several possible solutions for each one, of course.

After your network is purring as smoothly as the proverbial kitten, you'll walk proudly to the closest person on the planet and proclaim proudly, "I am . . . a *network administrator!*" (Feel free to throw confetti or have a T-shirt made. If you like, send me an e-mail message at mark@mlcbooks.com — use the subject line "Ohmygoodnessitworks" — and we can celebrate together.)

A Quickie Ethernet Primer

No, don't close this book! Of all the supposed technowizard technologies connected with PCs, Ethernet networking is the easiest to master. Windows has come a long way in taming the home networking beast. Sure, you used to need a gold medal in the Tech Olympics to install a small home network, but that was in the days of DOS and Windows 3.1. We've come a long way, baby.

In fact, Ethernet has been around since the days of stone-tipped spears. As the first widely used network structure, it's still the most popular structure for homes as well as offices with around 25 PCs or fewer. Sure, faster networking designs exist these days, but old faithful Ethernet is also the cheapest to set up and maintain, and it's directly supported within all flavors of Windows.

So how does Ethernet work? Surprisingly, it's much like ham radio. A PC that wants to share data (as in moving or copying a file or sending and receiving stuff from the Internet) broadcasts that data across the network cabling in discrete bursts called *packets*. Each packet is marked with an address (much like how an e-mail message always has a To address) of the receiving computer.

When the PC with the matching address receives the packet across the network (along with tons of other packets bound for other locations), it processes the packet; other computers simply ignore any packets that aren't addressed to them. Figure 2-1 represents an Ethernet network at its best.

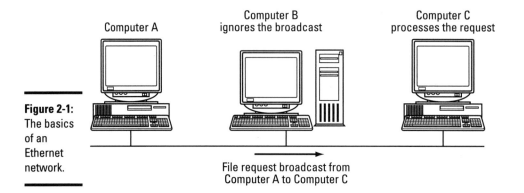

Figure 2-1: The basics of an Ethernet network.

Computer A

Computer B ignores the broadcast

Computer C processes the request

File request broadcast from Computer A to Computer C

This process sounds just nifty, but here's the catch: If two computers on your network try to broadcast packets at the same time, a network collision occurs, and everything stops until one computer successfully gets its data across the network. Collisions slow down the transfer of data, and that's why Ethernet networks are slower than other types of networks. (Of course, you see far fewer conflicts with fewer machines, so if you have only 4 PCs on your network, you typically get great performance. Only when 25 PCs are all trying to talk to each other at one time do conflicts start slowing things down dramatically.)

The first step when installing a small network is to create a chart that lists which computers need to be connected and where they are, plus the approximate distances between all the players. Because of the size limitations of this chapter, I can't provide you with a complete discussion of how to plan the cabling for your network — that's a book in itself. In fact, that book is *Home Networking For Dummies,* 4th Edition, written by Kathy Ivens (Wiley), which expands on all the basics I mention in this chapter.

The Hardware You Need

One benefit of Ethernet networks is their simplicity. You don't need a degree in Advanced Thakamology to install your network, and you can put four PCs in a simple Ethernet network for less than $75 (US) if you buy a kit.

In this section, I discuss the basic hardware requirements of any small Ethernet network.

Cables

In books I've written that cover Ethernet networking, I discuss two different kinds of cabling that connect computer to computer (or computer to network device):

✦ **Coaxial (coax):** The same type of cable that's used to connect your TV to your cable box. Coax is thick stuff and not easily routed or hidden. Also, each end of a coax Ethernet network must have a terminator to mark the end of the network circuit, which is a hassle (a small one, granted, but a hassle nonetheless).

✦ **Twisted pair:** Looks almost exactly like telephone wire or the cable that runs between a PC's dialup modem and the telephone wall jack. Twisted pair is easier to hide and much easier to route. (Figure 2-2 illustrates the connector — an RJ-45 connector — for a twisted pair cable.) The downside to using a twisted pair Ethernet network is that you need a *switch,* which acts as a central connection point. (See how it's used in Figure 2-3.) However, twisted pair cabling is much cheaper overall than coaxial cable.

I used to cover coax cabling, but in this book, I cover only twisted pair cabling. It's by far less-expensive and easier to install, which makes it the most popular standard — and that explains why Ethernet networks that use coaxial cabling are rapidly disappearing from the face of the globe. In fact, you have to go out of your way to find a late-model network interface card (NIC) that has a coax connector on it. (As the MCP said so eloquently in the classic movie *Tron,* "End of line.")

**Book VIII
Chapter 2**

**Ethernet to the
Rescue**

Figure 2-2:
Most
network
techs think
this RJ-45
connector
is rather
attractive.

RJ-45

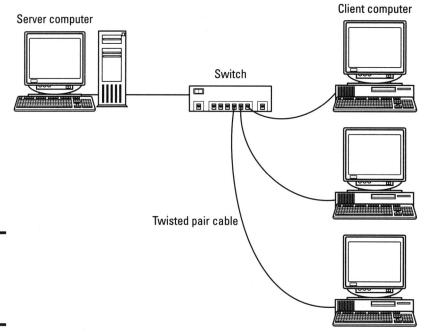

Server computer

Client computer

Switch

Twisted pair cable

Figure 2-3:
The basics
of an
Ethernet
network.

TIP

If you would rather eschew cables altogether (well, almost altogether), consider a wireless network. Although it's a bit slower, you have freedom of movement undreamed of by the wired crowd. Heck, you could even throw caution utterly to the wind and get a wireless switch or router that can provide both wired and wireless connections. (In fact, alternative wired networks can use your home or office's existing telephone or AC power lines. No, really!) I cover all these marvels of wireless (or almost wireless) networking in Chapter 3 of this minibook.

Switches

As I mention earlier in this chapter, a *switch* is essentially just an overgrown connection box, linking (via cabling) each computer on your network to all other network computers and peripherals, like a printer. It's about as visually interesting as a shoebox. (There's not much need to include a picture in this chapter. Imagine the most boring, nondescript box that you can, add a few lights and several RJ-45 jacks, and that's a switch.) On the inside, a switch prevents those dastardly collisions that I discuss earlier in this chapter. In effect, a switch narrows the broadcast of a packet to only the PC that needs it.

Most Internet sharing devices and routers designed to work with broadband connections have built-in switches — just keep in mind that you need some sort of switch for a twisted pair network. Switches are pretty inexpensive — how much you pay depends on how many ports the switch provides, ranging from about $50–$200.

Switches have virtually replaced the earlier, less-efficient Ethernet hub. Always choose a switch over an Ethernet hub. (I mention hubs in case you run across one whilst scavenging or encounter one on eBay.)

NICs

You need a network interface card (NIC) for each computer on your network. If your desktop or laptop PC doesn't have a built-in NIC, an internal adapter card is probably the best choice, but installing a NIC doesn't necessarily have to involve opening your PC's case. You can get a Personal Computer Memory Card International Association (PCMCIA; or PC Card) NIC for your laptop, and other network adapters can be connected through a Universal Serial Bus (USB) port. However, you probably don't need to buy a separate NIC for your PC because most PCs now include built-in network connectors. (Check your PC's manual or look for a port labeled Ethernet 10/100 or Network on the back of the computer.)

NICs are rated by the speed of the network. Most home networks use a 10/100 NIC (which means that your network can operate at either 10 Mbps or 100 Mbps), which sets you back about $25–$30. The third speed — Gigabit Ethernet — runs at a whopping 1000 Mbps, but you might not need that much throughput unless you regularly transfer huge multigigabyte files betwixt computers. (Gigabit hardware use to be as expensive as a meeting with a good lawyer, but prices for this faster equipment are now only slightly more expensive than 10/100 hardware.) Well-known Ethernet device manufacturers include D-Link, NETGEAR, and Linksys.

When shopping for your card, check the manufacturer's Web site and verify the drivers the card uses. The card should support at least Windows XP, Vista, and 7. (For me, the value of a NIC lies in direct proportion to its compatibility.) Also, check how often those drivers are updated; a two-year-old driver is not a good sign. In general, most manufacturers display certification statements (both on the box and on the company's Web site) guaranteeing that a NIC will work with specific operating systems.

Doing the Cable Dance

You have far fewer hassles when installing a twisted pair network as opposed to a coaxial network, as I mention earlier in this chapter. But even when you consider that the cables are easier to handle, I still make — from experience — a number of time-tested recommendations. You should always

✦ **Draft someone to help.** If you're wiring a small office, enlist the help of a steadfast friend (as a gofer, general cable handyperson, and sympathetic ear).

✦ **Buy premade cables!** Building a cable yourself is like cutting a diamond yourself: It can be done, but you had better be experienced or else you'll ruin a perfectly good, well, length of cable. Plus, first-timers can very easily create a cable that appears to be correct but doesn't work or that introduces all sorts of spurious problems later on that will be practically impossible to track down. (Can you say "electrical short"? I knew you could.) Instead, do what I do (and what everyone else who has already built one or two small networks does): Walk into your local computer store or online Web shop and buy premade cables in the lengths you need.

✦ **Buy extra cables.** Having a few spares never hurts. Hey, they're cheap. And buying cables that are at least a foot or two longer than what you think you'll need is a wise idea.

✦ **Test a cable before installing it.** Of course, you can buy a twisted pair cable tester (usually called a *remote cable tester*), but for those with lives outside of networking, simply connect the cable between your switch and a laptop to check it.

✦ **Consider pets!** Does Fluffy spend time in your home office unattended? Then prepare for the likelihood of chewed network cabling. (This can *really* test the relationship between pet and person.) To avoid these moments, use cable ties and anchors to run your Ethernet cabling underneath desktops and above the floor level whenever possible.

✦ **Avoid exposed cable.** Make sure that your cables are well out of reach of clumsy feet. Also, never cover a cable with tape or a rug where it can become a victim of foot traffic. The stress on the connectors and the wear from contact will destroy even the best cable over time and will likely result in eventual network errors.

Don't forget that a switch is a powered device, so it needs to be located close to an AC outlet.

Building a home? Now is the time to consider running your Ethernet cabling, at the same time your telephone cabling and AC wiring is installed. (Go with Gigabit Ethernet Cat6 cabling, and you'll thank me later.)

Configuring Windows 7 for Your Network

After your NICs are installed, the cabling is in place, and everything's plugged in, you're ready to flip that big Frankenstein-style leaf switch and start networking — and that's done from within Windows 7. In this section, I discuss what every home "network administrator" should know.

Your network allows you to share files and printers with other computers using the network, but it can also be configured to share an Internet connection with those computers. What you decide to share is up to you, as the administrator of your network. (I cover sharing your Internet connection in Chapter 4 of this minibook.)

Ah, sweet DHCP

You know, few acronyms in the computer world make me genuinely smile every time I see them. There's BBS (bulletin board system), of course. TWAIN (which most people think means *technology without an interesting name*) isn't even an acronym! It refers to a poem by Kipling; you know, "and never the twain shall meet." (It's not often that I get to quote Kipling.) But in networking, folks hold a fond spot in their hearts for *DHCP*, which stands for Dynamic Host Configuration Protocol.

What's so uplifting about a networking standard? It's the *dynamic* part. You see, DHCP was developed to automatically assign Internet Protocol (IP) addresses to the computers on your network. A computer's *IP address* is the address I mention at the beginning of the chapter: It's a unique number that identifies the specific PC on the network.

In days of yore, whoever set up a network had to keep track of which IP addresses were assigned to which computers. If a number was assigned twice, all sorts of carnage broke loose (at least on those two machines). A device with DHCP, such as an Internet sharing device or a PC acting as an Internet connection server, automatically assigns a number whenever needed.

If you're already using an Internet sharing device (such as a cable modem or digital subscriber line [DSL] Internet router that has DHCP built in) or a switch with DHCP built in and a connection port for your modem, you need to follow the steps in that device's manual. That's because you don't need a PC to act as the DHCP host for your network. I cover Internet connection sharing in Chapter 4 of this minibook.

**Book VIII
Chapter 2**

Ethernet to the
Rescue

Setting up the host

To set up a network under Windows 7 using DHCP and a shared Internet connection — where your DSL or cable modem connects directly to the PC — you need to configure settings on that PC. (That lucky computer becomes your Internet *host,* providing the DHCP functionality for your network. The other computers that connect to the host are *clients.*)

If your host PC is using a NIC to connect to a DSL or cable modem (as most do) and the switch *doesn't* accept a direct connection to your modem, *you need a second NIC installed in that computer* so that you can connect it to the switch! (Take a break and read the section "Using a Standard Switch with a Cable or DSL Modem," toward the end of this chapter, before you proceed. I explain things there.)

Ready to go? Follow these steps:

1. **Choose Start⇨Control Panel⇨Network and Sharing Center to display the window shown in Figure 2-4.**

   Make certain you're using an Administrator-level user account, so that you'll have full rights to set things up. (Simply log in using the account that you used to install Windows 7, and you'll be using an Administrator account.)

Figure 2-4: Displaying the existing network connection on my PC.

Make sure that all hardware has been installed, connected, and turned on. ("Now, Rochester, have you installed the network hardware like I asked?")

2. **Click the link for your Internet connection.**

   Windows 7 displays the Status dialog box for your Internet connection.

3. **Click the Sharing tab.**

   To see the Sharing tab, you'll need a second NIC, as I explain earlier.

4. **Select the Allow Other Network Users to Connect through This Computer's Internet connection check box.**

5. **Click OK to save your changes.**

Setting up the clients

After the host is configured, it's ready to accept connections from the other computers on your network. However, you also have to configure each of those PCs as network clients. Yep, that's where the buzz phrase *client/server* comes from. The good news is that you use your friend the Network and Sharing Center again, and the process is pretty similar.

Again, make sure that the host computer is connected to the Internet, and reboot each of the client PCs before continuing. Then follow these steps on each PC running Windows 7 that needs to join the network crowd:

1. **Choose Start⇨Control Panel⇨Network and Sharing Center.**

   Again, be sure you're using an Administrator-level user account.

2. **Click the local area connection for this client PC to display the Status dialog box, and then click the Properties button.**

   Windows 7 displays the Properties dialog box for your Internet connection.

3. **If the Internet Protocol Version 4 (TCP/IPv4) entry appears in the item list, click the Properties button to display the settings you see in Figure 2-5.**

4. **Select the Obtain an IP Address Automatically radio button.**

5. **Select the Obtain DNS Server Address Automatically radio button.**

6. **Click OK to save your changes.**

7. **If the Internet Protocol Version 6 (TCP/IPv6) entry appears in the item list, click it and click Properties.**

8. **Select the Obtain an IP Address Automatically radio button.**

9. **Select the Obtain DNS Server Address Automatically radio button.**

10. **Click OK to save your changes.**

**Book VIII
Chapter 2**

Ethernet to the Rescue

Figure 2-5:
Configuring
a client
PC for
that DHCP
goodness.

11. **Click OK in the Properties dialog box to return to the Connections window.**

12. **Click Close and restart the PC.**

When it completes the boot process, the added client PC should be a member of your network family.

Browsing the neighborhood

After you set up your network, you can easily see which other PCs are available. Windows 7 power users call this activity *browsing* your network, where you saunter around and admire what's connected. Choose Start⇨Network to display each of the PCs in your networked surroundings (as shown in Figure 2-6).

Whoops! I can hear all sorts of irate Windows 7 faithful growling in irritation, especially if you're working on a large office network with a number of different types of computers sharing resources. "Is that a (gasp) *Macintosh* that I see in my network?" That's right. As long as other computers conform to standard Ethernet protocols and have been recognized by the host PC (or DHCP device), they show up. (This includes PCs running Linux, Macs running Mac OS 9 or Mac OS X, and Unix machines.)

Figure 2-6:
The
Windows 7
Network
window.

"Wait! Where's Boopsie?" Well, if the client PC that you named Boopsie has been turned on *after* you opened the Network window, it doesn't show up. To see it, right-click any empty spot within the Network window and choose Refresh from the menu that appears, which rescans the network and updates the window's contents. (Whatever moved you to name a PC *Boopsie,* anyway? Are you a Doonesbury fan like I am?)

To display available folders and devices on each computer, simply double-click the computer icon to open it. Note that you might be greeted by a login dialog box, like the one you see in Figure 2-7; I see this one because I set up my media server as a *secure* (or *closed*) system, and I have to supply my username and password to my account. (If you set up your clients with the procedure in the preceding section, you shouldn't need a login to access their stuff — unless, of course, that computer's user has specifically configured Windows 7 to require a login.) If you've set up your account without a password (or you remove your password later from the User Accounts screen in Control Panel), your PC is essentially an *open* system.

**Book VIII
Chapter 2**

**Ethernet to the
Rescue**

Figure 2-7:
A closed
system
requires a
password.

Windows 7 automatically adds shared printers and displays them in the Network window — just double-click the name of the computer that the printer is attached to, and it appears (along with any shared files or drives). However, you can also manually add a new shared network printer to your Network window. Click the Add a Printer button on the Network window toolbar to run the Add a Printer Wizard, which guides you through the steps.

Sharing folders and documents

"So, Mark, what, precisely, controls what I can and can't see when browsing the network?" Now you've entered The Sharing Zone, where time and space have no meaning. What *does* matter are the shared files and folders that you set up on each computer in your network.

Sharing something across the network allows other computers to see it when browsing. (Note that network sharing is very different from sharing a local file among users of the same PC, which I cover in Book II, Chapter 4.)

Windows 7 takes the safe and conservative approach by default: Nothing is shared across a network until specifically set. (To be honest, I prefer that route over defaulting to a completely open machine.) However, you can share a folder and all its contents by following these steps:

1. **Double-click the Computer icon on your desktop to open the Explorer window; then navigate to the folder's location.**

2. **Right-click the folder and then choose Share With from the menu that appears.**

   Alternatively, you can click the Share With button on the Explorer window toolbar.

3. **To share a file — allowing full read/write access with your Homegroup — choose the Homegroup (Read/Write) entry.**

   You can choose the Homegroup (Read) entry from the menu if you want to allow others in your Homegroup to open and read files, but not make any changes to them.

4. To share the folder with only certain users (instead of everyone in your Homegroup), choose the Specific People entry.

You see the settings shown in Figure 2-8. Type the username to select an individual user to whom you're granting sharing privileges. You can click the Permission Level pop-up menu to set the read or read/write access to the folder and its contents. Then click the Share button to return to the Explorer window.

Windows 7 provides convenient links for e-mailing the location of your shared files and folders, or you can choose to copy the links into the Clipboard for pasting later into a document (like a Word document).

Figure 2-8:
Mark a folder as shared among specific users.

Note that shared files or folders are marked as such in the status display at the bottom of the Explorer window — you'll see the state marked as "shared" — so it's easy to tell which items on your system are shared.

You can also share a drive in the same fashion, but Microsoft cautions against it — and so do I. You should assign only one shared folder on each drive on each computer in your network.

When you share a folder, you place everything in that folder on the network. Therefore, if there's even one item (either a document or a subfolder) that you don't want to distribute with others inside a folder, *do not share that folder!*

After a folder is enabled with read/write access, its contents can be opened, saved, moved, or copied, including from within the File Open, Save, and Browse dialog boxes, which are common throughout Windows 7 and your applications. That's the neat thing: Everything works normally across the network by using the same functionality that I cover in Book II.

Printing across the Network

Although sharing an Internet connection is one of the prime advantages of using a network these days, one other resource has been shared across networks now for decades: the network printer. (Read all about Internet connection sharing in Chapter 4 of this minibook.) And, any printer connected to any PC on your network can be used by any other PC, which is a real boon when your office has only one large-format inkjet and only one color laser printer.

You can follow one of four avenues for network printing:

✦ **Hook up the printer to a PC so that it acts as a printer server.** As long as the printer receives only moderate use and it's in an open area, this option can work. (If the PC is in a private office, don't even think about it. You'll drive the occupant smackers.)

✦ **Set up a separate PC as a simple print server.** This is the traditional solution for high-traffic printers that need a central location. The client PC is basically just a doorman, existing only to queue print jobs for the connected printer. Expensive but efficient.

✦ **Buy a network printer box.** This standalone device is essentially an Ethernet card with a slightly more intelligent brain, and it provides the same functionality as a print server.

✦ **Buy a printer with onboard Ethernet network support.** Sure, it's more expensive, but a network-ready printer is *the* most elegant solution.

If you choose one of the latter two methods — either a network printer box or a network-ready printer — you have to follow the manufacturer's specific instructions to set things up. However, if you decide to use a client PC to provide printing services, Windows 7 makes it simpler than ever: any printer connected to your PC is automatically shared with your Homegroup! You'll find all the details about creating and managing a Homegroup in Book II, Chapter 4.

Using a Standard Switch with a Cable or DSL Modem

I discuss Internet sharing devices earlier in this chapter, and they're covered in detail in Chapter 4 of this minibook. Most have built-in switches, virtually all of them have DHCP support, and they have ports that allow a direct connection to your cable or DSL modem. That's great: In fact, as I mention earlier in this chapter, you don't even need a host PC in that case. Feel free to prance about.

What if your switch *doesn't* have a connection point (typically called wide area network [WAN] port or uplink port) for your DSL or cable modem? That's the situation I mention earlier, where your host PC needs two NICs, and you have to set your PC up using both cards.

To do this, connect your hardware and cables so that

✦ The cable or DSL modem is connected to one of the NICs on the host PC. (It should already be configured this way, so it's no big deal.)

✦ The other NIC on the host PC is connected to one of the ports on the switch.

✦ The client PCs on the network are connected to the switch.

Now follow the procedure that I provide earlier (in the section titled, "Setting up the host") for setting up the host PC and the client PCs, and all should function like butter.

Troubleshooting Your Network

I sure hope you're reading this section for fun — or because you thirst for knowledge, or just to be thorough. Why? Well, unfortunately, a misbehaving network can leave even the best techs with a four-bell headache. Your network is a mass of differing hardware, software, and data, all of which must work well in concert before you can send or receive a single packet.

Windows 7 does the best job it can to automate the process; and, if you've bought a networking kit, you can pretty much assume that everything is compatible. But if you have one bad cable or one faulty NIC driver, your state-of-the-art network becomes a family of dead cables and a little box with no lights. (Sounds like my last attempt at outdoor Christmas decorations.)

In this section, I provide the most common solutions to the most common problems.

Windows 7 doesn't recognize my NIC

Man, talk about starting with a problem from Step One! That's my kind of luck. Anyway, here are the possible problems and descriptions of their fixes:

✦ **An incompatible driver:** NIC drivers are legendary for their fickle behavior. Unlike some printers that allow you to use the same driver for both Windows Vista and 7, a network interface card simply demands the proper driver, or it doesn't work. Period. Reinstall the driver from the manufacturer's media (and make sure that you select the correct operating system version). If that doesn't work (and you still have access to the Internet on another computer), download the manufacturer's latest driver for your operating system from the company's Web site. (To download a driver, you must have access to another, working PC, and you might need a USB flash drive or a CD-R to install them.) Oh, by the way: You might have to uninstall the NIC and the reinstall it to reload the driver. Such fun.

✦ **A faulty NIC:** This is a definite possibility. If you have a NIC that you know is working, replace the misbehaving card (along with its drivers) to see whether the problem is solved.

✦ **A hardware conflict:** This problem is quite rare under Windows 7, but it can still happen. Use Device Manager to check whether Windows is having problems getting everyone to play nicely together; I demonstrate how to do this in Book II, Chapter 5.

No lights show up on my network card(s) or switch

This is classic stuff. It's not the most comforting thing to hear, but then again, it's good to know that others have been here before you. (To be precise, *I* have. I used to handle network problem calls at a major hospital.) Anyway, a lack of lights indicates that you're not getting a signal, which suggests a number of possible hardware problems:

✦ **Your cable is faulty.** An improperly made cable can short out and cause everything to come to a crashing halt. This is a likely culprit if all the other client PCs have illuminated signal lights and the switch's lights are lit. (If the computer store sold you a special *crossover* cable, march right back in and demand a standard twisted pair cable; crossover cables are meant to hook together two computers directly via their network ports. Unfortunately, it's hard to tell the difference with just your eyes unless you see the word *crossover* printed on the cable.)

✦ **Your NIC or switch is faulty.** If either has gone off the deep end, it needs to be replaced. If other client PCs are working, you can remove a working NIC from one of them and use it to test your switch.

✦ **Your switch isn't powered on.** (Whoops! — no need for embarrassment.) A switch needs AC power to operate.

✦ **You're using the WAN/uplink port.** This is a special port on your switch, as I explain in the previous section; it doesn't work for a client PC connection.

Nothing shows up when I browse

Just plain nasty. If everything seemed to go well when you set up your host PC and your client PCs but you still come up empty when you browse, here are the possibilities (and my recommended troubleshooting tips):

✦ **Client PCs are powered down.** Simple but effective. Boot up a client PC and then refresh the Network window — right-click at any empty spot in the window and choose Refresh from the menu. *The client should now be visible.*

✦ **A piece of hardware is faulty.** I use this term because any piece of your networking hardware might be experiencing problems, and you wouldn't be able to browse. See what I mean about the four-bell headache? Anyway, make sure that *all* your NICs and your switch have lighted activity/signal lights.

✦ **No network resources are shared.** Remember that Windows 7 doesn't share diddly by default, so when you first browse your Network window, it's likely to be absolutely blank (or, if you try to open a networked computer, nothing is there). After you create or join a Homegroup, however, your Network window will soon be crowded.

I can't connect (or print) to a shared printer

I saved the best for last because this problem is usually much easier to solve (apart from the obvious, such as running out of paper, ink, or toner). Try these stress relievers:

✦ **The printer is powered down.** I wish I had a dime for every time someone complained that they couldn't connect to Fred's printer, only to find that Fred was out of the office and (ahem) his PC (and the specific printer in question) was turned off. (Sound of hand slapping forehead.)

✦ **The printer isn't actually shared.** Yep, you guessed it; this is the other hot potato. Make sure that the shared printer hasn't been disabled (either accidentally or on purpose).

✦ **You have faulty NIC or cables.** Again, check the NIC for the PC that's connected to the printer. The easiest thing to do is to see whether you can browse or work with shared files on that PC. If not, there's a good chance that either the NIC or the twisted pair cable is giving you problems.

✦ **The printer has been placed offline.** Some printers have an Online/ Offline button. If a printer like this is offline, the printer goes comatose and doesn't respond.

Chapter 3: Going Wireless

In This Chapter

✔ Comparing wireless and wired networks

✔ Comparing wireless standards

✔ Using existing telephone and AC wiring

✔ Making a wireless connection under Windows 7

*W*elcome to the future: a world where network cables are on display in museums and your PCs can wirelessly access your home or office network from 100 feet away. Fast, convenient, and (most of all) as secure as a wired network, the wireless network of years to come will even bring other types of devices under its umbrella, such as cellphones, netbook PCs, and personal digital assistants (PDAs), just to name a few.

Hang on a second. Now that I think about it, all that stuff is available now! Wireless networks are rapidly overtaking traditional wired networks in homes and small offices. Even companies with extensive wired networks have added wireless access points (WAPs) for the laptop crowd, just to be hip.

In this chapter, I show you how wireless networking works, what's available, and how you can set up a wireless network under Windows 7.

Understanding Wireless Networking

In a sense, wireless networking isn't as revolutionary as you might think. In fact, it operates in the same manner as the standard wired Ethernet configuration, which I discuss in Chapter 2 of this minibook, complete with packets, collisions, and all the hoo-hah that accompanies networking. Of course, the method of transmitting and receiving packets is different when you're using wireless networking; instead of being sent over a wire, the packets are broadcast through the air like radio signals.

(However, you can't use your wireless network hardware to run a pirate radio station. Sorry about that, matey. Arrgh.)

Comparing wireless with wired

Other than the transmission method, here are the only three major differences between a wired network and its wireless sibling:

- ✦ **Speed:** *Wireless connections are slower.* This is the big 'un as well as the big reason why most larger networks still depend on wired Ethernet for the bulk of their connections. Even the fastest current wireless technology can pump data at only around 300 Mbps (and that figure would require perfect conditions, so you're more likely to end up with anywhere from 150 to 200 Mbps), but any run-of-the-mill wired network can easily deliver a steady 100 Mbps. Heck, the faster wired networks can hit gigabit (1000 Mbps) speeds! In fact, they can use fiber optic cabling rather than plain copper wire cabling to hit even faster speeds.

- ✦ **Semolians:** *Wireless hardware is more expensive.* Depending on the standard supported by your wireless hardware (read more about standards in the next section), you pay significantly more for wireless hardware than you do for 10/100 Mbps wired hardware.

- ✦ **Stuff:** *Wireless networks require no hubs or switches.* Most wireless base stations and WAPs (wireless access points, which I describe in a moment) can provide connections for up to 253 simultaneous users, so a larger wireless network (with 50 PCs or more) requires far less hardware and upkeep than a wired network that can handle the same number of computers.

Do you want to impress your network administrator? (Of course — don't we all? If you run your own home or small-office network, you can impress a hardware-savvy friend instead.) Use the technonerd buzzwords for network transmission technologies and refer to your wireless network as an *unguided* network — as opposed to a *guided* (wired) network.

Naturally, you can add a *wireless access point* — or, as it's commonly called, a *WAP* — to your wired network, which gives you the best of both worlds. Figure 3-1 illustrates a typical WAP device, which brings 802.11n wireless connectivity to an existing wired network; this baby runs about $75 (US). Most WAP units require two physical connections: one to your wired Ethernet network (naturally) and a Universal Serial Bus (USB) connection to the computer that controls it. You can also share your Internet connection with a dual router, which has both wired and wireless hardware built in (as I discuss in Chapter 4 of this minibook).

Keeping track of the standards involved

Like any other evolving PC technology, wireless networking suffers from competition between different standards — and, of course, some are compatible with others, but others are not. Readers of my other books are already acquainted with my overwhelming love for strange names and obfuscating acronyms in the PC world — *not.* Unfortunately, wireless networking has a handful of the most confusing names in the entire PC world, so make sure that you have a bottle of aspirin handy.

Figure 3-1:
A typical
WAP for
your LAN.
(Try to keep
a straight
face when
you say it.)

Here, in one easy-to-consume section, is the lowdown on the different wireless standards as well as which ones you should consider and which ones you should eschew.

The original standard: 802.11b

Commonly called *WiFi* (short for *wi*reless *fi*delity), the first 802.11b wireless base station (AirPort) was introduced by Apple Computer in 1999 — a fact that the good folks at Cupertino have been gloating over ever since. WiFi supports a maximum transfer rate of 11 Mbps, which is just a little faster than the slowest 10 Mbps wired Ethernet standard in common use.

A word about USB wireless connections

You can connect a desktop PC to a wireless network without even using an internal adapter card. Just use a *USB wireless adapter,* which uses a USB connection to your PC as a path for wireless network data packets. Hey, that USB is amazing, isn't it? (Note that this toy isn't the same as a simple USB cable network, which allows PCs to share files and printers over USB cabling.) The remote PC gets all the benefits of a wireless Ethernet connection.

As you can read in Book VII, Chapter 4, USB 1.1 ports can transfer a maximum of 12 Mbps, so they work just fine with 802.11b hardware. However, you would have to turn to a USB 2.0 wireless adapter to deliver the 54 Mbps top speed of an 802.11g connection or the 300

Mbps top speed of 802.11n. (Personally, I think that USB 2.0 is an example of overkill in this scenario. After all, you're moving either 54 or 300 Mbps over a cable that can reach as high as 480 Mbps! However, USB 1.1 doesn't cut it even at 54 Mbps, so what's a poor PC owner to do?)

Anyway, an external USB wireless adapter is an excellent way to add "temporary wireless" to a PC in your home or office. Many of these external adapters can also be used to make a printer a standalone wireless device, so you can place your printer in a central location that's convenient for everyone.

**Book VIII
Chapter 3**

Going Wireless

Distance is important in the wireless world, of course. It's one thing to be able to use your laptop on your network from across the room but yet another thing entirely to use it in your backyard. Although 802.11b devices are rated at a maximum distance of 300 feet from the base station, that figure is about as realistic as an African wildebeest wearing a hula skirt appearing in your living room. This idea of "theoretical top speed" also applies to "high-speed" dialup modems, which practically never delivered the top speed that the manufacturer listed on the box. From experience, I can tell you that you can count on 150 feet — and even fewer if a number of intervening walls stand between you and your network or if you're a victim of interference.

Oh, didn't I mention the interference? The 802.11b networking uses the 2.4 GHz broadcasting spectrum, which unfortunately is used by a horde of everyday household devices, including cellular phones, cordless phones, Bluetooth devices (which I cover in a bit), and even microwave ovens. Therefore, 802.11b wireless networks can slow down significantly because of interference from other devices. It's unlikely that your entire wireless network will shut down completely, but you will *definitely* be able to tell when your teenage daughter is using your cordless phone.

The misfit: 802.11a

Why is 802.11a such a misfit, and why did I list it after 802.11b? Well, you'll love this:

+ **The numbering is wrong.** Believe it or not, 802.11a is a more recent standard. (Can someone please explain to me why this select group of engineers decided to number successive standards in *reverse* order?)

+ **It has a shorter range.** Although 802.11a is officially rated at 150 feet under perfect conditions, in the real world, it can reach a distance of only 60 to 70 feet — your wireless world shrinks even further.

+ **It doesn't play well with others.** Because 802.11a is completely incompatible with both 802.11b and 802.11g, you're effectively limited to 802.11a equipment. (And there's not all that much out there.)

So why did folks develop 802.11a, anyway? It has two advantages:

+ **Speedy:** The first speed demon in wireless networking, 802.11a delivers up to 54 Mbps (more than five times as fast as 802.11b).

+ **Different broadcasting spectrum:** The 802.11a standard uses the 5 GHz spectrum, which prevents it from working in the 2.4 GHz range needed by 802.11b (hence the incompatibility). Because there's a lot less activity around most homes and offices in the 5 GHz spectrum, you get less interference and a better chance of achieving the best reception.

The mainstream: 802.11g

I know you're probably saying to yourself, "Self, I sure wish someone would get off their duff and produce a standard that is compatible with 802.11b *and* provides speeds as fast as 802.11a." Good news: Your wish has been heard! The 802.11g wireless standard does precisely that, combining the best of both worlds. At the time of this writing, 802.11g is still the most common wireless standard in use.

If you (or your company) have already invested in 802.11b wireless hardware, you can continue to use it on an 802.11g network. Naturally, you don't get 54 Mbps, but at least it works at 11 Mbps. New 802.11g hardware will transfer packets at that magic 54 Mbps — well, that's the top speed, anyway, but good luck in getting that kind of performance outside a laboratory.

The downside? Aw, jeez, we're back to the 2.4 GHz spectrum again, so once again your buddy in the next cubicle who loves microwave popcorn will introduce interference. It just goes to show you that nothing's perfect — except, perhaps, a 1964 Cadillac two-door coupe (when I can get it started, that is).

Raising the bar to 802.11n

Technology marches on, and now you can wave goodbye — eventually — to even 802.11g and 54 Mbps. Let me introduce the latest wireless standard from IEEE: 802.11n. Most third-party manufacturers have already introduced 802.11n wireless equipment. In fact, if you're buying a cutting-edge desktop or laptop with wireless hardware built-in, it's likely 802.11n (or easily upgraded to 802.11n later).

Why the hubbub? Oh, I forgot to mention that 802.11n can deliver throughput in excess of 300 Mbps! Don't bet your house that you get that kind of speed, though — like the other members of the 802.11 family, it's likely to be a theoretical maximum speed. As I mention earlier, look to 150–200 Mbps as a more likely speed.

Here's another feature you'll appreciate, especially if you have older wireless hardware: 802.11n networking equipment works with all members of the 802.11 family, including the black sheep 802.11a. Compatibility is A Good Thing, but note that to get the absolute best performance from your wireless network, *all* your hardware should be 802.11n. Otherwise, things slow down for the older standards.

You can't go wrong with the 802.11n standard: Think superfast wireless connections in your household or office.

The strangely named: Bluetooth

Okay now, here's a wireless standard name that sounds like some scriptwriter or concept artist in Hollywood was working overtime — but at least it breaks the 802.11*x* mold. Unlike the other four standards, Bluetooth isn't designed for full-scale wireless Ethernet networking. Instead, it was developed in 1995 as a specialized wireless technology for short distances to be used with cellphones, PDAs, laptops, palmtops, printers, and other external devices. The maximum distance for a Bluetooth network is about 30 feet.

The Bluetooth wave is even supposed to reach household appliances, like your TV and your stereo system. I'm sure there's a Bluetooth toaster out there. If you've seen it, drop me a line at mark@mlcbooks.com and tell me all about it.

Anyway, unlike the other standards I discuss here, Bluetooth requires very little power to use (befitting its design, which concentrates on battery-operated devices). It's also painfully slow compared with 802.11b — only about 1 Mbps — but that's not supposed to affect the small fry as much as it would your desktop PC. No base station is required for Bluetooth communications between devices. For example, after your laptop gets within 30 feet of your cellphone, they can update each other's telephone number directories. Eerie.

Oh, and Bluetooth also uses the — you guessed it — 2.4 GHz spectrum, so it conflicts with existing 802.11b and 802.11g networks! (The airwaves are getting so overpopulated that tin cans and string are starting to look attractive again.)

Table 3-1 compares wireless networking standards.

Table 3-1	Wireless Standards on Parade		
Standard	*Top Transfer Speed*	*Max Distance*	*Compatibility*
802.11b	11 Mbps	300 feet	802.11g, 802.11n
802.11a	54 Mbps	150 feet	802.11n
802.11g	54 Mbps	150 feet	802.11b, 802.11n
802.11n	300 Mbps	250 feet	802.11b, 802.11a, 802.11g
Bluetooth	1 Mbps	30 feet	None

You can buy an external wireless antenna for your base station or WAP. An 802.11n directional antenna typically costs about $40 or $50, and it can boost your existing signal quality as well as extend the range of your wireless network into every nook and cranny of your home or office. Check the documentation that came with your wireless base station or WAP to see whether it can accept an external antenna.

Using SideShow gadgets

Hey, Windows Vista and 7 users: Got your gadgets goin' on? In case you haven't used the SideShow feature yet, I had better explain. A *gadget* is a small add-on application running on an external device (like a cellphone, multimedia remote control, or PDA) that retrieves data wirelessly from your PC. The external device has a screen that can display information, like a program listing from Windows Media Center or your e-mail Inbox or a Web page. (See the following figure.)

Here's the kicker: SideShow works even if your PC is in sleep mode, or *turned off completely!* Now that's pretty slick, wouldn't you agree? This magic trick is easy if you set Windows Vista or Windows 7 to automatically wake your computer to update and transfer information to your devices. SideShow devices can connect

to your PC by using Bluetooth, standard wireless Ethernet, or even a USB cable connection.

Of course, you need a PC and external devices that are all Vista/7 SideShow–compatible. At the time of this writing, only a handful of devices support SideShow, but support for this new feature is sure to grow quickly.

Gadget applications are configured from within the Vista/7 Control Panel, using the Windows SideShow settings — make sure that the Set My Computer to Wake Automatically radio button is selected, and select the Automatically Wake My Computer check box to set up your Vista/7 "wake-up call." You can also assign a PIN (personal identification number) that gadgets must supply to receive data, which helps keep your PC secure.

AC and phoneline networking

Although wireless hardware has become quite popular over the past four years, here's another alternative to a traditional wired network: You can also build a network by using either existing standard AC power wiring (a *power-line* network) or telephone wiring (a *phoneline* network) in your home.

If running packets across your AC power lines sounds a little dangerous, let me put your fears to rest: Both these alternative wired networks have been around for several years — longer, in fact, than 802.11b — and they're perfectly safe. (If you're wondering, you can continue to use your telephone or your AC appliances with no changes.) The advantages of an alternative wired network over a wired or wireless network are clear:

✦ **No wires — at least, no Cat 5 or 6 cables:** Your home or office is already set up with all the "cabling" you need, and you likely have "ports" in every room.

✦ **Better security than a wireless network:** Although a wireless network can be made quite secure — I describe how to do this in the next section — you're still beaming a signal that might be picked up outside, in the street. On the other hand, the network packets transferred over a phoneline network or an AC network stay within the building and are practically impossible for anyone outside to intercept.

✦ **Easy to install:** A wireless network might be the easiest to install, but a phoneline network or an AC network is still much easier to set up than a traditional wired network.

So, why aren't phoneline and powerline networks more popular? Unfortunately, compared with wireless, both these network solutions leave much to be desired:

✦ **Slower than wireless:** The latest phoneline standard (from HomePNA, at www.homepna.org) delivers approximately 128 Mbps, whereas the HomePlug powerline standard (www.homeplug.org) is rated at only about 14 Mbps. The raw file-transfer speed of an 802.11n network wipes the floor with either alternative wired network.

✦ **Less convenient than wireless:** Even though you don't have to string Ethernet cabling all over your office, your networked PCs and peripherals are still tied down to certain areas (around either your telephone jacks or your AC power sockets). A wireless connection works wherever you are as long as you're in range.

✦ **Connect fewer computers:** A wireless network can accept twice as many users (or standalone network devices) as either a phoneline or powerline network.

When readers ask me to recommend a network solution for their homes or small offices, I almost always recommend either a traditional wired gigabit (Cat 6) network, for the fastest speeds and the best security, or a wireless network, which offers convenience and easy installation. The drawbacks of phoneline and powerline networks (along with the explosive popularity of wireless hardware) will likely doom them to gradual extinction.

Using Wireless Hardware in Windows 7

After you install your wireless base station or WAP, you're ready to configure your PC for use on your network.

Preparing to install

Before you begin the installation of an internal adapter card, make sure that you

+ **Read the manual.** Even if you already installed an adapter card in your PC, take a few minutes to check the documentation that shipped with the card. Here's a Mark's Maxim to live by:

   It's better to know about a "gotcha" before you install.™

+ **Gather the Big Four.** Find a Phillips screwdriver, a plastic bowl to hold any spare parts, a good light source, and some sort of static-free cover for your work surface. (Newspaper always works well if I'm away from my workbench.)

+ **Ground yourself.** After you remove the cover from your PC, touch the metal chassis of your computer to dissipate any static electricity that's stowing away on your body before it can cause damage to the card.

Installation tricks

All manufacturers of wireless adapter cards (for desktops) and wireless PC Cards (for laptops) include their own installation and setup programs — which also create the necessary wireless connection automatically within Windows — so I don't go into the gory details here. However, I can give you some suggestions that will help with the installation, no matter which type of card you're using:

+ **Choose between ad hoc and infrastructure.** You might be prompted to choose between ad hoc and infrastructure mode. In most cases, you want to choose *infrastructure* mode (where your laptop and PC workstations connect by using a base station or wireless access point) rather than *ad hoc* (where the devices talk directly to each other on a specific channel number that you determine, just like the CB radio days of old, without a base station or WAP). *Note:* If you're trying to connect your wireless device to your existing wired network, you must use infrastructure mode.

✦ **Check your WPA/WPA2 encryption.** When prompted for WPA/WPA2 information, use the highest level that the PC card supports. WPA2 is designed to automatically fall back to the encryption level used by your base station or WAP.

✦ **Assign your own passwords!** Base stations, wireless routers, and WAPs use an administrator name and password to identify you, and often this information even allows remote control. (Read that term as *hacker banquet.*) Therefore, you should *always* assign your own administrator name and password while configuring your wireless network!

✦ **Check your SSID.** You need an SSID (short for Service Set Identifier) that matches the SSID used by your base station or WAP. *Remember:* Change the SSID to the unique value that you used on your base station or WAP. For the best level of security, *don't* use the default SSID!

✦ **Keep your drivers and firmware current.** I sound like a broken record, but check for the latest drivers and firmware updates from the manufacturer's Web site every time you install new hardware — including wireless networking hardware.

Making the connection

Microsoft recommends that your wireless base station or WAP broadcast the SSID, as long as you're using WPA/WPA2 encryption in infrastructure mode. I heartily agree: This makes everything easier and more automatic, as long as you select an SSID of your own. (Yep, I'm saying it again: *Don't* use the default SSID, or else you'll leave a security hole in your wireless network.)

With a broadcasted SSID, connecting is as easy as plugging your wireless network card into your laptop. Windows XP, Vista, and 7 automatically search for and connect to your network. If you're using a desktop PC with a wireless card, this same process occurs when you log in to Windows. (See? I told you it was easy.) You see on the taskbar a notification icon letting you know that the connection has been made as well as how strong the signal is.

Chapter 4: Sharing Your Internet Connection

In This Chapter

✔ **Understanding the advantages of connection sharing**

✔ **Sharing your connection by using Windows 7**

✔ **Using a wired hardware sharing device**

✔ **Using a wireless hardware sharing device**

A high-speed Internet connection is a thing of beauty, especially when it's shared with everyone in your home or office over your network. After your network is set up and running smoothly, consider whether you want to share that connection through hardware or software as well as what sort of security you need in order to protect everyone on your network.

In this chapter, I discuss all the possibilities and show you how to set up Internet connection sharing within Windows 7.

Why Share Your Internet Connection?

"Don't I need a separate Internet connection for each PC on my network?" Actually, you just answered your own question: The network you installed allows for all sorts of data communications between PCs, including the ability to plug in to a shared Internet connection.

I should note here that it is indeed technically possible to share a dialup Internet connection by using the software connection-sharing feature in Windows 7. However, I don't think that you'll be satisfied with the results. (Sorry — it doesn't provide enough horsepower to handle more than one computer, and even then browsing the Web is as slow as molasses.) Therefore, I assume for the rest of this chapter that you're already using a digital subscriber line (DSL), a cable modem Internet connection, or a satellite connection.

Here's a list of benefits that help explain why Internet connection sharing — whether through a program or a dedicated hardware device — is so doggone popular these days:

+ **Cost effective:** As long as your Internet service provider (ISP) allows you to share your broadband connection, you save a bundle over the cost of adding completely separate connections for multiple machines in your home or office. (Naturally, this is the major benefit.)

+ **Convenient:** With a shared Internet connection, other PCs on your network are easy to configure, and each one is as content as a sleeping cat. Each PC on your network operates just as though it were directly connected to the Internet, and the computers on the network can all do their own thing on the Internet simultaneously.

+ **Centralized security:** With a *firewall* in place — either running on the PC (if you're sharing through software) or on the device itself (if you're sharing through hardware) — you can protect the Internet activity on all the PCs on your network at one time.

+ **Efficient:** Most folks I talk to are surprised that a shared Internet connection is so fast — even when multiple computers on the network are charging down the information superhighway at the same time.

A connection shared through a dedicated hardware device, however, is always faster than a connection shared through software.

Speaking of convenience and efficiency, I should also mention that many hardware sharing devices also double as Ethernet *switches* (devices offering several wired Ethernet ports that are used to build a home or office Ethernet network). Hardware sharing devices allow you to build your entire home or office network around one central piece of hardware rather than use a separate switch and a PC running a software sharing program.

Sharing through Hardware

With a hardware device, all the PCs on your network can concentrate on their own work, eliminating the need to leave a PC running constantly as an "Internet server" as is the case if you choose to use Windows 7 Internet Connection Sharing. (After all, a PC that's capable of running Windows 7 at a decent clip is an expensive resource compared with an investment of $50–$125 (US) on a hardware sharing device.)

In this section, I familiarize you with the two different types of hardware sharing devices.

Wired sharing devices

For PC owners who either already have a traditional wired Ethernet network — or who are considering building one — a device like the combination switch-firewall-DHCP-server-sharing-thing you see in Figure 4-1 is the perfect solution to Internet connection sharing. (The *Dynamic Host Configuration Protocol,* or *DHCP,* feature allows your hardware sharing device to automatically configure

IP addresses on your network. If all that sounds like an alien language, visit Chapter 2 of this minibook, where I wax enthusiastic about DHCP.)

Perhaps I should be a little more specific in my description. (Not even Google returns many results if you search for *switch-firewall-DHCP-server-sharing-thing.* The illustrated device is actually a cable/DSL router with a four-port switch.

Figure 4-1:
A candid shot of an Internet router.

For an idea of why hardware sharing is so popular, look at what you can buy — in one small, tidy box — online for a mere $50:

✦ **A built-in, four-port Ethernet 10/100 switch:** You can plug four PCs, to start with, directly into the router for an instant Ethernet network. (For more information about network speeds, see Chapter 2 of this minibook.)

✦ **A direct-connect port for your DSL or cable modem:** The port can also be used as a wide area network (WAN) connection to hook the sharing device to an existing external network.

✦ **A DHCP server:** It provides near-automatic network configuration for the PCs hooked into the device.

✦ **The hardware and software controls you need to block certain Internet traffic (both coming in and going out):** You can also lock out individual PCs from Internet access.

✦ **An easy-to-use, Web-based configuration screen:** You can use it on any PC connected to the router. Figure 4-2 illustrates the Web configuration screen from my router.

✦ **Built-in NAT functionality:** I dive into NAT in Chapter 5 of this minibook.

**Book VIII
Chapter 4**

**Sharing Your
Internet Connection**

Main Menu
- OnePage Setup

Advanced
- DHCP Settings
- Access Control
- Virtual Server
- Device Admin.
- Status Monitor
- Special App.
- DMZ Host
- RIP
- Static Routing
- PPPoE

Product Name: XRouter Pro

Administrator Password

Password Change: ••••

Password Confirm: ••••

External Admin.: ○ Enable ⊙ Disable

Block WAN Port Scanning: ⊙ Yes ○ No

Block WAN Ping Response: ⊙ Yes ○ No

Reset Device: ○ Yes ⊙ No

Factory Defaults: ○ Yes ⊙ No

Apply   Undo

Figure 4-2:
Most Internet routers are configured through your Web browser.

Pretty neat, eh? Remember that this device is used in tandem with your existing cable or DSL modem, which is typically included by your ISP as part of your Internet subscription (but you might be paying more because you're renting the modem).

I should also note that you can get a similar device with all these features *and* a built-in DSL or cable modem. Because you aren't charged a monthly rental fee for a modem, you can thumb your nose at your ISP and save money in the long run. (Please avoid mentioning my name when you glee-fully return your modem to your ISP, or do any visible nose-thumbing in the direction of your ISP.)

Naturally, the setup procedure for each device on the market is different, but here's a sample of what's in store when you take your new Internet sharing router out of the box. (Don't plug your new toy's power supply into the wall yet.)

1. **If you're running a typical standalone network switch, you can either unplug the existing Ethernet cables from all existing computers and plug them into the new sharing device or connect the WAN port from the existing hub into one of the ports on the Internet sharing device.**

Ethernet

The device manual tells you how to take care of the latter method.

If you're setting up a new network, naturally, you just connect each Ethernet cable directly to the sharing device. See Figure 4-3.

192.168.100.5   192.168.100.10   192.168.100.15

Cable/DSL Router
62.78.147.251

Internet

Figure 4-3:
An Internet
connection
shared
using a
hardware
device.

2. **Plug the power supply from the sharing device into the AC socket.**

3. **Configure one of the PCs on your new network with the default network settings provided by the device manufacturer.**

4. **Run Internet Explorer on the PC you configured in Step 3 and use the Web-based configuration utility to finish configuring the device.**

That's it! If you're running a typical home network or home office network, you'll likely keep the default settings for everything. For an idea of just what kind of power you can wield over your network as you share your Internet connection, take a gander at the sidebar "What the Sam Hill does *that* mean?" in Chapter 5 of this minibook. Luckily, you probably don't have to use any of those optional settings, but it's good to know that they're there.

Wireless sharing devices

Most folks think that sharing an Internet connection over a wireless network must be harder to set up than a traditional wired network — and that it's likely to be a tremendous security risk. I'm happy to tell you that both pre-conceptions are wrong. Wireless connection sharing with a hardware device is as simple to set up as the wired device that I discuss in the preceding section. And, with the settings I discuss in Chapter 5 of this minibook, you can make it very difficult (if not impossible) for someone to hack his way to your network or your Internet connection.

To see an example of a truly versatile all-in-one Internet sharing device, check out the device shown in Figure 4-4. Its antenna marks it as a wireless switch, but what you don't see is that it also sports four 10/100 Ethernet ports on the back for your old-fashioned wired network. Yep, you guessed it, this is just plain neat: It can accommodate multiple 802.11n wireless con-nections *and* four wired connections, all at the same time! (The somewhat spaghetti-fied world of wireless networking is covered in depth in Chapter 3 of this minibook.)

Figure 4-4:
Is it wired?
Is it
wireless?
This sharing
device is
both!

As you might expect, the cost on this puppy, about $125 online, is much higher than the wired-only device (see the preceding section). Another factor is the speed of the wireless connection; as you can read in Chapter 3 of this minibook, the older (and slower) 802.11g devices are rapidly disappearing from the market, so costs are dropping quickly on the faster 802.11n hard-ware. (And yes, if you opt for a wireless-only network, you can find a cheaper wireless sharing device that doesn't include any of those silly "antique" wired ports.) Wireless adapter cards (including the USB and PC Card varieties) are much more expensive than standard wired adapter cards, too.

As I mention in Chapter 5 of this minibook, don't forget to demand a wireless sharing device that offers Wi-Fi Protected Access (WPA2) private encryption. Use anything less and your wireless network will be much easier for outsiders to hack.

Sharing through Software in Windows 7

Time to be honest here; I think that using a hardware sharing device is *definitely* preferable to sharing a connection through software. For example, with a software solution

✦ At least one PC on your network must always remain turned on if anyone wants to use the Internet.

✦ You notice a significant slowdown on the sharing PC when several other PCs are using the Internet.

✦ You can't use software sharing on a network that already has domain controllers, DNS servers, gateways, or DHCP servers.

✦ You still need a switch or wireless base station.

If you decide to use the built-in Internet Connection Sharing (ICS) feature of Windows 7 — perhaps to avoid buying a hardware sharing device — first double-check to ensure that you already have everything in this list:

✦ **A working Ethernet network:** Emphasis on "working" — don't try to share your connection if your network isn't already running like a well-oiled machine. Chapter 2 of this minibook will guide you through these fast-moving waters.

✦ **A working broadband Internet connection to one of the PCs on your network:** Okay, you can use ICS with a dialup connection as well, but take my advice and *don't*. Everything works much faster with a DSL, cable, or satellite connection.

✦ **An installed copy of Windows 7 on the host PC that's connected to the Internet:** This PC also needs two network cards installed — one that leads to the network switch and one that leads to the cable or DSL modem (as shown in Figure 4-5). Because many flavors of network cards exist (using many different connections, such as USB, PC Card, and the more traditional internal adapter card), follow the installation instructions provided by the card manufacturer to add both cards to your PC.

**Book VIII
Chapter 4**

**Sharing Your
Internet Connection**

Standard 10/100/1000 switch

Desktop PC using DHCP
IP address 192.168.1.3

Laptop PC using DHCP
IP address 192.168.1.2

Figure 4-5:
An Internet
connection
shared
through
software
under
Windows 7.

PC with two network cards
IP address: 157.54.0.1

DSL or cable modem

The Internet

Everything shipshape? Good. Follow these steps to share that existing Internet connection on your host PC with the other computers on your network:

1. **Verify that you're connected to the Internet.**

I always open Internet Explorer and do the Google thing.

2. **Choose Start⇨Control Panel⇨Network and Sharing Center.**

3. **Click the Local Area Connection link you want to share to display the Status dialog box, and then click the Properties button.**

Windows 7 displays the Properties dialog box for your Internet connection.

4. **Click the Sharing tab.**

You won't see the Sharing tab unless you have at least two network connections (one to your DSL or cable modem, and one to your local network).

5. **Select the Allow Other Network Users to Connect through This Computer's Internet Connection check box.**

6. **Click OK to save your changes.**

Windows 7 indicates that a connection is shared by adding a "couple of friends" badge under the connection icon.

Chapter 5: Securing Your Home Network

In This Chapter

✔ Keeping your wired network secure

✔ Ensuring that your wireless network is secure

✔ Working with shared folders

✔ Understanding NAT security

✔ Setting up virtual private networking (VPN) in Windows 7

*P*robably the number-one question in my Outlook inbox these days is when readers ask me about home network security. "Am I opening my files to folks I don't know?" ranks right up there with "Am I sharing my Internet connection with the seedy teenager next door?" Frightening thoughts, indeed.

Regardless of whether you run a wired or wireless network — or some meld of both — I've got you covered in this chapter with a discussion of security tips and tricks you can use to help keep your network (and you) safe. Sure, a wired Ethernet network is easier to secure, but I have good news for the wireless network crowd, too. Read this chapter to see how to keep the private stuff private, even while sharing (using shared folders) the stuff you want to disseminate amongst others on your network.

And if you're always on the move, I also introduce you to the whiz-bang Windows 7 virtual private networking (VPN) feature, which allows you to reach your home network securely using any Internet connection!

Common Sense Tips for Wired Networks

Folks with wired home networks are often pretty doggone smug about their computer security because a connection to your network can occur only over a wired port or over the Internet. (In other words, you don't have to worry about broadcasting your address book across the street.)

What the Sam Hill does that mean?

When you're shopping for a wired or wireless Internet sharing device, you find that the side of the box mentions a number of nifty security features that seem to have been named by a very depressed engineer (who didn't speak common-folk English, either). Allow me to translate for you:

Static routing: This feature enables you to set up a preset network path between the device and an Internet host, which is likely to be an external network. Without static routing, you might not be able to use virtual private networking (VPN), which I discuss at the end of this chapter.

Dynamic routing: Basically, this concept is the reverse of static routing, which is a helpful feature for those who are continually yanking PCs, servers, and network hardware off the network and plugging stuff back in at other locations. With dynamic routing, the sharing device automatically compensates and adjusts for changes made to the *topology* (translation, *layout*) of your network.

Port forwarding: If you're running an e-mail, Web, or File Transfer Protocol (FTP) server on your network, you can set the router to automatically divert any incoming traffic of that type — HyperText Transfer Protocol (HTTP) for the Web server, for example — directly to the host PC. I use this feature at home to provide my Web site, FTP server, and bulletin board system (BBS) to my visitors.

IP filtering: This feature allows you to block certain users or PCs from Internet access. It's also a helpful feature to have when you're using VPN.

WAN blocking: This term sounds like something that happens in a nuclear reactor, doesn't it? Luckily, this feature just prevents other PCs on the Internet from *pinging* (scanning) for your network, so it's a good idea to leave this one on. Another Mark's Maxim is in order: **It's generally a good thing to be invisible to other computers on the Internet.™** (More on this in Book III, Chapter 3.)

Demilitarized zone (DMZ) host: Finally, here's a feature that's designed just for us Internet gamers: You can set up your router with a special set of "holes" to "reveal" your PC to others on the Internet when you're connecting to an Internet game server (or if you're hosting your own server). Without a DMZ, your router's NAT firewall would likely block your PC from communicating with others (as I explain later in this chapter), and you wouldn't be able to join or create an Internet gaming battleground. Anyone for a fragfest in *Borderlands*?

First, the good news: If you followed my advice in earlier chapters about using the Windows 7 Firewall on each of your network PCs — or if you installed a third-party firewall application on each PC — you can be reasonably sure that your Internet connection is secure from The Bad Guys.

However, it's still possible to be a little *too* complacent about your wired network's security: Don't forget that the seedy teenager next door might end up dating your kid and spending time within the comfortable confines of your own home. Yep, it's Mark's Maxim time again:

Unless you can be absolutely certain that no one else has access to your wired network, it still pays to practice good network security policy!™

With this Ultimate Truth in mind, here's a common sense checklist you can follow to help keep your wired network as secure as possible:

✦ **Use the armed guards supplied with Windows 7.** The moment you leave your PC unattended, you're opening the door for anyone else to step up and use it. For this reason, I recommend that you use a screen saver with the password feature enabled, and that you *always* assign a password to *every* account you create. Also, if security is an issue for your network, use the Windows 7 User Account Control (UAC) feature, which alerts you before running suspect applications or performing actions that could potentially harm your system. You can make this setting from the Windows 7 Control Panel. Choose Start➪Control Panel➪User Accounts and Family Safety➪User Accounts to display the User Accounts settings. Click the Change User Account Control Settings link, and make sure that the Notify slider is set to either Always Notify (the first position) or the default (the second position). Click OK to save the change.

✦ **Don't share passwords.** Do you regularly swap your credit card numbers with friends and relatives? I'm betting that you don't — and you should keep your login and screen saver passwords just as private.

✦ **Monitor your connections.** If you're using an Internet router or Internet sharing device, that device likely has a feature that allows you to see who's connected to your network (typically as part of the DHCP commands). Figure 5-1 illustrates my Internet router's DHCP connection table. Check your router's documentation to see how you can monitor who's connecting to it — and use this feature once a week or so, just to verify that the connections you see listed are the connections you *expected* to see. If you do encounter unwanted individuals who are using your wireless network, check your router's documentation to see whether it allows you to block them from connecting again.

✦ **Unplug unnecessary computers.** If a PC doesn't need a connection to your network, why keep it connected at all? Your wired network runs faster with fewer machines, and disconnecting that PC frees up a port on your switch or router for future use. (And, need I mention that another possible opening to your network has been closed?)

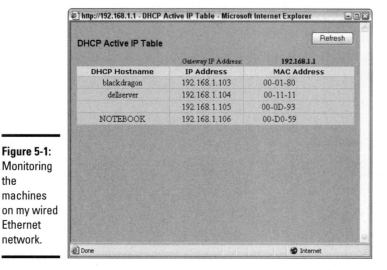

Figure 5-1:
Monitoring
the
machines
on my wired
Ethernet
network.

Ensuring Security on Your Wireless Network

If you're adding a wireless network to your home or office, security should be your first consideration before you send a single packet over the airwaves. First, if you're shopping for wireless hardware (as I discuss in Chapter 3 of this minibook), let me list the standards you should look for:

✦ **Do the WPA2.** WPA2 (blissfully short for *Wi-Fi Protected Access*) is a form of encryption that acts as your main defense against outside intrusion (as shown in Figure 5-2). Without the proper *key* (or, in human jargon, the proper *password*), a hacker is faced with a tough decoding job. The 256-bit WPA2 standard is the most common these days, and it does a creditable job of keeping your data secure. Choose hardware that supports the WPA2 standard whenever possible, and *make sure that WPA2 is enabled when you install the device.*

Make your WPA2 key as long as allowed by your hardware, and also use the same common sense that you use when choosing your Internet passwords. Keys should be completely random. Don't use your middle name or your Social Security number, and remember to mix letters and numbers.

✦ **LEAP for security.** Man, these acronyms are such a delight. (If you need an aspirin, I'll understand.) *Lightweight Extensible Authentication Protocol* (LEAP) is also an encryption protocol, but unlike WPA2, the key is automatically changed periodically while you're connected. Unfortunately, the LEAP key is easier for a hacker to uncover, so it's actually less secure than WPA2. For this reason, LEAP is being phased out in consumer wireless hardware in favor of WPA2.

Figure 5-2:
WPA2 in
action.
Thrilling,
isn't it?

After you configure your wireless network, here are the security guidelines I recommend that you follow:

✦ **Use virtual private networking (VPN) for extra security.** As you can read in this chapter, VPN is a hard nut for an outsider to crack. When security is all-important, set up a VPN session.

✦ **Secure your SSID.** I know that statement sounds weird, but your *SSID* (service set identifier) is, essentially, the name for your wireless access point (WAP) or base station. Change your SSID immediately when you install your wireless base station or access point, making sure that you configured your system so that your SSID isn't broadcast to the outside world. (You have to configure your wireless connections manually; your WAP or base station doesn't show up automatically when your PC is in range.) Determining your SSID is the first step in hacking your wireless network. After you turn off the broadcast of your SSID, I guarantee that it's practically impossible for an outsider to guess that your SSID is *Bullwinkle007* (or something similar). Visit Chapter 3 of this minibook for all the details on WAPs and wireless base stations.

✦ **Change your access point or base station password.** Naturally, you also don't want anyone to be able to guess the password that secures your wireless access point or base station, so change that hardware password to something unique.

If anyone asks you to jump in his vehicle for a bit of "war driving," you'll understand why wireless security is so important. *War driving* occurs when hackers rig their cars with laptop PCs, equipped with a wireless network cards and cheap, omnidirectional antennas, and then drive around neighborhoods in their towns looking for unsecured wireless networks. When easy pickings are found, the hacker can use any broadband connection that's hooked up to that network (read that as "free Internet connection") or — much worse — haul away copies of the shared files and documents found on that network.

**Book VIII
Chapter 5**

**Securing Your
Home Network**

Using Shared Folders (The Right Way)

In Book II, Chapter 4, I mention the Public folder that resides in each of your Windows 7 Libraries — any file you store in the Public Documents, Public Music, Public Pictures, or Public Videos folders (or subfolders within) is immediately available to everyone else using your PC. You can always access your Public folders within each Library at the left side of an Explorer window; click the triangle next to the desired Library heading to expand it.

By default, the contents of your Windows 7 Libraries are private — no one else but you can access your files, and the files in each top-level Library aren't shared with other PCs across your network. On the other hand, the contents of the Public subfolder that appears within each Library *are* shared across your local network and among the user accounts on that lone PC.

Don't forget that you can also enable HomeGroup sharing for your Libraries at any time, allowing other PCs running Windows 7 in your Homegroup to access files you specify inside your Libraries. If Homegroup sharing isn't turned on, open an Explorer window and click the Homegroup heading at the left of the window, and then click the Choose What You Want to Share, and View the Homegroup Password link.

For multiple users sharing only one PC, Public folders are the bee's knees: They're already set up as soon as you install Windows 7. Likewise, you can share the contents of your Libraries across your network using the Homegroup feature. But what if you need to share the contents of a folder *outside* the Windows 7 Libraries structure with others on your network? That's where *shared network folders* come in handy.

I show you how to create a shared network folder in Chapter 2 of this mini-book. I want to remind you, though, of these three important security guidelines that you should follow when using your Public Library folders, shared Libraries using Homegroup, or the shared folders you create:

✦ **Never, never, *never* share an item unless it's necessary!** Remember that Windows 7 doesn't differentiate who gets to open which documents within your Public folders. The contents are available to everyone using your network. Perhaps that updated copy of your resume should be withheld from prying eyes. . . . And, while we're at it, I'd like to stress that you should *never* share one of your PC's hard drives across your network! (Microsoft warns you against such a gaping hole in your security as well, if you decide to try sharing a drive.) Why? Well, you're also sharing *everything* on that drive — *every last file in every last folder,* including the stuff you probably either don't know about or forgot was there. Share only what you need to share: 'Nuff said.

✦ **Assign the Reader permission level.** When you share a folder, you set share permissions: that is, what rights you give the user. If you opt for the Owner permission level, that person can edit (or even delete) files. If you would rather keep these files pristine, go for the Reader permission level; that way, other network users can open and print the documents in the folder but can't edit or delete them. (I cover these permission levels in Book II, Chapter 4.)

✦ **Use descriptive names for your shared folders.** It just makes good sense. I generally create only one shared folder for each PC on a network, and that folder name reflects the PC's network name (like Shared Folder – Den or Shared Folder – Rm 321), which helps you keep track of which shared resources are on which PC.

Knowing Why You Need NAT

Okay, you might have heard of NAT (Network Address Translation), and you think that it's probably important — but what does it *do?* Well, check out Figure 5-3. If your Internet sharing device (or your Internet sharing software) supports NAT, a number of different PCs — each with a different Internet Protocol (IP) address — are masked behind the single IP address that your ISP assigned to your cable or DSL modem. No one can tell which individual IP addresses are used behind your NAT device.

Desktop PC using DHCP
IP address 192.168.1.2

Laptop PC using DHCP
IP address 192.168.1.3

Desktop PC using DHCP
IP address 192.168.1.4

DSL or cable modem

Figure 5-3:
With NAT on the job, individual PCs on your network are invisible.

Internet router or sharing device with built-in 10/100 switch
IP address 157.54.0.1

The ISP communicates only with IP address 157.54.0.1

The Internet

To hack a PC on your system, someone on the outside (meaning, elsewhere on the Internet) has to know the IP address of an individual computer on your system, and NAT prevents the intruder from learning just that. Instead, the only IP address that's visible is the modem or Internet-sharing device itself. Plus, a NAT blocks the most common weapon in the hacker arsenal: probing "port sniffers" that hunt for open, unprotected ports across the Internet.

NAT isn't a complete firewall, but when your connection-sharing hardware or software uses NAT in conjunction with the Windows 7 Firewall, you effectively shut the door on Internet intruders! By the way, I discuss the built-in Windows 7 Firewall in Book III, Chapter 3.

Marveling at the Magic of Virtual Private Networking

Imagine if you could take your networking one step further. Rather than use wires or even a wireless network, what if you could create a secure network connection over the Internet into your private network? You could enjoy the benefits of using your private home network anywhere in the world — as long as an Internet connection was handy.

Such is the reality of virtual private networking — and the emphasis, of course, is on the words *private* and *secure*. (It's one thing to have access to your files from across the country, but giving that same access to an interested hacker is another thing entirely.) Your data is protected by encryption when it passes over the Internet; so for all intents and purposes, your connection is as well protected as a correctly configured wireless network.

VPN places you squarely back into the realm of client/server networking, where the VPN *client* is the PC that you're using remotely and the VPN *server* is the machine on your home network that you're connecting to.

In this section, I demonstrate how to set up your laptop PC (or a remote desktop) as a VPN client under Windows 7, with the following assumptions (based on how VPN is used most often in real-world situations):

✦ **You're using either**

  • *A broadband connection to the Internet*

    VPN over a dialup modem connection is the definition of the word *frustrating*. Don't.

  • *Another company's network Internet connection*

✦ **Your network administrator has provided you with the IP address of the VPN server (in an office environment) or you've configured a VPN server on a PC on your home network.**

✦ **You'll use your regular network username and password to log in.**

Follow these steps to create and use a VPN connection:

1. **Choose Start➪Control Panel➪Network and Internet➪Network and Sharing Center➪Set Up a New Connection or Network➪Connect to a Workplace.**

2. **In the wizard that opens, click Next.**

The wizard displays the options shown in Figure 5-4.

Figure 5-4:
Build a
VPN client
connection
the wizard
way.

3. **Click Use My Internet Connection (VPN).**

4. **On the next wizard screen (see Figure 5-5), enter the following:**

- *The VPN server address,* provided by your network administrator or displayed by your home network's host PC (such as 157.54.0.1), into the Internet Address text box

  This address can also be in the form of a host name in good ol' English (like mlcbooks.com).

- A *descriptive name* to help you keep track of the connection (such as MLC Books VPN Client) in the Destination Name text box

5. **(Optional) If you want to allow other user accounts on your PC to use this connection, select the Allow Other People to Use This Connection check box.**

As Windows 7 indicates with the "shield" security icon, allowing anyone with access to your PC to use a VPN connection might not be a good idea. Unless more than one user account on your computer has to have this VPN connection, I recommend that you leave this check box deselected and prudently keep your VPN connection to yourself!

Book VIII
Chapter 5

Securing Your
Home Network

6. Click Next.

7. Fill out the next wizard window that opens:

- *Type the user name* — either provided by your network administrator or the account name you'll use on the host PC — into the User Name text box, as shown in Figure 5-6.

- *Type the password* for your VPN connection in the Password text box.

  Again, if security is an issue, I recommend that you leave the Remember This Password check box disabled. Of course, you have to enter your password each time you connect through VPN, but that may be a Very Good Thing.

8. Click Connect.

Windows 7 creates the connection.

If you need to make changes to your VPN connection properties — for example, if you have to change the IP address of the VPN server on your network — choose Start⇨Control Panel⇨Network and Internet⇨Connect to a Network. From the Network Connections dialog box that appears, right-click your VPN connection and then choose Properties, which displays the VPN Client Properties dialog box. From there, you can make any necessary changes.

When you're ready to use your VPN connection — and you're hooked up to the Internet during your travels — choose Start⇨Control Panel⇨Network and Internet⇨Connect to a Network, choose the VPN entry, and click Connect. Windows 7 prompts you for your username and password, as shown in Figure 5-7; type your user name and password and then click the

Connect button to begin your VPN session, and you'll find that you can now access all the network resources that you're accustomed to on your host PC.

Figure 5-6:
Enter
your user
name and
password
for a VPN
connection.

Figure 5-7:
Making
the VPN
connection.

Again, I'm a bit paranoid about enabling the Save This User Name and Password for the Following Users check box because anyone using your (unattended) computer can simply log on as you. Weigh carefully the possible results of convenience.

Now tell me that technology ain't grand!

Index

A

AAC format, 442
AC (powerline) networks. *See also* wireless
   networks
  advantages, 562
  defined, 562
  drawbacks, 562, 563
Access 2010
  database encryption, 291
  Datasheet view, 380
  defined, 290–291
  editing window, 380
  error checking and validation, 291
  features, 291
  fields, 380, 382–386
  File tab, 379
  Form Wizard, 382–384
  forms, 291, 381–385
  Navigation pane, 380
  New Screen settings, 378
  printing, 386
  queries, 291
  Quick Access toolbar, 380
  records, 380, 384–385
  reports, 291
  Ribbon, 379
  running, 378
  status bar, 380
  tables, 380–381
  templates, 386
  window illustration, 379
Access 2010 For Dummies (Ulrich Fuller and
   Cook), 377
access speed, hard drives, 502
accessibility, Internet Explorer (IE)
   options, 142
AceFTP Pro, 161, 162
Acquire dialog box (scanners), 422, 423
Add an E-mail Account Wizard (Windows
   Live Mail), 209–210
Add Hardware Wizard (Windows 7), 151
Add Items to DVD dialog box
   (DVD Maker), 459
Add New Account wizard (Outlook), 391
Address bar (IE), 188
Address toolbar (Windows 7), 99
Administrator accounts
  defined, 117
  troubleshooting and, 246

Advanced Micro Devices (AMD)
   processors, 45
AIFF (Audio Interchange File Format), 442
AIM (AOL Instant Messenger), 228
Alerts pane (Windows Live Messenger), 231
alignment
  photo, in rule of thirds, 474
  port card, 515
  Word, 317
all-in-one units, 26
Alt+F4, 83, 84
Alt (Alternate) key, 60
AMD (Advanced Micro Devices)
   processors, 45
animation (PowerPoint), 290
antivirus software
  entry points covered by, 268
  files, keeping up to date, 268
  types of, 267
  using, 186
AOL Instant Messenger (AIM), 228
applications
  AutoPlay options, 135
  backup, 261
  exiting, 83–84
  icons, 72, 73
  Internet function settings, 146–147
  moving and, 75
  network-ready, 535
  Office 2010 list, 286
  Office, Web-based, 412
  running, from CD-ROM/DVD-ROM, 82
  running, from hard drive, 81–82
  running, from network drive, 82–83
  running, from Start menu, 80–81
  sharing, with network, 531–533
  switching between, with taskbar, 96–97
  terminating, 100–101
  uninstalling, 147–149
  uninstalling in troubleshooting, 244
  Windows 7 compatibility, 85
appointments (Outlook)
  categories, 404
  comments, 404
  description, 403
  displaying, in Outlook Today, 405
  reminders, 291, 404
  schedule, printing, 405
  start/end times, 403
  status, 404

archive files, restoring, 200
arrow (navigation) keys, 59
Arrow Mailing List
    Server, 160
artwork/graphical tools (Word), 288
aspect ratio, DVD, 460
ATI graphics cards, 521
attachments (Outlook)
  file types, 397
  opening, 398
  in replying to e-mail, 395
  scanning, 398
  sending, 398
  size limit, 398
  using, 397–399
attachments (Windows
    Live Mail)
  adding, 218, 220
  defined, 220
  downloading, 221
  error message, 221
  illustrated, 160
  risky behavior, 181
  size, 221
attachments, digital photos as, 471, 481
AU (Audio Unix) format, 442
audio. *See also* sounds
  clips, importing, 447–448
  inserting in slides (PowerPoint), 367–369
Audio Interchange File Format (AIFF), 442
AutoComplete feature (IE), 145, 203
AutoFormatting (Word), 318–319
AutoPlay options, 135
avast! Antivirus Home Edition (ALWIL
    Software), 245, 267

B

background, desktop, 104–105, 132–133
Backup and Restore Center
  accessing, 262
  backing up files with, 262–265
  Restore option, 265
  Set Up Backup link, 262
backup drives, 32
backups
  applications, 261
  with Backup and Restore Center, 262–265
  creating, 261–265
  destination media, 262

e-mail accounts
    (Outlook), 392
  file selection for, 262, 264
  frequency recommendation, 261
  importance, 261
  media for, 261–262
  restoring, 265
  running, 263–264
  schedule time, 263
  unattended, 264
batteries, rechargeable, 471–472
Bcc messages
  Outlook, 395
  Windows Live Mail, 214–215
binary, 467
Bing, 188
bit rates, MP3 files, 435
BitLocker, 118
blocking (Windows Live Messenger),
    236–237
Blogger, 159
blogs, 159
Bluetooth. *See also* wireless standards
  defined, 559–560
  maximum distance, 560
  power requirement, 560
Blu-Ray recorders, 32
BMP format, 428
booting Windows 7
  defined, 49
  from last known good configuration, 270
  with Safe mode, 270
borders (Excel), 338–339
broadband Internet connections, creating,
    173–174
browsing history
  cache files, 140
  deleting automatically, 140–141
browsing networks
  closed system and, 547
  defined, 546
  folder and device display, 547
  open system and, 547
  shared printers, 548
*Build Your Own PC Do-It-Yourself For
    Dummies* (Chambers), 525, 534
Building Web Sites All-in-One For Dummies
    (Sahlin and Snell), 159
bullets (Word), 310–311
Burn a Disc dialog box, 124
burner speed, DVD, 461
business card scanners, 421

C

cable connections. *See also* Internet connections
  access speed variation, 166
  cons, 166
  creating, 173–174
  ISP information for, 170
  physical connection, 171
  pros, 165
cable modems
  routers with, 568
  switches, 550–551
cables
  checking, 243–244
  connectors, tightening, 276
  damage, checking for, 276
  labeling, 276
  maintaining, 275–276
  ties, 275
cables (network)
  coaxial (coax), 539
  exposed, avoiding, 542
  faulty, 552
  as hardware requirement, 534
  home building and, 543
  installing, 542–543
  pets and, 542
  premade, 542
  RJ-45 connector, 540
  testing, 542
  twisted pair, 539
Calendar (Outlook)
  appointment creation, 403–404
  appointment display, 405
  coloring, 292
  defined, 401
  display, 401–402
  feature overview, 291
  illustrated, 402
  pages, printing, 405, 406
  uses, 402
calendar display (Windows 7), 130
calibration
  color, 280
  onscreen controls, 281
  printer, 280–281
cameras. *See* digital cameras; film cameras
capture cards, 492
cases, removing, 497

Cc messages
  Outlook, 394
  Windows Live Mail, 214–215
CD-ROM/DVD-ROM, running applications from, 82
CDs
  for backups, 261
  burning from MP3 files, 443
  recording, 124
cells (Excel)
  aligning, 338
  blank, inserting, 335–336
  contents, printing, 349
  defined, 328
  editing, 331–332
  element types, 328
  entering data in, 328
  inserting from Clipboard, 336
  linking, 346–347
  moving among, 329–330
  selecting, 330–331
  shortcut keys, 329–332
central processing units (CPUs). *See* processors
certificates, 145
charts (Excel)
  adding, 344–346
  defined, 344
  display options, 344
  embedding, 344–346
  with Excel Chart Wizard, 344–346
  feature overview, 289
  illustrated, 346
  types of, 345
chat clients. *See also* Windows Live Messenger
  AOL Instant Messenger (AIM), 228
  function of, 228
  ICQ, 228–229
  selecting, 227–229
chatting. *See also* Windows Live Messenger
  defined, 161
  emoticons, 234
  message font attributes, 234
  message sending, 234
  name selection, 233
  sending message from menu system, 233
Check dialog box (Windows 7), 256–257
clean install, 47, 250

clients. *See also* Dynamic Host
  Configuration Protocol (DHCP)
  configuration illustration, 546
  defined, 544
  powered down, 553
  setting up, 545–546
  VPN, 580, 581
client/server, 545
clip art. *See also* graphics
  inserting (Excel), 343
  inserting (PowerPoint), 364
Clip Art task pane, 343, 364
Clipboard, Office, 292–293
clocks, displaying, 130–131
Close button, 65, 83
closed systems, 547
closing windows, 65
coaxial (coax) cabling, 539
coaxial digital (SPIDF) connector, 42
collaboration tools (Word)
  comments, 321–322
  feature overview, 287
  highlighting, 322–323
  revision marks, 320–321
colors
  calibration, 280
  display settings, 134
columns (Excel)
  inserting, 336–337
  resizing, 334–335
command buttons
  Outlook, 389
  Word, 300
comments (Word)
  defined, 321
  deleting, 322
  illustrated, 322
  reviewing, 322
CompactFlash, 467
composition, photo
  for first-rate photos, 473
  lighting, 477
  need for, 473
  process, 473–478
  rule of asymmetry, 475–476
  rule of thirds, 474–475
compressed air, 277
Computer icon, 75
computers. *See also* desktop PCs
  defined, 13
  form factor, 13–14
configuration (Windows 7), last known
  good, 270

Contact list (Windows Live Messenger),
  237
contacts (Outlook)
  adding photos to, 400
  displaying, 399
  editing, 401
  entering, 400–401
  going to, 399
  tracking, 291
  uses, 399
contacts (Windows Live Mail)
  creating, 224
  data, importing, 224–225
  editing, 224
  exporting in vCard format, 225
  sending e-mail messages to, 224
contacts (Windows Live Messenger)
  adding, 232–233
  removing, 233
  sharing, 233
Contacts list (Outlook), 393, 405
Contacts list (Windows Live Mail)
  accessing, 223
  adding contacts to, 212
  extracting addresses from, 215
  illustrated, 223
Content Advisor, 144–145
Content view (Windows 7), 109
Content window (IE), 190
contextual menus, 53
Control Panel
  accessing, 55, 128
  Apply button, 129
  AutoPlay, 135
  Backup and Restore, 262–265
  configuring as Start menu pop-up, 128
  Date and Time Properties, 129–131
  Devices and Printers, 92–93, 280
  Display, 134
  Fonts, 134
  HomeGroup, 115
  Internet Options, 140–147
  Keyboard, 138–139
  Mouse, 139–140
  Network and Sharing Center, 172, 174,
    544, 572, 581
  OK button, 129
  Personalization, 104–105, 131–134
  Phone and Modem, 150–151
  as pop-up, 129
  Power Options, 136–138
  Programs and Features, 147–149
  System and Security, 184

User Accounts, 149–150, 575
Windows Update, 271–272
conventions, this book, 2–3
Conversation window (Windows Live
    Messenger), 237
converting images, 427–428
cookies
    defined, 141
    deleting, 141
    handling, overriding, 143
    handling settings, 144
copyrights
    fallacies, 430–431
    irritation over, 430
    marks, 431
    scanning and, 431
CPUs. *See* processors
*Creating Web Pages All-in-One Desk
    Reference For Dummies* (Wagner and
    Mansfield), 159
cropping images. *See also* images, scan
    defined, 425
    illustrated, 427
    process, 425–426
    proportion, 426
CRT monitors, 15
Ctrl (Control) key, 59
cursors (Window 7), 53
Customize Start Menu dialog box, 95

D

DAT (Digital Audio Tape) backup drives, 490
databases (Access)
    access, 291
    blank table, 380
    encryption, 291
    recently used, opening, 380
Datasheet view (Access), 380
Date and Time Properties dialog box
    Additional Clocks tab, 130–131
    Date and Time tab, 130
    Internet Time tab, 131
dates, formatting (Excel), 332–334
DDR2 modules, 494
DDR3 modules, 494
DDR (double data rate) modules, 494
defragmenting hard drives. *See also* hard
    drives
    defined, 258
    with Disk Defragmenter, 259–260
    function, 259

manual, 260–261
process, 260–261
time needed for, 261
deleting
    browsing history, 140–141
    cookies, 141
    digital photos, 481
    files and folders, 87
    History list, 202
    with mouse and keyboard, 87
    Recycle Bin contents, 89
    slides (PowerPoint), 357
    special effects, 452
    tables (Access), 381
    thumbnails, 481
    transitions
        (Windows Live Movie Maker), 451
demilitarized zone (DMZ) host, 574
desktop
    background, changing, 104–105
    background, setting, 132–133
    personalizing, 104–108
desktop PCs
    components, 13–17
    computer, 13–15
    CPUs, 19
    expansion, 18
    GPUs, 19
    keyboard, 16
    lunchbox, 14
    minitower, 14
    monitor, 15–16
    mouse, 17
    pizza box, 14
    RAM, 19
    speakers, 17
    standard tower, 13
    touchpad, 17
    trackball, 17
Desktop toolbar, 99
Details view, 109
Device Manager
    defined, 253
    illustrated, 254
    opening, 254
    steps for using, 254–256
    troubleshooting with, 247–248
    in updating drivers, 254–256
devices
    conflicting, 254
    disabling, 254
    enabling, 254
    status, 255

Devices and Printers window (Windows 7), 92–93, 280
DHCP. *See* Dynamic Host Configuration Protocol
dialup connections
 cost savings, 170
 creating (Windows 7), 171–173
 ISP in setting up, 172–173
 local access numbers, 172
 not use recommendation, 170
 physical connection, 171
 pros/cons, 164
 setting up, 170
 troubleshooting, 175
dialup modems
 adding/removing, 151
 dialing rules, 150–151
 PCMCIA, 151
 provider list, 151
digital audio extraction, 434
Digital Audio Tape (DAT) backup drives, 490
digital cameras
 battery requirements, 470
 benefits, 30
 cable, 479
 external card readers, 471
 extras, 471–473
 film cameras versus, 466, 467
 floppy drives, 468
 functioning of, 466–468
 hard drives, 467
 illustrated, 30
 lenses, 472
 macro lenses, 472
 misconceptions, 466
 motion capture, 470
 older storage mediums, 468
 photosensors, 467
 plugging into PCs, 479
 RAM cards, 467
 reasons for using, 465
 rechargeable batteries, 471–472
 recordable CD and DVD drives, 468
 software, 479
 telephoto lenses, 472
 tripods, 473
 USB connections, 124, 479
 USB ports, 510
 wide angle lenses, 472
digital photos
 camera angles, 476
 composing, 473–478
 in craft projects, 471
 deleting, 481

downloading, 124, 478–481
 editing, 469
 as e-mail attachments, 471, 481
 exposure, 477
 first-rate (FRPs), 473
 lighting, 477–478
 managing, 469
 organizing, 478
 printing, 470, 481
 pros and cons, 468–471
 rotating, 481
 rule of asymmetry, 475–476
 rule of thirds, 474–475
 selecting, 481
 shadows, 477–478
 in slide shows, 471, 481
 thumbnails, 478
 versatility, 468
 viewing, 123
 on Web sites, 470
digital subscriber line. *See* DSL connections
Digital Video Disc. *See* DVDs
DIMM slots, 497–498
discs, 125
Disk Cleanup utility, 89
Disk Defragmenter. *See also* defragmenting hard drives
 defined, 259
 illustrated, 260
 running, 260–261
 scheduling, 260
display messages, this book, 3
Display settings (Windows 7), 134
document sharing, 548–550
documents (Word)
 double-clicking to open Word and document, 298
 formatting, 287, 315–319
 inserting into PowerPoint slides, 358–359
domain names, blocking, 222
double data rate (DDR) modules, 494
downloading files
 MP3, 440–441
 pictures, 200
 recommendations, 199–200
 video clips, 448
 warning, 199–200
downloading photos
 cables, 479
 PC connection, 479
 prerequisites, 478–479
 software for, 479
 with Windows 7, 479–480

Draft view (Word), 301
drafts, creating/sending, 218
drive cage kits, 502
drive thrashing, 501
drivers
  defined, 254
  incompatible, 551–552
  network adapter card, 535
  network interface cards (NICs), 541–542,
    551–552
  updating, 254–256
  wireless networks, 564
drives. *See also* hard drives
  backup, 32
  DVD/Blue-Ray recorders, 32
  external, 31–33
  portable, 31
  sharing, 549
  USB flash, 33
DSL (digital subscriber line) connections.
    See also Internet connections
  cons, 165
  creating, 173–174
  ISP information for, 170
  physical connection, 171
  pros, 164–165
  splitters, 165
DSL modems
  routers with, 568
  switches, 550–551
D-SUB video port, 40
dust bunnies, avoiding, 274–275
DVD+R format, 459
DVD+RW format, 459
DVD authoring programs, 459
DVD Menu Style dialog box
    (DVD Maker), 463
DVD movies, watching, 125
DVD Options dialog box (DVD Maker), 460
DVD/Blu-Ray recorders, 32, 510
DVD-R format, 459
DVD-RW format, 459
DVDs
  aspect ratio, 460
  for backups, 261
  burner speed, 461
  burning, 464
  creating, 457–464
  defined, 458
  formats, 459
  labels, 464
  menu customization, 462–463
  menu style, 461
  menu system, 459

playback settings, 460
previewing, 463–464
settings, configuring, 460–461
titles, changing, 460
video clips, navigating to, 460
video format, 461
watching, 464
with Windows DVD Maker, 457–464
DVI-I port, 40
DVI-VGA adapter, 40
dye-sub printers, 24
Dynamic Host Configuration Protocol (DHCP)
  client setup, 545–546
  defined, 543
  functioning of, 543
  hardware device sharing with, 566–567
  host setup, 544–545
  switched-firewall, 567
dynamic routing, 574

E

editing
  cells (Excel), 331–332
  contacts (Outlook), 401
  digital photos, 469
  fields (Access), 385–386
  text (PowerPoint), 361–362
  text (Word), 305–306
editing window
  Access, 380
  Excel, 327
  PowerPoint, 352
  Word, 301
EIDE (Enhanced Integrated Drive
    Electronics) hard drives, 502, 505
802.11a standard, 558
802.11b standard. *See also* wireless
    standards
  defined, 557
  distance, 558
  interference, 558
802.11g standard, 559
802.11n standard, 559
e-mail (Outlook)
  addressing, 397
  attachments, 395
  composing, 396–397
  forwarding, 395
  message format, 393
  printing, 405
  prioritizing, 396
  reading, 392–393

e-mail (Outlook) *(continued)*
  replying to, 393–396
  sending, 397
  threading display, 393
e-mail (Windows Live Mail)
  attachments, 160, 181, 218
  Bcc, 214–215
  Cc, 214–215
  creating, 216–217
  drafts, 218
  flagging, 219
  formatting, 217–218
  forwarding, 214
  importance, 205
  moving to outbox, 217
  name, 209
  password, 209
  privacy, 182–183
  read verification, 220
  reading, 211–212
  receiving, 211
  replying to, 213–214
  settings, automatic configuration, 210
  spam, 180, 222–223
  spell check, 218–219
  Web-based, 160
e-mail accounts (Outlook)
  adding, 390–392
  backing up, 392
  passwords, 391
  removing, 392
emoticons, 228, 234
encryption
  SSL, 188
  transparent, 118
  WPA/WPA2, 564
Enhanced Integrated Drive Electronics
    (EIDE) hard drives, 502, 505
Enter key, 59
ergonomic keyboards, 16
eSATA
  adapter card, 512
  plug and play, 512
  recorders, 490
eSATA ports
  adding, 488
  illustrated, 510
  speed comparison, 511
Escape (Esc) key, 59
Ethernet networks. *See also* networks
  browsing, 546–548
  cables, 539–540, 542–543
  coaxial (coax) cabling, 539

components illustration, 540
connections, displaying, 544
defined, 538
device manufacturers, 541
document sharing, 548–550
folder sharing, 548–550
hardware, 539–542
illustrated, 538
inkjet printer connections, 23
NICs, 541–542
packets, 538
primer, 537–539
printer connections, 550
process, 538–539
RJ-45 connector, 540
security, 573–576
switches, 541
troubleshooting, 551–553
twisted pair cabling, 539
Windows 7 configuration for, 543–550
wireless network comparison, 555–556
Excel 2010
  borders and shading, 338–339
  cell alignment, 338
  cells, 328–332, 346–347
  charts, 289, 344–346
  defined, 288
  editing window, 327
  features, 289
  File tab, 326, 412
  font formatting, 337
  formatting, 337–340
  forms, 289
  formulas, 289, 340–343
  functions, 289
  graphics, 343–344
  headers and footers, 347–348
  lists, 289
  number formats, 332–334
  printing in, 348–349
  Quick Access toolbar, 326
  reports, 289
  Ribbon, 326
  rows and columns, 334–337
  running, 326
  screen controls, 326–328
  selection appearance, changing, 340
  sheet tabs, 326
  shortcut keys, 329–332
  smart tags, 289
  status bar, 327
  styles, 340
  templates, 342–343

Web-based version, 412
window, 327
workbooks, 327–328, 344
worksheets, 328–330, 347–348
Excel 2010 Bible (Walkenbach), 343
Excel Chart Wizard, 344–346
exiting
  programs, 83–84
  saving and, 84
  Windows 7, 49–50
expansion upgrades, 488
Explorer window
  copying in, 85–86
  file management with, 84–88
  folder creation in, 86–87
  illustrated, 81
  moving in, 86
  Navigation pane, 109–110
  opening, 81
  Preview pane, 110, 123
  running, 64
  views, 108–109
exposure, digital photos, 477
extensions, Web site, 159
external card readers, 471
external devices, removing during
    troubleshooting, 244
external drives
  backup drives, 32
  USB flash drives, 33
external hard drives
  internal hard drives versus, 503–504
  portable, 31–32
  selecting, 489

F

F (Function) keys, 60
Favorites (IE)
  adding, 194–195
  order, changing, 196
  organizing, 195–196
  URL, modifying, 196
  using, 195
Favorites Center (IE), 189–190, 201
faxes
  receiving, 121
  sending, 120–121
  setting up for, 119–120
fields (Access)
  defined, 380
  editing, 385–386

entering, 385–386
form, 382–383
incrementing, 384
file servers, 533
File tab
  Access, 379
  Excel, 326, 412
  OneNote, 412
  Outlook, 389
  PowerPoint, 352, 412
  Word, 299, 412
file transfer, network, 530–531
File Transfer Protocol (FTP)
  with AceFTP Pro, 161, 162
  defined, 161
  Internet Explorer support, 161
  servers, 161
files
  adding to SkyDrive, 408–411
  archive, restoring, 200
  backing up, 262–265
  compression, 200
  copying, 85–86
  deleting, 87
  downloading, 199–200
  icons, 72–73
  managing, 84–88
  managing on network, 530
  moving, 86
  MP3, 122–123
  properties, displaying, 87–88
  saving within Office applications
      (SkyDrive), 412–413
  selecting, for backup, 262, 264
  sending, in chat session, 235
  sound, 107
  transferring (SkyDrive), 410
  vCard, 225
film cameras
  cost of, 469–470
  digital cameras versus, 466, 467
  motion capture, 470
  reasons for not using, 465
filters, spam, 182–183
Find and Replace (Word)
  accessing, 306
  formatting searches, 308
  More options, 307–308
  next occurrence, 307
  replacing matches, 307
  steps, 306–307

firewalls
  defined, 183
  functions, 183
  hardware versus software, 184
  third-party, 185
  Windows Firewall, 184–185
FireWire
  control over connections, 512
  defined, 37
  device support, 512
  hard drives, 32
  hubs, 488
  illustrated, 37
  as plug-and-play connection, 38
  recorders, 490
FireWire ports
  adding, 488
  availability, 38
  800 version B, 511
  hubs, 513
  icon, 510
  illustrated, 510
  port card, 513
  sound cards, 519
  speed comparison, 511
firmware, 11
first-rate photos (FRPs), 473
flagging e-mail messages, 219
flash drives
  ReadyBoost and, 497
  USB, 33, 102
flatbed scanners. *See also* scanners
  features, 421
  film adapter, 421
  FireWire connections, 421
  42-bit color, 421
  illustrated, 419
  one-button operation, 421
  optical resolution, 421
  recommendation, 419
  scan quality, 419
  sensor head, 419
  single-pass operation, 421
  USB connections, 421
  versatility, 420
flat-panel speakers, 17
Flip 3D, 96
floppy disks, 101–102, 261
Folder pane (Windows Live Mail), 207
folders
  copying, 85–86
  creating, 86–87
  creating (SkyDrive), 409–411
  deleting, 87

  icons, 74
  in libraries, 112
  moving, 86
  Music, 438
  orphan, 149
  properties, displaying, 87–88
  Public, 113–114
  sharing, 548–550, 578–579
  Users, 110–112
Font dialog box (PowerPoint), 362
fonts (Excel), 337
fonts (Word)
  attributes, 315–316
  color, 316
  families, 315
  formatting, 315–316
  size, 316
  spacing, 316
Fonts settings
  Internet Explorer (IE), 142
  Windows 7, 134
footers (Excel), 347–348
force feedback, 29
Form Wizard (Access), 382–384
Format Cells dialog box (Excel)
  Alignment tab, 338
  Border tab, 338–339
  Font tab, 337
  Number tab, 333–334
formatting (Excel)
  borders and shading, 338–339
  cell, 338
  font, 337
formatting (Word)
  applying, 315–319
  AutoFormatting, 318–319
  feature overview, 287
  font, 315–316
  marks, 317
  paragraph, 316–318
formatting e-mail messages (Windows Live
  Mail), 217–218
Formatting toolbar (Windows Live Mail),
  217–218
forms (Access)
  creating, 381–385
  deleting, 384
  feature overview, 291
  fields, 382–383
  layout, 383
  save default, 382
  tables, 382
  use benefits, 381–382
  using, 384

forms (Excel), 289
Formula bar (Excel), 326
formulas (Excel)
  cell changes and, 341
  defined, 340
  examples, 340
  Excel calculation of, 340
  feature overview, 289
  inserting, 341
  templates, 342–343
  using, 340–343
forwarding e-mail messages
  Outlook, 395
  Windows Live Mail, 214
fragmentation, hard drive, 258, 259
frames, printing with, 203
freeware, 12
FRPs (first-rate photos), 473
FTP. *See* File Transfer Protocol
Full Screen Reading view (Word), 302–303
functions (Excel), 289

G

gadgets. *See also* Sidebar
  adding, 108
  defined, 107
  options/settings, 108
  SideShow, 561
game controllers, 29
game ports, sound cards, 519
gamer's video cards, 491–492
games
  LAN parties, 531
  multiplayer, 531, 532
  network, 531
Gigabit Ethernet, 541
Google
  Groups, 162
  Web-based e-mail, 160
GPUs. *See* graphics processing units
graphics (Excel)
  adding, 343–344
  illustrated, 344
  moving, 343
graphics (PowerPoint)
  feature preview, 290
  installing in slides, 363–364
  pasting, 364
  resizing, 363
graphics (Word)
  adding, 319–320
  illustrated, 320

graphics cards. *See* video cards
graphics processing units (GPUs), 19
graphics tablets
  characteristics, 28
  defined, 27
  illustrated, 27
group scheduling (Outlook), 292
Guest accounts
  access, 118
  defined, 118
  turning on/off, 150

H

handouts (PowerPoint), 289
hard drives
  access speed, 502
  characteristics, 501–503
  checking, 256–258
  checking during troubleshooting, 245
  contiguous space, 258
  defragmenting, 258–261
  digital cameras, 467
  drive cage kit, 502
  EIDE, 502, 505
  external, 489, 503–504
  fragmentation, 258, 259
  internal, 489, 503–508
  misconceptions, 256
  performance, 258
  power options, 137
  rpm, 502–503
  running applications from, 81–82
  SATA, 502
  scanning, 245, 256–258
  SCSI, 502
  size, 502
  solid-state, 261
  speed, 502
  upgrading, 489
  virtual memory space, 500
  Windows 7 requirement, 48
hardware
  conflicts, checking for, 255
  defined, 10
  Ethernet networks, 539–542
  examples, 10
  icons, 71–72
  maintaining, 273–282
  network requirements, 534
  properties, 255
  resource allocation, 254
  shared Internet connection, 531, 566–571

hardware *(continued)*
  TWAIN-compatible, 448
  wireless, 563–564
headers (Excel), 347–348
Help (Windows 7)
  displaying, 60
  functions, 60
  illustrated, 61
  links, 61
  Microsoft support, 62
  searching in, 61–62
  technical articles, 62
  troubleshooting with, 251, 256
Help system (Office)
  defined, 293
  displaying, 294
  Online links, 294
  Show Table of Contents button, 295
  Type Words to Search For box, 294–295
  use illustration, 294
  using, 293–295
hibernation, 51
highlighting (Word), 322–323
History list
  deleting, 202
  displaying, 201
  searching, 201
  settings, 141
  tracking with, 201–202
Home Networking For Dummies (Ivens), 539
home page
  choosing, 193
  setting, 140, 193
Home Premium edition (Windows 7), 47
HomeGroup
  automatic creation, 114
  defined, 114
  file sharing, 548
  folder sharing, 549
  illustrated, 115
  joining, 115
  Library sharing, 578
  networks and, 531
  settings, 115
hosts
  defined, 544
  DMZ, 574
  NICs and, 544, 551
  setting up, 544–545
hot keys, 57
hovering, 57, 63
HTML (HyperText Markup Language), 217
HTTP (HyperText Transfer Protocol)
  servers, 391

hubs. *See also* ports
  adding, 488
  Ethernet, 541
  network, 513
  USB, 513
Hulu, 163
HyperText Markup Language (HTML), 217
HyperText Transfer Protocol (HTTP)
  servers, 391

1

Icon view (Windows 7), 109, 123
icons
  defined, 52
  digital photos, 123
  field guide, 70–76
  file, 72–73
  folder, 74
  hardware, 71–72
  multiple contiguous, selecting, 76–77
  multiple separated, selecting, 77
  program, 72, 73
  selecting, 76–77
  shortcut, 74–76
  system, 75
  taskbar notification area, 97–98
  this book, 5
  Windows 7, 52–53, 70–77
ICQ. *See also* chat clients
  defined, 228
  downloading, 228
  options, 229
ICS (Internet Connection Sharing), 571
IDE (Integrated Drive Electronics) drives, 489
IE. *See* Internet Explorer
IEEE 1394. *See* FireWire; FireWire ports
image-cataloging programs, 478
images, scan
  acquiring, 422–424
  boundaries, 424
  converting, 427–428
  cropping, 424–427
  dimensions, 424
  dpi (resolution), 424
  fine-tuning, 424
  outdated formats, 430
  output type, 424
  rotating, 424–425
  saving, 428–429
  scale, 424
indentation (Word), 317
infrared ports, 39

inkjet printers
advantages, 23
cartridges, changing, 279–280
cartridges, cleaning, 281–282
cartridges, refilling, 282
ink levels, checking, 279
nozzles, 281, 282
onscreen ink alerts, 279
InPrivate, 144
Insert Chart dialog box (Excel), 345
Insert Picture dialog box (PowerPoint), 363
Insert Picture dialog box (Word), 319
Insert Table dialog box (Word), 309
inserting (Excel)
blank cells, 335–336
cell from Clipboard, 336
formulas, 341
rows and columns, 336–337
inserting (PowerPoint)
audio, 367–369
slides, 357–358
video, 367–369
Word documents into, 358–359
instant messaging, 161
Integrated Drive Electronics (IDE) drives, 489
Intel processors, 45
internal hard drives. *See also* hard drives
external hard drives versus, 503–504
recommendation, 503
second, adding, 504–508
selecting, 489
Internet
connection description, 156–157
digital media over, 163
illustrated view, 156
as Internet connection requirement, 167
navigating, 193–199
potential, 158–163
privacy protection, 177–186
radio, 163
risky behavior, 180–183
sharing connection with networks, 531
Internet Accounts dialog box (Windows
Live Mail)
accessing, 209
Add button, 209
Properties button, 210
Internet audio streaming, 440
Internet Connection Sharing (ICS), 571
Internet connections
adding to Windows 7, 169–175
cable, 165–166, 171
dialup, 164, 170, 171
DSL, 164–165, 171

ISP information for, 170
minimum requirements, 167
physical, 171, 175
Properties dialog box, 545–546
satellite, 166, 171
sharing, 531, 565–572
testing, 175
in troubleshooting, 246
troubleshooting tips, 175
Internet Explorer (IE)
accessibility options, 142
Add to Favorites Bar button, 191
Address bar, 188
AutoComplete, 145, 203
Back button, 190
browsing history, 140–141
Content window, 190
controls, 188–193
as default browser, 147
default search engine, 142, 188
Favorites button, 191, 194
Favorites Center, 189–191, 194–196
fonts specification, 142
Forward button, 190
FTP support, 161
Help button, 193
Home button, 191
language specification, 142
link color specification, 142
Live Search box, 188, 191, 196
Page button, 192, 204
Print button, 192
Read Mail button, 192
Refresh button, 191
RSS feeds, 145, 199
RSS Feeds button, 191
running, 187–188
Safety button, 192
search suggestions, 198
searching with, 196–198
security options, 142–143
Status bar, 190
Stop button, 191
Suggested Sites button, 191
tabbed window display settings, 142
tabs, 191, 198
toolbar, 189
toolbar buttons, 191–193
Tools button, 192
Web Slice Gallery button, 191
Web Slices, 145, 194
window, 188–193
Zoom level menu, 190

Internet Options
  accessing, 140
  Advanced tab, 147
  Connections tab, 145–146
  Content tab, 144–145
  General tab, 140–142
  Privacy tab, 143–144
  Programs tab, 146–147
  Security tab, 142–143
Internet Protocol (IP) addresses, 157, 543
Internet service providers (ISPs)
  in broadband connection setup, 174
  in dialup connection setup, 172–173
  information for connections, 170
  locating Web sites, 157
  PC connection to, 156
Internet time synchronization, 131
IP (Internet protocol) addresses, 157, 543
IP filtering, 574
iPods, as MP3 player, 440
ISPs. *See* Internet service providers
iTunes, 438

J

joysticks, 29
JPEG format
  scanned images, 424, 428
  Web page, 428
Jump Lists (Windows 7), 96
jumpers, 505–506
junk mail. *See* spam

K

key sequences, 84
Keyboard Properties dialog box
  Hardware tab, 139
  Speed tab, 138–139
keyboards
  Alt (Alternate) key, 60
  arrow (navigation) keys, 59
  cleaning, 277
  Ctrl (Control) key, 59
  deleting with, 87
  Enter key, 59
  ergonomic, 16
  Escape (Esc) key, 59
  F (Function) keys, 60
  illustrated, 58

  in moving slide elements (PowerPoint), 363
  Num Lock key, 59
  one-touch buttons, 16
  Page Up/Page Down keys, 65
  port, 42
  properties, 138–139
  PS/2, 42
  repeat delay, 138
  repeat rate, 139
  Shortcut key, 59
  Windows keys, 58–59
  wireless, 26–27
keying, 508

L

label printers. *See also* printers
  convenience, 25
  defined, 24
  illustrated, 25
  items produced by, 24
labels, DVD, 464
LabelWriter 450 Turbo printer, 24–25
LAN (local area network) connections,
    145–146
languages, IE specification, 142
Laptop PCs
  connectivity, 39
  CPUs, 19
  desktop PCs versus, 18
  drawbacks, 18
  GPUs, 19
  infrared ports, 39
  PC Cards, 39
  RAM, 19
laser printers. *See also* printers
  advantages, 22
  cleaning, 278
  cost, 22
  illustrated, 23
  toner, 278
LCD monitors. *See also* monitors
  defined, 15
  DVI-I port, 40
  illustrated, 15
  recommendation, 16
leaders, 315
LEAP (Lightweight Extensible
    Authentication Protocol), 576
legalities, MP3 files, 433, 436, 444

lenses, digital camera, 472
libraries
  browsing, 113
  creating, 112
  defined, 112
  folders in, 112
lighting. *See also* composition, photo;
    digital photos
  exposure do's/don'ts, 477
  shadows, 477–478
Lightweight Extensible Authentication
    Protocol (LEAP), 576
Line Out/Speaker jacks, 41
links
  cell, creating, 346–347
  colors, specifying, 142
  Help system, 61
  index, printing, 203
  Start menu, 55
liquid crystal display. *See* LCD monitors
List view (Windows 7), 109
lists (Excel), 289
lithium-ion (Li-Ion) batteries, 472
Live Search box (IE), 188, 191, 196
local area network (LAN) connections,
    145–146
locking (Windows 7), 52
logging off (Windows 7), 51–52
Logitech MOMO steering wheel, 29
lunchbox case, 14

M

*Mac OS X Snow Leopard All-in-One For
    Dummies* (Chambers), 533
McAfee AntiVirus Plus 2010, 267
macro lenses, digital camera, 472
macros (Word), 288
Mail Properties dialog box
    (Windows Live Mail), 210–211
mailing lists, 160
maintenance
  antivirus, 267–268
  backing up, 261–265
  boot and recovery, 269–270
  cables, 275–276
  device and driver, 253–256
  with Device Manager, 253–256
  hard drive check, 256–258
  hard drive defragmentation, 258–261

keyboard, 277
  monitors, 276–277
  mouse, 177
  PC, 273–277
  printer, 278–282
  restore points, 265–267
  scanners, 176–177
  spyware elimination, 268–269
  updates, 271–272
Manage Add-Ons dialog box (IE), 188
margins (Word)
  current indication, 312
  setting from Ribbon, 313
  setting with ruler, 312–313
Maximize button, 68
Media Player Library, 438
memory. *See also* random access memory
    (RAM)
  physical, 501
  virtual, 499–501
memory cards, digital cameras, 467
memory packs, 487
Memory Stick cards, 467
menu commands, this book, 3
menus
  contextual, 53
  hot keys, 57
  Windows 7, 56, 57
Message list
  Outlook, 389
  Windows Live Mail, 208, 212
Messages pane (Windows Live
    Messenger), 231
Microsoft
  Knowledge Base, 251
  tech support, 62, 252
  Web site, 252
Microsoft Paint (MSP) images, 430
MIDI (Musical Instrument Digital Interface)
    format
  defined, 442
  ports, 519–520
  support, 442–443
Minimize button, 66, 67
minimizing windows, 66–68
minitower case, 14
mini-tripods, 473
MLC Radio, 163, 440
modems
  cable, 550–551, 568
  dialup, 150–151

modems *(continued)*
  DSL, 550–551, 568
  installation, 151
  as Internet connection requirement, 167
  PCMCIA, 151
  removing, 151
monitors
  cleaning, 276–277
  CRT, 15
  LCD, 15
  multiple, video card support, 522
  port connections, 40
  power settings, 137
  recommendation, 16
monopods, 473
motherboards
  built-in sound/video cards, 490
  defined, 486
  illustrated, 486
  PCI slots, 514
  upgrading, 486–487
Motion Picture Experts Group. *See* MPEG
mouse
  acceleration setting, 140
  buttons, 17
  cleaning, 277
  cordless, 17
  deleting with, 87
  middle button function, 139–140
  in moving slide elements (PowerPoint), 363
  optical, 17, 277
  pointer settings, 140
  port, 42
  PS/2, 42
  right clicking, 53
  scrolling setting, 140
  settings, 139–140
  trails setting, 140
  USB, 42
movies
  building, 448–449
  clips/images, importing, 447–448
  creating, 445–456
  flow, mapping, 449
  previewing, 254–255
  saving, 455
  sharing, 256
  sound, 452–453
  special effects, 451–452
  titles, 453–454
  transitions, 450–451
  viewing, 254
  with Windows Live Movie Maker, 445–446

moving PCs, 273–274
moving windows, 68
MP3 cards, 491, 519
MP3 files
  applications running, 439
  association, changing, 439
  audio quality, 434, 435
  benefits of, 122
  bit rates, 435
  burning audio CDs from, 443
  CDs versus, 434
  defined, 434
  double-clicking, 438
  downloading, 440–441
  folder placement, 438
  legality, 433, 436
  listening to, 438–440
  playback, pausing, 439
  playing, 122–123
  playlists, 440, 441
  primer, 434–435
  recording, 434
  right-clicking, 439
  ripping, 435–438
  saving, 435
  tracks, 439
  uses, 434–435
MP3 players
  downloading to, 440–441
  iPod, 440
  USB ports, 510
  Windows Media Player support, 441
MPEG (Motion Picture Experts Group)
  cards, 492
  encoding/decoding, 522
  files, 522–523
  hardware support, 522
MSP (Microsoft Paint) images, 430
multifunction devices
  printers, 26
  scanning hardware, 419
multiplayer games, 235
multiuser operations
  Administrator accounts, 117
  booting PC and, 117
  examples, 116
  Guest accounts, 117, 118
  logging in, 117
  logging off, 117
  Standard accounts, 117
  switching users, 117
  user account levels, 117
music, adding to movies, 452–453

Music folder, 438
Musical Instrument Digital Interface (MIDI)
    format, 442–443
My Book drive, 32

N

NAT (Network Address Translation),
    579–580
Navigation pane
    Access, 380
    Explorer window, 109–110
    Outlook, 389
    Word, 303
negative scanners, 420
netbooks, 18
Netflix, 163
Network
    icon, 75
    running applications from, 82–83
network adapter cards
    drivers, 535
    installation, 534
    as required networking hardware, 534
Network Address Translation (NAT),
    579–580
network administrators, 537
Network and Sharing Center
    Set Up a New Connection or Network
        option, 172, 174, 581
    Sharing tab, 545, 572
network interface cards (NICs)
    certification statements, 542
    coax connectors, 539
    defined, 541
    drivers, 541–542
    drivers, incompatible, 551–552
    faulty, 552
    Gigabit, 541
    hardware conflict, 552
    host setup and, 544, 551
    manufacturers, 541
    no lights show up on, 552
    ratings, 541
    shopping for, 541–542
    troubleshooting, 551–552
    Windows 7 doesn't recognize, 551–552
network kits, 534
network management software, 535
network printer boxes, 550

network security
    NAT and, 579–580
    shared folders, 578–579
    VPN and, 580–583
    wired networks, 573–576
    wireless networks, 576–577
Network window (Windows 7)
    Add a Printer button, 548
    displaying, 546
    illustrated, 547
network-ready applications, 535
networks
    advantages, 529–533
    application sharing, 531–533
    browsing, 546–548
    connections, adding, 94
    connections, viewing, 94
    creation chart, 539
    document sharing, 531–533, 548–550
    Ethernet, 537–553
    file transfer, 530–531
    folder sharing, 548–550
    games, 531
    hardware connections, 533
    hardware requirements, 534
    HomeGroup and, 531
    hubs, 513
    Internet sharing, 531
    Macintosh/Linux computer
        connections, 533
    PC connections, 533
    PDA connections, 533
    printer connections, 534, 550
    RJ-45 connector, 540
    routers, 534
    setting up, 94
    software requirements, 535
    switches, 534, 541
    troubleshooting, 551–553
    Windows 7 configuration for, 543–550
    wired versus wireless, 555–556
    wireless, 540, 555–564
    working with, 94, 537
newsgroups
    defined, 162
    risky behavior, 180
    troubleshooting with, 252
    use benefits, 162
nickel-cadmium (NiCad) batteries, 472
nickel-metal-hydride (NiMH) batteries, 472
NICs. *See* network interface cards
Normal view (PowerPoint), 354
Norton AntiVirus (Symantec), 186

Norton Disk Doctor (Symantec), 258
Norton Internet Security (Symantec), 185
notes (PowerPoint)
  defined, 366
  entering, 366–367
  feature overview, 289
  printing, 375
Notes Page view (PowerPoint), 355, 356
Notes pane (PowerPoint), 366–367
notification area. *See also* taskbar
  customizing, 98
  defined, 97
  icons, 97
  icons, adding, 98
  illustrated, 98
  Live Messenger icon, 229
Num Lock key, 59
number formats (Excel)
  characteristics of, 332
  default, 333
  defined, 332
  General, 333, 334
  specifying, 333–334
  types of, 332
numbered lists (Word), 310–311
NVIDIA graphics cards, 520

O

objects (PowerPoint), selecting, 361
OCR (optical character recognition), 25, 417
Office 2010. *See also specific applications*
  applications list, 286
  Clipboard, 292–293
  components, 286–292
  Help system, 293–295
  New command, 412
  Web site, opening, 294
  Web-based applications, 412
Office 2010 All-in-One For Dummies
  (Weverka), 286
OneNote, 412
online backup, 32
online stores, 181
Open dialog box (Windows Live Mail), 220, 221
open systems, 547
OpenGL, 521
opening windows, 64–65

operating systems. *See also* Windows 7
  compatibility in saving images, 428
  functions, 20
  types of, 20
optical (TOSLINK) connector, 42
optical character recognition (OCR), 25, 417
optical mice/trackballs, 277
optical mouse, 17
Options dialog box (Windows Live
    Messenger)
  accessing, 230
  Alerts pane, 231
  exiting, 232
  illustrated, 230
  Messages pane, 231
  Personal pane, 231
  Privacy pane, 23
  Sign In pane, 231
organization, this book, 3–4
orphan folders, 149
Outline pane (PowerPoint), 353–354
Outline view (Word), 301–302
Outlook 2010
  Add New Account wizard, 391
  appointments, 291, 403–405
  attachments, 395, 397–399
  Calendar, 292, 401–405
  command buttons, 389
  composing messages, 396–397
  contacts, 291, 399–401
  Contacts list, 393
  defined, 291
  event calendar, 291
  features, 291–292
  File tab, 389
  Find function, 292
  group scheduling, 292
  Hotmail account support, 292
  mail account configuration, 390–392
  mailbox cleanup, 292
  Message list, 389
  Navigation pane, 389
  onscreen reminders, 292
  printing, 405–406
  reading e-mail, 392–393
  Reading pane, 389, 392
  Reply window, 394
  replying to e-mail, 393–396
  Ribbon, 389
  running, 388

sending messages, 397
Startup Wizard, 390
status bar, 389
tabs, 389
window design, 387
window illustration, 388
Outlook 2010 For Dummies (Dyszel), 387

P

Package for CD (PowerPoint)
  creating, 272–273
  defined, 372
  package contents, 373
  presentation updates and, 373
  using, 272–273
packets, 538
Page Setup dialog box (Word), 313
Page Up/Page Down keys, 65
PaintShop Photo Express, 478
Paragraph dialog box (Word), 314
paragraph formatting (Word)
  alignment, 317
  attributes, 317–318
  indentation, 317
  qualifications for, 316
  spacing, 317
paragraph marks (Word), 317
Parallel ATA (PATA), 505
parallel ports, 39
Parental Controls
  accessing, 144
  enabling/disabling, 150
  illustrated, 145
  user account selection, 144
passwords
  application remembering of, 180
  AutoComplete and, 180
  changing, 150
  different, using, 179
  e-mail account (Outlook), 391
  e-mail account (Windows Live Mail), 209
  guidelines, 179–180
  ISP, 172–175
  not sharing, 575
  random, 179
  sleep mode wakeup, 138
  VPN, 582, 583
  wireless networks, 564
PATA (Parallei ATA), 505

PC Cards, 39
PCI Express, 520, 524
PCMCIA (Personal Computer Memory Card International Association) modems, 151
PCs. *See also* desktop PCs; laptop PCs
  cleaning, 275
  dusting, 274–275
  moving, 273–274
  as open system, 547
  upgrading, 485–492
  wrapping in towels, 274
PDAs. *See* personal digital assistants
pen scanners, 421
peripherals. *See also specific peripherals*
  adding, 21
  connections to computer, 13
  defined, 12
  examples, 12
Personal Computer Memory Card International Association (PCMCIA) modems, 151
personal digital assistants (PDAs), 467, 583
personal information
  divulging, 180
  not giving, 182
  phishing, 181
Personal pane (Windows Live Messenger), 231
Personalization settings
  accessing, 131
  Desktop Background option, 132–133
  Screen Saver option, 133–134
  Sounds option, 133
  Theme option, 131–132
phishing, 181
Phone and Modem dialog box
  Advanced tab, 151
  Dialing Rules tab, 150–151
  Modems tab, 151
phone calls, from Windows Live Messenger, 235
phoneline networking. *See also* wireless networks
  advantages, 562
  defined, 562
  drawbacks, 562, 563
photo printers, 24
photographs. *See* digital photos
photosensors, digital camera, 467

physical Internet connections, 171, 175
pictures, downloading, 200
pipelines, 157
pixels, 418
pizza box case, 14
Player window (Windows Live Movie
    Maker), 446
playlists
  adding MP3 tracks to, 441
  creating, 440
  defined, 440
pointers, setting, 140
POP3 servers, 391
pop-up blockers, 144
port cards
  aligning, 515
  cost, 513
  installation disc, 516
  installing, 513–516
  slot, 514
  slot cover, 515
port forwarding, 574
portable hard drives, 31–32
ports
  adding, 488
  audio, 41–42
  eSATA, 488, 510
  FireWire, 37, 38, 488, 510, 519
  game, 519
  hubs, 512–513
  infrared, 39
  keyboard, 42
  laptop, 39
  MIDI, 519–520
  mouse, 42
  parallel, 39
  peripheral connections with, 13
  PS/2, 42
  serial, 38
  speed comparison, 511
  USB, 17, 33, 42, 488, 510
  video, 40
power button, action specification, 138
Power Options
  Power Button/Sleep Button Action
    option, 138
  power plan, 136
  Put the Computer to Sleep option, 137
  Require a Password on Wakeup option, 138
  Turn Off Hard Disk After option, 137
  Turn off the Display option, 137
power plans, 136
powerline networks, 562–563

PowerPoint 2010
  animation and transition effects, 290
  defined, 289
  design tools, 289
  editing window, 352
  features, 289–290
  File tab, 352, 412
  fonts, 362
  graphics controls, 290
  graphics installation, 363–364
  handouts, 289
  multimedia, 367–369
  multiple screen support, 290
  Normal view, 354
  notes, 289, 366–367
  Notes Page view, 355, 356
  Notes pane, 366–367
  Outline pane, 354
  Package for CD, 272–273
  presentation illustration, 290
  presentation print preview, 289
  printing, 374–375
  Quick Access toolbar, 352
  Reading view, 355
  Reuse Slides pane, 357–358
  Ribbon, 352
  ruler, 353
  running, 352
  shortcut keys, 360–362
  slide creation, 356–359
  Slide pane, 353–354
  Slide Show view, 356
  slide shows, 369–371
  Slide Sorter view, 354–355
  status bar, 354
  text, working with, 359–363
  themes, 364–366
  transitions, 371–372
  views, 354–356
  Web-based version, 412
  window illustration, 353
PowerPoint 2010 For Dummies (Lowe), 351
presentations (PowerPoint)
  print preview, 289
  slides, adding to, 357
  slides, printing, 374–375
  updates, Package for CD and, 373
Preview mode (Windows DVD Maker),
    463–464
Preview pane (Explorer window), 110, 123
previewing
  DVDs, 463–464
  movies, 254–255

presentations (PowerPoint), 289
screen savers, 133
in Windows Live Mail, 254–255
Print dialog box (IE), 202–203
Print Layout view (Word), 302
printers
  accessing, 92–93
  adding to network, 94
  calibrating, 280–281
  cleaning, 278
  default, 92
  defined, 22
  dye-sub, 24
  inkjet, 23, 281–282
  inkjet cartridges, cleaning, 281–282
  inkjet cartridges, refilling, 282
  label, 24–25
  laser, 22–23
  multifunction, 26
  photo, 24
  preference settings, 93
  properties, 280
printers (network)
  adding, 548
  can't connect to, 553
  connections, 550
  displaying, 548
  Ethernet network support, 550
  as network connection element, 534
  network printer box, 550
  network-ready, 550
  offline, 553
  as printer server, 550
  troubleshooting, 553
printing
  cell contents (Excel), 349
  with cell grid (Excel), 349
  data (Access), 386
  digital photos, 470, 481
  with frames, 203
  index of links, 203
  jobs, displaying, 93
  methods for, 93
  within Outlook, 405–406
  slides (PowerPoint), 374–375
  Web pages, 202–203
  worksheets (Excel), 348–349
printing (Word)
  feature overview, 288
  methods, 323
  Print pane, 323

Printing Preferences dialog box
    (Windows 7), 92–93
prioritizing messages (Outlook), 396
privacy
  e-mail, 182–183
  firewalls, 183–185
  hacker difficulty in invading, 178
  InPrivate, 144
  level, 143
  options, 143–144
  passwords, 179–180
  personal information, 180–182
  pop-up blocker, 144
  potential violations, 178
  protecting, 177–186
  risky behavior, 180–182
  SkyDrive storage, 408
  targets, 177–178
  Web site, 144
Privacy pane (Windows Live Messenger), 231
processors
  AMD, 45
  Celeron, 487
  Core 2 Duo, 487
  Intel, 45
  type, displaying, 19
  types of, 19
  upgrading, 486–487
  Windows 7 requirement, 48
Professional edition, Windows 7, 47
programs. *See* applications
Programs and Features window
  accessing, 148
  closing, 149
  for uninstalling and repairing programs,
    147–149
properties
  displaying, 87–88
  hardware, 255
  Internet connection, 545–546
  keyboard, 138–139
  printer, 280
  Recycle Bin, 89
  shortcuts, 116
  Start button, 91
Properties dialog box, 87–88
PS/2 keyboards, 42
Public folders, 113–114, 578
Public sharing, 113–114

Q

queries (Access), 291
Quick Access toolbar
Access, 380
Excel, 326
PowerPoint, 352
Word, 300

R

RAM. *See* random access memory
RAM cards. *See also* digital cameras
defined, 467
number of images on, 468
types of, 467
Rambus (RDRAM) modules, 494
random access memory (RAM)
amount selection, 496–497
benefits, 19
cost, 487
DDR, 494
DDR2, 494
DDR3, 494
digital camera cards, 467–468
DIMM slots and, 497–498
existing module inspection, 495
installation ease, 487–488, 493
installing, 497–498
memory packs, 487
minimum, by operating system, 496
RDRAM, 494
SDRAM, 494–495
selecting, 495
specifications, 495
types of, 493–495
upgrading, 487–488, 493–498
video cards, 521
Windows 7 requirement, 48
RCA jacks, 41
RDRAM (Rambus) modules, 494
Reading pane
Outlook, 389, 392
Windows Live Mail, 208, 212
Reading view (PowerPoint), 355
Ready to Burn DVD dialog box (DVD Maker), 462
ReadyBoost, 497
Recent Applications list. *See also* Start menu
disabling, 90–91
location, 54
in running applications, 80

Recent Items list, 90
rechargeable batteries, 471–472
recorders, adding, 489–490
records (Access)
defined, 380
displaying, 385
moving between, 384
Recycle Bin
emptying, 88–89
icon, 75
properties, 89
recovering items from, 89–90
refilling inkjet cartridges, 282
reinstalling Windows 7
applications, effect on, 250–251
backing up before, 250
clean install and, 250
defined, 250
product key, 251
reactivation, 251
System Restore disc and, 250
with Windows 7 installation disc, 250–251
remote access, 181
Remote Assistance (Windows Live Messenger), 235
remote cable testers, 542
removable disks, scanning, 245
repair installation. *See* reinstalling Windows 7
replying to e-mail (Outlook)
attachments, 395
Bcc, 395
Cc, 394
copy, saving, 395
drafts, 395
forwarding, 395
prioritizing, 396
process, 393–396
replying to e-mail (Windows Live Mail), 213–214
reports
Access, 291
Excel, 289
resizing windows, 69
resolution
display, 134
scanner, 421, 424
video card, 521
restarting PCs, 50
restore points
applying, 265
creating, 265
defined, 265
loss of, 251

saving, 265
  using, 266–267
restoring backups, 265
restoring windows, 66–68
Reuse Slides pane (PowerPoint), 357–358
revision marks (Word), 320–321
Ribbon
  Access, 379
  Excel, 326
  Outlook, 389
  PowerPoint, 352
  Windows Live Movie Maker, 446
Ribbon (Word)
  defined, 299
  Insert tab, 319
  minimizing, 300
  Page Layout tab, 313, 314
  setting margins from, 313
  setting tabs from, 314–315
right click, 53
ripping
  legalities, 444
  MP3 files, 435–438
risky Internet behavior, 180–183
RJ-45 connectors, 540
rotating images, 424–425, 481
routers. *See also* networks
  defined, 534
  DHCP, 543
  functions, 567
  illustrated, 567
  with modems, 568
  setting up, 568–569
rows (Excel)
  inserting, 336–337
  resizing, 334–335
Roxio Creator, 124
rpm, hard drives, 502–503
RSS feeds
  information display, 199
  Internet Explorer support, 145, 199
  using, 199
RSS Feeds button, 191
rule of asymmetry. *See also* composition,
    photo; digital photos
  defined, 475
  illustrated, 476
  relationship, 475
rule of thirds. *See also* composition, photo;
    digital photos
  alignment, 474
  defined, 474
  illustrated, 474, 475
ruler (PowerPoint), 353

ruler (Word)
  feature overview, 301
  setting margins with, 312–313
  setting tabs with, 314
Run dialog box, 91–92
running applications
  from CD-ROM/DVD-ROM, 82
  from hard drive, 81–82
  from network drive, 82–83
  from Start menu, 80–81
RW/RE (rewritable), 32

S

Safe mode
  with command prompt, 270
  defined, 270
  with networking, 270
  troubleshooting with, 248
  using, 270
SATA (Serial ATA) hard drives, 489, 502
satellite Internet connections. *See also*
    Internet connections
  creating, 173–174
  defined, 166
  ISP information for, 170
  physical connection, 171
  transfer speeds, 166
Save Webpage dialog box (IE), 204
saving
  exiting and, 84
  movies, 455
  MP3 files, 435
  restore points, 265
  scan images, 428–429
  Web pages, 203–204
scanners
  business card, 421
  cleaning, 276–277
  cost, 25, 417
  drivers, 429
  features, 421
  film adapter, 421
  FireWire connections, 421
  flatbed, 419–421
  42-bit color, 421
  functioning of, 417–418
  functions, 25
  glass, cleaning, 429
  illustrated, 26
  manufacturers, 422
  negative, 420
  one-button operation, 421

scanners *(continued)*
  optical character recognition (OCR), 417
  optical resolution, 421
  pen, 421
  sensor, 418
  sheet-fed, 419, 420
  single-pass operation, 421
  specialized, 26
  TWAIN standard, 422
  USB connections, 421
  USB ports, 510
  versatility, 417
scanning
  copyrights and, 431
  don'ts, 429–430
  do's, 429
  image acquisition, 422–424
  image boundaries, 424
  image conversion, 427–428
  image cropping, 424–427
  image dimensions, 424
  image dpi (resolution), 424
  image fine-tuning, 424
  image rotation, 424–425
  image saving, 428–429
  image scale, 424
  original size, 429
  output type, 424
  PC memory for, 429
  with Windows Live Photo Gallery, 422–429
scanning drives
  with avast! Antivirus Home Edition, 245
  commercial utilities, 258
  messages, 257–258
  steps, 256–257
  time needed for, 257
screen savers
  caution, 133
  previewing, 133
  setting, 133–134
  troubleshooting and, 246
scrolling
  mouse setting, 140
  windows, 65–66
scrubber bar, 455
SCSI (Small Computer System Interface),
    242–243, 502
SDRAM (SyncDRAM) modules, 494–495
search and replace (Word), 288
search providers
  default, IE, 188
  default, selecting, 142
search suggestions (IE), 198
searches (IE), 196–198

second hard drives. *See also* hard drives
  adding, 504–508
  benefits of, 504
  cable, 507
  cable connector, 508
  installation process, 504–508
  jumper settings, 505–506
  keying, 508
  multiple drives setting, 506
  plugging in, 506
  sliding into drive bay, 506, 507
Secure Sockets Layer (SSL) encryption, 188
security
  BitLocker, 118
  network, 573–583
  Web browser, 142–143
seek time, hard drives, 502
selections
  shortcut (Word), 305
  text (Word), 304–305
sensors, scanner
  in flatbed scanners, 419
  in multifunction devices, 419
  in scanning process, 418
  in sheet-fed scanners, 419
Serial ATA (SATA) hard drives, 489, 502
serial ports, 38
servers, VPN, 580–582
Service Set Identifiers (SSIDs)
  checking, 564
  defined, 564
  securing, 577
Set Up Backup Wizard, 262–264
Set Up Show dialog box (PowerPoint), 370
shading (Excel), 338–339
shadows, digital photos, 477–478
shared applications, 531–533
shared folders. *See also* folders
  guidelines, 578–579
  naming, 579
  Public, 113–114, 578
  Reader permission level, 578–579
  read/write access, 549–550
  status display marking, 549
  steps, 548–549
  using, 578–579
shared Internet connections
  with all-in-one sharing device, 570
  convenience, 566
  cost effectiveness, 566
  efficiency, 566
  with hardware, 531, 566–571
  methods, 531
  monitoring, 575, 576

reasons for, 565–566
security, 566
with software, 531, 571–572
with wired sharing devices, 566–569
with wireless sharing devices, 570–571
shared locations, 94
shared network hardware, 533
shareware, 12
sharing
  applications, 531–533
  contacts (Windows Live Messenger), 233
  defined, 548
  documents, 531–533, 548–550
  drives, 549
  files, 548
  with HomeGroup, 114–115, 578
  movies (Windows Live Movie Maker), 456
  Public, 113–114
sheet-fed scanners
  document condition for, 420
  illustrated, 420
  sensor hardware, 419
ShieldsUP!! (Gibson Research
    Corporation), 185
Shortcut key, 59
shortcut keys (Excel)
  cell editing, 331–332
  cell selection, 330–331
  movement, 329–330
shortcut keys (PowerPoint)
  object selection, 361
  slide show control, 371
  text field movement, 360–361
  text field selection, 361, 362
shortcut keys (Word)
  editing, 306
  movement, 304
  selection, 305
shortcuts
  benefits, 75
  creating, 116
  defined, 74
  icons, 74–76
  key sequences, 84
  multiple copies, 75
  properties, 116
Shut Down button (Start menu), 49
Sidebar
  defined, 107
  gadgets, adding, 108
  starting, 107
SideShow gadgets, 561
Sign In pane (Windows Live Messenger), 231

SkyDrive
  Add Files link, 410
  adding files to, 409–411
  All Folders link, 408
  cost, 408
  defined, 407
  document icons, 412
  file access, 407
  file transfer, 410
  folder creation, 409–411
  Options menu, 409
  organizing, 409
  privacy, 408
  Recent Folders list, 408
  safety, 407
  saving files within Office applications,
    412–413
  screen, 408–409
  screen illustration, 410
  signing into, 408–409
  space, 407
  space remaining, 409
  storage contents, 407
  transfer speed, 408
  use requirements, 408
  working with, 407–413
sleep mode
  defined, 50, 137
  using, 50
  wakeup passwords, 138
Slide pane (PowerPoint), 353–354
Slide Show view (PowerPoint), 356
slide shows (PowerPoint)
  building, 369–370
  control keys, 371
  running, 371
  slide selection, 370
  slide transitions, 371–372
  slides, moving between, 369
Slide Sorter view (PowerPoint), 354–355
slides (PowerPoint)
  audio, 367–369
  creating, 356–359
  deleting, 357
  elements, moving, 362–363
  graphics installation in, 363–364
  inserting, 357–358
  inserting documents into, 358–359
  jumping to, 353
  as model, 357
  moving between, 369
  moving through, 354
  multimedia, 367–368

slides (PowerPoint) *(continued)*
  printing, 374–375
  selecting, 370
  transitions, 371–372
  video, 367–369
Small Computer System Interface (SCSI),
    242–243, 502
smart tags (Excel), 289
SmartMedia, 467
smileys, 228
sneakernet, 532
software
  defined, 11
  digital camera, 479
  examples, 11
  firmware, 11
  freeware, 12
  network management, 535
  network requirements, 535
  operating system, 20
  shared Internet connections with, 531,
    571–572
  shareware, 12
solid-state hard drives, 261
sound cards
  audio cables and, 525
  built-in, 490
  FireWire port, 519
  game port, 519
  installation disc, 525
  installing, 523–525
  MIDI ports, 519–520
  MP3, 491, 519
  shopping for, 517–520
  slot, 524
  speaker connection, 41
  surround sound, 491, 518
  3D spatial imaging, 518
  24-bit, 491
  upgrading, 490–491
Sound Control Panel dialog box, 133
Sound dialog box, 106–107
sound formats
  AAC, 442
  AIFF, 442
  AU, 442
  MIDI, 442–443
  MP3, 433–441
  WAV, 441
  WMA, 442
sounds
  assigning, 106
  changing, 106–107

  scheme, building, 133
  testing, 107
  WAV file format, 107
soundtracks
  adding, 452–453
  importance, 452
  overlaying, 453
spacing (Word), 316–317
spam
  defined, 222
  domain names, blocking, 222
  filters or rules, 182–183
  getting rid of, 222
  replying to, 180
  unsubscribing and, 223
speakers, 17
special effects. *See also* movies
  adding, 451–452
  deleting, 452
  experimenting with, 452
  types of, 451
spell-checking
  Windows Live Mail, 218–219
  Word, 287
spyware
  defined, 268
  terminating, 268–269
SQL servers, connection with, 291
SSIDs. *See* Service Set Identifiers
SSL (Secure Sockets Layer) encryption, 188
Standard accounts, 117
Start button, 91
Start menu (Windows 7)
  All Programs list, 54, 80
  Computer item, 81
  configuring, 95–96
  Control Panel item, 55
  defined, 54
  Documents item, 54
  Games item, 55
  Help and Support item, 60, 256
  illustrated, 54
  Jump Lists, 96
  Music item, 55
  Network item, 55, 82, 94, 546
  Pictures item, 55
  Properties dialog box, 90–91
  Recent Applications list, 54, 80, 90–91
  Recent Items list, 90
  right-arrow button options, 50–51
  Run item, 91–92
  running applications from, 80–81
  Shut Down button, 49

Start Search text box, 55
using, 54
Startup Repair, 249
Startup Wizard (Outlook), 390
static electricity, dissipating, 497, 523, 563
static routing, 574
status (Windows Live Messenger), 235–236
status bar
  Access, 380
  Excel, 327
  Outlook, 389
  PowerPoint, 354
  Windows Live Mail, 208
  Word, 301
Status bar (IE), 190
storage upgrades, 489–490
Storyboard (Windows Live Movie Maker)
  adding items to, 448–449
  defined, 446
  item deletion, 449
  item order, changing, 449
storyboarding, 446
styles (Excel), 340
surge protectors, 33
surround sound cards, 491, 518
switches. *See also* Ethernet networks;
    networks
  built-in, 541
  cable modem, 550–551
  defined, 534
  DHCP, 543
  DSL modem, 550–551
  as Ethernet hub replacement, 541
  faulty, 552
  function, 541
  as powered devices, 542
  troubleshooting, 552
switching
  users (Windows 7), 51, 117
  windows, 69–70
SyncDRAM (SDRAM) modules, 494–495
System and Security, 184–185
System Configuration utility, 246–247
system icons, 75
System Image Recovery, 249
System Properties
  displaying, 19
  in troubleshooting, 244
System Recovery Options, 249
system requirements, Window 7, 48–49
System Restore utility
  defined, 265
  disc, 250
  restore point creation, 265
  restore point loss, 251
  restore point use, 244, 266–267
  Wizard, 265

T

tables (Access)
  creating, 380–381
  Datasheet view, 380
  defined, 380
  deleting, 381
  fields, 380, 382–383
  forms, 382
  illustrated, 381
  records, 380
tables (Word)
  building, 308–310
  feature overview, 287
  illustrated, 310
  inserting with grid, 309
  uses, 308
tablets, graphics, 27–28
tabs (IE)
  clearing, 315
  defined, 191
  grouping, 198
  opening, 198
  switching between, 198
tabs (Outlook), 389
tabs (Word)
  leader, 315
  setting from Ribbon, 314–315
  setting with ruler, 314
tape drives, adding, 489–490
Task Manager
  accessing, 100
  Applications tab, 100
  logging off from, 101
  Performance tab, 101
  terminating programs with, 100–101
taskbar (Windows 7)
  configuring, 99
  defined, 55, 96
  expanding, 99
  locking/unlocking, 98
  moving, 99
  notification area, 97–98
  for switching between programs, 55, 56,
    96–97
  toolbars, adding to, 99
  uses, 55
  window grouping, 67

tech support, Microsoft, 62, 252
technical articles, 62
telephoto lenses, digital camera, 472
templates (Access), 386
text (PowerPoint)
  adding, 359–360
  editing, 361–362
  fields, moving, 360–361
  fields, moving within, 360–361
  fonts, 362
  movement shortcut keys, 360–361
  selecting, 361
  selection keys, 361
text (Word)
  editing, 305–306
  selecting, 304–305
  typing, 304
  working with, 303–306
themes (PowerPoint)
  applying, 364–366
  illustrated use, 365, 366
  selecting, 365
  uses, 364
themes (Windows 7)
  choosing, 105–106
  color schemes, 131
  creating, 106, 132
  defined, 105
  elements, 131
threading, 393
3D spatial imaging, 518
3DMark Vantage, 520
thumbnails
  defined, 478
  deleting, 481
  digital photo, 478
TIFF format
  operating system compatibility, 428
  scanned images, 424, 428
Tiles view (Windows 7), 108
time
  Internet, synchronizing, 131
  setting, 130
time zone, setting, 130
title bar, window, 68
titles, movie, 253–254
toner, laser printer, 278
toolbars
  adding to taskbar, 99
  Address, 99
  defined, 57
  Desktop, 99
  IE, 189
  locations, 77

using, 57, 77
Windows 7, 56, 57
Windows Fax and Scan, 120
Windows Live Mail, 206–207
tooltips, 57, 63
Total Commander, 84–85, 530
touchpads, 17
tower case, 13
TPM (Trusted Platform Module), 118
trackballs
  benefits, 28
  characteristics, 28
  defined, 17
  illustrated, 28
  optical, 277
transitions (PowerPoint)
  adding, 371–372
  defined, 371
  duration, 372
  feature overview, 290
  sound, 372
transitions (Windows Live Movie Maker)
  adding, 450–451
  cardinal rule, 451
  defined, 450
  deleting, 451
  jarring, 450
  selecting, 451
tripods, 473
troubleshooting
  Administrator access check, 246
  backing up data and, 242
  cable checking in, 243–244
  with Device Manager, 247–248
  dialup connections, 175
  drastic measures, 249–251
  external device removal in, 244
  hard drive check in, 245
  with Help system, 251, 256
  Internet connection verification, 246
  with Microsoft tech support, 252
  with Microsoft Web site, 252
  networks, 551–553
  with newsgroups, 252
  NICs, 551–552
  program uninstallation in, 244
  relaxation as key, 241–242
  resources, 242, 251–252
  restarting PC in, 243
  with Safe mode, 248
  screen saver check, 246
  shared printers, 553
  steps, 243–248
  switches, 552

with System Configuration utility, 246–247
with System Recovery Options, 249
Windows 7, 241–252
Windows 7 Firewall, 185
with Windows 7 Help system, 251
Windows 7 reinstallation and, 250–251
Trusted Platform Module (TPM), 118
TV output, video cards, 522
TV tuner, video cards, 522
TWAIN
  compatibility, 448
  defined, 447
  drivers, 422
  function, 447
  scanners, 422
24-bit sound cards, 491
twisted pair cabling, 539
typing text (Word), 304

U

UAC (User Account Control), 575
unattended backups, 264
uninstalling programs
  checking after, 149
  in Programs and Features window, 147
  steps, 148
  warning, 147
uninterruptible power supplies. *See* UPSs
Universal Resource Locators (URLs)
  characteristics of, 192
  defined, 157
  Favorites, 196
Universal Serial Bus. *See* USB connections;
    USB ports
Update Driver Software Wizard, 255
upgrading
  CPU, 486–487
  expansion, 488
  firmware, 11
  hard drive, 489
  memory, 487–488, 493–498
  motherboard, 486–487
  ports, 488
  recorders, 489–490
  requirements, 485
  sound cards, 490–491
  storage, 489–490
  tape drives, 489–490
  video cards, 491–492
  to Windows 7, 47

UPSs
  benefits, 34
  characteristics, 33
  power life, 34
  warning, 33
URLs. *See* Universal Resource Locators
USB connections
  backup hard drives, 32
  benefits, 36
  cable connectors, 36–37
  device support, 36
  digital cameras, 124, 479
  flash drives, 33, 102
  inkjet printers, 23
  label printers, 24
  mouse, 42
  as plug and play, 36
  ports, 17, 33
  speakers, 17
  speed, 36
  wireless access points (WAPs), 556
  wireless adapters, 557
USB ports
  adding, 488
  as audio connector, 42
  comparing, 510–511
  defined, 35
  digital cameras, 510
  DVD/Blue-Ray recorders, 510
  FireWire ports versus, 38
  hubs, 488, 513
  icon, 510
  illustrated, 510
  MP3 players, 510
  parallel ports versus, 39
  plugging into, 33
  power support, 511
  scanners, 510
  serial ports versus, 38
  speed comparison, 511
  USB 2.0, 510
USB recorders, 490
User Account Control (UAC), 575
user accounts
  creating, 150
  fine-tuning, 149–150
  levels, 117
  names/passwords, changing, 150
users, switching (Windows 7), 51, 117
Users folder
  defined, 110
  locating, 112
  subfolder creation, 112
  subfolders, 111

V

vCards
  defined, 224
  exporting, 225
  importing, 224–225
VERA (Virtual Entity of Relevant
    Acronyms), 447
video camcorders
  benefits, 30
  illustrated, 30
  webcam, 30
video capture, 522
video cards
  ATI, 521
  built-in, 490
  capture, 491
  chipsets, 520–521
  driver and standards support, 521
  gamer, 491–492
  installation disc, 525
  installing, 523–525
  MPEG, 492
  MPEG hardware support, 522–523
  multiple monitor support, 522
  NVIDIA, 520
  onboard RAM, 521
  PCI Express, 520
  resolution, 521
  shopping for, 520–523
  slot, 524
  TV output, 522
  TV tuner, 522
  upgrading, 491–492
  video capture, 522
  Windows 7 requirement, 49
video ports, 40
videos
  in chat session, 235
  clips, importing, 447–448
  compression, 522
  inserting in slides (PowerPoint), 367–369
Videos Library (Windows DVD Maker), 459
views (PowerPoint)
  changing, 354–356
  Normal, 354
  Notes Page, 355, 356
  Reading, 355
  Slide Show, 356
  Slide Sorter, 354–355
views (Windows 7)
  Content, 109
  Details, 109
  Explorer, 108–109
  Icon, 109, 123
  List, 109
  Tiles, 108
views (Word)
  Draft, 301
  Full Screen Reading, 302–303
  Outline, 301–302
  Print Layout, 302
  switching between, 301
  Web Layout, 302
Virtual Entity of Relevant Acronyms
    (VERA), 447
virtual memory
  amount of, 500
  checking, 501
  defined, 499
  leaving space for, 500
  operating system use of, 500
  speed, 501
  use as drive trashing, 501
virtual private networking (VPN)
  client, 580, 581
  connection names, 581
  connection properties, 582
  connections, 145–146, 582–583
  defined, 580
  password, 582, 583
  for security, 577
  server, 580–582
  server address, 581
  setting up, 580–582
VirusScan Plus (McAfee), 186
VPN. See virtual private networking

W

WAN blocking, 574
WAPs. See wireless access points
war driving, 577
WAV (Windows Audio/Video) format, 441
Web addresses, 192
Web browsing
  with Favorites, 194–196
  navigation, 193–199
  searches, 196–198
  tracking, 201–202
Web Layout view (Word), 302
Web pages
  creating (Word), 323–324
  JPEG format, 428
  printing, 202–203
  saving, 203–204

Web servers, 157
Web sites
  building, 159
  extension, 159
  Favorites, 194–196
Web Slices
  automatic update, 145
  defined, 194
  icon, 194
Web videoconferencing, 163
Web-based Office applications, 412
webcams, 30, 163
wide angle lenses, digital camera, 472
WiFi
  defined, 557
  distance, 558
  interference, 558
Wi-Fi Protected Access (WPA2), 576
Windows 7
  advantages, 45–47
  broadband Internet connection creation,
    173–174
  clean install of, 47
  controls, 52–57
  cursor, 53
  dialup Internet creation, 171–173
  downloading photos with, 479–480
  graphics card requirement, 49
  hard drive space requirement, 48
  Help system, 60–62
  hibernation mode, 51
  Home Premium edition, 47
  icons, 52–53, 70–77
  Internet Connection Sharing (ICS), 571
  Internet connections, adding to, 169–175
  last know good configuration, 270
  locking, 52
  logging off of, 51–52
  maintaining, 253–272
  managing, 63–70
  menus and toolbars, 56–57, 77
  minimum RAM, 496
  network configuration, 543–550
  primer, 45–49
  processor and RAM requirements, 48
  Professional edition, 47
  recommendation, 20
  reinstalling, 250–251
  restarting, 50
  shutting down, 49–50
  sleep mode, 50
  Start menu, 54–55, 80–83
  starting, 49
  system requirements for, 48–49

taskbar, 55–56, 96–99
troubleshooting, 241–252
Ultimate edition, 47
upgrading to, 47
users, switching, 51
wireless networks, 563–564
Windows 7 Firewall
  enabling, 184–185
  testing, 185
  troubleshooting, 185
  when to use, 184
windows
  active, 69
  arranging, 68
  closing, 65
  Explorer, 64
  inactive, 69
  maximizing, 68
  minimizing, 66–68
  moving, 68
  opening, 64–65
  resizing, 69
  restoring, 66–68
  scrolling, 65–66
  switching, 69–70
  title bar, 68
Windows Defender
  checking, 268–269
  defined, 268–269
  illustrated, 269
Windows DVD Maker. *See also* DVDs
  accessing, 457
  Add Items button, 459
  Burn button, 464
  Burn DVD screen, 461, 462
  Choose Photos and Videos button, 458, 459
  defined, 457
  initial window, 458
  Menu button, 464
  Menu Text button, 462
  Preview button, 463
  Preview mode, 463–464
  Videos Library, 459
Windows Fax and Scan utility
  accessing, 119
  illustrated, 119
  receiving faxes with, 121
  sending faxes with, 120–121
  setting up, 119–120
Windows File Protection feature, 249
Windows Flip 3D, 96
Windows keys, 58–59

Windows Live Mail. *See also* e-mail
    (Windows Live Mail)
  account modification, 210–211
  Attach button, 220
  Bcc box, 215
  Blocked list, 222–223
  Cc box, 215
  Check Spelling button, 218
  Contacts list, 212, 215, 223–225, 237
  Conversation window, 237
  default account, 210
  defined, 160, 205
  downloading, 205
  Folder pane, 207
  Folders list, 211
  Formatting toolbar, 217–218
  Forward button, 214
  Junk E-mail option, 222
  mailbox setup, 209–210
  menu system, 206
  Message list, 208, 212
  New button, 216
  Play button, 255
  previewing in, 254–255
  Reading pane, 208, 212
  Reply All button, 213
  Reply button, 213
  Save button, 218
  scrubber bar, 255
  status bar, 208
  toolbar, 206–207
  window, 206–208
Windows Live Messenger
  access methods, 229
  Activities menu, 235
  activity support, 234–235
  adding contacts to, 232–233
  blocking with, 236–237
  chatting with, 233–235
  configuring, 230–232
  defined, 161
  Emoticon option, 234
  as free download, 227
  Hotmail ID and, 229
  Invite button, 234
  menu bar, 233
  Menu button, 230
  Options dialog box, 230–232
  Personal pane, 231
  removing contacts from, 233
  Request Remote Assistance, 235
  running, 229–230
  Send a Single File option, 235

  sharing contacts with, 233
  Start a Video Call option, 235
  status, selecting, 235–236
  unblocking with, 237
Windows Live Movie Maker
  Add Music command button, 453
  Add Videos and Photos command
    button, 447
  Animations tab, 450
  availability, 445
  downloading, 445
  format support, 447
  Home tab, 253, 453
  illustrated, 446
  Movie Maker tab, 455, 456
  Player window, 446
  Publish Movie option, 456
  Ribbon, 446
  saving movies, 455
  sharing movies, 456
  for slideshow movies, 481
  soundtracks with, 452–453
  Special Effects tab, 451
  special effects with, 451–452
  Storyboard, 446, 448–449
  Title command button, 253
  titles, 253–254
  transitions with, 450–451
Windows Live Photo Gallery
  acquiring images with, 422–424
  crop box handles, 426
  Crop Photo button, 426
  cropping images, 424–427
  Delete button, 481
  downloading, 422
  Editing pane, 425–426
  E-mail button, 481
  Fix button, 425, 481
  illustrated, 480
  image conversion, 427–428
  image saving, 428–429
  main window, 423
  Make button, 481
  manipulating images in, 481
  Next button, 481
  opening after photo download, 480
  Previous button, 481
  Print button, 481
  Rotate Clockwise button, 425, 481
  Rotate Counter-clockwise button, 425, 481
  rotating images, 424–425
  Send the Scan Now button, 424
  Slide Show button, 481

Windows Media Player
  Burn tab, 443
  burning audio CDs with, 443
  Internet radio, 440
  Media Player Library, 438
  MP3 player support, 441
  music information retrieval, 436
  Next button, 439
  opening, 436
  playing MP3 files with, 122–123
  Playlist button, 440
  Previous button, 439
  Rip Settings button, 437, 438
  in ripping MP3s, 436–438
  watching DVD movies with, 125
Windows Memory Diagnostic, 249
Windows Registry, 251
Windows Update
  configuring, 271–272
  defined, 271
  illustrated, 271
  running, 272
Windows Vista, 20
Windows XP, 20, 188
wired networks. *See* Ethernet networks
wired sharing devices, shared Internet
    with, 566–569
wireless access points (WAPs)
  defined, 555, 556
  encryption, 564
  illustrated, 557
  physical connections, 556
  security, 577
  USB connection, 556
wireless adapter cards, 571
wireless hardware
  ad hoc mode, 563
  adding, 94
  connections, 564
  drivers, 564
  infrastructure mode, 563–564
  installation preparation, 563
  installation tricks, 563–564
  passwords, 564
  SSID, 564
  WPA/WPA2 encryption, 564
wireless keyboards, 26–27
wireless networks
  AC (powerline), 562–563
  cables and, 540
  hardware expense, 556
  hardware installation, 563–564
  phoneline, 562–563

primer, 555–563
security, 576–577
speed, 556
USB wireless adapters, 557
with Windows 7, 563–564
wired network comparison, 555–556
wireless standards
  Bluetooth, 559–560
  comparison, 560
  competition, 556
  802.11a, 558
  802.11b, 557–558
  802.11g, 559
  802.11n, 559
WMA (Windows Media Audio) format, 442
Word 2010
  artwork/graphical tools, 288
  AutoFormatting, 318–319
  bullets, 310–311
  collaboration tools, 287, 320–323
  command buttons, 300
  comments, 321–322
  defined, 286
  document formatting, 287
  Draft view, 301
  editing window, 301
  elements of, 298–301
  feature overview, 287–288
  File tab, 299, 412
  Find and Replace operation, 306–308
  font formatting, 315–316
  formatting, 315–319
  Full Screen Reading view, 302–303
  graphics, 319–320
  group headings, 300
  highlighting, 322–323
  macros, 288
  margins, 312–313
  movement shortcut keys, 304
  Navigation pane, 303
  numbered lists, 310–311
  Outline view, 301–302
  paragraph formatting, 317–319
  Print Layout view, 302
  printing from, 288, 323
  Quick Access toolbar, 300
  revision marks, 320–321
  Ribbon, 299–300, 313–315
  ruler, 301, 312–314
  running, 298
  search and replace, 288
  spell-checking, 287
  status bar, 301

Word 2010 *(continued)*
  tables, 287, 308–310
  tabs, 300, 314–315
  text editing, 305–306
  text selection, 304–305
  text typing, 304
  uses, 286
  Web Layout view, 302
  Web page creation, 323–324
  Web-based version, 412
  window, 299
workbooks (Excel)
  chart sheets within, 344
  defined, 327–328
worksheets (Excel)
  defined, 328
  embedded objects within, 344
  footers, 347–348
  headers, 347–348
  moving around, 328–330
  printing, 348–349

workspace, keeping clean, 275
WPA2 (Wi-Fi Protected Access), 576

X

Xnews, 162

y

Yahoo! Mail, 160
YouTube, sharing movies on, 456

Z

Zip standard, 200
Zoom level menu (IE), 190

Business/Accounting & Bookkeeping

Bookkeeping For Dummies
978-0-7645-9848-7

eBay Business
All-in-One For Dummies,
2nd Edition
978-0-470-38536-4

Job Interviews
For Dummies,
3rd Edition
978-0-470-17748-8

Resumes For Dummies,
5th Edition
978-0-470-08037-5

Stock Investing
For Dummies,
3rd Edition
978-0-470-40114-9

Successful Time
Management
For Dummies
978-0-470-29034-7

Computer Hardware

BlackBerry For Dummies,
3rd Edition
978-0-470-45762-7

Computers For Seniors
For Dummies
978-0-470-24055-7

iPhone For Dummies,
2nd Edition
978-0-470-42342-4

Laptops For Dummies,
3rd Edition
978-0-470-27759-1

Macs For Dummies,
10th Edition
978-0-470-27817-8

Cooking & Entertaining

Cooking Basics
For Dummies,
3rd Edition
978-0-7645-7206-7

Wine For Dummies,
4th Edition
978-0-470-04579-4

Diet & Nutrition

Dieting For Dummies,
2nd Edition
978-0-7645-4149-0

Nutrition For Dummies,
4th Edition
978-0-471-79868-2

Weight Training
For Dummies,
3rd Edition
978-0-471-76845-6

Digital Photography

Digital Photography
For Dummies,
6th Edition
978-0-470-25074-7

Photoshop Elements 7
For Dummies
978-0-470-39700-8

Gardening

Gardening Basics
For Dummies
978-0-470-03749-2

Organic Gardening
For Dummies,
2nd Edition
978-0-470-43067-5

Green/Sustainable

Green Building
& Remodeling
For Dummies
978-0-470-17559-0

Green Cleaning
For Dummies
978-0-470-39106-8

Green IT For Dummies
978-0-470-38688-0

Health

Diabetes For Dummies,
3rd Edition
978-0-470-27086-8

Food Allergies
For Dummies
978-0-470-09584-3

Living Gluten-Free
For Dummies
978-0-471-77383-2

Hobbies/General

Chess For Dummies,
2nd Edition
978-0-7645-8404-6

Drawing For Dummies
978-0-7645-5476-6

Knitting For Dummies,
2nd Edition
978-0-470-28747-7

Organizing For Dummies
978-0-7645-5300-4

SuDoku For Dummies
978-0-470-01892-7

Home Improvement

Energy Efficient Homes
For Dummies
978-0-470-37602-7

Home Theater
For Dummies,
3rd Edition
978-0-470-41189-6

Living the Country Lifestyle
All-in-One For Dummies
978-0-470-43061-3

Solar Power Your Home
For Dummies
978-0-470-17569-9

DUMMIES.COM®

How-to?
How Easy.

Go to www.Dummies.com

From hooking up a modem to cooking up a casserole, knitting a scarf to navigating an iPod, you can trust Dummies.com to show you how to get things done the easy way.

Visit us at Dummies.com

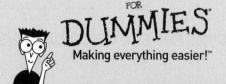

Notes

Notes